Heavy Weather Guide

SECOND EDITION

HEAVY WEATHER GUIDE

By Rear Admiral William J. Kotsch, USN (Retired)
and Richard Henderson

Naval Institute Press
Annapolis, Maryland

Library of Congress Cataloging in Publication Data

Kotsch, William J.
  Heavy weather guide.

Bibliography: p.
  Includes index.
  1. Meteorology, Maritime. 2. Seamanship.
I. Henderson, Richard, 1924– . II. Title.
QC994.K636 1984   551.69162   84-16615
ISBN 0-87021-263-X

Printed in the United States of America on acid-free paper ∞

10 9 8 7 6 5 4 3 2

Contents

Publisher's Preface
to the Second Edition

To some people, two decades must seem like a rather long time. To others, time passes almost as swiftly as the speed of light, and twenty years seems more like a long pause.

During the twenty years that have passed since publication of the first edition, so much scientific progress has been made in the disciplines of meteorology and oceanography, and the advances in high technology have been so rapid, that one is infused with a feeling of wonderment and admiration for the ingenuity and creative activity of man. That feeling temporarily evaporates, however, when indiscriminate and uncoordinated organizational changes in scientific programs are dictated by governments, and when geopolitical decisions and mutations are thrust upon individuals. All of these factors have had their impact on making the first edition obsolete.

When the manuscript of the first edition was put to bed in 1964, polar-orbiting and geostationary weather satellites were not yet the routine operational tools of meteorologists. Special communications satellites were usually discussed in secrecy. And computer microchips were not even a gleam in anyone's eye.

During the last two decades, many constructive criticisms and suggestions to enhance the book's usefulness have been received from users of the first edition. A valid point made on many occasions by critics was that the book was directed primarily toward highly experienced oceangoing mariners with a considerable knowledge of meteorology and oceanography. Meteorological terms were not clearly defined for the weekend sailor and weather novice. It had been assumed incorrectly that the reader would have a rather broad background in weather science, which proved not to be the case.

Another consistent suggestion by first edition users was that the book should contain a section devoted to weather warnings and visual displays, information pertaining to marine weather and oceanographic services and broadcasts, and sources and methods of obtaining weather and oceanographic information. All of this material has now been incorporated and appears in the first chapter, profusely illustrated.

Basically, hurricanes, typhoons, cordonazos, baguios, etc., are the same meteorological phenomenon. They have the same intriguing and destructive characteristics, but are known by different names in various parts of the world. Above all, these storms must be respected. With proper knowledge and preparedness, however, they can be successfully dealt with at sea.

Hurricanes and typhoons are tropical (warm-core) cyclones with many similar features. To avoid the repetition that appeared in the first edition, chapter two of this second edition encompasses the characteristics common to all tropical cyclones, regardless of geographical location. This chapter is also profusely illustrated—with photos, diagrams, and weather satellite images. Information pertinent to hurricanes only—such as hurricane havens—is contained in chapter three, and data pertinent to typhoons only—such as conditions of readiness and typhoon havens—is contained in chapter four. Both of these chapters contain a wealth of illustrations.

The overall scope of the second edition has been significantly increased. Not included in the first edition, extratropical (cold-core) low-pressure systems (cyclones) and storms are somewhat different phenomena, but they can be as serious a hazard at sea as a hurricane or typhoon. Consequently, a new chapter five, describing these phenomena, including secondary lows and meteorological "bombs," has been added. Also, some of the meteorological aspects of the 1979 Fastnet Yacht Race disaster are discussed here. This chapter, too, is more than amply illustrated.

A new chapter six, encompassing yacht and vessel design for heavy weather, features wholesome characteristics for sailing yachts, safety features for other vessels, and vessel inspections and modifications. Two other new chapters, seven and eight, discuss in detail storm gear and storm preparations and contain recommendations for courses of action in tropical storms, ship and power-vessel handling, and sailing yacht tactics. Chapters six, seven, and eight continue the policy of bountiful illustrations for easy understanding and clarity.

Appendices I through VIII of the first edition, which sparked so much interest, controversy, and comment on the part of so many readers, have been retained in their entirety. In accordance with further suggestions through the years, appendix IX, containing a list of recommended books and information sources, has been added, as has a new appendix X, "Conversion Tables and Conversion Factors."

Heavy Weather Guide, second edition, can hardly be called a new edition of an old book. Because of the enormous increase in scope plus update, and the profusion of timely and pertinent illustrations, totaling almost 300 tables, photos, and line drawings, it is really a brand new book. But the title is appropriate, for this book now constitutes a true heavy weather guide for seafarers of *all* echelons and *all* experience levels and in *both* hemispheres—the weekend sailors, the yachtsmen, the busy merchant skippers, or naval officers on the bridge. There is something in this book for all who follow the sea.

To the uninformed and uninitiated, heavy weather at sea can be as unexpected as it can be disastrous. And even to widely experienced and salty oceangoing mariners, heavy weather at sea can present problems of dangerous—sometimes life-threatening—magnitude.

This book will help significantly in minimizing the dangers of heavy weather at sea and in promoting safety at sea for all who sail the oceans and coastal waters of the world.

Publisher's Preface to the First Edition

Sweeping up from tropical zones into the colder latitudes of the Northern Hemisphere, vast cyclonic storms each year leave in their wakes death and devastation. In the Atlantic these storms are called hurricanes; in the Pacific they are called typhoons. Both kinds of storms carry inconceivable amounts of energy and have greater potential for destruction than the most powerful atomic bombs. They are mysterious, yet they follow generally predictable behavior patterns; they are terrifying, yet their approach need not lead to panic. The purpose of this book is to discuss the theory, origin, and habits of these storms, and to show how to evade or survive them.

This book treats hurricanes and typhoons separately, and so there is some repetition, because in most ways hurricanes and typhoons are alike. Yet due to the far-ranging scale of operations of both naval and merchant vessels, both kinds of storms are included in one book, for the skipper who is concerned about a hurricane off Bermuda this month may well face the prospect of a typhoon off Guam a few weeks hence.

The reader, whether he be deep-draft skipper, weekend sailor, or shore-side dweller, can learn about hurricanes and typhoons from this book without actually experiencing one. For those who wish the vicarious experience of weathering one of these awesome storms, there are included excerpts from *Typhoon*, by Joseph Conrad, as well as other accounts of tropical storms by seamen who have experienced them.

Introduction

Give me the courage, Lord, to sail
  my boat out from the shore.
I'd rather know the ocean's gale
  and hear the tempest's roar
Than anchor safely in some bay
  because fear conquered me.
Let craft less daring inland stay . . .
  be mine the pathless sea.
                —Joseph Morris

Ever since man first began to use the waters of the world many centuries ago, the sea has been—and will continue to be—a simultaneously dangerous yet very helpful and soothing mistress. So it is most important, for weekend sailors as well as oceangoing mariners, to know in advance when this mistress intends to threaten the safety of life, vessel, or cargo. Also, what to do after the threat has been implemented.

This requires a certain fundamental knowledge of meteorology and oceanography, and the essentials of sailing, powerboating, and overall seamanship.

Seafarers of all classes and experience levels should have some insight into the vagaries of the atmosphere and the hydrosphere, and the nature of storms—and other threats—at sea. It goes without saying that to cope successfully with the raging elements at sea or in coastal waters requires a special resourcefulness and an expertise in boat and shiphandling.

It is the purpose of this *Heavy Weather Guide* to provide, in a single volume, much of the basic information required to promote safety at sea prior to and during heavy weather. Recommendations for heavy weather precautions, maneuvering, and storm evasion tactics are included.

While it is true that: "In a calm sea, every man is a pilot" (John Ray 1670), it is the hope of the authors that this *Guide* will assist in providing the information to extend that capability to include situations when the sea is other than calm.

1

Weather Definitions, Displays, and Warnings

Definitions are good things, if only
we did not employ words in making them.
—Jean Jacques Rousseau, 1712–1778

Some days, one is almost inclined to agree with Rousseau's philosophy expressed above. But meteorology is a complex and fascinating science, and definitions are an integral part of it. If one is to be aware of the severity of meteorological and oceanographic threats, and if one is to understand the nature of such threats, a few basic definitions must be stashed in one's mental gear locker. For if we do not understand the terminology used by meteorologists in their weather bulletins, advisories, and warnings; if we are confused by the words and phrases of commentators, newscasters, and weathermen on TV and radio; and if the language of automatic telephone-answering weather services and weather broadcasts makes little sense, then one is a prime candidate for steering a meteorological course into harm's way—and perhaps to disaster.

The following terms and definitions should have "instant recall" by all who use the sea for recreation, livelihood, commerce, and for military purposes.

TERMINOLOGY USED BY METEOROLOGISTS

The terminology used throughout this book—words, phrases, definitions, and so forth—is consistent with the *Glossary of Meteorology*, American Meteorological Society, Boston, Mass., 1959; the *National Hurricane Operations Plan*, National Oceanic and Atmospheric Administration, Washington, D.C. (1984); and the *Commander in Chief, Pacific Instruction (CinCPacInst)3140.1(x)*, Camp H.M. Smith, Hawaii (1984).

There can be neither mutiny nor compromise where basic meteorological definitions are concerned. A consistent and solid "words and wording foundation" is essential. Otherwise, our structure would collapse and be swept out to sea. To ease digestion, an attempt has been made to present the definitions in a simple and easily understandable manner for the inexperienced boating enthusiast while maintaining a palatable approach for the knowledgeable and experienced mariner.

In General

Air Mass. A widespread body of air, the properties of which can be identified as (a) having been established while that air was situated over a particular region of the earth's surface (air mass source region), and (b) undergoing specific modifications while in transit away from the source region. An air mass is also defined as "a widespread body of air that is approximately homogeneous in its horizontal extent, particularly with reference to temperature and moisture distribution. In addition, the vertical temperature and moisture variations are approximately the same over its horizontal extent." Another way of saying it is that an air mass is a huge dome, or "glob," of air (enveloping many thousands of cubic miles) in which the temperature and moisture (humidity) conditions in a horizontal plane are very similar. (See figure 1-1.)

Anticyclone (or High-Pressure System, High-Pressure Cell, or simply High). An area within which the pressure is high relative to the surroundings. The wind circulation is *clockwise* around an anticyclone *in the Northern Hemisphere*, with the wind crossing the isobars at an angle and blowing from higher toward lower pressure. The wind circulation is *counterclockwise* around an anticyclone *in the Southern Hemisphere*, with the wind crossing the isobars at an angle and blowing from higher toward lower pressure. (See figure 1-2.)

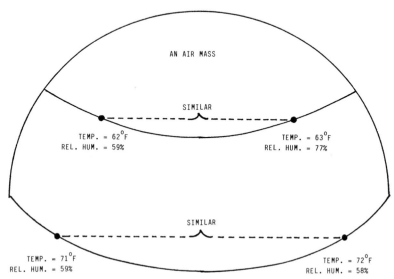

Figure 1-1. In an *air mass*, the temperature and humidity (moisture) conditions in a horizontal plane are very similar.

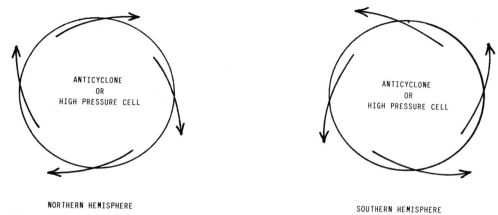

NORTHERN HEMISPHERE   SOUTHERN HEMISPHERE

Figure 1-2. The winds spiral outward from the center of an anticyclone in a *clockwise* circulation in the *Northern Hemisphere*. They spiral outward in a *counterclockwise* circulation in the *Southern Hemisphere*.

Beaufort Wind Scale. A system of estimating and reporting wind speeds. For over 175 years, wind force (speed) has been conveniently expressed by means of the *Beaufort Scale*, a numerical scale devised in 1808 by Admiral Sir Francis Beaufort of the British Navy. It was based originally on the amount of canvas that a man-o'-war of the period could carry with different winds. The numbers on the scale ranged from zero (representing calm conditions) to 12 (representing a hurricane "such that no canvas could withstand"). Through the years, with the gradual disappearance of sailing ships, the scale as originally designed became unsuitable and has been revised on several occasions. Today, by international agreement, all wind reports are encoded and plotted on weather maps in knots. This may be changed in the future to conform to the metric system (meters per second, kilometers per hour, etc.). Frequent reference, however, is still made, and will continue to be made, to the Beaufort Scale. (See table 1-1.)

Buys Ballot's Law. This is a law describing the relationship of the horizontal wind direction in the atmosphere to the pressure distribution. "If one stands with his back to the wind in the *Northern Hemisphere, lower pressure* will always be to the *left,* and *higher pressure* to the *right."* "In the *Southern Hemisphere,* if one stands with his back to the wind, lower pressure will always be to the right, and higher pressure to the left." This law was first formulated in 1857 by the Dutch meteorologist, Buys Ballot, and bears his name. It is also known as the *Baric Wind Law.* An explanation of the wind direction-pressure distribution relationship is given in the section *Wind* (and balance of forces), on page 12.

Col. The saddle-back region between two anticyclones and two cyclones, arranged as shown in figure 1-3. It is also called a saddle point, or neutral point. It can be described as the point of intersection of a trough of low pressure and a ridge of high pressure on weather maps. It can also be described as the point of relatively lowest pressure between two high-pressure systems

Table 1–1. The Beaufort Wind Scale, Speed Conversions, Descriptions, and Symbols.

Beaufort Number	Knots	Miles per Hour	Description	Effect at Sea	Wind Symbols on Weather Maps
0	0–0.9	0–0.9	Calm	Sea like a mirror.	Calm
1	1–3	1–3	Light air	Scale-like ripples form, but without foam crests.	Almost calm
2	4–6	4–7	Light breeze	Small wavelets, short but more pronounced. Crests have a glassy appearance and do not break.	5 Knots
3	7–10	8–12	Gentle breeze	Large wavelets. Crests begin to break. Foam has glassy appearance. Perhaps scattered white horses.	10 Knots
4	11–16	13–18	Moderate breeze	Small waves, becoming longer. Fairly frequent white horses.	15 Knots
5	17–21	19–24	Fresh breeze	Moderate waves, taking a more pronounced long form. Many white horses are formed. Chance of some spray.	20 Knots
6	22–27	25–31	Strong breeze	Large waves begin to form. White foam crests are more extensive everywhere. Some spray.	25 Knots
7	28–33	32–38	Moderate gale	Sea heaps up and white foam from breaking waves begins to be blown in streaks along the direction of the wind. Spindrift begins.	30 Knots

8	34–40	Fresh gale	Moderately high waves of greater length. Edges of crests break into spindrift. Foam is blown in well-marked streaks along the direction of the wind.	35 Knots
9	41–47	Strong gale	High waves. Dense streaks of foam along the direction of the wind. Sea begins to roll. Spray may affect visibility.	45 Knots
10	48–55	Whole gale and/or storm	Very high waves with long overhanging crests. The resulting foam in great patches is blown in dense white streaks along the direction of the wind. On the whole, the surface of the sea takes a white appearance. The rolling of the sea becomes heavy and shocklike. Visibility is affected.	50 Knots
11	56–63	Storm and/or violent storm	Exceptionally high waves. Small- and medium-sized vessels might for a long time be lost to view behind the waves. The sea is completely covered with long white patches of foam lying along the direction of the wind. Everywhere, the edges of the wave crests are blown into froth. Visibility is seriously affected.	60 Knots
12	64 or higher	Hurricane and Typhoon	The air is filled with foam and spray. Sea is completely white with driving spray. Visibility is very seriously affected.	75 Knots

NORTHERN HEMISPHERE

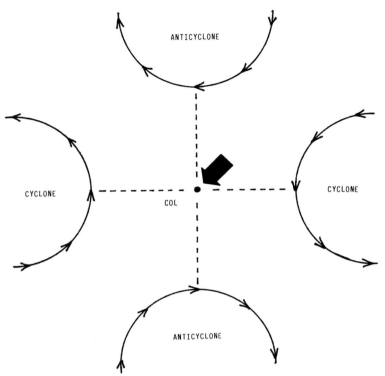

Figure 1-3. The saddle-back region between two anticyclones and two cyclones is called a *col*. It is also called a *saddle point* or *neutral point* where the ridges of high pressure and trough lines of low pressure intersect.

and the point of relatively highest pressure between two low-pressure systems. It is important because the area is usually one of very light winds. Unfortunately, there are exceptions to contend with.

Convergence. The contraction of a vector field. In meteorology, the term is used in a broad sense to include the "coming together," or meeting, of winds (air particles) from different directions or areas (horizontally or vertically). Mathematically, convergence is negative *divergence*. (See figure 1-4.)

Cyclone (or Low-Pressure System, or simply Low, or Depression). An area within which the pressure is low relative to the surroundings. An atmospheric "closed circulation" with the winds blowing *counterclockwise* around cyclones in the *Northern Hemisphere*, and clockwise around cyclones in the Southern Hemisphere. The winds cross the isobars at an angle (15° over water and 30° over land), and blow from higher toward lower pressure. (See figure 1-5.)

Divergence. The expansion, or spreading out, of a vector field. In meteorology, the term is used in a broad sense to include the "spreading apart," or

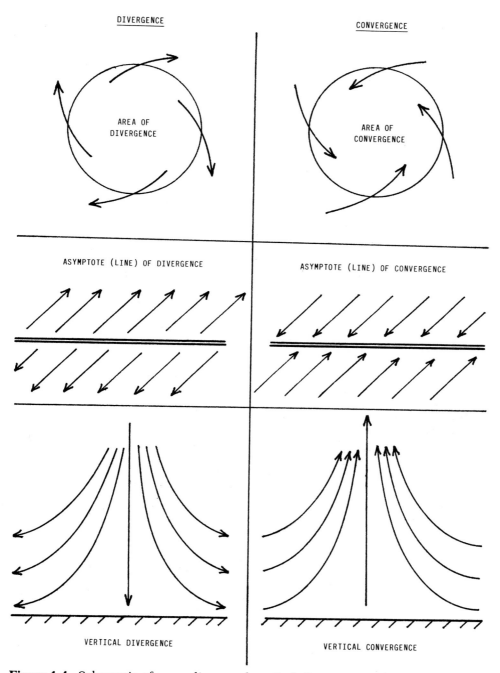

Figure 1-4. Schematic of areas, lines, and vertical divergence and convergence.

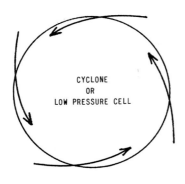 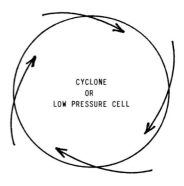

NORTHERN HEMISPHERE   SOUTHERN HEMISPHERE

Figure 1-5a. The winds spiral inward toward the center of a cyclone in a *counter-clockwise* circulation in the *Northern Hemisphere*. They spiral inward in a *clockwise* circulation in the *Southern Hemisphere*.

drawing apart, of winds (air particles) either horizontally or vertically. (See figure 1-4.)

Front (or Weather Front).   The interface, or transition zone, between two air masses of different density. Since the temperature distribution is the most important "regulator" of atmospheric density, a front usually separates air masses of different temperature. Fronts are drawn as "lines" separating different air masses on weather maps. (See figure 1-6.) Following are the four types of fronts:

- *Cold Front*—A front along which colder air replaces warmer air. Usually accompanied by cumulus-type low clouds and heavy showers, sometimes thundershowers with violent squalls. Wind normally shifts abruptly from S or SW to W or NW as the front passes. After the front passes, wind remains gusty for a time, visibility improves, and temperature drops.
- *Warm Front*—A front along which warmer air replaces colder air. Usually preceded by gradually lowering and thickening stratus-type clouds, a steady type of rain or drizzle, and falling pressure. Wind usually veers from E or SE to S or SW as the front passes. After the front passes, temperature rises and visibility may deteriorate because of possible fog formation in the warm, moist air.
- *Occluded Front*—A front resulting when a cold front overtakes a warm front and the warm air is "lifted" off the earth's surface (forced aloft). Weather and clouds preceding occluded fronts are similar to those preceding warm fronts. There is no warm air at the earth's surface, however, as the front passes.
- *Stationary Front*—A front along which one air mass does not replace another air mass. The front is not moving.

Gale. In general (and in popular) use, an unusually strong wind. In storm-warning terminology, a wind of 28–47 knots (13.9–24.4 mps). In the Beaufort Wind Scale, a wind of 28–55 knots (13.9–28.4 mps), and categorized as follows:

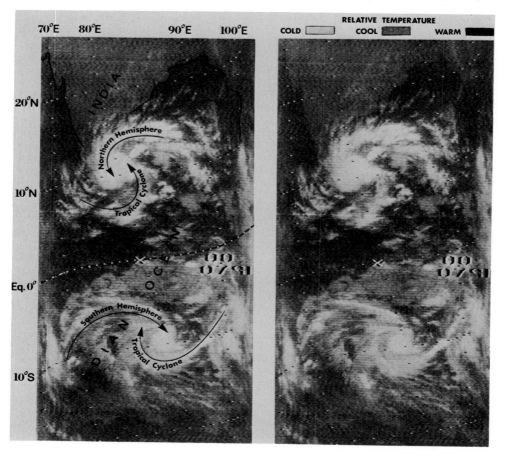

Figure 1-5b. Two tropical cyclones are seen in this Nimbus 4 nighttime Temperature Humidity Infrared Radiometer (THIR) image of 19 November 1970. The storms have the expected mode of circulation: counterclockwise in the Northern Hemisphere and clockwise in the Southern Hemisphere. (Courtesy of NASA Goddard Space Flight Center)

- Moderate Gale, 28–33 knots (13.9–17.1 mps).
- Fresh Gale, 34–40 knots (17.2–20.7 mps).
- Strong Gale, 41–47 knots (20.8–24.4 mps).
- Whole Gale, 48–55 knots (24.5–28.4 mps).

Isobar. A line of equal or constant pressure. On weather maps, isobars are lines drawn through all points of equal atmospheric pressure along a given reference surface (such as mean-sea-level on surface weather maps). Isobars are usually drawn at four-millibar intervals. (See figure 1-7.)

Kona. A stormy, rain-bringing wind from the SW or SSW in Hawaii. It occurs about five times per year on the southwest slopes, which are in the lee of the prevailing NE trade winds. *Kona* is the Polynesian word meaning "leeward."

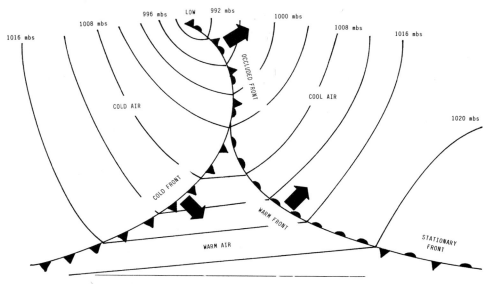

Figure 1-6. On weather maps, fronts (or weather fronts) are drawn as "lines" separating different air masses.

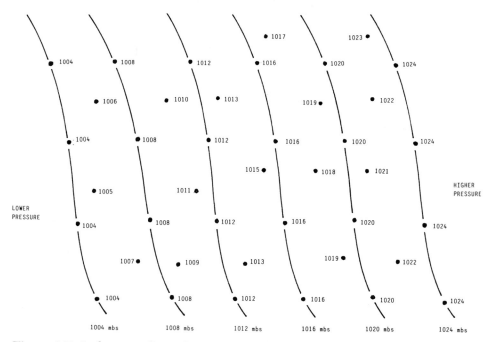

Figure 1-7. Isobars are lines drawn on weather maps through points of equal atmospheric (or barometric) pressure.

Pressure (Atmospheric). The earth's atmosphere has weight, which is manifested by a downward pressure. A column of air extending from the earth's surface to the top of the atmosphere exerts a pressure on the earth's surface equivalent to a column of mercury 29.92 inches, or 76 centimeters, or 760 millimeters high, or a column of water 34 feet high. This pressure is 1,013.2 *millibars* (units normally used on weather maps). The atmosphere exerts a pressure on the earth's surface amounting to about 14.7 pounds per square inch, or about one ton per square foot.

Quadrant (in Storm Warnings). The 90-degree sector of the storm centered on a designated cardinal point of the compass. An eight-point compass rose is used when referring to quadrants. *Example*: The north quadrant refers to the sector of the storm from 315° through 360° to 045°. (See figure 1-8.)

Semicircle (in Storm Warnings). The 180-degree sector of the storm centered on the designated cardinal point of the compass. A four-point compass rose is used when referring to a semicircle. *Example*: The south semicircle refers to the segment of the storm from 090° through 180° to 270°. (See figure 1-8).

Storm. Any disturbed state of the earth's atmosphere, especially as affecting the earth's surface, and strongly implying destructive or otherwise unpleasant weather (tornadoes, thunderstorms, tropical cyclones, extratropical cyclones, blizzards, ice storms, sandstorms, dust storms, etc.). Winds of 48

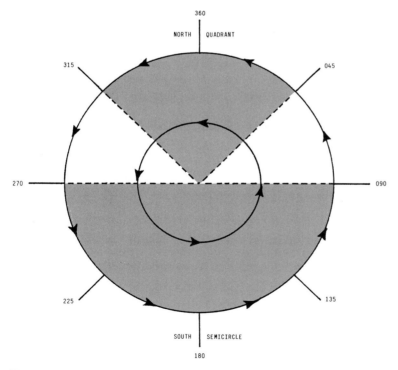

Figure 1-8. Storm quadrants and semicircles.

knots (24.5 mps) or greater, when not associated with tropical weather systems. (See *Tropical Storm* in the section titled "The Tropical Weather Systems.")

Subsidence. A descending motion of air in the atmosphere, usually with the implication that the condition extends over a rather broad area. As the air descends, it is heated *adiabatically* (no transfer of heat or mass; the air is warmed by *compression* as it descends), and becomes more dry. Good weather is usually associated with subsidence.

Subtropics. The indefinite "belts" in each hemisphere between the tropic and temperate regions. The polar boundaries are considered to be roughly 35°–40° N and S latitudes, but vary greatly according to continental influence. They are farther poleward on the west coasts of continents and farther equatorward on the east coasts.

Tropics. The zone of earth's surface which lies between the Tropic of Cancer (approx. 23° 27′N lat.) and the Tropic of Capricorn (approx. 23° 27′S lat.). Same as the *Torrid Zone.*

Warning (Winter Storm, Hurricane, Flood, etc.). A warning means that (the predicted phenomenon) conditions are expected within 24 (or as otherwise specified) hours. The warnings usually describe phenomenon intensity, expected time of arrival, areas that will be affected, precautions to take, etc. Do not delay; *take action immediately.*

Watch (Winter Storm, Hurricane, Flood, etc.). A watch is established, covering a specified area and indicating the duration, when the *threat* (of the predicted phenomenon) is a real possibility. It does *not* mean that the threat is imminent. Everyone in the area covered by the "watch" should listen for further advisories and *be prepared* to act quickly if warnings are issued.

Wind (and balance of forces). Air in motion relative to the surface of the earth. Wind is a balance of three forces (if we neglect curvature): (1) the coriolis (or horizontal deflecting) force, (2) the frictional force, and (3) the pressure force. This balance results in the wind blowing across the isobars at angles of about 15° over water (because friction is less) and about 30° over land (where friction is greater), in the direction from higher toward lower pressure. (See figure 1-9.)

Regarding Tropical Weather Systems—Anywhere in the Tropics

Center. The axis or pivot of a tropical cyclone. Usually determined by wind, temperature, or pressure distribution.

Center Fix. The location of the center of a tropical or subtropical cyclone obtained by means other than reconnaissance aircraft penetration.

Extratropical. In meteorology, typical of occurrences poleward of the belt of tropical easterly winds.

Eye. The relatively calm center of a tropical cyclone that is more than one-half surrounded by wall cloud. (See figure 1-10.)

Hurricane Season. That portion of the year having a relatively high incidence of hurricanes. In the Atlantic, Caribbean, and Gulf of Mexico, this is the period from June through November; in the eastern Pacific, June through

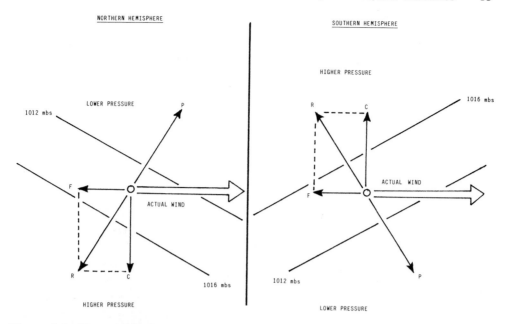

Figure 1-9. If we neglect curvature, the actual wind is a balance of three forces: (1) the coriolis (or horizontal deflecting) force (C), (2) the frictional force (F), and (3) the pressure (gradient) force (P). From the diagrams above, we see that: C + F = R; P = R; and the actual wind is a balance of the three forces C, F, and P. R = resultant vector, equal and opposite to the vector P.

November 15; and in the central Pacific, the period is from June through October.

Maximum Sustained Wind (and Gusts). The highest surface wind speed of a cyclone averaged over a one-minute period of time. (Note: Wind is subject to gusts which bring a sudden, temporary increase in speed. Maximum sustained wind speeds of 30 knots may have superimposed gusts of 50 knots.)

Present Movement. The best estimate of the movement of the center of a tropical cyclone at a given time and at a given position. This estimate does not reflect the short-period, small-scale oscillations of the cyclone center.

Relocated. A term used in an advisory to indicate that a vector drawn from the preceding advisory position to the latest known position is not necessarily a reasonable representation of the cyclone's movement.

Typhoon Season. There is no true typhoon season. Typhoons in the western Pacific can—and do—occur in every month of the year. However, 90 percent of the typhoons occur between early June and late December. A maximum (22.6 percent) of the total occurs in August, and a minimum (0.6 percent) in February.

Vortex Fix. The location of the surface and/or flight level center of a tropical or subtropical cyclone obtained by reconnaissance aircraft penetration.

Wall Cloud. An organized band of cumuliform clouds immediately surrounding the center of a tropical cyclone. Wall cloud and *eye wall* are used synonymously.

Regarding Tropical Weather Systems—In the Western North Pacific Only (West of 180°)

Conditions of Readiness (COR).

- Condition ONE: Destructive winds of (***knots) are occurring or anticipated within 12 hours.

Figure 1-10. An almost perfect "eye" of a hurricane (at tip of arrow) as viewed from a weather satellite in space on 1 September 1977. (Courtesy of NASA Goddard Space Flight Center)

- Condition TWO: Destructive winds of (***knots) are anticipated within 24 hours.
- Condition THREE: Destructive winds of (***knots) are possible within 48 hours.
- Condition FOUR: Destructive winds of (***knots) are possible within 72 hours.

***Wind speed inserted by forecaster

Significant Tropical Cyclone. A tropical cyclone becomes "significant" with the issuance of the first numbered warning by the responsible warning agency.

Significant Tropical Weather Advisory. A daily message describing significant tropical activity and the Joint Typhoon Warning Center/Guam's evaluation of its potential for development into a significant tropical cyclone.

Super Typhoon. A warm core tropical cyclone in which the maximum sustained surface wind (one-minute mean) is 130 knots or greater.

Suspect Area. An area suspected of containing a developing or existing tropical cyclone.

Tropical Cyclone Formation Alert. A message advising of the possible or probable formation of a tropical cyclone.

Tropical Cyclone Warning. A message issued by responsible forecast activities which provides details of tropical cyclone location, intensity, size, and movement.

The Tropical Weather Systems

Tropical Disturbance. A discrete system of apparently organized convection—generally 100–300 miles in diameter—originating in the tropics or subtropics, having a nonfrontal migratory character and maintaining its identity for 24 hours or more. It may or may not be associated with a detectable perturbation of the wind field. As such, it is the basic generic designation, which, in successive stages of intensification, may be classified as a tropical wave, depression, storm, or hurricane.

Tropical Wave (or Easterly Wave). A trough or cyclonic curvature maximum in the trade-wind easterlies. The wave may reach maximum amplitude in the lower middle troposphere, or may be the reflection of an upper-troposphere cold-low or equatorward extension of a middle-latitude trough.

Tropical Cyclone. A nonfrontal low-pressure system of synoptic scale developing over tropical or subtropical waters and having a definite organized circulation. The center is normally warmer than the surroundings.

- *Tropical Depression*—A tropical cyclone in which the maximum sustained surface wind (one-minute mean) is 33 knots or less.
- *Tropical Storm*—A warm-core tropical cyclone in which the maximum sustained surface wind (one-minute mean) ranges from 34–63 knots, inclusive.
- *Hurricane* (or Typhoon)—A warm-core tropical cyclone in which the maximum sustained surface wind (one-minute mean) is 64 knots or higher.

Subtropical Cyclones

These are nonfrontal, low-pressure systems comprising initially baroclinic (surfaces of constant pressure intersect surfaces of constant density) circulations developing over subtropical waters. There are two types: (1) A cold low with circulation extending to the surface layer and maximum sustained winds generally occurring at a radius of 100 miles or more from the pressure center. These cyclones sometimes metamorphose and become tropical storms or hurricanes. (2) A mesoscale cyclone originating in or near a frontolyzing zone or horizontal wind shear, with radius of maximum sustained winds generally less than 30 miles. The entire circulation sometimes encompasses an area initially no more than 100 miles in diameter. These marine cyclones may change in structure from cold core to warm core (center warmer than the surroundings). While generally short-lived, they may ultimately evolve into major hurricanes or typhoons, or into extratropical wave cyclones. Subtropical cyclones are classed according to intensity as follows:

- *Subtropical Depression*—A subtropical cyclone in which the maximum sustained surface wind (one-minute mean) is 33 knots or less.
- *Subtropical Storm*—A subtropical cyclone in which the maximum sustained surface wind (one-minute mean) is 34 knots or greater.
- *Kona Cyclone* (or *Kona Storm*)—A slow-moving, extensive cyclone that forms in subtropical latitudes during the winter season. See also *Kona* in a previous section titled, "In General."

VISUAL WARNING DISPLAYS

It goes without saying that few people are more sensitive to the elements than those who sail the seas of the world. And few individuals have a greater need for routine, accurate, and timely information and forecasts concerning the earth's environment. This information is readily available from the national and commercial weather services of most countries of the world, who regularly provide marine weather and sea condition reports, forecasts, and warnings (as well as other services) for all seafarers. All sorts of information, advice, and services are available in the form of pamphlets, maps, charts, radio broadcasts, facsimile broadcasts, telephone and radiotelephone services, satellite photos, and warnings. Not taking full advantage of these excellent facilities and services could result in serious difficulties and perhaps disaster. But as Syrus so aptly put it: "Many receive advice, but only the wise profit by it."

The most universally accepted—and the most meaningful—basis for classifying and describing the various types of weather warnings in coastal waters and at sea is that of *wind speed*. Wind warnings may relate to middle- or high-latitude rotary or non-rotary weather systems, to closed cyclonic (rotary) circulations of tropical origin inside or outside the tropics, or to weather systems of tropical origin other than closed cyclonic (rotary) circulations.

Warnings associated with weather systems located *in latitudes outside the tropics*, or with weather systems of tropical origin other than closed cyclonic (rotary) circulations are as follows:

Terminology	*Equivalent Wind Speeds*
Small Craft Warning	Winds up to 33 knots (38 mph, 17.1 mps, 61 kph), and used mostly in coastal and inland waters.
Gale Warning	Winds of 34–47 knots (39–54 mph, 17.2–24.4 mps, 62–88 kph).
Storm Warning	Winds of 48 knots (55 mph, 24.5 mps, 89 kph) or greater.

Warnings associated with *closed cyclonic* (rotary) *circulations of tropical origin* are expressed in the following way:

Terminology	*Equivalent Wind Speeds*
Tropical Depression	Winds up to 33 knots (38 mph, 17.1 mps, 61 kph)
Tropical Storm	Winds of 34–63 knots (39–74 mph, 17.2–32.6 mps, 62–117 kph)
Hurricane or Typhoon	Winds of 64 knots (74 mph, 32.7 mps, 118 kph) or greater

Visual displays of pennants, flags, and lights (for nighttime), as shown in figure 1-11, are used at designated coastal points along the seacoasts of the United States and many other countries around the world when winds (or sea conditions generated by the winds) dangerous to navigation exist or are

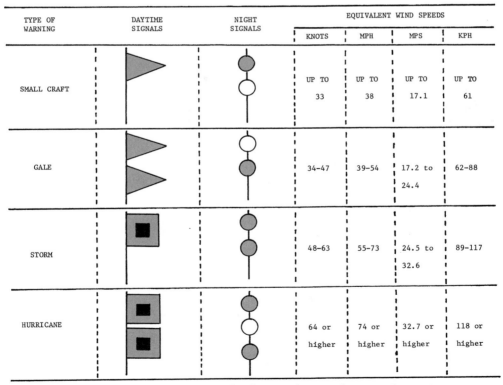

Figure 1-11. Visual weather warning displays and equivalent wind speeds.

predicted for any coastal sea, bay, inlet, etc., area. These visual warning displays follow.

Small Craft Warning. One red pennant displayed by day and a red light over a white light at night indicate that winds up to 33 knots (38 mph) or sea conditions dangerous to small-craft operations exist or are predicted for the area.

Gale Warning. Two red pennants by day and a white light over a red light at night indicate that winds of 34–47 knots (39–54 mph) exist or are forecast for the area.

Storm Warning. A single red flag with a black center displayed by day and two red lights at night, one above the other, indicate that winds of 48 knots (55 mph) and above exist or are predicted for the area. If the winds are associated with a tropical cyclone (hurricane), storm warnings indicate forecast winds of 48–63 knots (55–73 mph).

Hurricane Warning. Two square red flags with black centers displayed by day, one above the other, and a white light between two red lights at night indicate that winds of 64 knots (74 mph) or higher exist or are forecast for the area. This display is used *only* in connection with hurricanes.

Most skippers, regardless of the size of their craft or vessel, are vitally concerned about the safety and well-being of their passengers, crew, and cargo. And it seems that the more experienced the skipper, the more thorough the precautions taken. It is usually the less-experienced skippers and the over-confident weekend sailors that we have to be most concerned about. Quite obviously, if one is to "follow the sea" for recreational, commercial, or military purposes, one must be thoroughly familiar with the various wind and weather warning criteria and what they mean. And one must recognize—*and heed!*—the four types of warning displays. This cannot be overemphasized. But as Samuel Taylor Coleridge wrote so beautifully: "Advice is like snow; the softer it falls, the longer it dwells upon, and the deeper it sinks into, the mind." So, enough said on that subject.

By international agreement, all wind reports are encoded and plotted (either by hand or by computer) on weather maps in *knots*. This may change in the future to conform to the metric system. Instead of 40 *knots*, we may be saying 20.7 *meters per second* (mps), or 74 *kilometers per hour* (kph). See Conversion Table J-4 in Appendix J. Frequent reference, however, is still made, and will undoubtedly continue to be made, to the Beaufort Wind Scale. Consequently, one should have an easy familiarity with this wind scale (table 1-1, pages 4 and 5) and the excellent photographs illustrating the sea conditions associated with various magnitudes of Beaufort wind force (figures 1-12 to 1-24, inclusive).

MARINE WEATHER AND OCEANOGRAPHIC SERVICES AND BROADCASTS*

The U.S. Government and the governments of many other countries around the world provide a variety of weather and oceanographic forecasts, warnings,

---

*With the kind permission of the U.S. National Weather Service, much of the information in this section has been derived from the NWS publication, *Operations of the National Weather Service.*

and other services of exceptional quality. This information is available to all seafarers, from novice weekend sailor to expert global sea-dog, for little or no cost. More detailed and highly specialized forecasts and services "tailored" to meet the unique requirements of clients are also available from commercial meteorological organizations in the United States and abroad.

In the United States, the National Weather Service (NWS), under the National Oceanic and Atmospheric Administration (NOAA), has a vast and outstanding program. In the period of one year, roughly three and a half million observations are taken and about two million forecasts and warnings are issued. Also, innumerable individual briefings and services are provided on a routine but unscheduled basis. It is inconceivable that anyone would even remotely consider selling off parts of the NWS or the government's weather and Landsat satellite programs to private interests! Yet, this is the case at this writing.

The provision of forecasts and warnings to the general public and to specialized users is the core of the NWS operations. The offices most involved in the production of *forecasts* are the Weather Service Forecast Offices (WSFOs) and the River Forecast Centers (RFCs), while *warnings* are issued by both WSFOs and the more localized Weather Service Offices (WSOs).

Forecasts issued by the WSFOs include state, zone, local, agricultural, environmental quality, *marine*, and other specialized forecast products. The National Meteorological Center (NMC), located in the World Weather Building at Camp Springs, Maryland (a suburb of Washington, D.C.), serves as the operating nerve center for weather and oceanographic information for the

Figure 1-12. Beaufort Force 0
Wind speed less than 1 kt
Sea criterion: Sea like a mirror.

Beaufort 1-10
(Courtesy Canada,
Atmospheric Environment
Service)

Date/Time of photograph: 5 June 1960, 2340 GMT.
Height of camera above sea: 35 ft.
Waves at time of picture

	Direction (° true)	Period (sec)	Height (ft)
Sea waves	—	—	—
Swell	100	5	2

Figure 1-13. Beaufort Force 1
Wind speed 1–3 kt, mean 2 kt
Sea criterion: Ripples with the appearance of scales are formed, but without foam
            crests.
Date/Time of photograph: 22 May 1960, 2000 GMT.
Height of camera above sea: 35 ft.
Waves at time of picture

	Direction (° true)	Period (sec)	Height (ft)
Sea waves	—	—	—
Swell	290	10	3

Figure 1-14. Beaufort Force 2
Wind speed 4–6 kt, mean 5 kt
Sea criterion: Small wavelets, still short, but more pronounced—crests have a
            glassy appearance and do not break.
Date/Time of photograph: 26 May 1961, 1700 GMT.
Height of camera above sea: 45 ft.
Waves at time of picture.

	Direction (° true)	Period (sec)	Height (ft)
Sea waves	120	—	—
Swell	050	6	1

Figure 1-15. Beaufort Force 3
Wind speed 7–10 kt, mean 9 kt
Sea criterion: Large wavelets. Crests begin to break. Foam of a glassy appearance.
　　　　　　Perhaps scattered white horses.
Date/Time of photograph: 19 Feb 1961, 2000 GMT.
Height of camera above sea: 45 ft.
Waves at time of picture.

	Direction (° true)	Period (sec)	Height (ft)
Sea waves	—	—	—
Swell	180	7	8

Figure 1-16. Beaufort Force 4
Wind speed 11–16 kt, mean 13 kt
Sea criterion: Small waves, becoming longer, fairly frequent white horses.
Date/Time of photograph: 3 July 1960, 2240 GMT.
Height of camera above sea: 35 ft.
Waves at time of picture

	Direction (° true)	Period (sec)	Height (ft)
Sea waves	310	5	3
Swell	—	—	—

Figure 1-17. Beaufort Force 5
Wind speed 17–21 kt, mean 19 kt
Sea criterion: Moderate waves taking a more pronounced long form, many white
horses are formed. (Chance of some spray.)
Date/Time of photograph: 7 Apr 1961, 2315 GMT.
Height of camera above sea: 35 ft.
Waves at time of picture

	Direction (° true)	Period (sec)	Height (ft)
Sea waves	280	6	7
Swell	240	8	6

Figure 1-18. Beaufort Force 6
Wind speed 22–27 kt, mean 24 kt
Sea criterion: Large waves begin to form; the white foam crests are more exten-
sive everywhere. (Probably some spray.)
Date/Time of photograph: 10 Feb 1961, 2115 GMT.
Height of camera above sea: 20 ft.
Waves at time of picture

	Direction (° true)	Period (sec)	Height (ft)
Sea waves	280	6	11
Swell	—	—	—

Figure 1-19. Beaufort Force 7
Wind speed 28–33 kt, mean 30 kt
Sea criterion: Sea heaps up and white foam from breaking waves begins to be
            blown in streaks along the direction of the wind.
Date/Time of photograph: 28 Feb 1961, 1900 GMT.
Height of camera above sea: 45 ft.
Waves at time of picture

	Direction (° true)	Period (sec)	Height (ft)
Sea waves	300	6	13
Swell	250	9	10

Figure 1-20. Beaufort Force 8
Wind speed 34–40 kt, mean 37 kt
Sea criterion: Moderately high waves of greater length; edges of crests begin to
            break into the spindrift. The foam is blown in well-marked streaks
            along the direction of the wind.
Date/Time of photograph: 15 Jan 1961, 1955 GMT.
Height of camera above sea: 35 ft.
Waves at time of picture

	Direction (° true)	Period (sec)	Height (ft)
Sea waves	260	7	18
Swell	—	—	—

Figure 1-21. Beaufort Force 9
Wind speed 41–47 kt, mean 44 kt
Sea criterion: High waves. Dense streaks of foam along the direction of the wind.
Crests of waves begin to topple, tumble, and roll over. Spray may affect visibility.
Date/Time of photograph: 17 Jan 1961, 2130 GMT.
Height of camera above sea: 35 ft.
Waves at time of picture

	Direction (° true)	Period (sec)	Height (ft)
Sea waves	120	7	20
Swell	—	—	—

Figure 1-22. Beaufort Force 10
Wind speed 48–55 kt, mean 52 kt
Sea criterion: Very high waves with long overhanging crests. The resulting foam, in great patches, is blown in dense white streaks along the direction of the wind. On the whole, the surface of the sea takes on a white appearance. The tumbling of the sea becomes heavy and shocklike. Visibility affected.
Date/Time of photograph: 14 Mar 1961, 2330 GMT.
Height of camera above sea: 15 ft.
Waves at time of picture

	Direction (° true)	Period (sec)	Height (ft)
Sea waves	340	9	22
Swell	—	—	—

Figure 1-23. Beaufort Force 11
Wind speed 53–63 kt, violent storm
Sea criterion: Exceptionally high waves, sea covered with white foam patches;
        visibility still more reduced. From *Marine Observer's Handbook*, 8th
        edition, London, 1963. Courtesy of the Controller of Her Britannic
        Majesty's Stationery Office.

Figure 1-24. Beaufort Force 12
Wind speed 64–71 kt. hurricane
Sea criterion: Air filled with foam; sea completely white with driving spray; visi-
        bility greatly reduced. From *Marine Observer's Handbook*, 8th edi-
        tion, London, 1963. Courtesy of Her Britannic Majesty's Stationery
        Office.

United States and much of the rest of the world. The NMC provides analyses and all sorts of forecast guidance material to the WSFOs and other consumers in order to meet their requirements.

The WSFOs and WSOs issue warnings for severe weather such as storms, hurricanes, tornadoes, severe thunderstorms, flash floods, and extreme winter weather. The National Severe Storms Forecast Center (NSSFC) in Kansas City, Missouri, and the National Hurricane Center in Miami (Coral Gables), Florida, provide the main support for the NWS warning program.

The River Forecast Centers (RFCs) issue river stage forecasts as well as special flow forecasts for use by irrigation, *navigation*, and hydroelectric power generation interests. The RFCs disseminate most special flow forecasts directly to users. The WSFOs interact with other agencies in their area and disseminate flood warnings and river stage forecasts to disaster officials, news media, and the general public. Most WSFOs and WSOs support the RFCs by the collection and relay of hydrologic data, and issue generalized flash flood watches and warnings.

Oceanographic Program and Services

This program provides oceanographic services necessary for safe and efficient marine activities along the seacoasts, offshore, and on the high seas. The oceanographic services program has a three-tiered structure. The Ocean Services Group at NMC assimilates ocean data from all sources and develops guidance products for the entire program. Ocean Service Units (OSUs) in selected coastal WSFOs provide regional focus for user liaison, and for development of improved ocean service products. Other coastal WSFOs and WSOs retain local forecast and warning responsibilities, and emphasize local dissemination of ocean products.

Analyses and forecasts of oceanographic phenomena are provided to support shipping, fishing, offshore drilling and mining, and marine recreation activities. Advisory and summary information on storm surges from both tropical and extratropical storms are provided to alleviate the loss of life and property along seacoasts, bays, and estuaries.

The services provided include ocean frontal analyses of the Gulf Stream, the Gulf of Mexico Loop Current, and Pacific Coast Upwelling. Objective analyses are also made of regional and global sea surface temperature (SST) and anomalies. Products range from daily analyses to monthly summaries, and are disseminated via mail, radio broadcasts, and facsimile broadcasts. Regional spectral wave and boundary current forecast products are now also included.

Marine Weather Program

This program measurably increases the safety of life and property, and greatly improves the efficiency of operations on the high seas, offshore, along the coasts, on the Great Lakes, and on other inland waterways, such as lakes, rivers, and reservoirs. Making use of the analyses and forecast guidance provided by the NMC, the marine weather forecasters issue specialized wind, wave, weather, and ice forecasts, warnings, and other information essential to the conduct of safe and effective marine operations and for the protection of the boating public.

The principal products include coastal, offshore, and high-seas forecasts; small-craft advisories; gale, storm, tropical cyclone, and storm-surge warnings; sea and swell forecasts; and sea and lake ice advisories. Special weather and trajectory forecasts are prepared to aid in the containment and cleanup of oil spills and other hazardous substances in the marine environment. Marine services in capsulated form showing coastal, offshore, and lakeside radio stations that make scheduled marine weather broadcasts are contained in the following figures:

- 1-25: High Seas Areas
- 1-26: Coastal and Offshore Areas
- 1-27: The Great Lakes
- 1-28: Alaska

High Seas Areas. High-seas services include warnings and special forecasts of weather, waves, and sea ice, and provide data in support of navigation and other operations on the high seas. Service in the western North Atlantic is furnished by the WSFOs, Washington, D.C., and Miami, Florida. Service in the North Pacific is furnished by the WSFOs in San Francisco and Honolulu. High-seas forecasts, based on NMC guidance and regional analyses, consist of three parts: (1) warnings (gale, storm, and tropical cyclone conditions), (2)

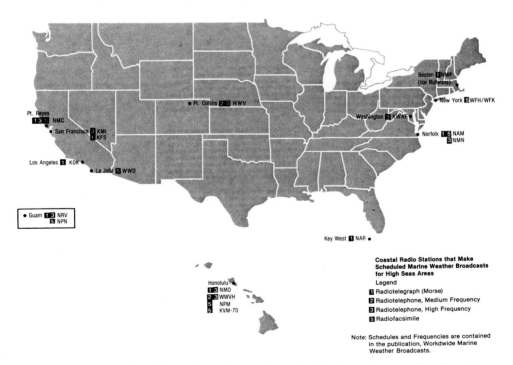

Figure 1-25. Coastal radio stations that make scheduled marine weather broadcasts for high seas areas. (Courtesy of NOAA National Weather Service)

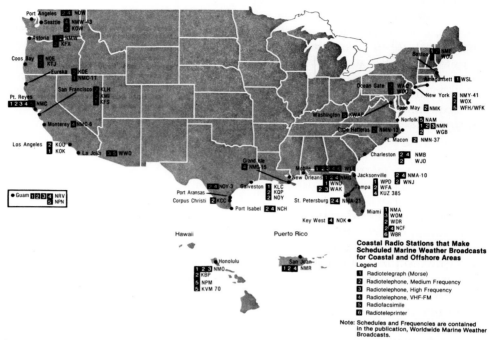

Figure 1-26. Coastal radio stations that make scheduled marine weather broadcasts for coastal and offshore areas. (Courtesy of NOAA National Weather Service)

synopses, and (3) forecasts of winds, waves, and sea ice. WSFO Honolulu also provides service as needed for the South Pacific to 25° S from 110° W to 160° E, and San Francisco furnishes support to fisheries as needed off South America from the equator to 25° S, east of 110° W.

These products are disseminated by the U.S. Coast Guard, the U.S. Navy, and commercial radiotelegraph stations; Coast Guard and commercial high-seas radiotelephone stations; and by Coast Guard radiofacsimile. National Marine Fisheries Radio Station WWD in La Jolla, California, provides fishing vessels in the Eastern Pacific with specialized fisheries information by radiotelephone and radiofacsimile.

In cooperation with the National Bureau of Standards, the NWS has established a High Seas Storm Information Service (HSSIS) consisting of brief, hourly broadcasts of information about major storms on the high seas using the facilities of the time signal station WWV for the North Atlantic and eastern North Pacific, and WWVH for the North and South Pacific. The WSFOs Washington, San Francisco, and Honolulu prepare the scripts for these broadcasts.

In cooperation with the U.S. Navy, the NWS also publishes *Worldwide Marine Weather Broadcasts*, the sole U.S. directory of principal marine weather broadcasts for the high seas, offshore, and coastal waters. The NWS also provides marine weather radio dissemination information through the

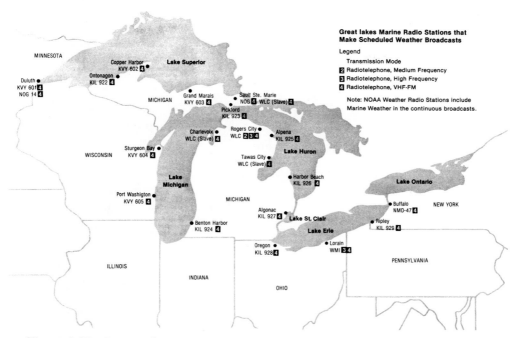

Figure 1-27. Great Lakes marine radio stations that make scheduled marine weather broadcasts. (Courtesy of NOAA National Weather Service)

Environmental Data Information Service (EDIS) publication, *Mariners' Weather Log*. Figure 1-29 depicts the U.S. high-seas forecast and warning areas.

Coastal and Offshore Waters. The services provided include specialized forecasts, warnings, and data in support of commercial operations and marine recreational activities in offshore and coastal waters. Services for coastal activities are furnished by 19 WSFOs and about 50 WSOs. Seven of the WSFOs prepare forecasts for offshore areas. These forecasts stress wind, weather, visibility, and wave heights, and are supplemented by synopses, small craft advisories, gale and storm warnings, short-fuze severe local storm warnings, and statements supplementing tropical cyclone advisories (issued by the National Hurricane Center (NHC)) including coastal flooding and shore erosion. In addition, warnings and forecasts of surf and breakers are prepared for selected beaches, plus information for selected ports and local areas. In Alaska, ice advisories are prepared for Cook Inlet, the Bering Sea, and the coastal areas of the East Chukchi and Beaufort Seas.

The warnings and forecasts are disseminated by NOAA Weather Radio, Coast Guard and commercial radiotelephone stations, and by regular AM and FM radio and television stations. In Alaska, the NWS supplements the commercial and Coast Guard weather broadcasts with five medium-frequency radio broadcast stations of its own. In most large metropolitan areas, marine

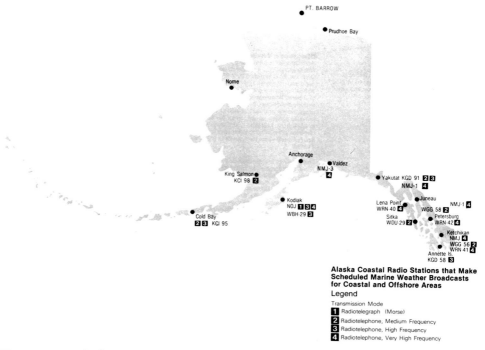

Figure 1-28. Alaska coastal radio stations that make scheduled marine weather broadcasts for coastal and offshore areas. (Courtesy of NOAA National Weather Service)

weather information is available on automatic telephones. Fifteen Marine Weather Services Charts, described in the following section titled "Sources of Weather Information," list the marine radio broadcasts in the areas covered by the charts, and show the locations of visual warning display stations. Figures 1-30, 1-31, and 1-32 show the coastal and offshore marine forecast areas.

The Great Lakes. These services include special forecasts and warnings in support of commercial shipping, fishing, and marine recreational activities on the Great Lakes. Forecasts and warnings for open lake shipping in the U.S. portion of the Great Lakes are provided by the WSFOs at Chicago, Ann Arbor, Cleveland, and Buffalo. During the boating season, these offices plus WSFO Milwaukee and 10 WSOs issue forecasts, small-craft advisories, and warnings for recreational boating for 32 nearshore areas (out to 5 miles). WSFO Chicago also issues forecast charts and a Great Lakes Storm Summary Bulletin to aid shipping operations. WSFO Cleveland alerts mariners to the expected onset of unusual, widespread storm conditions requiring special advance planning to safeguard life and property.

Day-to-day ice advisories and information relative to ice formation and movement at the end of the normal Great Lakes navigation season, and predictions of ice breakup in the spring are furnished to the Coast Guard,

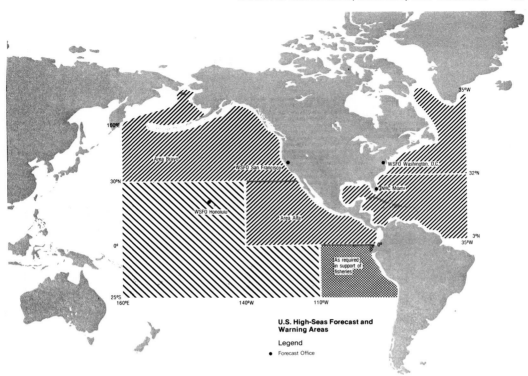

Figure 1-29. U.S. high-seas forecast and warning areas. (Courtesy of NOAA National Weather Service)

shipping interests, and anyone desiring or having a need for them by the WSFO Ann Arbor. Advisories are issued by WSFO Cleveland for storm surges and low water levels in Lake Erie. The WSFO Chicago issues seiche (oscillation of surface of lake) warnings for southern Lake Michigan, and the WSFO Ann Arbor does the same for Saginaw Bay in Lake Huron.

The warnings and forecasts are disseminated by NOAA Weather Radio, Coast Guard radio stations, the commercial marine VHF radiotelephone networks, and by regular AM and FM radio and television stations. The Marine Weather Services Charts list the marine radio broadcasts and show the locations of visual warning display stations. The Great Lakes marine forecast and warning areas (including nearshore marine forecast areas) are as shown in figure 1-33.

The Joint Ice Center Program. This program provides sea/lake ice data, analyses, and forecast services in support of operational and climatological ice programs. In collaboration with the Department of the Navy, NOAA has established a Joint Ice Center (JIC) composed of NWS, NESS, and Navy personnel. The JIC provides ice information to the two agencies. This also includes guidance for the WSFOs with sea/lake ice responsibilities.

Global and regional ice analyses are produced as a synthesis of information from ships and shore stations, aerial ice reconnaissance missions, ice analyses

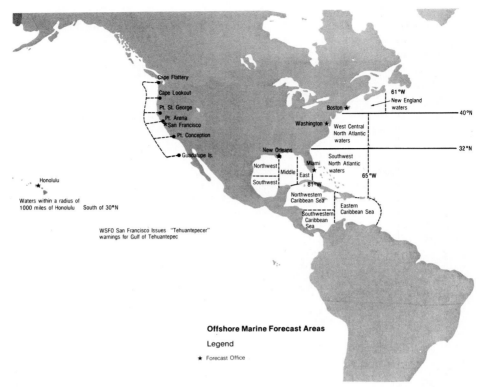

Figure 1-30. Offshore marine forecast areas. (Courtesy of NOAA National Weather Service)

from other domestic and foreign centers, and from satellites. Quite obviously, this information also has strategic value and implications. Prediction services include short-term specialized forecasts, weekly, monthly, and seasonal regional and hemispheric forecasts. In addition, the JIC weekly ice charts are published as yearly Arctic and bi-yearly Antarctic atlases.

The Tsunami Warning System Program

Tsunamis are ocean waves produced by a submarine earthquake, a landslide, or a volcanic eruption. They are also correctly called *seismic sea waves*. But they are popularly and incorrectly called *tidal waves*. Tsunamis have no connection whatever with tides. The popular name, tidal wave, is entirely misleading. Tsunamis may reach enormous dimensions, and they have sufficient energy to travel across entire oceans at high speed, sometimes approaching 440 knots (500 mph, 820 kph, 226 mps)! They proceed as ordinary *gravity waves* with a period between about 15 and 60 minutes. Tsunamis steepen and increase in height on approaching shallow water, completely inundating low-lying areas. Where local submarine topography causes extreme steepening, they may break and cause very extensive damage.

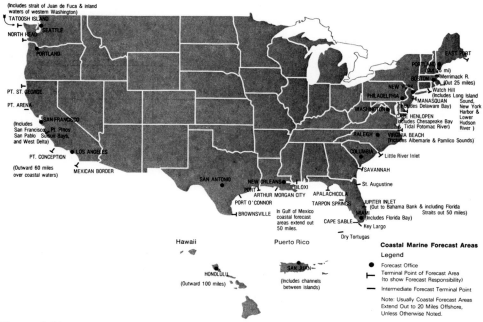

Figure 1-31. Coastal marine forecast areas. (Courtesy of NOAA National Weather Service)

Returning to Norfolk, Virginia, from the world's first hydrogen-bomb detonation at Eniwetok in November 1952, several navy colleagues and the author took a few days of annual leave in Honolulu to "rest, fall back, and regroup" on the way home. One night, we heard on the radio that a tsunami warning had been issued for the Hawaiian Islands. Since none of us had ever seen a tsunami, it was decided to take binoculars, cameras, picnic baskets, and chilled wine and glasses to Waikiki Beach for a first-hand and spectacular view of the phenomenon. That was a foolish and almost fatal mistake. In scrambling away from the beach at high speed at the last minute to avert personal catastrophe, all equipment and supplies had to be hurriedly abandoned and fell victim to the terrifying tsunami. But it was another lesson learned by several navy junior officers.

The Tsunami Warning System provides timely and effective tsunami information and warnings to Pacific communities and boating interests in order to minimize the hazards of tsunamis. The Pacific Tsunami Warning Center (PTWC) at Ewa Beach, Oahu, Hawaii, is responsible for releasing public watches and warnings of tsunamis for all U.S. territories and states bordering on the Pacific Ocean. Watches and warnings are disseminated to WSFOs, state civil defense agencies, the Federal Emergency Management Agency (FEMA), military organizations, and others, who, in turn, furnish the information to users. In accordance with bilateral agreements, tsunami watch and warning

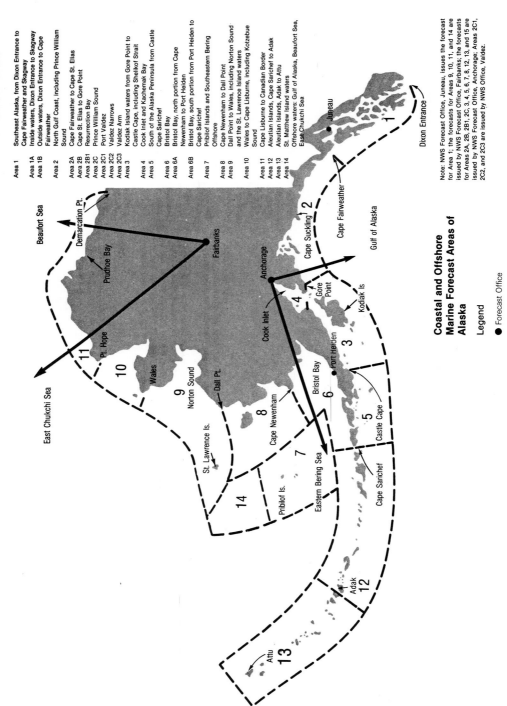

Figure 1-32. Coastal and offshore marine forecast areas of Alaska. (Courtesy of NOAA National Weather Service)

Figure 1-33. Great Lakes marine forecast and warning areas (including nearshore marine forecast areas). (Courtesy of NOAA National Weather Service)

information is also disseminated by the PTWC to countries and territories throughout the Pacific basin.

Seismograph stations participating in the system detect earthquakes and submit reports to the PTWC, where the earthquake location and magnitude are determined. Tide stations in the system detect the tsunami and furnish the information on the nature of the local wave to the PTWC.

A regional tsunami warning system is operated for the protection of Alaska and the Aleutian Island chain. This system is headquartered at the Alaska Tsunami Warning Center (ATWC) in Palmer, Alaska. Figure 1-34 shows the U.S. Tsunami Warning System.

Private and Commercial Weather Organizations

Although the services and products of the National Weather Service are timely, diversified, and excellent, it is impossible for the NWS to meet each and every unique requirement of all users of meteorological and oceanographic data and information. This is why there are private and commercial weather organizations performing special environmental tasks and studies for consumers and providing highly specialized, "tailored" forecasts and other services to meet client requirements. A listing of these private and commercial companies is contained in the Professional Directory section of each monthly issue of the *Bulletin of the American Meteorological Society*.

From a marine standpoint, the "Rolls-Royce" (but affordable) of commercial weather and oceanographic companies is *Oceanroutes, Inc.*, headquar-

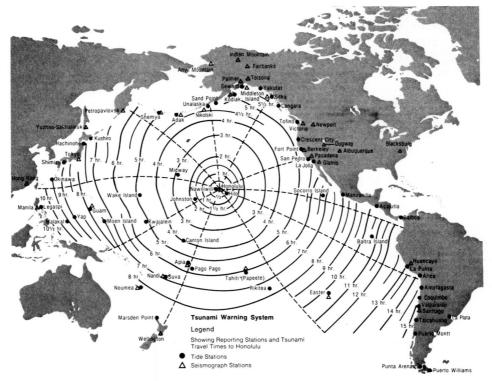

Figure 1-34. The Tsunami Warning System. (Courtesy of NOAA National Weather Service)

tered in Palo Alto, California (about 40 miles SSE of San Francisco). For mariners with a "weather eye" for safety and efficiency, this company is the largest, best-staffed, best-equipped, and overall most capable commercial organization in the business of:

- Ship/Ocean Routing—more than a thousand routings monthly for over 700 different companies;
- Marine Forecasting—daily operational weather and sea-condition forecasts for over 100 offshore projects;
- Ocean-Tow and Rig-Move Strategies—route evaluation, tow simulation, and en route monitoring;
- Offshore studies—historical data profiles, hindcast studies, and weather-related simulations for major offshore oil producers and contractors.

To enable the closest of client relationships, *Oceanroutes, Inc.,* also maintains offices in New York, NY; Houston, TX; Aberdeen, Scotland; London and Gravesend, England; Tokyo, Japan; Seoul, Korea; Hong Kong; Singapore; Perth, Australia; and Abu Dhabi, U.A.E.

As every experienced sailor knows, a great-circle track is the shortest route between two points on our planet. But it is frequently not the shortest in time nor the safest route. High winds, heavy weather, fog, ice, and other navigational hazards, and/or high seas often render a great-circle track time-consuming, uneconomical, and hazardous or downright dangerous. In the period of a year, it is not unusual for world shipping to experience more than 6 percent heavy-weather damage and over 4 percent collisions and groundings caused by heavy weather and/or sea conditions. World ship casualties from weather-related causes for the period 1967–1975, inclusive, are listed in table 1-2. In view of these statistics, it is imperative that skippers and shipping interests avail themselves of the mandatory and excellent services provided by organizations such as *Oceanroutes*.

Over the last three decades, *Oceanroutes* has amassed extensive archives of world weather and oceanographic data and information and has compiled detailed ship performance characteristics for all major hull geometries. Not too many years ago, coastal and ocean routing services provided little more than a least-threatening route to avoid or minimize weather damage. Techniques were cumbersome and slow. Weather observations were sparse or non-existent in many areas. Data were transmitted by slow-speed telex. And weather maps were plotted by hand. Then, along came four events that advanced the sciences of meteorology and oceanography immeasurably: (1) extremely high-speed computers, (2) remote sensing satellites, (3) communications satellites, and (4) the formulation of theoretical models that effectively simulate the interaction of marine weather (and sea conditions) and sea-going vessels.

The routing of ships and smaller craft today is an extremely modern and complex operation of planning, guiding, and tracking the passage of vessels embarked on long coastal cruises and/or transocean voyages, using the sciences of meteorology, oceanography, seamanship, vessel dynamics, navigation, satellite technology, naval architecture, computer technology, and maritime economics. Quite obviously, this requires advanced computer capabilities and a global communications network, including access to polar-orbiting and geostationary satellites.

Continuous weather and oceanographic observations are received from sources around the world by landline communications networks, marine

Table 1-2. World ship casualties from weather-related causes for the period 1967–1975, inclusive.* Courtesy of *Oceanroutes, Inc.*

Heavy weather	96
Dense fog	15
Typhoons	10
Fog	6
Hurricanes	3
Cyclones	2
Monsoons	2
Storms	1
Heavy rain and fog	1
Poor visibility	1
Lightning	1
TOTAL	138

*Over 5,000 tons DW.

radio, computer-to-computer links, and satellites. But even the most modern and most efficient physical resources require management and staffing by knowledgeable, competent, and dedicated professionals. This is precisely the case at *Oceanroutes, Inc.*, where the staffs consist of senior professional meteorologists, oceanographers, climatologists, ocean engineers, computer experts, systems analysts, naval architects, statisticians, master mariners, and a variety of consultants.

The operational forecasting staffs (see figure 1-35) and the routing staffs (see figure 1-36) determine the routes that will provide the *fastest passage*, with the *maximum safety* for the crew and passengers, and the *greatest security* for the cargo and hull, considering the predicted weather and oceanographic conditions along the proposed route or course. By entering the ship's basic speed capability into the computer that contains the weather and oceanographic data for the selected tracks, the effect of the wind and sea on the ship's speed for all feasible routes is determined. Only then is the decision/recommendation made for the least-time-route (staying well within the ship's safety limits).

But conditions other than heavy weather and ocean currents affect transit time. Areas of fog can slow a ship. Sea ice and ship icing conditions in higher latitudes can present serious sources of danger. And navigational hazards and restricted zones can all add to the sailing time. All environmental factors are taken into account to determine the theoretical fastest time route during the first planning stage.

The theoretical route determined from the computer is then evaluated by the operational forecast specialists to incorporate the requirements imposed

Figure 1-35. Operational analysts and forecasters preparing ships' routings and voyage advisories. (Courtesy of Oceanroutes, Inc.)

Figure 1-36. Route analysts receive a daily morning briefing—more often if necessary—of current weather and oceanographic patterns over the world's oceans. (Courtesy of Oceanroutes, Inc.)

by the cargo, the conditions of load and trim, the sea-handling characteristics of the ship or smaller craft, the vessel's navigational equipment, the schedules to be met, the insurance restrictions, the fuel consumption, etc., etc. Nothing is left to chance, and one can easily see that this is an extremely detailed and complex business. The various ship routing selection factors are shown in table 1-3.

Once under way, all vessels are "followed" by the *Oceanroutes'* tracking program and become the 24-hours-per-day, seven-days-per-week responsibility of the on-duty route analysts, who are backed by a team of highly experienced meteorologists, oceanographers, master mariners, etc. Supported by unique computer programs and graphic plots, satellite data and images, a ship's passage is continuously tracked. If unexpected adverse weather or sea conditions require a change from the original route, the skipper is alerted in advance and given diversions that will enable him to avoid or circumnavigate the worst conditions. This requires a global communications network as illustrated in figure 1-37.

Figure 1-38 shows the large difference in times of passage, distances traveled, weather encountered, etc., by routed and unrouted ships on North Atlantic and North Pacific ocean crossings.

On the completion of each transit, an appraisal of the voyage is made by an End of Voyage Summary and a Post-Voyage Analysis, as shown in figure 1-39. These reports include a track chart of the voyage, a communications log, and a daily summary of position, distance sailed, and speed of advance (SOA). This

Table 1-3. Ship-routing selection factors. Courtesy of *Oceanroutes, Inc.*

Environment	*Ship* or *Craft*
Weather pressure patterns and storm paths	Type
	Speed capability
Winds, seas, swells	Draft, trim
Hurricanes, typhoons, tropical storms	Stability
	Deck load, ballast
Ocean currents	Sea-handling characteristics
Localized weather and geographic anomalies	Navigational aids
Seasonal weather	
Operational	*Cargo*
Schedule	Kind
Fuel economies	Special requirements
Insurance restrictions	(temperature, humidity, etc.)
Navigational hazards	Protection from the sea
Restricted zones	

report provides a vital record of environmental impact on vessel peformance for the skipper, the charterer, and the owner. By studying such post-voyage reports, skippers enlarge their professional fund of knowledge about their ships and the elements, learn the uses and benefits of ocean routing, and how to apply this knowledge to their personal operating procedures. Not to avail oneself of the superb marine services of the National Weather Service and commercial organizations such as *Oceanroutes, Inc.*, is tantamount to conning a ship through a narrow channel blindfolded.

SOME SOURCES AND METHODS OF OBTAINING WEATHER AND OCEANOGRAPHIC INFORMATION

Charts and Publications

Marine Weather Services Charts. The broadcast schedules of radio stations, NWS office telephone numbers, the locations of warning display stations, and all sorts of good and pertinent information for mariners is reprinted on these charts. The charts are issued periodically for the following areas and numbered as follows:

- MSC-1 Eastport, Maine, to Montauk Point, N.Y.
- MSC-2 Montauk Point, N.Y., to Manasquan, N.J.
- MSC-3 Manasquan, N.J., to Cape Hatteras, N.C.
- MSC-4 Cape Hatteras, N.C., to Savannah, Ga.
- MSC-5 Savannah, Ga., to Apalachicola, Fla.
- MSC-6 Apalachicola, Fla., to Morgan City, La.
- MSC-7 Morgan City, La., to Brownsville, Tex.
- MSC-8 Mexican Border to Point Conception, Calif.
- MSC-9 Point Conception, Calif., to Point St. George, Calif.

Figure 1-37. The communications center at corporate headquarters links Ocean-routes to offices and ships around the world. (Courtesy of Oceanroutes, Inc.)

- MSC-10 Point St. George, Calif., to Canadian Border
- MSC-11 Great Lakes; Michigan and Superior
- MSC-12 Great Lakes; Huron, Erie, and Ontario
- MSC-13 Hawaiian Waters
- MSC-14 Puerto Rico and Virgin Islands
- MSC-15 Alaskan Waters

Copies of the Marine Weather Services Charts are available at local marinas, at marine chart dealers, or one can obtain them by ordering from the National Ocean Survey, Distribution Division (C-44), 6501 Lafayette Avenue, Riverdale, Maryland 20840.

Notice to Mariners. Boating enthusiasts and mariners of all experience levels should be familiar with, and subscribe to, this publication. It is published weekly by the Defense Mapping Agency Hydrographic/Topographic Center (DMAHTC), and is prepared jointly by NOAA's National Ocean Survey (NOS) and the U.S. Coast Guard (USCG). All issues contain a wealth of information of interest to sailors of all descriptions and levels of expertise. Among other items, important matters affecting navigational safety, including new hydrographic discoveries, changes in channels and navigational aids, etc., are included in each issue. The *Notices* contain selected items from various *Local Notices to Mariners* and other reported marine information required by ocean-going vessels. The *Notices* also contain specific information that is useful for updating the latest editions of nautical charts and publications produced by the DMAHTC, the NOS, and the USCG.

Local Notices to Mariners are issued by each U.S. Coast Guard district to disseminate important information affecting navigational safety within that particular district. Since temporary information, known or expected to be of short duration, is not included in the weekly *Notice to Mariners*, the appropriate *Local Notice to Mariners* may be the only source of such information. Small craft using the Intercoastal Waterway and other waterways and small harbors that are not normally used by ocean-going vessels will require the *Local Notices to Mariners* to keep charts and related publications up-to-date. *Local Notices* may be obtained from the Commander of the local Coast Guard District at no cost.

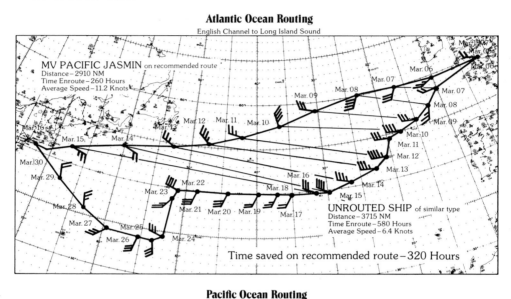

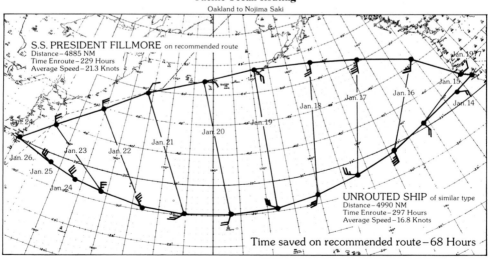

Figure 1-38. Comparative studies of routed and unrouted ships. Note the large differences in times en route, distances traveled, average speed, etc. (Courtesy of Oceanroutes, Inc.)

Important contributions are made to the *Notice to Mariners* by the U.S. Army Corps of Engineers and by foreign hydrographic offices and cooperating observers of all nationalities. These *Notices* are global in scope. The contents are presented in three sections:

- Section I—Catalog Corrections, Geographic Index, Chart Corrections, New Charts and Publications, Chartlets and Depth Tabulations, Sailing Directions, and Coast Pilot Corrections.
- Section II—Light List Corrections, Radio Aids Corrections, Other Publication Corrections.
- Section III—Broadcast Warnings and Marine Information, Miscellaneous.

Figure 1-39. At the end of each routed voyage, an analysis is made of the ship's actual and potential performance through the weather and sea conditions encountered en route. (Courtesy of Oceanroutes, Inc.)

Issues of *Notice to Mariners* may be obtained from local offices of the DMAHTC, or the NOS, or the USCG, or by writing to one of the following: Defense Mapping Agency Hydrographic/Topographic Center (Attn: Code-NS), Washington, D.C. 20315; the U.S. Coast Guard (Attn: GWAN-174), Washington, D.C. 20590; or the National Ocean Survey (Attn: C-44), Riverdale, Maryland 20840.

Mariner's Weather Log. This excellent periodical, published bi-monthly by NOAA's Environmental Data Service, is a must for all who sail upon the sea. Each issue contains numerous photographs, charts, diagrams, and other illustrations covering subjects of particular interest to weekend sailors and deep-sea mariners. Among other things, each issue contains fascinating weather-related articles by meteorologists, oceanographers, and mariners, hints to observers, tips concerning radio operations, special subjects, interesting letters to the editor, marine weather reviews of the North Atlantic and North Pacific, and monthly marine weather diaries. Also included are special articles and tips regarding heavy weather situations. This publication is available from NOAA's Environmental Data Service, Page Building (D-762), 2001 Wisconsin Avenue, Washington, D.C. 20235.

Worldwide Marine Weather Broadcasts. This publication is now the principal source of information on marine weather broadcasts. It has replaced Publication H.O. 118, published for many years by the Naval Oceanographic Office. It is revised annually, and interim changes and corrections are made by means of the weekly *Notice to Mariners* issued by the DMAHTC. The table of contents of this excellent publication is as follows:
- Introduction—(A description and explanation of the material presented)
- Section 1—Radiotelegraph Broadcasts
- Section 2—Radiotelephone Broadcasts
- Section 3—Radiofacsimile Broadcasts
- Section 4—Radioteleprinter Broadcasts
- Section 5—Weather Broadcasts for the Great Lakes Continuous Broadcasts—NOAA Weather Radio (VHF-FM)
- Figures—(Marine Weather Forecast Areas)
- Appendix—(Explanation of Terms, Symbols, and Codes)

This publication is for sale by: Superintendent of Documents, U.S. Government Printing Office, Washington, D.C. 20402.

International Meteorological Codes and Worldwide Synoptic Broadcasts. This publication has replaced Section 3 (Synoptic Broadcasts) and Section 5 (Codes) of the now obsolete H.O. Publication 118, Radio Weather Aids. Changes to the publication are provided by the Commander Naval Oceanography Command. The contents are as follows:
- Introduction—(A detailed description of the contents)
- Section A—Lists of International Code Forms and Corresponding Standard Coding Procedures
- Section B—Lists and Meanings of Symbolic Words and Groups Appearing in Coded Reports
- Section C—Lists of Symbolic Letters which are to be Replaced, Generally

by Figures in Coded Reports, Analyses, or Forecasts, with their Specifications

- Section D—Specifications of Code Figures in the Form of Code Tables
- Section E—Description of the System of Station Index Numbers
- Section F—The Beaufort Scale of Wind for Ease of Reference (and in order to provide the equivalent wind speeds for Beaufort numbers used in some codes)
- Attachment—(Common Code—FM12-VII and FM13-VII—for reporting surface observations from different types of surface stations)

This publication is obtainable from the Commander, Naval Oceanography Command, NSTL Station, Bay St. Louis, Mississippi 39529.

Information for Shipping. Details of all foreign weather broadcasts are contained in this publication. It should be on the checklist of all vessels and craft that travel internationally. The publication identifier is Publication Number 9, TP-4, Volume D, and may be obtained from The World Meteorological Organization (WMO), Case Postale No. 7, CH 1211, Geneva, 20, Switzerland.

Environmental Data Buoys

NOAA's National Data Buoy Center (NDBC) at Bay St. Louis, Mississippi, has several programs under way to correct major voids that exist in the marine environmental observational network in the waters contiguous to the United States and other areas. One of these voids is the U.S. coastal region. Very few marine weather and oceanographic observations are reported routinely from this region, which is heavily congested with traffic.

Observations in the coastal region were previously furnished by U.S. Coast Guard personnel assigned to light stations and lightships along the coast and at major harbor entrances. These light stations and lightships have been replaced by automatic lights and Large Navigational Buoys (LNBs). All personnel have been assigned to other duties. As a result, very few weather observations have been available from coastal regions. To correct this deficiency, the NDBC has been installing and operating automated marine environmental observing and reporting stations on LNBs (as shown in figure 1-40).

Other moored environmental data buoys, which are of great importance to weather and hurricane forecasters, are deployed off the coasts of the United States, in the Great Lakes, and in the Gulf of Mexico. The NDBC has engaged in a continuing buoy development process based on its experience and technological expertise gained through the design, fabrication, deployment, and maintenance of environmental data buoys. Through this process, the NDBC has developed a network of highly reliable environmental buoys that require considerably less maintenance and service than previously deployed buoy systems. And the information obtained from these buoys is invaluable.

Since deployment of the prototype environmental data buoy in July 1975, the moored buoy network has been expanded to over 25 buoys. Approximately 17 of these buoys are dedicated to NWS support, with five located in the

Atlantic, four in the Gulf of Mexico, six in the northeast Pacific, and two in the Great Lakes. The remaining buoys are special stations, which include support of Bureau of Land Management studies, salt dome environmental monitoring, and experimental buoys. Figure 1-41 is a plot of moored data buoy locations. At this writing, DISCUS hull type (D) and NOMAD hull type (N) environmental buoys are deployed at the following locations:

Figure 1-40. A Large Navigational Buoy (LNB) of the U.S. Coast Guard with NOAA Data Buoy Center automated marine environmental observing and reporting equipment installed. (Courtesy of NOAA Data Buoy Center)

D 34.9N–72.9W	N 40.5N–69.4W	D 46.1N–131.0W
N 32.3N–75.3W	N 48.0N–87.6W	D 40.8N–137.6W
N 29.3N–77.3W	N 45.3N–86.3W	N 46.2N–124.2W
D 25.9N–89.7W	N 45.3N–82.8W	D 34.9N–120.9W
D 26.0N–93.5W	N 47.2N–86.5W	N 37.4N–122.7W
D 26.0N–86.0W	N 41.7N–82.5W	D 38.2N–123.3W
D 30.1N–88.9W	N 47.3N–90.0W	D 39.2N–124.0W
28.7N–95.3W (Platform)	N 42.7N–87.1W	N 40.8N–124.5W
29.6N–93.5W (Platform)	N 44.3N–82.4W	N 34.3N–120.7W
N 40.8N–68.5W	N 56.3N–148.3W	D 32.8N–119.2W
D 38.5N–70.7W	D 42.5N–130.3W	N 33.6N–119.0W
D 42.7N–68.3W	D 51.9N–155.7W	N 37.8N–122.7W
N 43.5N–70.1W	D 50.9N–135.9W	N 23.4N–162.3W

There are also four environmental data buoys independently operated and maintained by EXXON, transmitting data every three hours, from the following locations:

63.3N–170.3W (Platform)	57.2N–170.3W (Platform
60.3N–172.3W (Platform)	55.9N–168.0W (MAREX 5)

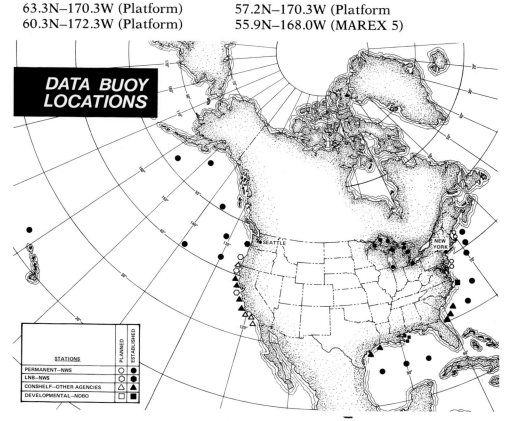

Figure 1-41. Locations of the moored environmental data buoys of the NOAA National Data Buoy Center. (Courtesy of the NOAA Data Buoy Center)

The deep-ocean moored buoys are either 33-feet (10 meters) or 40-feet (12 meters) in diameter DISCUS buoys as shown in figure 1-42. Or they are 20-foot (6 meters) long, boat-shaped NOMAD buoys, as shown in figure 1-43, which are

Figure 1-42. The 12-meter (40-foot) discus-hull-type environmental buoy under tow by the U.S. Coast Guard, en route to its offshore station. (Courtesy of NOAA Data Buoy Center)

Figure 1-43. The six-meter (20-foot) NOMAD boat-shaped environmental data buoy. (Courtesy of NOAA Data Buoy Center)

located in near-shore areas and in the Great Lakes. Some recent stability tests by the elements, which were unplanned, have shown these platforms to be more stable than expected in high seas. And this will, undoubtedly, have an impact on future deployments of these hulls.

The NOAA NDBC moored buoys gather and report meteorological and oceanographic data every three hours. However, in the event of severe weather, hourly observations may be taken. The parameters measured by the buoys include the following:

- Wind speed
- Wind gusts
- Wind direction
- Air temperature
- Barometric pressure
- Significant wave height
- Wave period
- Wave spectra
- Surface water temperature

So, if you encounter one of these buoys while you're cruising or sailing, you will know it isn't a special effects prop from "Star Wars" or "Return of the Jedi," floating on the surface of the sea.

A complete communications network, as shown in figure 1-44, has been

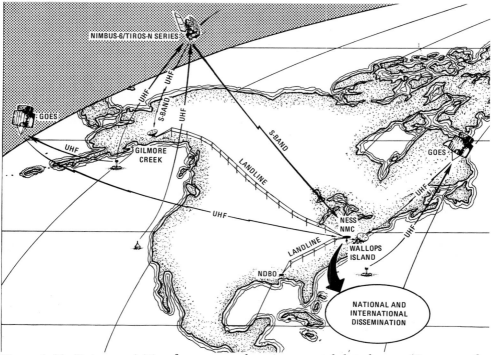

Figure 1-44. Data acquisition from moored environmental data buoys. (Courtesy of NOAA Data Buoy Center)

established to receive and disseminate the data acquired from these buoys. The system uses the GOES satellite system and other facilities operated by the National Environmental Satellite Service (NESS) and the National Weather Service (NWS).

NDBC's drifting environmental buoys (as opposed to the moored buoys) are versatile and the lowest cost of all NDBC buoy systems. They measure and report a simple set of meteorological and oceanographic parameters, as well as fix and report their geographical position. These drifting buoys are popular oceanographic tools for mapping ocean currents using Lagrangian tracking techniques. They report position fixes and environmental data at UHF frequencies via the polar-orbiting TIROS-N series satellites. The satellite transmits the information to NESS facilities in Anchorage, Alaska, or Wallops Island, Virginia, where it is relayed by landline to Service ARGOS in Toulouse, France, for processing and distribution over the Global Telecommunications System. These data are available at least once per day.

These TIROS meteorological drifting buoys of the NDBC were deployed in the South Pacific Ocean in 1978–79 for the First GARP Global Experiment (FGGE). The buoys reported barometric pressure, sea surface temperature, and position via the satellite. American and Argentine ships deployed 51 buoys, and 14 buoys were successfully air-dropped by the U.S. Air Force as shown in figure 1-45. Figure 1-46 shows some of the tracks of the U.S. FGGE drifting buoys in the Southern Hemisphere. The data from these drifting buoys have proven to be extremely valuable in overcoming real-time forecasting problems in the Southern Hemisphere oceans, where persistent cloudiness hinders satellite observations and where weather observation stations and reporting ships are extremely sparse or do not exist at all. During 1985–86, the National Weather Service hopes to deploy 40–50 of these drifting buoys in the Pacific Ocean and Gulf of Mexico to assist weather and hurricane forecasters.

NOAA (National Weather Service) VHF-FM Radio Weather Transmissions

The NOAA National Weather Service provides weather, river, and marine information, forecasts and warnings, and provides positive alerts by demuting receivers to warn of hazardous conditions. This is an outstanding service for all coastal and inland boating enthusiasts and mariners. These VHF-FM radio weather transmissions repeat taped messages every four to six minutes. The tapes are updated every two to three hours and modified as necessary to include the latest information. The transmissions are broadcast 24 hours per day on one of seven high-band frequencies ranging from 162.400–162.550 MegaHertz (MHz) from many stations along U.S. mainland coastal areas, rivers, and lakes as well as inland. Also, they are broadcast from Alaska, Hawaii, and Puerto Rico, as shown in figure 1-47. (MHz = MegaHertz; one Hertz = one cycle per second; MegaHertz = one million Hertz = one million cycles per second.)

The messages include weather and radar summaries, wind observations, visibility, sea and river and lake conditions, detailed local and area forecasts, and other information tailored to meet the needs of professional mariners and amateur boatmen. During severe weather, NWS forecasters interrupt the

Figure 1-45. The drifting environmental buoy being air-dropped into the ocean. (Courtesy of NOAA Data Buoy Center)

routine weather broadcasts and substitute special warning messages. They also activate specially designed warning receivers. Such receivers either sound an alarm indicating that an emergency exists, which alerts the listener to turn the receiver up to an audible volume, or when operated in a muted mode, are automatically turned on so that the warning message is heard.

The frequencies used (162.400–162.550 MHz) are not found on the average home-type radio. More recently, however, many radio manufacturers offer special weather radios that operate on these frequencies—with and without the emergency warning alarm. There are also many radios on the market now that offer standard AM/FM frequencies plus the so-called "weather band" as an additional feature.

The NOAA VHF-FM broadcasts can usually be received 20–60 miles from the transmitting antenna, depending on terrain and the quality of the receiver used. Frequencies between 162.400–162.550 MHz lie above the commercial FM frequencies (which end at 108 MHz). Receivers are available in a variety of

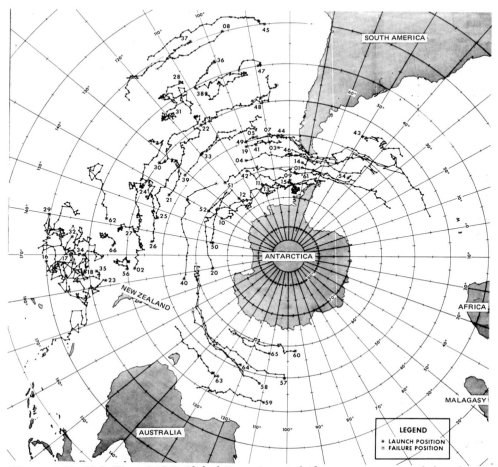

Figure 1-46. U.S. First GARP Global Experiment drifting environmental data buoy tracks in the Southern Hemisphere. (Courtesy of NOAA Data Buoy Center)

types, sizes, and prices. In selecting a suitable receiver, one should pay special attention to the manufacturer's rating of the receiver's *sensitivity*. A receiver with a sensitivity of *one microvolt or less* should pick up a broadcast at a distance of 40–60 miles.

A "listening guide" to be used when buying a receiver for the reception of NOAA VHF-FM radio transmissions is contained in table 1-4. The data used in constructing table 1-4 are based on the following parameters: (1) transmission over clear terrain, (2) standard 300-watt transmitting station, (3) transmitter antenna height 300 feet, (4) receiver antenna height six feet, and (5) narrow-band FM receiver (deviation 15 kHz). (kHz = kiloHertz; kiloHertz = one thousand Hertz = one thousand cycles per second.) No conscientious coastal sailor or recreational boating enthusiast should be without this equipment.

Radiofacsimile (Radiofax)

Through the years, radiofax has become almost as important a "tool" to men of the sea as a sextant. From naval captain to master mariner to fisherman to pleasure boating and yachting enthusiasts, the aspect of *safety* has always been a primary consideration. Rightly so. And one of the *major threats* to that safety will always be *heavy weather.*

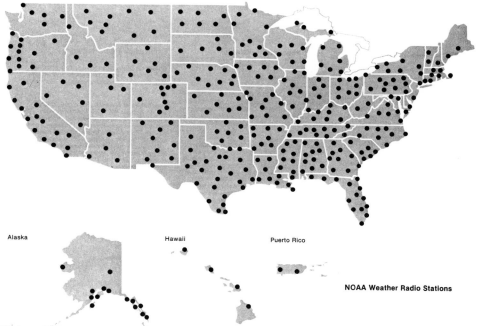

Figure 1-47. Locations of the NOAA VHF-FM weather radio stations. (Courtesy of NOAA National Weather Service)

Table 1-4. A guide to be used when buying a radio receiver for the reception of NOAA VHF-FM radio weather transmissions. Courtesy of NOAA National Weather Service.

Distance of Receiver from Transmitter Site	Sensitivity of Receiver
60 miles	0.6 microvolts
50 miles	0.9 microvolts
40 miles	1.2 microvolts
30 miles	2.5 microvolts
20 miles	6.0 microvolts
10 miles	20.0 microvolts

The development and extensive use of many navigational and safety aids such as radar, Loran, Omega, and radiofax have made transocean planning and operations, and coastal and inland commercial shipping and pleasure boating much easier and safer. And radiofax has been a major contributor to safety at sea.

I.S. Turgenev said it so well: "A picture shows me at a glance what it takes dozens of pages of a book to expound." And radiofax is primarily a broadcast of pictures, charts, maps, and satellite images, thereby saving many, many man-hours that would otherwise be required to copy weather broadcasts, plot the data, and analyze the maps, etc. Radiofax is far more useful than only voice, plain language, or coded weather broadcasts, and is an unbeatable combination when used together with other broadcasts and/or ocean routing services.

Radiofax weather and oceanographic maps and charts, and satellite images, are now available almost everywhere in the world. Transmitter sites are located in seven geographic areas: North and Central America, South America, Europe, Africa, Asia, the Southwestern Pacific, and the Antarctic. At this writing, there are over 50 transmitters, located in over 20 countries, transmitting weather and oceanographic maps and charts and/or satellite images. Table 1-5 is an Abbreviated Directory of Worldwide Radiofax Transmitter Sites and Frequencies (kHz).

As a communications technique, radiofax provides the desired characteristics of redundancy. Even with the presence (and frustrations) of ambient noise, information that would normally be "garbled" and lost in radiotele-type transmissions can usually be understood via radiofax. And with an elementary knowledge of meteorology and oceanography, naval captains, merchant masters, fishing skippers, yachtsmen, and pleasure boat owners of all types with radiofax equipment on board are well equipped to minimize heavy weather threats and optimize environmental factors.

Radiofax transmissions are available around the world to anyone who has the equipment to receive them. All that is required is a high-frequency (HF) radio receiver (tunable or crystal controlled), an appropriate antenna, and a suitable facsimile (fax) recorder.

Radiofax equipments today are usually solid state and very simple to operate. After minimal training, the user finds that operation of the radiofax system quickly becomes as routine as with other electronic gear on board. There are several features, however, that one should look for when selecting a radiofax system:

- *Map Printout Size*—The various systems available range from 8" in width to a full size 18" weather map. On-board space and map readability must be considered in selecting a system.
- *Automatic Operation*—Some systems operate automatically upon receipt of the appropriate signals from the transmitter. Some systems do not, and require an operator to start, frame, and stop the recorder. This is a nuisance and sometimes not feasible. As a rule, automatic systems are much simpler to operate, require minimum attendance, and are recommended by the author.

Table 1-5. Abbreviated directory of worldwide radiofacsimile (radiofax) transmitter sites, geographical areas covered, and frequencies (kHz). Source: *Worldwide Marine Weather Broadcasts*, pp. 60–74.

North Atlantic

Frobisher, Canada
Area: Hudson Strait, Hudson Bay, East Coast Baffin Island, Foxe Basin, Lancaster Sound, Queen Elizabeth Islands
Freq: 3253, 7710, 15644

Halifax, N.S. Canada
Area: Western North Atlantic
Freq: 4271, 6330, 9890, 13510, 122.5

Boston, MA
Area: Western North Atlantic
Freq: 8502, 12750

Brentwood, NY
Area: Western North Atlantic (Transmissions beamed toward Caribbean, Central and South America)
Freq: 9290, 9389.5, 11035, 17436.5

Norfolk, VA
(U.S. Navy Fleet Broadcast)
Area: North Atlantic Ocean
Freq: 3357, 4975, 8080, 10865, 16410, 20015

Washington, D.C.
(U.S. Air Force Broadcast)
Area: North Atlantic Ocean
Freq: 4793.5, 6912.5, 10185, 12201, 13472.5, 14671.5, 15620.5, 17670.5, 19955, 23068.5

Bracknell, England
Area: Eastern North Atlantic
Freq: 3289.5, 4610, 8040, 11086.5, 14582.5

Bracknell, England
Area: Eastern North Atlantic
Freq: 4782, 9203, 14436, 2618.5, 18261

Northwood, England
Area: Northeast Atlantic
Freq: 4247.85, 6492.35, 8494.85

Norrkoping, Sweden
Area: Northeast Atlantic and Baltic Sea
Freq: 119.85, 4037.5, 6901, 8077.5

Helsinki, Finland
Area: Baltic Sea
Freq: 83.1, 8018

Copenhagen, Denmark
Area: North Sea, North Atlantic, Greenland
Freq: 5850, 9360, 13855, 17510

Moscow, U.S.S.R.
Area: Eastern North Atlantic
Freq: 5355, 7750, 10980, 15950, 2815

Offenbach, Germany
Area: Northeastern North Atlantic and Mediterranean Sea
Freq: 134.2

Hamburg, Germany
Area: Northeastern North Atlantic
Freq: 3855, 7880, 13657

Paris, France
Area: North Atlantic Ocean and Mediterranean Sea
Freq: 4047.5, 8185, 12305, 131.8

Dakar, Senegal
Area: Eastern Atlantic — Equator
Freq: 13667.5, 19750, 7587.5

Mediterranean

Rota, Spain
(U.S. Navy KFAX Broadcast)
Area: Eastern North Atlantic and Mediterranean Sea
Freq: 8100, 3713, 5206, 12903, 15941.5, 7626

Madrid, Spain
Area: Eastern North Atlantic and Mediterranean Sea
Freq: 3650, 6918.5, 10250

Athens, Greece
(U.S. Navy KFAX Broadcast)
Area: Eastern North Atlantic and Mediterranean Sea
Freq: 5206, 8100, 12903

Monsanto, Portugal
Area: North Atlantic and Western Mediterranean Sea
Freq: 4235, 8526, 13002

Rome, Italy
Area: North Atlantic, Mediterranean, Black and Caspian Seas
Freq: 4777.5, 8146.6, 13600

Beograd, Yugoslavia
Area: Mediterranean Sea
Freq: 5800, 3520

Sofia, Bulgaria
Area: 30°N, 20°W, 28°N, 34°E; 64°N, 45°W, 60°N, 63°E
Freq: 3259, 5093

Ankara, Turkey
Area: Mediterranean Sea
Freq: 3377, 6790

Cairo, Egypt
Area: Mediterranean Sea, Red Sea and waters around Africa
Freq: 4526, 10123

South Atlantic

Rio de Janeiro, Brazil
Area: South Atlantic
Freq: 12025, 8291.1

Buenos Aires, Argentina
Area: Outlined by 48°S, 12°E; 48°S, 132°W; 04°N, 30°W; 04°N, 90°W
Freq: 5185, 10720, 18093

Pretoria, South Africa
Area: South Atlantic east of 40°W, Indian Ocean west of 80°E
Freq: 4014, 7508, 13773, 18238

Table 1-5. (continued)

North Pacific Ocean

Esquimalt, B.C., Canada
Area: N. Pacific, N. Polar Region
Freq: 4268, 6946, 12125

Edmonton, A.B., Canada
Area: Eastern North Pacific
Freq: 8160, 11615.5, 15770.5

San Francisco, CA
Area: Eastern North Pacific, South Pacific
Freq: 4346, 8682, 12730, 17151

La Jolla, CA
Area: 05°S, 30°N, east of 140°W
Freq: 8646, 17410

Honolulu, Hawaii
(U.S. Navy Fleet Broadcast)
Area: North Pacific Ocean
Freq: 2122, 9440, 13862.5, 4802.5, 16398, 21785

Honolulu, Hawaii, USA (KVM 70)
Area: 25°S-40°N, 160°E-110°W
        (Broadcast is broadly beamed to the west)
Freq: 5037.5, 7770, 9982.5, 11090, 13627.5, 16135, 23331.5

Kodiak, Alaska
Area: Gulf of Alaska and Bering Sea
Freq: 4296, 8457

Guam, Marianas Islands
(U.S. Navy Fleet Broadcast)
Area: Western North Pacific and Eastern Indian Oceans
Freq: 4975, 7645, 10255, 13807.5, 18620, 23880

Khabarovsk, U.S.S.R.
Area: Territory and the neighboring Pacific waters.
Freq: 4516.7, 7457, 9230, 14737, 19275

Tokyo, Japan
Area: Western North Pacific
Freq: 3622.5, 7305, 9970, 13597, 18220, 22770

Peking, Peoples Republic of China
Area: West Pacific, E. China Sea
Freq: 5525, 8120, 10115, 12110, 14365

Bangkok, Thailand
Area: 30°S, 50°N; 45°E, 160°E
Freq: 6765, 7395, 17520

South Pacific, Indian Ocean and Persian Gulf

Darwin, Australia
Freq: 5755, 7535, 10555, 15615, 18060

Canberra, Australia
Area: South of 10°N; 70°E, 150°W
Freq: 5100, 11030, 13920, 19690

Nairobi, Kenya
Area: Indian Ocean
Freq: 9043, 17365

Tehran, Iran
Area: 58°N, 20°E; 28°N, 85°E; 23°N, 20°E; 08°N, 65°E
Freq: 8715

New Delhi, India
Area: 45°N, 25°S, 30°E, 125°E
Freq: 7405, 14842, 18227

Reunion-Saint Denis
Freq: 8176, 16335

Antarctic

Orcades
Area: 50°S-Pole, 20°W, 90°W
Freq: Summer:
        2422.5, 8818, 8195, 11147
        Winter:
        2422.5, 4250, 6454

- *Radio Receiver*—Some systems have built-in radios that are synthesized or fully tunable and do not require any crystal storage. Also, most fax systems can be tied in to a separate HF-SSB radio receiver or transceiver. If you already have one on board, make certain that it is stable enough to allow good radiofax reception.

Some systems have built-in HF-SSB crystal-controlled radios from 6 to 23 crystal slots. *A word of caution*: because most transmitter sites broadcast simultaneously on several frequencies, if you are planning an extensive cruise or voyage, it would be better to install a system with a built-in or fully tunable receiver. This type of installation will assure your receiving the maps and charts without interruption anywhere in the world. Also to be considered is the fact that radio crystals range in price from about $30 to $150 each. If you require a large number of frequencies, this can become quite expensive. And you will need additional space for crystal storage. Also, you will have to plug in different crystals as you change geographical locations. An expensive nuisance.

- *System Size and Weight*—This is more of a problem for smaller craft. There is a wide variety of sizes and weights available. In any case, space requirements must be considered along with voltage and available power.
- *Power Drain*—Recorders draw about 100–135 milliamps while in a standby, and about 260–300 milliamps while recording.
- *Cost*—Radiofax equipment is manufactured by several companies. Prices range from about $2,500 to over $6,000, depending on specific system characteristics and features.

In the author's view, the best overall facsimile equipment is designed and built by the *Alden Electronics and Impulse Recording Equipment Co., Inc.*, of Westborough, Massachusetts. Of particular interest to owners and skippers of smaller craft and pleasure boats—ships, also—are *Alden's* Radio Marinefax Recorders, as shown in figure 1-48. From left to right are the Alden Marinefax II Recorder, designed specifically for mariners who already have an HF single sideband radio or ham rig on board; the Alden Marinefax III Recorder, which is the same as the Marinefax IV, but without the built-in radio. The Marinefax III is desirable for those already having an HF radio, but who want to have all operating speeds. The recorder on the right is the Alden Marinefax IV Recorder, the ultimate marine weather chart recorder. This is the facsimile recorder world's "gem of the ocean."

The latest design of this Marinefax IV Recorder is also shown separately in figure 1-49. This outstanding and unique piece of electronic equipment has a self-contained radio. The radio is designed specifically for receiving radiofax maps and charts from all of the 50 international transmitting sites. It features solid-state, phase-locked, digital synthesized tuning with winking lights to

Figure 1-48. From left to right are the Alden Electronics Marinefax II Recorder (for mariners who already have an HF single-sideband radio or ham rig on board), the Marinefax III Recorder (for those already having a radio on board, but who want to have all operating speeds), and the Marinefax IV Recorder (the ultimate marine weather and oceanographic chart recorder). (Courtesy of Alden Electronics)

Figure 1-49. The Alden Electronics Marinefax IV. This remarkable equipment is smaller than an attaché case, has a self-contained, synthesized radio designed to receive radiofax charts worldwide, and can be mounted almost anywhere—on the bridge, in the navigator's area, in the skipper's quarters, on a table top, or on a bulkhead. (Courtesy of Alden Electronics)

permit easy tuning of all frequencies worldwide from 100 kHz to 29.999 MHz. Coverage is continuous with no gaps, eliminating the need to buy and store expensive crystals. And in addition to receiving facsimile charts, the radio can copy Low-Frequency (long-wave) weather transmissions and SSB marine coast station voice weather broadcasts, as well as WWV time ticks. It is a "lightweight" in the field (14.2 lbs., or 6.5 kg.), compact in size (810 cu. in., or 0.5 cu. ft.—smaller than an attaché case), is easy to install, simple to use, extremely reliable, and is a power miser that does it all. For interested radio fans, figure 1-50 is a simplified block diagram of radiofacsimile signals.

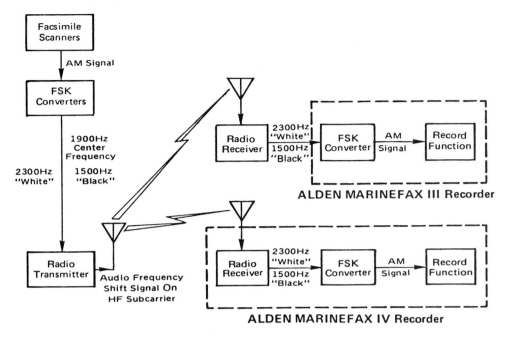

Figure 1-50. Simplified block diagram of radiofax signals. The radiofax weather broadcasts as received by the radio consist of 1500 Hz and 2300 Hz signals that must be converted to black and white analog signal information for use by your recorder so as to print the map. Two tuning lights on the control panel of the recorder provide a visual indication of the presence of the incoming 1500 Hz and 2300 Hz signals. Built into the recorder is a frequency shift-to-analog converter that changes the 1500 Hz black to a pulse for printing a mark and converts the 2300 Hz white to a minimum level to provide a "space." (Courtesy of Alden Electronics)

The standard symbols used on weather facsimile charts transmitted all over the world are as shown in figure 1-51.

The various types of radiofax charts available around the world in accordance with table 1-5 are as follows:

- *Surface weather analyses* showing the latest weather systems and patterns based on the latest synoptic weather observations.
- *Surface weather prognostic charts* indicating the predicted positions of highs, lows, fronts, etc., for 12 and 24 hours into the future. On some broadcasts, the predictions extend to 36 and 48 hours into the future. And on a few, up to 5 days.
- *Surface wind analyses* show the direction and speed of the surface wind.
- *Surface wind prognostic charts* show the predicted direction and speed of surface winds for the next 12–48 hours.
- *Wave analyses* depict the characteristics of sea and swell height and direction of movement.

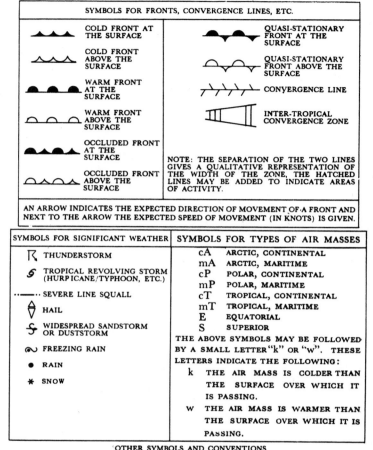

Figure 1-51. Standard weather facsimile chart symbols used around the world. (Source: *Worldwide Marine Weather Broadcasts*, p. 121)

- *Wave prognostic charts* show the predicted state-of-the-sea conditions for the next 12–24 hours.
- *Sea ice charts* delineate the sea ice areas with their known characteristics, in addition to known positions of icebergs.
- *Significant weather depiction charts* show frontal systems with associated cloud patterns, and areas of precipitation and fog.
- *Satellite weather images* show cloud patterns and the positions of extra-tropical storms and disturbances, and hurricanes, typhoons, tropical storms, and the intertropical convergence zone (ITCZ).
- *Oceanographic charts* provide a variety of information (some still experimental). This information includes sea surface temperature (SST), color zones, areas of convergence and divergence, mixed layer depth (MLD) data, and ocean current data (including eddies). For obvious reasons, oceanographic charts are of tremendous interest to submarine skippers, anti-submarine tacticians, commercial fishermen, master mariners, and many other breeds of seagoing folk.

§ The symbol is not plotted for "ww" when "00" is reported. When "(1, 02, or 03" is reported for "ww", the symbol is plotted on the station circle.
† Refers to "hail" only.   †† Refers to "Soft hail", "small hail", and "hail".

ww
PRESENT WEATHER

00 Cloud development NOT observed or NOT observable during past hour.§	01 Clouds generally dissolving or becoming less developed during past hour.§	02 State of sky on the whole unchanged during past hour.§	03 Clouds generally forming or developing during past hour.§	04 Visibility reduced by smoke.	05 Haze.
10 Light fog.	11 Patches of shallow fog at station, NOT deeper than 6 feet on land.	12 More or less continuous shallow fog at station, NOT deeper than 6 feet on land.	13 Lightning visible, no thunder heard.	14 Precipitation within sight, but NOT reaching the ground.	15 Precipitation within sight, reaching the ground, but distant from station.
20 Drizzle (NOT freezing and NOT falling as showers) during past hour, but NOT at time of ob.	21 Rain (NOT freezing and NOT falling as showers) during past hour, but NOT at time of ob.	22 Snow (NOT falling as showers) during past hour, but NOT at time of observation.	23 Rain and snow (NOT falling as showers) during past hour, but NOT at time of observation.	24 Freezing drizzle or freezing rain (NOT falling as showers) during past hour, but NOT at time of observation.	25 Showers of rain during past hour, but NOT at time of observation.
30 Slight or moderate duststorm or sandstorm, has decreased during past hour.	31 Slight or moderate duststorm or sandstorm, no appreciable change during past hour.	32 Slight or moderate duststorm or sandstorm, has increased during past hour.	33 Severe duststorm or sandstorm, has decreased during past hour.	34 Severe duststorm or sandstorm, no appreciable change during past hour.	35 Severe duststorm or sandstorm, has increased during past hour.
40 Fog at distance at time of observation, but NOT at station during past hour.	41 Fog in patches.	42 Fog, sky discernible, has become thinner during past hour.	43 Fog, sky NOT discernible, has become thinner during past hour.	44 Fog, sky discernible, no appreciable change during past hour.	45 Fog, sky NOT discernible, no appreciable change during past hour.
50 Intermittent drizzle (NOT freezing) slight at time of observation.	51 Continuous drizzle (NOT freezing) slight at time of observation.	52 Intermittent drizzle (NOT freezing) moderate at time of observation.	53 Continuous drizzle (NOT freezing), moderate at time of observation.	54 Intermittent drizzle (NOT freezing), thick at time of observation.	55 Continuous drizzle (NOT freezing), thick at time of observation.
60 Intermittent rain (NOT freezing), slight at time of observation.	61 Continuous rain (NOT freezing), slight at time of observation.	62 Intermittent rain (NOT freezing), moderate at time of observation.	63 Continuous rain (NOT freezing), moderate at time of observation.	64 Intermittent rain (NOT freezing), heavy at time of observation.	65 Continuous rain (NOT freezing), heavy at time of observation.
70 Intermittent fall of snow flakes, slight at time of observation.	71 Continuous fall of snow flakes, slight at time of observation.	72 Intermittent fall of snow flakes, moderate at time of observation.	73 Continuous fall of snow flakes, moderate at time of observation.	74 Intermittent fall of snow flakes, heavy at time of observation.	75 Continuous fall of snow flakes, heavy at time of observation.
80 Slight rain shower(s).	81 Moderate or heavy rain shower(s).	82 Violent rain shower(s).	83 Slight shower(s) of rain and snow mixed.	84 Moderate or heavy shower(s) of rain and snow mixed.	85 Slight snow shower(s).
90 Moderate or heavy shower(s) of hail†, with or without rain or rain and snow mixed, not associated with thunder.	91 Slight rain at time of observation; thunderstorm during past hour, but NOT at time of observation.	92 Moderate or heavy rain at time of observation; thunderstorm during past hour, but NOT at time of observation.	93 Slight snow or rain and snow mixed or hail†† at time of observation; thunderstorm during past hour, but NOT at time of observation.	94 Moderate or heavy snow, or rain and snow mixed or hail†† at time of observation; thunderstorm during past hour, but NOT at time of observation.	95 Slight or moderate thunderstorm without hail†, but with rain and/or snow at time of observation.

Figure 1-52. Weather code figures and symbols with their meanings.

C_L — Clouds of type C_L	C_M — Clouds of type C_M

06. Widespread dust in suspension in the air, NOT raised by wind, at time of observation.

07. Dust or sand raised by wind, at time of ob.

08. Well developed dust devil(s) within past hour.

09. Duststorm or sandstorm within sight of or at station during past hour.

0 (C_L). No Sc, St, Cu, or Cb clouds.

0 (C_M). No Ac, As or Ns clouds.

16. Precipitation within sight, reaching the ground, near to but NOT at station.

17. Thunder heard, but no precipitation at the station.

18. Squall(s) within sight during past hour.

19. Funnel cloud(s) within sight during past hour.

1 (C_L). Ragged Cu, other than bad weather, or Cu with little vertical development and seemingly flattened, or both.

1 (C_M). As, the greatest part of which is semitransparent through which the sun or moon may be faintly visible as through ground glass.

26. Showers of snow, or of rain and snow, during past hour, but NOT at time of observation.

27. Showers of hail, or of hail and rain, during past hour, but NOT at time of observation.

28. Fog during past hour, but NOT at time of observation.

29. Thunderstorm (with or without precipitation) during past hour, but NOT at time of ob.

2 (C_L). Cu of considerable development, generally towering, with or without other Cu or Sc; bases all at same level.

2 (C_M). As, the greatest part of which is sufficiently dense to hide the sun or moon, or Ns.

36. Slight or moderate drifting snow, generally low.

37. Heavy drifting snow, generally low.

38. Slight or moderate drifting snow, generally high.

39. Heavy drifting snow, generally high.

3 (C_L). Cb with tops lacking clear-cut outlines, but are clearly not fibrous, cirriform, or anvil-shaped; Cu, Sc, or St may be present.

3 (C_M). Ac (most of layer is semitransparent) other than crenelated or in cumuliform tufts; cloud elements change but slowly with all bases at a single level.

46. Fog, sky discernible, has begun or become thicker during past hour.

47. Fog, sky NOT discernible, has begun or become thicker during past hour.

48. Fog, depositing rime, sky discernible.

49. Fog, depositing rime, sky NOT discernible.

4 (C_L). Sc formed by spreading out of Cu; Cu may be present also.

4 (C_M). Patches of semitransparent Ac which are continuously changing; cloud elements are continuously changing.

56. Slight freezing drizzle.

57. Moderate or thick freezing drizzle.

58. Drizzle and rain, slight.

59. Drizzle and rain, moderate or heavy.

5 (C_L). Sc not formed by spreading out of Cu.

5 (C_M). Semitransparent Ac in bands or Ac in one or more continuous layer gradually spreading over sky and usually thickening as a whole; the layer may be opaque or a double sheet.

66. Slight freezing rain.

67. Moderate or heavy freezing rain.

68. Rain or drizzle and snow, slight.

69. Rain or drizzle and snow, moderate or heavy.

6 (C_L). St in a more or less continuous layer and/or ragged shreds, but no Fs of bad weather.

6 (C_M). Ac formed by the spreading out of Cu.

76. Ice needles (with or without fog).

77. Granular snow (with or without fog).

78. Isolated starlike snow crystals (with or without fog).

79. Ice pellets (sleet, U.S. definition).

7 (C_L). Fs and/or Fc of bad weather (scud) usually under As and Ns.

7 (C_M). Double-layered Ac or an opaque layer of Ac, not increasing over the sky; or Ac coexisting with As or Ns or with both.

86. Moderate or heavy snow shower(s).

87. Slight shower(s) of soft or small hail with or without rain or rain and snow mixed.

88. Moderate or heavy shower(s) of soft or small hail with or without rain or rain and snow mixed.

89. Slight shower(s) of hail††, with or without rain or rain and snow mixed, not associated with thunder.

8 (C_L). Cu and Sc (not formed by spreading out of Cu); base of Cu at a different level than base of Sc.

8 (C_M). Ac with sprouts in the form of small towers or battlements or Ac having the appearance of cumuliform tufts.

96. Slight or moderate thunderstorm, with hail† at time of observation.

97. Heavy thunderstorm, without hail†, but with rain and/or snow at time of observation.

98. Thunderstorm combined with dust storm or sandstorm at time of observation.

99. Heavy thunderstorm with hail† at time of observation.

9 (C_L). Cb having a clearly fibrous (cirriform) top, often anvil-shaped, with or without Cu, Sc, St, or scud.

9 (C_M). Ac, generally at several layers in a chaotic sky; dense Cirrus is usually present.

C_H — Cloud of type C_H	C_L — Type of Cloud	W — Past Weather	N — Total amount of clouds	a — Barometer characteristic
0 No Ci, Cc, or Cs clouds.	**0** Ci	**0** Cloud covering ½ or less of sky throughout the period.	**0** No clouds.	**0** Rising then falling. Now higher than, or the same as, 3 hours ago.
1 Filaments, strands, or hooks of Ci, not increasing.	**1** Cc	**1** Cloud covering more than ½ of sky during part of period and covering ½ or less during part of period.	**1** One-tenth or less, but not zero.	**1** Rising, then steady; or rising, then rising more slowly. Now higher than 3 hours ago.
2 Dense Ci in patches or twisted sheaves, usually not increasing; or Ci with towers or battlements or resembling cumuliform tufts.	**2** Cs	**2** Cloud covering more than ½ of sky throughout the period.	**2** Two- or three-tenths.	**2** Rising (steadily or unsteadily). Now higher than 3 hours ago.
3 Ci, often anvil-shaped, derived from or associated with Cb.	**3** Ac	**3** Sandstorm, or duststorm, or drifting or blowing snow.	**3** Four-tenths.	**3** Falling or steady, then rising; or rising then rising more rapidly. Now higher than 3 hours ago.
4 Ci, hook-shaped and/or filaments, spreading over the sky and generally becoming denser as a whole.	**4** As	**4** Fog, or thick haze.	**4** Five-tenths.	**4** Steady. Same as 3 hours ago.
5 Ci, often in converging bands, and Cs or Cs alone but increasing and growing denser as a whole; the continuous veil not exceeding 45° above horizon.	**5** Ns	**5** Drizzle.	**5** Six-tenths.	**5** Falling, then rising. Now lower than, or the same as, 3 hours ago.
6 Ci, often in converging bands, and Cs or Cs alone but increasing and growing denser as a whole; the continuous veil exceeds 45° above horizon but sky not totally covered.	**6** Sc	**6** Rain.	**6** Seven- or eight-tenths.	**6** Falling, then steady; or falling, then falling more slowly. Now lower than 3 hours ago.
7 Veil of Cs completely covering the sky.	**7** St	**7** Snow, or rain and snow mixed, or ice pellets (sleet).	**7** Nine-tenths or more, but not ten-tenths.	**7** Falling (steadily or unsteadily). Now lower than 3 hours ago.
8 Cs not increasing and not completely covering the sky.	**8** Cu	**8** Shower(s).	**8** Ten-tenths.	**8** Steady or rising, then falling; or falling, then falling more rapidly. Now lower than 3 hours ago.
9 Cc alone or Cc accompanied by Ci and/or Cs, but Cc is the predominant cirriform cloud.	**9** Cb	**9** Thunderstorm, with or without precipitation.	**9** Sky obscured, or cloud amount cannot be estimated.	**9** Indicator figure. Regionally agreed elements and NOT "pp" are reported by the next two code figures.

2

Tropical Cyclones

Blow, winds, and crack your cheeks! rage! blow!
You cataracts and hurricanes, spout
Till you have drench'd our steeples.
      —Shakespeare, *King Lear*, III, 2

Despite the advent of extremely high-speed computers, microchips, geostationary and polar-orbiting weather satellites, and communications satellites, there remain many unsolved problems today regarding tropical cyclones and tropical meteorology. For example, there is still no universally accepted theory on the formation of tropical cyclones (hurricanes, typhoons, cordonazos, willy-willys, etc.). The primary reasons for this are the lack of funds and personnel earmarked for basic and applied research and the extreme paucity of meteorological data in tropical latitudes. The newer satellites with the latest remote sensing instrumentation are helping to solve the latter problem.

It is known, however, that all motion in the earth's atmosphere results from inequalities in heating and cooling—particularly the net radiation differences between the tropical and polar regions. And since the temperature averaged over many years at all places is nearly constant, these differences must be balanced by the heat exchange between polar and tropical latitudes. The air currents that are set in motion blowing toward the poles and toward the equator largely effect the exchange. Still unknown, though, are the *exact* details of how the exchange takes place.

Nevertheless, the considerable knowledge we do have of the tropics and tropical cyclones can be put to good operational use by ships' captains, yachting skippers, and many other marine decision makers.

The term *cyclone* (which means "the coil of a snake") was first suggested about the year 1850 by a gentleman by the name of Henry Piddington, who was president of the Marine Courts at Calcutta. The word was quickly adopted universally.

When fully developed, tropical cyclones are the most destructive of all storms because of their great size coupled with their intensity. Tornado winds blow with greater fury, but they are confined to a relatively narrow path (about 1,200 feet in average width) and travel distances of only a few miles. The violent winds of tropical cyclones, on the other hand, cover many thousands of square miles and travel distances of many hundreds (and sometimes several thousand) miles. Mountainous waves are associated with intense tropical cyclones at sea. The destructive forces of the winds and waves are evidenced by the appalling record of ships sunk and cast ashore in both peacetime and in war. The high tides caused by these cyclones completely inundate low coastal areas. Entire cities and towns have been wiped out and never rebuilt. In some of the most severe tropical cyclones, the loss of life has been in the hundreds of thousands, and the property damage has exceeded one billion dollars. Although conceived in the tropics, tropical cyclones travel long distances and devastate areas (and ships) far away from their point of origin.

The effect of some great tropical cyclones has been so profound that they have been credited with affecting the course of history. In March 1889, for example, war between Germany and the United States was prevented by a tropical cyclone. This event was made an important part of the Report of the Secretary of the Navy, 1889. And it was beautifully described by Ivan Ray Tannehill in his classic, *Hurricanes*, copyright 1938, 8th edition. The copyright was renewed in 1980 by the Princeton University Press. In the latter part of 1888, a German naval force removed the native chief of the Samoans and put another king on the throne. The natives rebelled, and in one skirmish 22 German soldiers were killed. The Germans retaliated by shelling a native village, and in doing so, inadvertently destroyed the property of American citizens. An American flag raised by a U.S. citizen to protect his property was torn down and burned. The then-Secretary of State Bayard strongly protested. And American warships were immediately ordered to Samoa to guard the rights of American citizens there—a distance of over two thousand miles from the Hawaiian Islands and four thousand miles from the west coast of the United States.

On 16 March 1889, seven warships—three German, three American, and one British—were in the harbor at Apia, Samoa.

Then, with relations between Germany and the United States strained to the breaking point and with very little warning, a severe tropical cyclone (hurricane) zeroed in on Apia.

The British warship *Calliope* steamed from the inner harbor during the fury of the hurricane and survived. The U.S. and German warships, and also six merchant ships, were slammed on the reefs, sent to the bottom, or beached by the hurricane. Over 150 sailors lost their lives.

During the fury of the hurricane, national differences were quickly forgotten; American and German sailors became comrades against the storm, and many acts of heroism were recorded. Also, the natives came to the rescue of both American and German sailors. The U.S. Navy Department expressed its appreciation for the courage of the natives, especially to Chief Seumanu, the native leader, and recommended that he be presented with a double-banked whaleboat with all the fittings, and that his men be suitably rewarded. A severe tropical cyclone (hurricane) brought about a temporary peace—but at a cost of many lives and twelve ships.

Thus, in 1889, a hurricane accelerated action to settle political differences in the U.S. Congress and in the treaty of Berlin. This tropical cyclone has also been credited with being responsible, indirectly but most assuredly, for the founding of the modern, well-equipped United States Navy.

A BRIEF NOTE ON THE EARTH'S GENERAL CIRCULATION

The process that accomplishes the necessary transfer of heat between the tropics and the polar regions (for a balanced heat exchange) is called the *general circulation* of the earth's atmosphere. Even though all facets of the general circulation are not known in great detail, a good idea of the major features of the circulation can be obtained. This is done by using the statistical and climatological means and averages at many points over the globe for a period of a great many years. Figure 2-1 is a highly simplified diagram of the earth's general circulation.

The Doldrums

Almost encircling the earth near the equator lies a "belt," or trough, of low pressure. It lies approximately midway between the zones, or "belts," of high pressure usually found in the Northern Hemisphere near latitude 30–35N, and

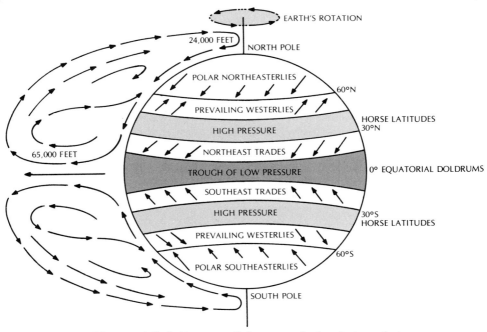

Figure 2-1. Highly simplified diagram of the general circulation of air over our rotating earth. (*Weather for the Mariner*, Naval Institute Press, 1983)

in the Southern Hemisphere near latitude 30–35S. Except for slight diurnal changes (occurring at 0400, 1000, 1600, and 2200 local time every day), atmospheric pressure along the equatorial trough is almost uniform. Winds are usually very light and variable in direction. Hot and sultry days are common. The sky is often overcast. And heavy showers and thundershowers frequently occur.

This equatorial trough of low pressure is relatively narrow, usually having a greater width in the eastern regions of the world's oceans than in the western regions. Both the north-south geographical positions and the east-west extent of this low-pressure belt vary with the seasons. During the winter months in each hemisphere (Dec., Jan., Feb. in the Northern Hemisphere; June, July, Aug. in the Southern Hemisphere), it lies slightly on the poleward side of the equator (except in the South Atlantic Ocean). During the summer months in each hemisphere (June, July, Aug. in the Northern Hemisphere; Dec., Jan., Feb. in the Southern Hemisphere), the trough, or "belt," of low pressure is centered near latitude 7–9 degrees in each hemisphere, and sometimes penetrates as far as latitude 22 degrees in western oceanic areas (a north-south meandering in each hemisphere of some 800 + nautical miles), except, again, in the South Atlantic Ocean. During the summer months, the trough may be as much as 250 miles in width.

The Trade Winds

If the earth had a uniform surface, and if our planet neither rotated on its axis nor revolved around the sun, a simple atmospheric circulation would result. Since this is not the case, constantly changing large-scale movements of air take place. And a part of this air movement is called the *trade winds*. The trade winds are the winds of the tropical regions of earth.

In each hemisphere, there exists a "belt" of high pressure, centered along latitudes 30–35N and 30–35S. Actually, this is a series of anticyclonic (high-pressure) cells rather than a continuous belt, as shown in figures 2-2a, 2-2b, and 2-2c. The trade winds in each hemisphere blow outward from these belts, or cells, of high pressure and toward the equatorial trough of low pressure. Because of the earth's rotation, the moving air is deflected to the *right* in the *Northern Hemisphere*, and to the *left* in the *Southern Hemisphere*. So, in the Northern Hemisphere, we have *northeast trade winds* instead of north trade winds. And in the Southern Hemisphere we have *southeast trade winds* instead of south trade winds.

Over the eastern regions of the oceans, the trade winds reach much greater distances from the equator. Also, their direction is more N'erly and NNE'erly (in the Northern Hemisphere) and more S'erly and SSE'erly (in the Southern Hemisphere) than in the western regions of the oceans.

As one would expect, the NE trades of the Northern Hemisphere on approaching and crossing the equator become N'erly and NW'erly winds in the Southern Hemisphere because they are then deflected to the left. And the SE trades of the Southern Hemisphere on approaching and crossing the equator become S'erly and SW'erly winds in the Northern Hemisphere because they are then deflected to the right. The winds of the SW *monsoons*

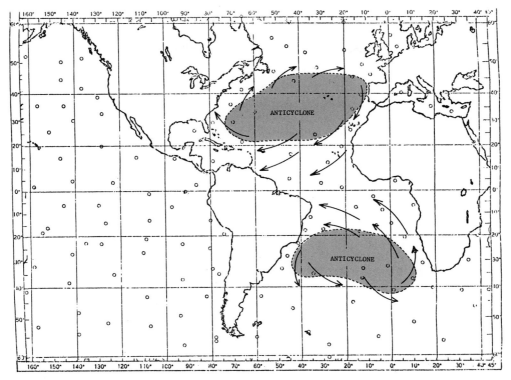

Figure 2-2a. Mean positions of the oceanic high-pressure cells, or anticyclones, in the North Atlantic and South Atlantic.

(discussed in a following section) of the Northern Hemisphere are a combination of Northern Hemisphere westerly-component winds and diverted Southern Hemisphere trade winds that have crossed the equator.

The trade winds in each hemisphere (averaging between 11–19 knots, and stronger during the winter months than during summer) encompass most of the tropics, and are perhaps the most constant portion of the earth's wind regime. Figure 2-3 is a profile of "wind constancy" versus latitude, and shows that the trade winds attain a constancy as high as 80 percent. The greatest constancy occurs in the South Atlantic and in the South Indian Oceans.

Occasionally the trade winds, like all people and all things, weaken or change direction. And there are regions where their normal pattern is disrupted. Temperate-latitude cyclonic storms seldom move into the regions of the trade winds. *But*, tropical storms, hurricanes, and typhoons usually form in these areas!

The Horse Latitudes

On the poleward side of each trade-wind belt, and corresponding roughly with the zone of high pressure in each hemisphere, is another region with weak pressure gradients and associated light and variable winds. These regions are

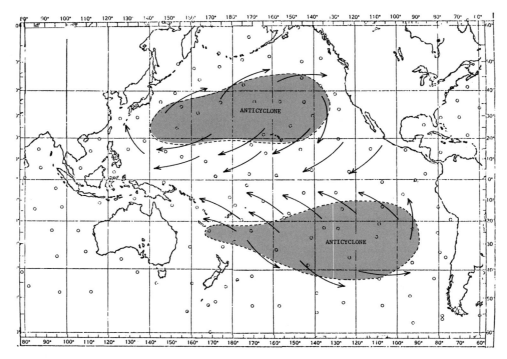

Figure 2-2b. Mean positions of the oceanic high-pressure cells, or anticyclones, in the North Pacific and South Pacific.

called the *horse latitudes*. In the days of sail, when ships became becalmed, horses were thrown overboard to conserve water. At least that's the story. But unlike the weather in the doldrums, the weather is usually clear and fresh. Periods of "stagnation" are less persistent. They are more of an intermittent nature. The difference results primarily from the fact that the rising currents of warm air in the equatorial trough of low pressure carry aloft large amounts of moisture that condense as the rising air expands and cools at higher levels. In the horse latitudes, on the other hand, the air is descending (subsiding) and becomes less humid as it is warmed (adiabatically—remember from chapter 1?) at the lower altitudes.

The Prevailing Westerlies

On the poleward side of the high-pressure zone or belt in each hemisphere, the atmospheric pressure again decreases. See, again, figure 2-1. The air currents moving toward the poles are deflected by the earth's rotation to the east (to the right) in the Northern Hemisphere and to the left (to the east) in the Southern Hemisphere. They become southwesterly winds in the Northern Hemisphere and northwesterly winds in the Southern Hemisphere. These two wind systems are called the *prevailing westerlies* of the temperate zone in each hemisphere.

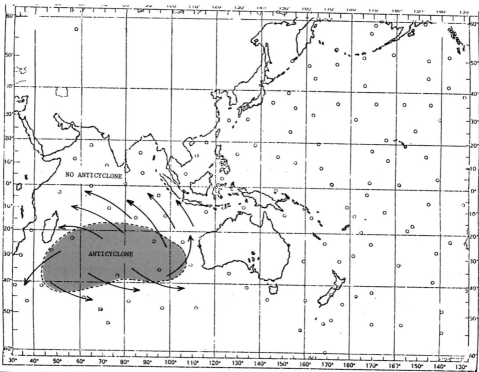

Figure 2-2c. Mean position of the oceanic high-pressure cell, or anticyclone, in the South Indian Ocean. There is no anticyclone in the North Indian Ocean because of the land mass–oceanic areal configuration and the resulting NE (winter) and SW (summer) monsoon circulations.

    This simple pattern is distorted considerably in the Northern Hemisphere because of the presence of the large land masses (the continents). Between latitudes 40–50N in the North Atlantic, for example, winds blow from some direction between NW and S about 75 percent of the time, less persistent in summer than in winter. Also, they are stronger in winter, averaging about 25–30 knots as compared to 10–18 knots in summer.

    In the Southern Hemisphere, the westerlies blow throughout the year with a steadiness almost as great as that of the trade winds. Wind speed, although somewhat variable, is usually between 18–30 knots. These winds occur between latitudes 40–55S and are called the *roaring forties*. The higher speed and greater persistence of the westerlies in the Southern Hemisphere are caused by the difference in the atmospheric pressure pattern—and its variations—from that of the Northern Hemisphere. There is comparatively little land mass in the Southern Hemisphere, and the average annual pressure decreases much more rapidly on the poleward side of the high-pressure belt. Put another way, there are fewer "irregularities" caused by the presence of large land masses (continents), as is the case in the Northern Hemisphere.

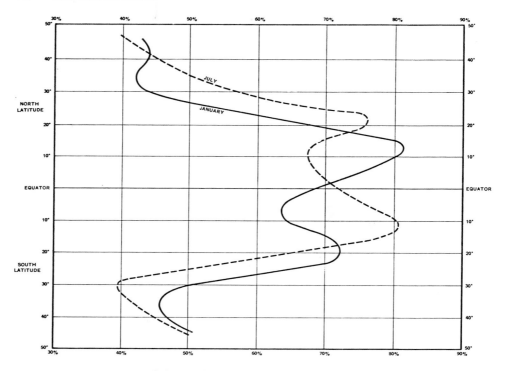

Figure 2-3. Constancy of the surface wind direction versus latitude expressed in percent. Note that the trade winds attain a constancy as high as 80 percent.

Winds in the Polar Regions

Temperatures are quite low near the geographical poles of the earth. Because of this, pressure tends to remain higher at the poles than in the surrounding areas. As a result, the winds blow outward from the poles and are deflected to the right in the Northern Hemisphere (to the west), and to the left in the Southern Hemisphere (to the west), by the earth's rotation. These winds become *northeasterlies* in the Arctic, and *southeasterlies* in the Antarctic. They meet the prevailing westerlies near latitudes 60N and 60S.

In the Arctic, the general circulation is modified considerably by the surrounding land masses. Winds over the Arctic Ocean are somewhat variable, and strong surface winds are not encountered very often.

In the Antarctic region, however, a high, central land mass is surrounded by water. This is a condition that augments, rather than diminishes, the general circulation in the area. The high pressure is much stronger than in the Arctic, and has great persistence near the south pole. The upper-level air descends (subsides) over the high, south polar continent, where it becomes intensely cold. As it travels outward (and downward) toward the sea, it is deflected toward the west (to the left) by the earth's rotation. These winds remain strong throughout the year. They frequently reach hurricane and typhoon speeds (greater than 64 knots or 74 mph). Sometimes, they attain speeds as high as

200 knots (230 mph)! With the exception of hurricane, typhoon, and tornado winds, these are the strongest surface winds encountered anywhere in the world.

Figures 2-4a and 2-4b are a more accurate presentation of the prevailing winds over the world's oceans between latitudes 60N and 60S.

The Semipermanent Highs (Anticyclones)

The high pressure in the horse latitudes is really not distributed uniformly in zones or belts all around the globe. Actually, it is accentuated at various points around the globe, and appears as high-pressure cells on weather maps and

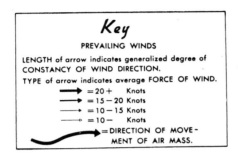

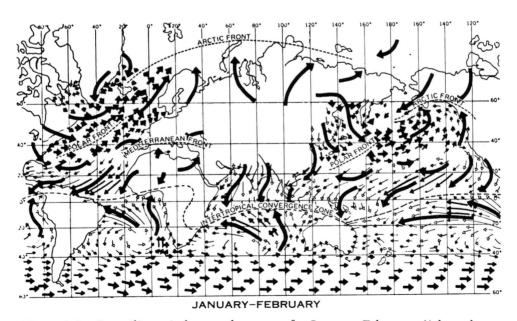

Figure 2-4a. Prevailing winds over the oceans for January–February. (Adapted from Bowditch, *American Practical Navigator*, U.S. Navy Hydrographic Office, 1958)

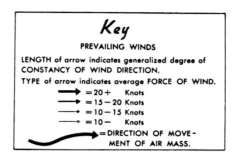

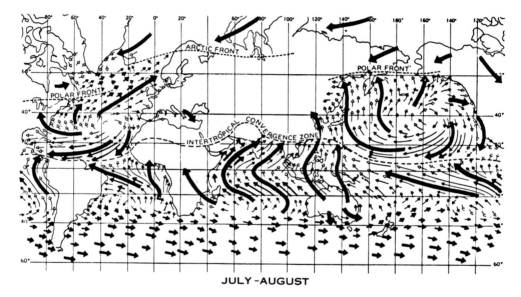

Figure 2-4b. Prevailing winds over the oceans for July–August. (Adapted from Bowditch, *American Practical Navigator*, U.S. Navy Hydrographic Office, 1958)

charts. However, these oceanic high-pressure cells, or anticyclones, as shown in figure 2-5, remain at about the same places with great persistence, expanding and contracting like the giant lungs of great sea monsters.

The Semipermanent Lows (Cyclones)

These phenomena also occur in various places around the world. In the Northern Hemisphere, the prominent ones occur in the area to the west of Iceland and over the Aleutians in the winter. In the Southern Hemisphere, they are located in the Ross Sea and the Weddell Sea in the Antarctic. These areas are sometimes called by weathermen "the graveyard of lows," since many low-pressure systems move directly into these areas and are absorbed into the semipermanent lows which they reinforce. The low pressure in these areas is maintained largely by the migratory lows that come to a standstill in these regions. It is also partly maintained by the sharp temperature difference between the polar regions and the warmer ocean areas.

The Monsoons

Another factor that causes variations in the earth's general circulation is *land*. During summer months, a continent is warmer than its surrounding oceans. Also, it undergoes greater temperature *changes* than does the sea. As a result, lower pressures tend to prevail over the land in summer. When a belt of high pressure encounters such a continent, its pattern is interrupted, or distorted. A belt of low pressure, on the other hand, is intensified. And the winds associated with belts of high pressure or low pressure are distorted accordingly. The opposite effect takes place in winter months. In this case, belts of high pressure are intensified over land masses, and belts of low pressure are interrupted.

Perhaps one of the most striking examples of a wind system produced by the alternate heating and cooling of a land mass is the *monsoons* of the Indian Ocean and the China Sea. Referring to figure 2-5a, in the summer months, low pressure dominates the warm continent of Asia. High pressure dominates the adjacent sea. Between these two major wind systems, the winds blow in a nearly steady direction. The lower portion of the pattern extends to about 10°S in the Southern Hemisphere. Here, the earth's rotation causes a deflection to the left. But as these winds cross the equator, the SE trades of the Southern Hemisphere are deflected to the right in the Northern Hemisphere, and they become SW'erly winds. In the winter months, as shown in figure 2-5b, the positions of the high- and low-pressure systems are reversed (high over land, and low over water) and , consequently, the air flow is reversed, and the area is enveloped by NE'erly and E'erly winds.

In the China Sea, the summer monsoon blows steadily from the SW, from about May to September. These strong winds are accompanied by heavy squalls and thunderstorms. Rainfall is very much heavier—sometimes torrential—than during the winter monsoon. As the season advances, rainfall and squalls become less frequent. In some places, the wind becomes light and unsteady. In other places, it continues reasonably steady.

The winter monsoon blows from the NE, from about October to April. It is a rather steady wind, frequently attaining a speed of 35 knots (40 mph). Except for the windward slopes of mountainous or hilly areas, skies are generally clear to partly cloudy during the winter monsoon, and there is relatively little rain (except for the windward slopes of mountains). However, some low cloudiness and/or light fog (yes, even at low latitudes) may occur along coastal areas.

THE INTERTROPICAL CONVERGENCE ZONE (ITCZ)

Compared to the frequently rapid weather changes associated with mid- and high-latitude low-pressure systems, the weather in the tropics follows an almost routine schedule most of the time. The frequent alternating between cold north winds and warm south winds (in the Northern Hemisphere; the

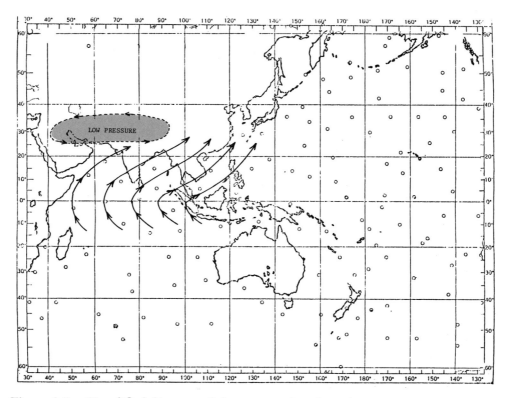

Figure 2-5a. Simplified diagram of the summer (southwest) monsoon.

reverse in the Southern Hemisphere), accompanied by large temperature falls and rises, does not occur. Instead, temperatures and winds experience a daily cycle that is dictated largely by orographic, island, coastal, or other terrain features. A daily, rather dull weather cycle so dominates life that very little of an unusual nature ever seems to occur—*except* for cyclones, hurricanes, and typhoons. But this is a viewpoint not shared by enthusiastic tropical meteorologists and forecasters.

In the tropics, a cycle of wet and dry seasons replaces the four seasons of middle and higher latitudes. There is a definite sequence of weather changes during the dry (winter) and the wet (summer) seasons. Perhaps surprisingly, perturbations (or disturbances) of one kind or another in tropical regions produce more than 90 percent of the rainfall. And a large fraction of the rainfall occurs in a few intense spurts during the rainy season(s).

Largely influencing the weather of the tropics is an almost-continuous trough or belt of low pressure around the globe in the equatorial regions. This trough, or belt, is where the NE trade winds (of the Northern Hemisphere) and the SE trades (of the Southern Hemisphere) converge, or come together. This belt of converging trade winds is known by many different names: the Intertropical Convergence Zone (ITCZ), the Equatorial Trough, the Equatorial Front, the Intertropical Front, the Equatorial Convergence Zone, etc. In this

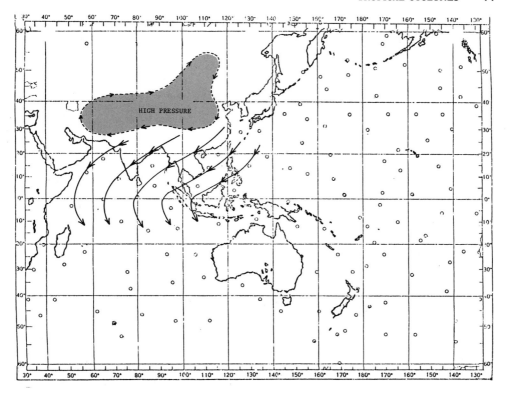

Figure 2-5b. Simplified diagram of the winter (northeast) monsoon.

Heavy Weather Guide, we'll refer to it as the *Intertropical Convergence Zone—* the *ITCZ.* We choose this title because there is no real density discontinuity involved, as is the case with higher latitude weather fronts.

Most of the "weather" in tropical regions is associated with the ITCZ— directly or indirectly. Because the ITCZ is where the trade winds of each hemisphere converge, the ITCZ is usually characterized by strong, ascending air currents, large areas of overcast skies, and frequent heavy showers and thunderstorms. The intensity, however, does vary greatly. At times, the ITCZ has the appearance of a tremendous wall of black clouds, with cloud tops extending to 55,000–65,000 feet. At other times, it is so weak and inconsequential that it is difficult to locate with certainty on a weather map, because the winds are relatively light and there is little cloudiness or weather associated with it. The latitudinal width of the ITCZ varies from about 20 to 150 nautical miles, and as a general rule, the narrower the zone, or trough (i.e., the greater the convergence), the more extensive is the cloudiness and the more intense is the weather associated with it.

Seasonally, the ITCZ migrates from the winter hemisphere into the summer hemisphere (except in the South Atlantic), so that the winter hemisphere controls a larger part of the oceanic tropics than does the summer hemisphere. Figure 2-6 shows the mean position of the ITCZ during the winter and summer

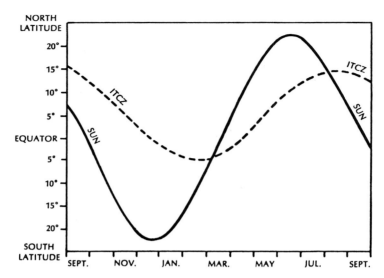

Figure 2-6. Seasonal meandering of the ITCZ compared to the overhead position of the sun. Note the two-month lag of the ITCZ.

periods of the Northern Hemisphere. And remember, when it is winter in the Northern Hemisphere, it is summer in the Southern Hemisphere and vice versa.

In general, as we see in figure 2-6, as the ITCZ migrates north and south in the course of a year, it passes the latitudes between its extreme north-south positions twice, lagging behind the sun by about two months. As a result, many regions in the tropics—but by no means all regions—have two rainy seasons and two dry seasons. In regions where the ITCZ moves as shown in figure 2-6, the peaks of the rainy seasons occur in December and April on the equator, in November and May at latitude 5 degrees north, and in June and October at latitude 10 degrees north. At latitudes 15 degrees north and 5 degrees south, the two rainy seasons merge into a single broad peak during the summer months.

The ITCZ never penetrates the South Atlantic because of the land mass—oceanic configuration and distribution. Consequently, no hurricanes are to be found in the South Atlantic. See, again, figures 2-4a and 2-4b for the mean winter and summer positions of the ITCZ.

It's a different story, however, in the Pacific and Indian Oceans. In these oceans, the total annual meandering of the ITCZ in both hemispheres sometimes amounts to as much as 44 degrees of latitude (over 2,600 nautical miles) in extreme cases. See figures 2-7, 2-8, and 2-9.

As shown in figures 2-4b, 2-6, and 2-8, in the Northern Hemisphere, the ITCZ reaches its northernmost latitude in August, and as shown in figures 2-4a, 2-6, and 2-7, its southernmost latitude in February. It must be realized, however, that the day-to-day variations in the positions of the ITCZ may differ substantially from the mean positions during both the winter and summer months.

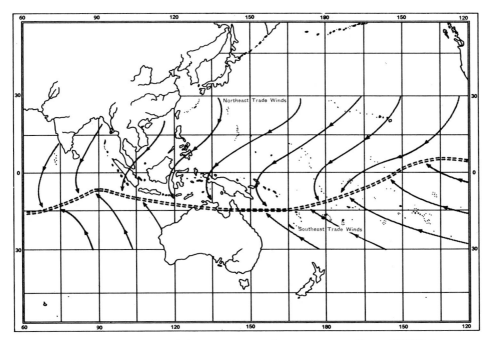

Figure 2-7. Mean position of the Intertropical Convergence Zone (ITCZ) for February.

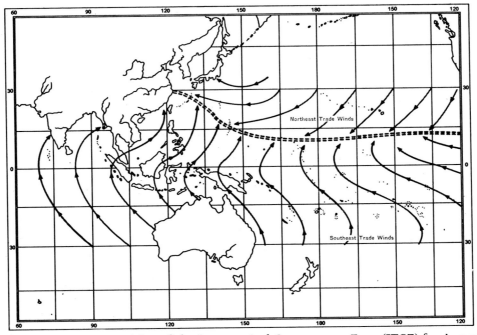

Figure 2-8. Mean position of the Intertropical Convergence Zone (ITCZ) for August.

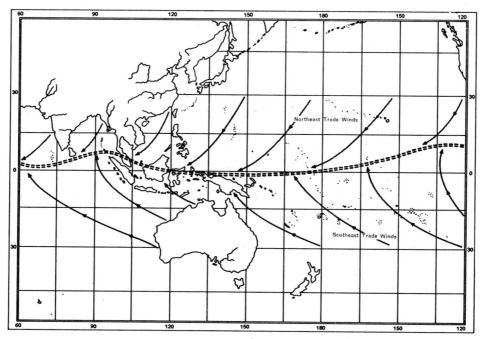

Figure 2-9. Mean position of the Intertropical Convergence Zone (ITCZ) for May and November.

When the ITCZ is located at or near the equator (where the coriolis—or horizontal deflecting—force is very small, or zero), only small and weak cyclonic circulations (vortices) can develop within it. But when it migrates away from the equator (at least 5 degrees of latitude or more), the influence of the earth's rotation (the coriolis force—which varies directly as the sine of the latitude and is strongest at the poles) becomes great enough to transfer sufficient "spin" to the converging air currents to permit dangerous tropical cyclones, hurricanes, and typhoons to develop. And this is one reason why aircraft weather reconnaissance and weather satellites are so very important over tropical oceanic areas where weather data are normally very sparse. Figure 2-10 is a weather satellite's view of the earth during a Northern Hemisphere summer day, showing the cloudiness conditions and weather patterns and storms for each hemisphere.

Figure 2-11 is another weather satellite view of the earth during a Southern Hemisphere late summer–early fall day, showing the cloudiness conditions and weather patterns and storms for each hemisphere.

In figure 2-12, we see a magnificent weather satellite image of two intense hurricanes on 8 August 1980: the easternmost one in the Gulf of Mexico and the westernmost one located SSW of the southern tip of Baja, California. Both hurricanes have clearly discernible "eyes," even from an altitude of 22,300 miles up in space.

In figure 2-13, we see an intense typhoon located 420 miles to the east of Taiwan (at point of white arrow) in the western Pacific on 19 October 1981. Note that the "eye" is elliptical in shape, measuring almost 70 nautical miles in a NE-SW direction, and about 30 miles in a NW-SE direction.

Figure 2-14 is a late season, nighttime, polar-orbiting NIMBUS III satellite HRIR (high resolution, infrared radiometer) image of a tropical cyclone over Hyderabad, Southern India. This storm, with its torrential rains, had moved westward from the Bay of Bengal.

In figure 2-15, we see a well-developed tropical cyclone in the southern Arabian Sea, 700 miles to the east of the Gulf of Aden, on 30 October 1971. Note

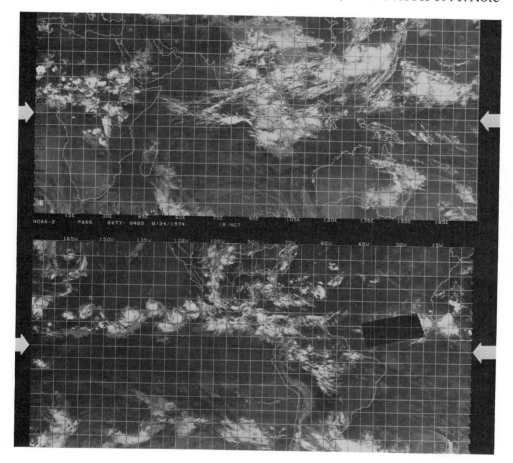

Figure 2-10. The tropical and subtropical regions of the earth as seen by the NOAA-2 polar-orbiting weather satellite on 24 August 1974, the Northern Hemisphere summer. The white arrows at the edges indicate the earth's equator. The latitude-longitude lines are at 5-degree intervals. Note the great variability of cloudiness associated with the ITCZ. Note, also, the total of seven tropical cyclones and hurricanes at one time in the North Pacific Ocean. (Courtesy of the National Air Survey Center Corp.)

the extreme narrowness of the Strait of Hormuz (at tip of white arrow), which is the entrance to the Persian Gulf. Tankers carrying so much of the world's oil must navigate this narrow strait. One can easily see how vulnerable this strategic "choke point" really is!

And figure 2-16 is a satellite view of a dissipating tropical cyclone (at tip of arrow) over Mozambique in the Southern Hemisphere. Note the reverse of the wind circulation from that of the Northern Hemisphere. When the supply of moisture (which is the energy engine of these phenomena) is cut off over land, tropical cyclones dissipate fairly rapidly.

So, as a "breeder" area of dangerous tropical cyclones, hurricanes, and

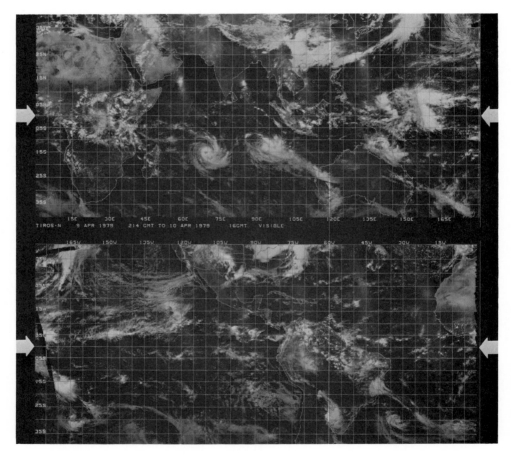

Figure 2-11. The tropical and subtropical regions of the earth as seen by the polar-orbiting TIROS-N weather satellite on 9–10 April 1979. The white arrows at the edges indicate the earth's equator. The latitude-longitude lines are at 5-degree intervals. Again, note the great variability of cloudiness associated with the ITCZ. Also, note the three tropical cyclones (willy-willies, hurricanes) in the Southern Hemisphere, off the NE coast of Australia and in the South Indian Ocean. (Courtesy of the National Air Survey Center Corp.)

typhoons, the ITCZ must be a familiar phenomenon to all who sail the seas of the world.

WAVES IN THE TRADE WIND EASTERLIES
OR EASTERLY WAVES (EWs)

The subject of easterly waves (EWs), or waves in the tropical easterlies, is a somewhat controversial subject among meteorologists. But then, several subjects and theories are. Two of the reasons for this are that: (1) one still cannot "crank in" finite values for all of the variables in the complicated equations of the meteorologists, and (2) it is not feasible to conduct strictly controlled laboratory experiments in the earth's atmosphere.

Some meteorologists, and other scientists, refer to "waves" in a flow current when that current exhibits fairly sinusoidal oscillations. As we mentioned earlier, and as shown in figure 2-3, two of the most constant air currents in the

Figure 2-12. A weather satellite's magnificent view (from 22,300 miles in space) of two intense hurricanes on 8 August 1980. The easternmost hurricane is located in the Gulf of Mexico. The westernmost hurricane is located to the SSW of the southern tip of Baja, California. Note the well-developed and clearly discernible "eye" of each hurricane. (Courtesy of the National Air Survey Center Corp.)

earth's atmosphere are the NE and SE trade winds of the tropical and subtropical oceanic areas of our planet. At times, the easterly trade wind currents oscillate in a wave-like manner, as shown in figure 2-17. And thus, some weathermen speak of "waves" in the tropical easterlies, or easterly waves (EWs).

In the author's opinion, easterly waves are extremely important phenomena because of their relation to tropical cyclone, hurricane, and typhoon formation. Fundamentally, these waves are (inverted) troughs of low pressure which are embedded in the deep easterly currents located on the equator side of the large oceanic high-pressure cells centered near 30–35 degrees north and south latitude. On average, easterly waves occur about every 15 degrees or so of longitude during the summer season primarily, and have an average length

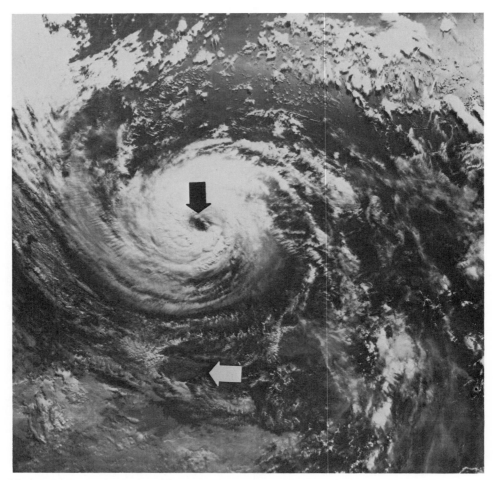

Figure 2-13. An intense typhoon located 420 miles to the east of Taiwan (at tip of white arrow) in the Western Pacific on 19 October 1981. Note the elliptical (rather than circular) shape of the "eye" (at tip of black arrow). (Department of Defense photo)

of about 15–18 degrees of latitude. They extend vertically in the atmosphere from the earth's surface to approximately 26,000 feet, and travel *from east to west* at an average speed of 10–13 knots. Note in figure 2-17 that EWs are at 90 degrees to the air flow, and that the wave amplitude decreases with increasing latitude. Rather than being distinct air-mass boundaries (such as the weather fronts of higher latitudes), easterly waves are "zones of transition," 30 to 100 miles wide, in which the weather changes rather gradually—but very definitely.

Figure 2-18 is a vertical model of the "standard" type of easterly wave. Note that the average slope is in a ratio of about 1/70, and that the EW slopes upward from west toward the east. The slope orientation, coupled with the convergence of the air flow to the east of the EW, and the divergence of air flow

Figure 2-14. Tropical cyclone with winds in excess of 60 knots over Hyderabad, southern India. Storm moved westward from the Bay of Bengal. (Courtesy of NASA Goddard Space Flight Center)

to the west of the EW, result in the bad weather occurring behind—to the east of—the EW, as shown in figures 2-17 and 2-18.

In almost all tropical—and other—weather disturbances, the associated cloud patterns and arrays are best displayed over the open oceans, free from the disrupting influences of land surfaces. But this, unfortunately, is also where the data are most sparse. And this is another reason why aircraft weather reconnaissance and weather satellites are so very important.

Figure 2-19 is a plan-view sketch of the cloud patterns of a "standard" easterly wave, as might be seen from a high-flying reconnaissance aircraft or a weather satellite. Note that the clouds are arranged almost in rows, forming "cloud streets." To the west of the EW, the rows, or "streets," of clouds are

Figure 2-15. A tropical cyclone in the Southern Arabian Sea, 700 miles east of the Gulf of Aden, is viewed by the image dissector camera system on board the Nimbus 4 meteorological satellite, 19 months after launch. (Courtesy of NASA Goddard Space Flight Center)

oriented from the NE toward the SW. The clouds here are small, fair-weather, cumulus clouds, dying out farther west. To the east of the EW, the clouds are oriented from the SE toward the NW. Heavy cloudiness and bad weather prevail to the east of the "standard" EW. A brief summary of easterly wave weather is contained in table 2-1.

Why are easterly waves important to professional and amateur sailors? Not only because of the unpleasant weather usually associated with them. But far more importantly, because of the role they frequently play in the formation of tropical cyclones, hurricanes, and typhoons. This will be discussed in the following section.

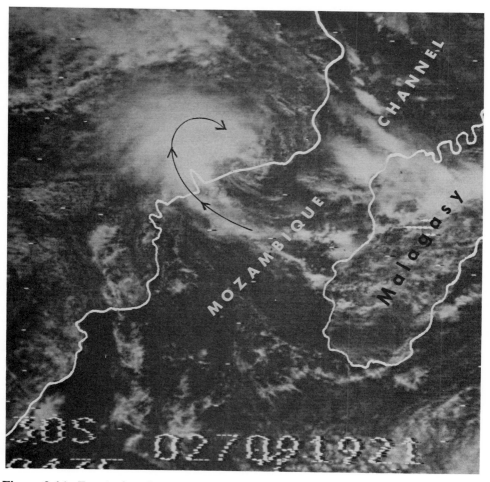

Figure 2-16. Tropical cyclone over Mozambique as viewed by the Nimbus 4 image dissector camera system. (Courtesy of NASA Goddard Space Flight Center)

LIFE CYCLE AND CHARACTERISTICS

As so beautifully put by Professor Richard A. Anthes in his book, *Tropical Cyclones—Their Evolution, Structure and Effects* (published by the American Meteorological Society, 1982), tropical cyclones are "conceived over warm tropical oceans, born amid torrential thundershowers, and nurtured by water vapor drawn inward from far away . . ." To that exceptionally fine prose I could only add, ". . . and are transformed or perish when the warm water and water vapor nutrients are withdrawn" (as by land masses, cold ocean currents, etc.).

Fully mature tropical cyclones (hurricanes, typhoons, etc.) are large rotating storms of extraordinary violence, where the temperatures in the center of

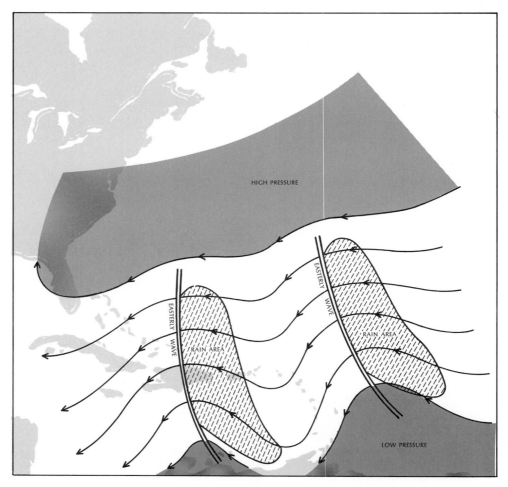

Figure 2-17. A schematic plan view of two easterly waves (EWs) moving westward in the western tropical Atlantic region. The double lines are the EWs. The streamlines show the air flow in the lower levels of the atmosphere. Note that the wave amplitude decreases with increasing latitude.

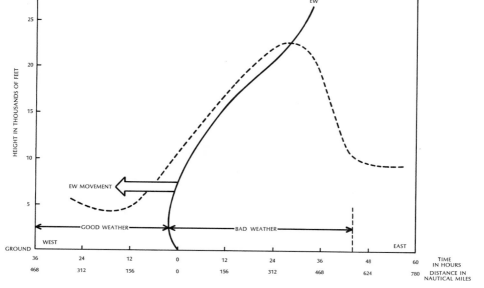

Figure 2-18. Vertical model of a "standard" easterly wave moving from east to west at 13 knots. The dashed line indicates the depth of the moist layer.

the storm are higher than those in the storm's periphery (called "warm-core"). Although these storms are neither the largest in horizontal extent (the winter storms of middle latitudes cover more area) nor the most intense from the standpoint of wind speed (the concentrated fury of tornadoes is unmatched), their considerable *size coupled with* their great *intensity* have made them the most dangerous and destructive phenomena on earth over the years.

To put these rampages of nature in proper perspective, consider the following isolated events. On 8 Sept. 1900, the death toll of the Galveston, Texas, hurricane reached 6,000. On 15–16 Oct. 1942, an intense tropical cyclone took the lives of 11,000 people in Bengal, India. During the period 4–8 Oct. 1963, a severe hurricane in the Caribbean caused over 6,000 deaths in Cuba and Haiti. And on 13 Nov. 1970, 300,000 unfortunate souls in Bangladesh lost their lives to a devastating tropical cyclone! That's almost as many people as the entire population of the city of Norfolk, Virginia.

Over the years, intense tropical cyclones have caused almost twice as many deaths as earthquakes, tidal waves, floods, tornadoes, avalanches, volcanic eruptions, and heat and cold waves combined! Each year, about 20,000 deaths and economic losses of almost $7 billion are attributed to these destructive phenomena. And through the years, these meteorological devastators have also taken their toll of warships, merchant vessels, pleasure craft, and the mariners who man them.

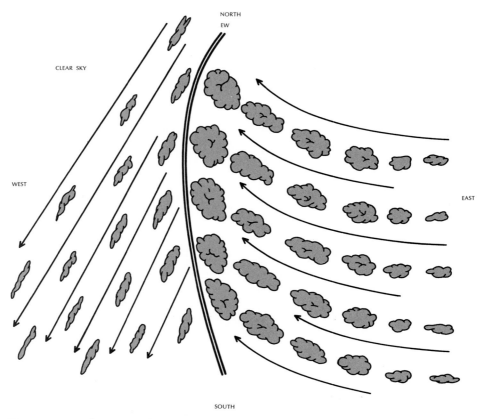

Figure 2-19. Plan-view sketch of "cloud streets" associated with a "standard" easterly wave, as they might be seen from a high-flying reconnaissance aircraft or a weather satellite. (Adapted from J.S. Malkus and H. Riehl.)

Formation

Although many scientific papers have been written on the subject of tropical cyclone formation, there is still no universally accepted theory of formation. There is the "convectional hypothesis," the "dynamic instability" theory, the "waves in a baroclinic easterly current" theory, the "thermal theory," and several others. Each theory, however, deals with only one or two specific aspects of tropical cyclone formation, and to the author's knowledge, there is still no composite treatment of all aspects. Outstanding work and research in this field is being accomplished at NOAA's NWS National Hurricane Center and the National Hurricane and Experimental Meteorology Laboratory in Coral Gables, Florida, at NASA's Goddard Space Flight Center in Greenbelt, Maryland, at various universities throughout the world, and at the National Center for Atmospheric Research in Boulder, Colorado.

In 1967, when he was Director of the Prediction Development Branch of the National Hurricane Research Laboratory, Dr. Banner I. Miller wrote: "One

Table 2-1. A brief summary of "standard" easterly wave weather conditions.

	West of Trough	Close to Trough	At Trough Line	East of Trough
Clouds	Fair-weather cumulus. Few build-ups.	Cumulus build-ups. Some high and middle clouds.	Heavy cumulus build-ups. Broken to overcast high and middle clouds.	Heavy cumulus and thunder-heads. Layers of high and middle clouds.
Visibility	Strong haze.	Improving.	Good, except in showers.	Fair to poor in showers.
Precipitation	Usually none.	Scattered showers.	Frequent showers.	Heavy showers, thundershowers, and rain.
Surface winds	ENE to NE.	ENE to E.	Easterly, some gusts.	ESE to SSE, with frequent gusts.

may say that meteorologists know less about the formation of hurricanes (and typhoons) than about their existence." And 20 years ago, Dr. H. Riehl, one of the world's foremost tropical meteorologists wrote: "The formation of a hurricane (typhoon) is a rare event, and we do not yet understand all the links in the chain which cause these events to occur."

Unfortunately, even after 20 years, we still do not have all the answers. But with the advances being made in the field of ultra-high-speed computers, the encouraging progress being made in the computer modelling of hurricanes, and the phenomenal advances in weather satellite remote sensing instrumentation, these answers will surely come. For our purposes, however, an exact, universally accepted theory is not necessary.

Severe tropical cyclones occur in almost all warm-water oceans. The two exceptions are the South Atlantic and the *extreme eastern* South Pacific Ocean. This is because the ITCZ does not invade these areas. In order for a cyclonic circulation to develop, the converging air currents must be able to concentrate their *vorticity* (local rotation, or "spin," in a fluid flow) at any altitude. The vorticity is very small near the equator, and zero at the equator. Consequently, tropical cyclones almost never form within 5 degrees north or south of the equator. The absorption of heat from the ocean by the air is greater when a circulation develops in the areas and during the seasons with the highest ocean-surface temperature. This occurs over the western parts of the oceans during August–October in the Northern Hemisphere, and during January–March in the Southern Hemisphere.

Most meteorologists—both theoretical and operational—agree that the sea-surface temperature must exceed 26°C (78.8°F) to enable the formation of a tropical cyclone. In 1954, Dr. A. Kasahara of Japan did considerable work in this regard. Figure 2-20 is a schematic chart of the results he obtained. This chart shows the average sea-surface temperatures in the western North Pacific during the summer months, and the number of tropical cyclones in each 5° × 5° latitude/longitude square during the 10-year period 1940–1949, inclusive.

One situation that is very conducive to the formation of an intense tropical cyclone (hurricane, typhoon)—if other conditions are favorable—occurs when an easterly wave (EW) moves into juxtaposition with a northward (or in the Southern Hemisphere, southward) "bulge" of the ITCZ, as depicted in figure 2-21. The NE trade winds of the Northern Hemisphere have already developed a cyclonic pattern because of the presence of the EW. As the SE trade winds of the Southern Hemisphere (where winds are deflected to the left) cross the equator and intrude into the Northern Hemisphere, they are then deflected to the right and become SW winds, virtually completing a closed cyclonic circulation. A more complicated situation—and a forecaster's nightmare—is shown in figure 2-22.

Hurricanes and typhoons derive their tremendous energy (and violence) from the latent heat of condensation (598 calories per gram) released into the atmosphere as the water vapor condenses. As long as the cyclonic center remains over warm water, the supply of energy is almost limitless. As more and more moist equatorial and/or tropical maritime air spirals inward toward the low-pressure center to replace the heated and rapidly ascending air, more

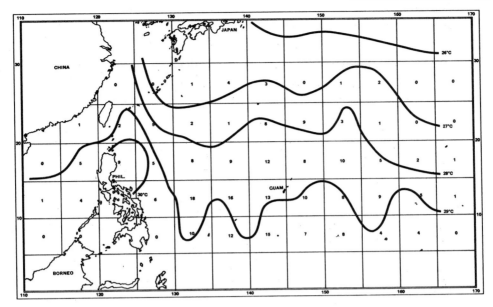

Figure 2-20. Schematic chart showing average sea-surface temperatures in the western North Pacific during summer months, and the numbers of tropical cyclones in each 5° × 5° latitude/longitude square during the 10-year period 1940–1949, inclusive. Note that tropical cyclones form where sea-surface temperatures exceed 26°C (78.8°F). (After Dr. A. Kasahara, 1954)

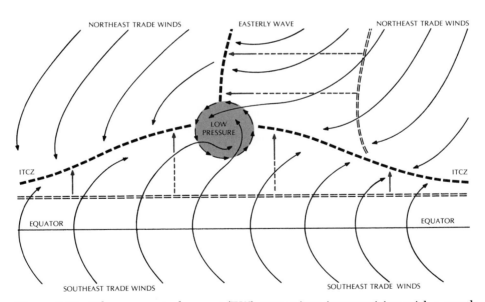

Figure 2-21. When an easterly wave (EW) moves into juxtaposition with a northward "bulge" of the ITCZ, the low-level air currents are favorable for the formation of a hurricane or typhoon. The dashed lines indicate the previous positions of the EW and the ITCZ. The dashed arrows show the movements of the EW and the ITCZ. (After Lt. Col. L.H. Hutchinson, USAF, 1956)

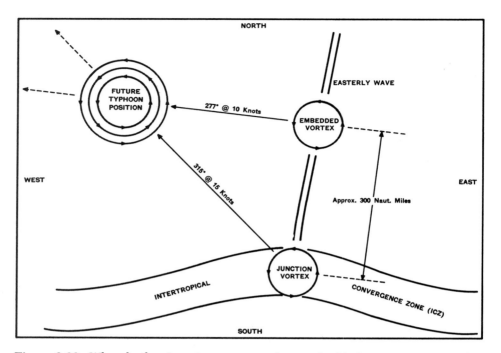

Figure 2-22. When both a junction vortex and an embedded vortex exist, it is frequently difficult to predict well in advance *which* vortex will develop to full hurricane or typhoon intensity. Sometimes one vortex "masks" the existence of the other, leading to erroneous forecasts of speed and direction of movement. (After Lt. Col. L.H. Hutchinson, USAF, 1956)

and more heat is released into the atmosphere, and the wind circulation continues to increase. The heat energy is converted into potential energy that is converted into kinetic energy. Professor H. Riehl has compared the hurricane to a simple, though inefficient, heat engine, since only about 3 percent of the total latent heat released is converted into kinetic energy—most fortunately for us all! When the wind speeds exceed 64 knots (74 mph, 33mps, or 119 kph), we have, by definition, a hurricane or typhoon.

Although we have no universally accepted, detailed theory of formation, most meteorologists agree that certain conditions are favorable (or necessary) for hurricane and typhoon formation. These conditions are contained in table 2-2.

Areas of Formation and Frequency of Occurrence

As we mentioned earlier, severe tropical cyclones occur in all of the tropical oceans except the South Atlantic and the extreme eastern South Pacific. And the southwestern portion of the North Pacific has more severe tropical cyclones (typhoons) than any other place on earth. Because of the newspaper headlines and TV segments devoted to the havoc and devastation wreaked by these phenomena, it may seem surprising that less than 10 percent of tropical

Table 2-2. Conditions favorable (or necessary) for the formation of hurricanes and typhoons.

1. Sea-surface temperature higher than 26°C (78.8°F).
2. Below-normal pressure in low latitudes (less than 1004 millibars, or 29.65 inches).
3. An existing tropical disturbance of some sort at the earth's surface.
4. Movement of the disturbance at a speed less than 13 knots.
5. Easterly winds decreasing in speed with height, but extending upward to at least 30,000 feet.
6. Moderate to strong outflow (divergence) at high levels in the atmosphere.
7. Special dynamic and kinematic conditions in the air flow near and above 40,000 feet.
8. Heavy rain or rainshowers in the area.

disturbances develop into full-blown hurricanes or typhoons. Even in a very active year (meteorologically) in the tropics, seldom will there be more than 50–80 *severe* tropical cyclones per annum with winds exceeding 64 knots. Compare this number to the average of about 2,500 extra-tropical cyclones in the winter months in the Northern Hemisphere, alone.

The number of severe tropical cyclones varies within wide limits from year to year. In the North Atlantic area, for example, the number has ranged from zero to 12 during the hurricane season. Taken over a long period of time, table 2-3 shows the monthly and annual average number of tropical cyclones per year for each major oceanic basin. And figure 2-23 shows the world's source regions of tropical cyclones, adapted from Dr. William M. Gray's Atmospheric Science Paper No. 114, "Global View of the Origin of Tropical Disturbances and Storms."

Tracks and Movement

Forecasting the future tracks and speeds of movement (and stalls) of hurricanes and typhoons is one of the most challenging and difficult—and exhilarating, when you "hit" the forecast right on the button—tasks that any operational meteorologist has to face. So much depends on the accuracy of the forecasts: the potential large loss of human life, the evacuation of many thousands of people from coastal and low-lying areas, the possibility of ships and smaller craft being sunk or ending up "high and dry," the expenditure of many millions of dollars in boarding up properties and moving ships and aircraft away from the threatened area(s), and so forth. In addition to these vital forecasts themselves, a hurricane/typhoon operational meteorologist has a score of other things on his mind as well—such as all sorts of deadlines, etc.

As a result of aircraft reconnaissance, shipboard, land station, and aircraft weather and radar reports, geostationary and polar-orbiting weather satellites, and the accumulation of large quantities of weather and oceanographic data over many years, we know that simple solutions to hurricane and typhoon movement seldom provide the correct answer. So-called *unusual* tracks occur far too often. Too many tracks exhibit loops, humps, staggering motions, abrupt course and/or speed changes, and so forth.

Table 2-3. Monthly and annual average number of tropical cyclones per year for each major oceanic basin. (Source: *Mariners' Worldwide Climatic Guide to Tropical Storms at Sea*, NAVAIR 50-1C-61, 1974)

Basin and Stage	JAN	FEB	MAR	APR	MAY	JUN	JUL	AUG	SEP	OCT	NOV	DEC	ANNUAL
North Atlantic													
Tropical Storms	*	*	*	*	0.1	0.4	0.3	1.0	1.5	1.2	0.4	*	4.2
Hurricanes	*	*	*	*	*	0.3	0.4	1.5	2.7	1.3	0.3	*	5.2
Tropical Storms and Hurricanes	*	*	*	*	0.2	0.7	0.8	2.5	4.3	2.5	0.7	0.1	9.4
Eastern North Pacific													
Tropical Storms	*	*	*	*	*	1.5	2.8	2.3	2.3	1.2	0.3	*	9.3
Hurricanes	*	*	*	*	0.3	0.6	0.9	2.0	1.8	1.0	*	*	5.8
Tropical Storms and Hurricanes	*	*	*	*	0.3	2.0	3.6	4.5	4.1	2.2	0.3	*	15.2
Western North Pacific													
Tropical Storms	0.2	0.3	0.3	0.2	0.4	0.5	1.2	1.8	1.5	1.0	0.8	0.6	7.5
Typhoons	0.3	0.2	0.2	0.7	0.9	1.2	2.7	4.0	4.1	3.3	2.1	0.7	17.8
Tropical Storms and Typhoons	0.4	0.4	0.5	0.9	1.3	1.8	3.9	5.8	5.6	4.3	2.9	1.3	25.3

Southwest Pacific and Australian Area

	JAN	FEB	MAR	APR	MAY	JUN	JUL	AUG	SEP	OCT	NOV	DEC	ANNUAL
Tropical Storms	2.7	2.8	2.4	1.3	0.3	0.2	*	*	*	0.1	0.4	1.5	10.9
Hurricanes	0.7	1.1	1.3	0.3	*	*	0.1	0.1	*	*	0.3	0.5	3.8
Tropical Storms and Hurricanes	*3.4*	*4.1*	*3.7*	*1.7*	*0.3*	*0.2*	*0.1*	*0.1*	*	*0.1*	*0.7*	*2.0*	*14.8*

Southwest Indian Ocean

	JAN	FEB	MAR	APR	MAY	JUN	JUL	AUG	SEP	OCT	NOV	DEC	ANNUAL
Tropical Storms	2.0	2.2	1.7	0.6	0.2	*	*	*	*	0.3	0.3	0.8	7.4
Hurricanes	1.3	1.1	0.8	0.4	*	*	*	*	*	*	*	0.5	3.8
Tropical Storms and Hurricanes	*3.2*	*3.3*	*2.5*	*1.1*	*0.2*	*	*	*	*	*0.3*	*0.4*	*1.4*	*11.2*

North Indian Ocean

	JAN	FEB	MAR	APR	MAY	JUN	JUL	AUG	SEP	OCT	NOV	DEC	ANNUAL
Tropical Storms	0.1	*	*	0.1	0.3	0.5	0.5	0.4	0.4	0.6	0.5	0.3	3.5
Cyclones[1]	*	*	*	0.1	0.5	0.2	0.1	*	0.1	0.4	0.6	0.2	2.2
Tropical Storms and Cyclones[1]	*0.1*	*	*0.1*	*0.3*	*0.7*	*0.6*	*0.6*	*0.4*	*0.5*	*1.0*	*1.1*	*0.5*	*5.7*

* Less than .05   [1] Winds ≥ 48 Kts.

Monthly values cannot be combined because single storms overlapping two months were counted once in each month and once in the annual.

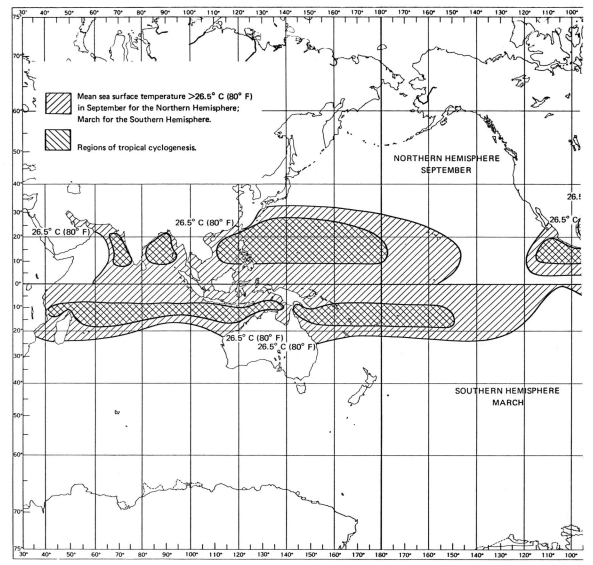

Figure 2-23. The world's source regions of tropical cyclones. (Source: *Mariners' Worldwide Climatic Guide to Tropical Storms at Sea*, NAVAIR 50-1C-61, 1974)

No two recorded severe tropical cyclone tracks have ever been *exactly* the same in any ocean. This is understandable when one considers the infinite number of variables involved. However, an examination of many hundreds of tracks by the author in 1963 revealed that there are about 12 different basic tracks that severe tropical cyclones tend to follow. To these 12 have been added 3 more by the scientific personnel at NOAA's National Climatic Center in Asheville, North Carolina, making a total now of 15 basic tracks. These

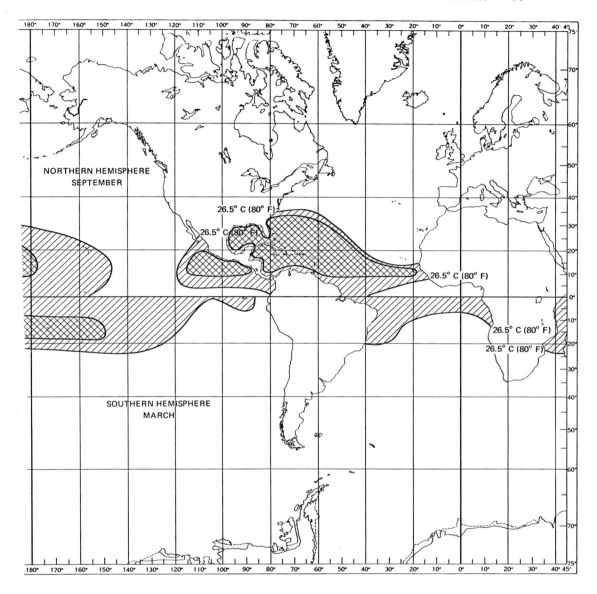

tracks are illustrated in figure 2-24. It must be remembered, however, that even these 15 basic tracks (in each hemisphere) have many minor variations.

Hurricanes and typhoons tend to move under the influence of both internal and external forces or influences. Internal forces arise within the circulation of the hurricane/typhoon itself. External forces are applied by the air currents that surround the tropical cyclone on all sides and "carry it along." Despite all of the unusual facets and irregularities of movement illustrated in figure 2-24,

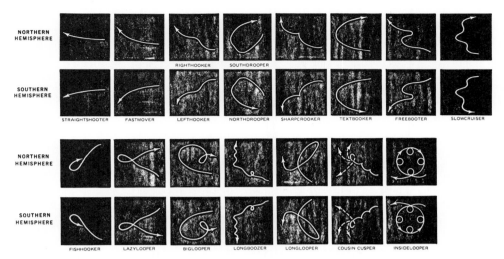

Figure 2-24. The basic tracks of severe tropical cyclones in both hemispheres. The tracks "Longlooper," "Cousin Cusper," and "Insidelooper" have been added by personnel of NOAA's National Climatic Center to the author's original basic tracks.

all severe tropical cyclones have one thing in common: a tendency to move eventually toward higher latitudes. And this tendency, shared by cyclones at all latitudes (and in both hemispheres), suggests propulsion by an internal force. Also, it can be demonstrated mathematically that severe tropical cyclones will move in the general direction of the "steering air current" in which they are embedded and with a certain percentage of the current's speed. A *steering current* is defined as the pressure-weighted, mean air flow from the earth's surface upward to about 30,000 feet (a pressure of about 300 millibars) and over a latitudinal band width of about 8 degrees and centered over the severe tropical cyclone.

In the language of most meteorologists, the term *recurvature* in tropical cyclone work refers to the change in the direction of movement from a westerly to an easterly component of movement. That is, a hurricane or typhoon *curves* from a course of 270° to 340° (it is still moving toward the west). But it *recurves* from a course of 340° to 030° (when the direction of movement passes 360° and continues turning toward the right, it is heading toward the east). Forecasting the exact recurvature of tropical cyclones in either hemisphere is one of the most difficult problems confronting meteorologists. Especially if one must predict the recurvature many hours in advance.

Prior to recurvature, the small-scale track of tropical cyclones is usually close to being sinusoidal, as shown in figure 2-25, leading some forecasters astray in their predictions. The speed of forward movement at this stage is quite slow (4–13 knots). During the recurvature, movement is usually very slow and very erratic (2–8 knots). After recurvature, however, when the tropical cyclone has moved into higher latitudes, the track is often reasonably "straight-line" and forward translational speeds of 40–50 knots are not uncommon. Figure 2-26 shows the worldwide principal tracks of severe tropical cyclones.

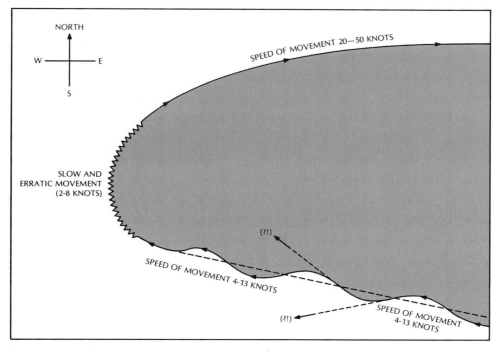

Figure 2-25. The speed, direction, and nature of movement of tropical cyclones before, during, and after recurvature. Note the sinusoidal nature of the track when the cyclone is developing and heading toward the west, and how this can easily mislead forecasters. Also note the rapid speed after recurvature.

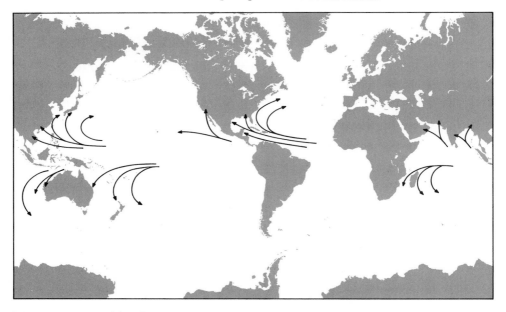

Figure 2-26. Worldwide principal tracks of severe tropical cyclones (hurricanes and typhoons), greatly simplified. Note that there are no tracks in the South Atlantic Ocean nor in the extreme eastern South Pacific Ocean. Why?

Size and Vertical Extent

The so-called "size" of a hurricane or typhoon is usually expressed in one of three ways, depending upon the particular author: (1) the diameter of the 64-knot (and higher) winds, (2) the diameter of the 50-knot winds, or (3) the diameter of the outer closed isobar (circular, or most usually elliptical).

In the western North Pacific, the average diameter of typhoon-force winds is about 325 nautical miles. However, in this respect, typhoons are subject to great individual variations. In the case of Typhoon Carmen in August 1960, for example, the typhoon-force winds extended more than 350 miles from the center in all directions, with gale-force winds almost 1,800 miles in diameter at one time! The average diameters of hurricanes in the North Atlantic and in other oceans of the world are somewhat smaller.

As a rule, in the early stages of development and even for the first day or two after the storm reaches hurricane/typhoon intensity, the diameter of the 64-knot winds is usually relatively small—on the order of 120 nautical miles. As the storm increases in age, it also expands laterally. Sometimes the wind speeds increase markedly, and sometimes rather gradually, depending upon meteorological conditions both in the upper and lower levels of the earth's atmosphere.

The vertical extent of hurricanes and typhoons, for many decades, was a source of puzzlement to meteorologists. And not too many years ago, the subject of the vertical extent of these phenomena was a "heavy" controversy amongst some of the best theoreticians. Some insisted that these circulations must disappear above 10,000 feet. Others insisted just as emphatically that the circulations must extend to very great heights. As the result of high-level balloon weather observations, high-flying weather reconnaissance aircraft, and the geostationary and polar-orbiting weather satellites, we now have the answer.

Although hurricanes and typhoons usually first develop as low-level phenomena, the tops of these mature storms extend all the way up to the tropopause (the zone between the troposphere and the stratosphere). However, the wind direction reverses completely between the earth's surface and at a height of about 40,000 feet. Above the low-level cyclonic circulation, there exists an anticyclonic circulation at high levels in the atmosphere. *Ahead* of the storm center, the winds turn *clockwise* with increasing height. And to the *rear* of the storm center, the winds turn *counterclockwise* with increasing height. Available data further indicate that the stratospheric easterly winds continue to blow undisturbed, despite nature's rampage taking place underneath.

The "Eye"

The "eye" of a hurricane or typhoon is unique. It is not observed in any other phenomenon on earth. Through the years, it has always been one of the favorite subjects of writers and scientific investigators, for in some respects, it is the most spectacular part of the hurricane's anatomy.

As we mentioned in a previous section, the winds in a hurricane or typhoon spiral violently inward toward the center of lowest pressure. There, the strongly converging air is whirled upward by convection, by the mechanical thrusting of other converging air, and by the pumping action of high-altitude circulations. This spiral is marked by the thick "wall clouds" that surround— and form the outer edge of—the hurricane's center. The wall cloud of a hurricane or typhoon is the area of most violent winds, heaviest precipitation, and greatest release of heat energy. This "ring" of strongest winds and torrential rain is usually 5–30 miles from the storm's center, with the average eye diameter being about 15 nautical miles. Inside the eye wall cloud, the winds decrease rather abruptly to 12 knots or less, and the torrential rain also ceases abruptly. This area is the celebrated "eye"—a term coined many decades before the advent of radar, high-speed computers, weather satellites, etc.

The eye offers a brief, *but very deceptive*, respite from the violent conditions of the eye wall. Inside the eye, the winds are light and there are intermittent bursts of blue sky through the thin middle and high clouds. Occasionally, low clouds form miniature spirals inside the eye. Across the eye, however, at the opposite wall, the violent winds and torrential rains resume—*but* the *winds* are from the *opposite direction* because of the cyclonic circulation of the storm.

To primitive man, this fantastic transformation from great violence to comparative calm, and from calm into great violence again from another quarter—all in a very short interval of time—must have seemed an excessive whim of the gods. Nevertheless, it *is* spectacular. Just ask anyone who has undergone the experience! The eye's relative calm and abrupt existence in the midst of such meteorological violence is never forgotten by anyone experiencing it.

Although the eye of a hurricane or typhoon is usually described as being "circular," it is frequently observed by weather reconnaissance crews and weather satellites to be elliptical. See figure 2-27, a satellite's view of Typhoon Kit on 17 December 1981, for an example of an almost perfect circular eye of a typhoon. Then thumb back a few pages and compare this circular eye to the elliptical eye of figure 2-13, an earlier typhoon on 19 October 1981. When the eye of a hurricane or typhoon is elliptical, the longest axis is usually parallel to the direction of the storm's movement. Aircraft weather reconnaissance crews have also observed that the diameter of the eye is constantly undergoing transformation. This is hardly surprising, however, when one considers the extreme conditions at the boundary of the eye.

While the average diameter of hurricane and typhoon eyes is about 15 nautical miles, in immature storms eye diameters of only 4.5 miles have been observed. And at the other extreme, when the mature Typhoon Carmen passed over Okinawa on 20 August 1960, the diameter of the eye of this monstrous typhoon was observed (and radar-photo verified) to be 200 nautical miles!

The length of time it takes for an eye to pass over a ship or station depends upon the size and shape of the eye, the length of the eye's chord which passes over the ship or station, the speed of movement of the hurricane or typhoon, and the direction and speed of movement of the ship—although any ship so caught will not be making much headway!

Dr. Robert H. Simpson (former Director, National Hurricane Center) has made many flights into tropical cyclones, as has the author. But Dr. Simpson's

Figure 2-27. Typhoon Kit, located to the WNW of Guam on 17 December 1981, packing more than 115 knots of wind. Note the almost perfect circular eye (at tip of arrow). Compare this eye to the elliptical typhoon eye shown in figure 2-13. (Department of Defense photo)

descriptions of events are far superior to the author's. His description of his entrance into the eye of a hurricane (Marge) is as follows:

> The plane flew through bursts of torrential rain and severe turbulent bumps. Then, suddenly, we were in the dazzling sunlight and bright blue sky. Around us was an awesome display. Marge's eye was a clear space 40 miles in diameter surrounded by a coliseum of clouds whose walls on one side rose vertically and on the other were banked like galleries in a great opera house. The upper rim, about 35,000 feet high, was rounded off smoothly against a background of blue sky.

Three quick words of caution regarding hurricane and typhoon eyes: (1) elliptical eyes, wherein the longest axis is usually parallel to the direction of the storm's movement, have been observed by aircraft crews and by radar to rotate, (2) double eyes have been observed, and (3) concentric eyes have also been observed—all adding to the complications of the problem of "maneuvering to avoid."

The Wind

As one can imagine, it's very difficult to obtain the highest winds of the super- and killer-hurricanes/typhoons because the storm's full fury usually causes the instrument shelters and masts to collapse and be carried away before the highest intensity of the storm is reached. Much of the current data and estimates are based primarily upon: (1) aircraft reconnaissance flights, (2) calculations from pressure-gradient measurements and pressure-temperature relationships, and (3) detailed studies of the structural damage to buildings, etc.

Many typhoons over the open ocean areas of the western North Pacific have maximum sustained surface winds as high as 140–150 knots sometime during their life histories. Also, there is considerable evidence available from gust recordings, which indicated that the extreme gusts frequently exceed the maximum sustained winds by as much as 30 to 50 percent. This means that for a 150-knot typhoon, one should prepare for extreme gusts as high as 225 knots!

The distribution of wind speed around a 150-knot tropical cyclone is shown for each hemisphere in figure 2-28. This diagram shows the maximum of 150 knots (173 mph) to the right of the direction of movement of the tropical cyclone in the Northern Hemisphere, and to the left of the direction of movement in the Southern Hemisphere, looking downstream. This is typical and due, in part, to the fact that (in the Northern Hemisphere) on the *right* side, the forward movement of the storm is *added* to the observed wind velocity. And on

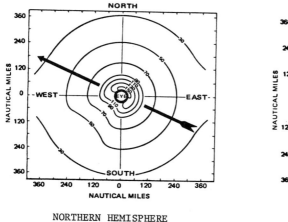

NORTHERN HEMISPHERE

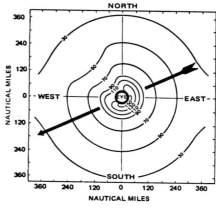

SOUTHERN HEMISPHERE

Figure 2-28. Distribution of surface wind speed (in knots) around 150-knot tropical cyclones over open water, moving on a track of 295° in the Northern Hemisphere, and on a track of 245° in the Southern Hemisphere. Note that the highest winds occur to the right of the center in the Northern Hemisphere, and to the left in the Southern Hemisphere.

the left side, the forward movement of the storm is *subtracted* from the observed wind velocity. The opposite is true in the Southern Hemisphere. On the *left* side, the storm's translational speed is *added* to the observed wind velocity. In the case of a stationary tropical cyclone, the distribution of wind speeds is much more symmetrical.

Again, remember that winds blow counterclockwise around tropical cyclones in the Northern Hemisphere, and clockwise around them in the Southern Hemisphere, as shown in figure 2-29. Note that the winds tend to blow toward the center until they reach the edge of the "eye." The angle of inflow is not the same in every quadrant of the storm, but it averages about 20°–30° across the isobars, except near the inner edge of the wall cloud, where there is no longer any inflow. Here, the winds are almost parallel (or tangential) to the wall clouds. Wind directions in the diagram have been exaggerated for purposes of illustration.

The angle of inflow of the wind varies considerably with individual tropical cyclones, their size, maturity, latitude, and other meteorological conditions. As a general rule, the intense, slowly-moving immature tropical cyclones have the most symmetrical wind fields, and the strongest winds are located in and under the wall cloud surrounding the eye. In poorly developed and/or rapidly moving tropical cyclones, the highest winds are usually found in only one quadrant, to the *right* of the direction of movement in the Northern Hemisphere and to the *left* of the direction of movement in the Southern Hemisphere.

Pressure

Motion in the earth's atmosphere—the wind—is caused by the pressure differences between two points. That's putting it very simply. Winds tend to blow

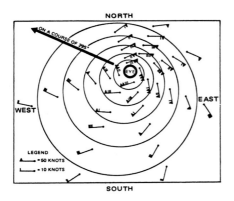

NORTHERN HEMISPHERE

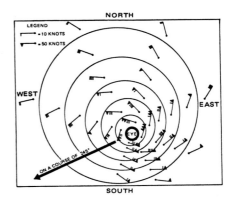

SOUTHERN HEMISPHERE

Figure 2-29. The wind circulation around 150-knot tropical cyclones in the Northern and Southern Hemispheres. Note how the circulations are reversed in each hemisphere. Each pennant indicates 50 knots of wind, and each long barb indicates 10 knots. Thus, two pennants and two long barbs equal 120 knots, and one pennant and two long barbs equal 70 knots. (A short barb equals 5 knots.)

across the isobars at an angle (about 30° over land and about 15° over water where the friction is less), from higher pressure toward lower pressure. And the greater the pressure differences between those two points, the faster the wind blows. Obviously then, the extremely strong winds, such as those found near the centers of hurricanes and typhoons (and tornadoes, of course), can only exist in areas where the pressure differences are extremely large.

The pressure at the center of intense tropical cyclones must be very low in order to concentrate a rapid decrease in pressure in a short horizontal distance, resulting in the devastating winds characteristic of hurricanes and typhoons. So, in a very general way, the pressure at the center of a hurricane or typhoon is a measure of its intensity—although not an absolute measure. To the author's knowledge, the lowest scientifically accepted sea-level barometer reading occurred in Typhoon Tip on 12 October 1979 in the western North Pacific with a pressure reading of 870 millibars (25.691 inches of mercury)! As a general rule, the lower the central pressure, the more intense the tropical cyclone.

Over 20 years ago, Dr. Robert D. Fletcher (then Director, Scientific Services, USAF Air Weather Service) developed a rather simple formula for calculating the maximum sustained winds of an intense tropical cyclone. In the absence of other detailed and definitive information, this formula can be used to great advantage by "sea dogs" of all experience levels to get an idea of a storm's intensity. It's a matter of simple substitution in the following formula:

Maximum Wind $= 16 \times \sqrt{P_n - P_o}$

Where: P_n = pressure in millibars along the hurricane's or typhoon's periphery.

P_o = pressure in millibars at the storm's center.

During Typhoon Karen (later dubbed a "killer" typhoon), the night of 11–12 November 1962, when that storm blew the island of Guam apart, the author used Fletcher's formula and compared the results to the aircraft reconnaissance data and sea-level pressure readings on the island, with the following result:

Maximum Wind $= 16 \times \sqrt{1010 - 907}$

$= 16 \times \sqrt{103}$

$= 16 \times 10.1$

$= 161.6$ knots

The actual maximum sustained winds (over a one-minute interval) of Typhoon Karen were 150 knots—a close comparison. The formula has been used by the author on many tropical storms, with quite good results.

Barograph traces at shore stations during a hurricane's or typhoon's passage furnish a measure of the pressure field in the core if the rate of movement is known. Figure 2-30 is a typical example of a barograph trace as an intense tropical cyclone approaches, passes over, and leaves a ship's position or station. On the day before the storm's arrival, local weather is often unusually good, with the barometer reading slightly above normal. Then the pressure begins to fall slowly (in excess of the diurnal value), and the wind may start blowing from an unusual direction. Finally, the pressure falls at an extremely rapid rate (usually for about three hours) as the eye itself approaches, and rises almost equally rapidly as the eye moves away. Pressure falls of as much as 40 millibars (1.181 inches) in 20 minutes have been recorded, and total pressure drops of 60 millibars (1.772 inches) in 50 miles horizontally are not uncommon.

Figure 2-31 is a tracing of the actual barograph record at the U.S. Fleet Weather Central/Joint Typhoon Warning Center, Guam, as the geometric center of Typhoon Karen passed nine miles to the south of the instrument on that fateful night.

Dr. H. Ito of Japan did some outstanding work on the statistical pressure aspects of tropical storms and typhoons in the western North Pacific during the 10-year period 1950–1959, inclusive, most of which were penetrated by aircraft reconnaissance flights. Table 2-4 is based on Dr. Ito's research, and

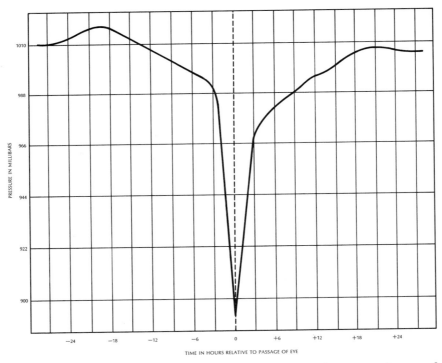

Figure 2-30. Typical example of a barograph (pressure) trace as the eye of a hurricane or typhoon approaches, passes over, and departs a ship or station.

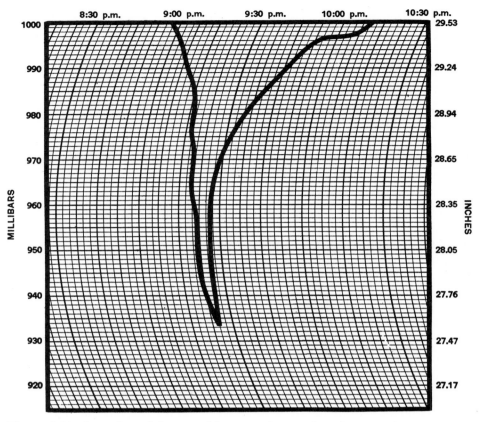

Figure 2-31. A tracing of the actual barograph record at the U.S. Fleet Weather Central/Joint Typhoon Warning Center, Guam, as the eye of Typhoon Karen passed nine miles to the south of the instrument the night of 11–12 November 1962.

shows the frequency of occurrence of tropical storms and typhoons, as classified by the lowest surface pressure that each typhoon attained in its life cycle. And figure 2-32 illustrates the relation between the lowest central pressure and the maximum 24-hour pressure fall for each typhoon. Dr. Ito also found that, on average, the central pressures of typhoons begin to drop rapidly about 3–4 days after their formation, and that the pressures attain their minimum value about 4–5 days after the birth of the typhoon.

Clouds and Precipitation

Even though the detailed cloud sequence varies from one intense tropical cyclone to another, the precursory signs are remarkably uniform. On the day before the storm's arrival, local weather is frequently unusually good and the barometer above normal. The arrival of a long swell is sometimes the first warning sign—coming from the general direction of the storm's center. Then, the pressure begins to fall slowly, and the wind may start blowing from an unusual direction. There are only a few cumulus clouds, and these do not extend very high.

Table 2-4. Frequency of occurrence of tropical storms and typhoons, classified by the lowest surface pressure which each typhoon attained in its life cycle. (After Dr. H. Ito, 1962.)

	Millibars												
≧1000	999 to 990	989 to 980	979 to 970	969 to 960	959 to 950	949 to 940	939 to 930	929 to 920	919 to 910	909 to 900	899 to 890	889 to 880	879 to 870
14	51	41	24	31	13	14	15	11	11	8	6	3	1
≧29.53	29.50 to 29.24	29.21 to 28.94	28.91 to 28.64	28.62 to 28.35	28.32 to 28.05	28.02 to 27.76	27.73 to 27.46	27.43 to 27.17	27.14 to 26.87	26.84 to 26.58	26.55 to 26.29	26.25 to 25.99	25.96 to 25.69
	Inches												

Late in the afternoon—or during the early evening—on the day before the storm's arrival, high-level cirrus clouds approach from the direction of the hurricane or typhoon. These are followed in order several hours later by lowering and thickening cirrostratus, altostratus, and altocumulus clouds. Then, several brief periods of tall cumulus clouds with showers are experienced.

The barometer begins to fall much more rapidly, the showers become much heavier, and the wind begins to increase markedly. Finally, a dark wall of clouds approaches—the *bar* of the storm. And with its arrival, the full fury of the hurricane or typhoon is unleashed.

The fury of the storm, however, does not persist constantly. Periods of extreme violence alternate with periods of comparative "lull." Even the central area of the storm is not uniformly filled with clouds. Rather, relatively narrow, elongated spiral bands of very heavy rain are interspersed with areas of relatively light rain—and sometimes no rain at all. Some of these spiral bands have their origin several hundred miles distant from the center of the storm. See figure 2-33 for a good example of this. These spiral bands head inward toward the eye wall cloud.

The number of spiral bands around a hurricane or typhoon seems to vary within rather wide limits. The width of each spiral band further seems to increase from a minimum of about two miles near the center of the storm to a maximum of about 40 miles near the storm's periphery. The general shape of these bands is close to that of a logarithmic spiral.

Some of the world's heaviest rainfalls have occurred in connection with intense tropical cyclones. One typhoon, for example, in 1911, dumped 88 inches of rain on the Philippines in a four-day period. This is close to the *annual* average rainfall on Guam.

The rainfall associated with hurricanes and typhoons is always heavy; however, the exact rainfall is not always known. After the wind speed exceeds 50 knots, it is unlikely that the rain gauges catch more than 50 percent, and when the winds go much higher, the rain gauges frequently become a part of the lethal flying debris. The total accumulation of rain is, of course, greatly dependent upon the speed of movement of the storm, simply because in slowly moving storms the rain lasts a lot longer.

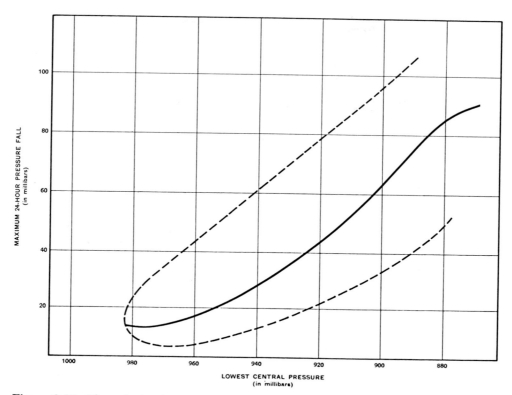

MAXIMUM 24-HOUR PRESSURE FALL (in millibars)

LOWEST CENTRAL PRESSURE
(in millibars)

Figure 2-32. The relation between the lowest central pressure and the maximum 24-hour pressure fall for each typhoon between 1950–1959, inclusive. The solid curve represents the "mean." The dashed curve shows the "limits." (After Dr. H. Ito, 1962)

Life Cycle

On average, the life span of hurricanes and typhoons is about six to seven days from the time they first form until they either enter a land area or recurve into higher latitudes. Some storms last for only a day or so; others continue for over two weeks. I like to divide the lifetime of intense tropical cyclones into the following four stages.

Formative Stage. Hurricanes and typhoons form only in pre-existing low latitude disturbances. The fall of barometric pressure can be a slow process, requiring several days for the organization of a large area with diffuse winds. It can also be explosive, with a well-formed eye developing within 12 hours. The winds usually remain below 64 knots during the formative stage. The strongest winds are concentrated in one quadrant, usually to the north and east of the center of the developing vortex in the Northern Hemisphere, and to the south and east of the developing vortex in the Southern Hemisphere. The surface pressure drops to about 1002 millibars (29.59 inches).

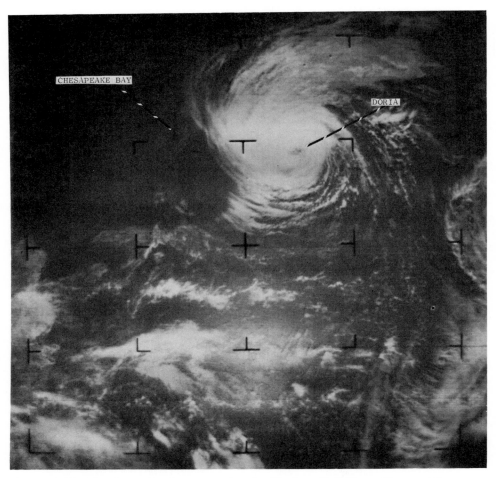

Figure 2-33. Hurricane Doria as seen by the Nimbus II APT satellite on 15 September 1967. Note that the "spiral bands" originate at large distances from the storm's center. (Courtesy of NASA Goddard Space Flight Center)

Immature Stage. All incipient tropical cyclones do not become hurricanes and/or typhoons. Some have been observed to die within 24 hours, even though the winds had attained hurricane force (64 knots). Others travel over very long distances as shallow tropical depressions (maximum sustained winds not exceeding 33 knots). If intensification takes place, the pressure in the center drops rapidly below 1,000 millibars (29.53 inches), and winds of 64 knots or higher form a tight band around the center. The cloud and rain pattern changes from disorganized squalls to narrow organized bands spiraling inward toward the center. Up to this point, only a relatively small area is involved.

Mature Stage. The surface pressure at the center no longer falls, and maximum sustained wind speeds have been attained. The lateral area of the circulation expands, and may continue to do so for six or seven days. Whereas 64-knot winds may blow only within a 35–50 mile radius during the immature stage, the radius can now increase to 350 miles or more in the mature stage. However, with the great expansion of the system, the symmetry is lost, as the area of gales and bad weather extends much farther to the right of the direction of movement (looking downstream) in the Northern Hemisphere, and to the left of the direction of movement (looking downstream) in the Southern Hemisphere.

Dissipation Stage. As a hurricane or typhoon recurves from tropical latitudes to temperate latitudes and enters the belt of westerly winds, its size usually decreases. At times, it even dissipates within a day or so. But at other times, only the storm's tropical characteristics decay, and as the storm travels toward the subpolar latitudes, it assumes a middle-latitude character (a "cold core"). When this happens, the storm frequently attacks anything in its path with renewed vigor.

Not all tropical cyclones recurve into temperate latitudes. Many dissipate over land masses. A few even die over the tropical oceans.

Hurricanes and typhoons, as such, die when: (1) they leave the environment of warm, moist tropical air, (2) they move over a large land mass, and (3) when they travel under an unfavorable large-scale circulation of air currents at high levels in the earth's atmosphere.

FORCES OF DESTRUCTION

When one considers the fantastic energy associated with hurricanes and typhoons, the tremendous destruction and loss of life wrought by these systems is entirely understandable. Consider, for example, that an ordinary afternoon thunderstorm has the energy equivalent of about 13 20-kiloton atomic bombs. And that even a small hurricane or typhoon will release about 20-billion tons of water. This is an energy equivalent of almost 500,000 atomic bombs, or about six atomic bombs per second!

The Wind

Since it is the gustiness of the wind that results in the "uneven" intermittent pressures and the wrenching effects, the speed of peak gusts must be considered in designing ships and structures to withstand the onslaught of intense tropical cyclones.

Another vital consideration in relation to ship and shore construction vis-à-vis tropical cyclone damage is the rapid rise in the actual force of the wind at higher speeds. The force exerted by the wind does not increase proportionately with the velocity, but rather with the *square of the velocity*. In other words, *doubling* the velocity results in *four times the force*.

If the wind is normal (at 90 degrees) to a face of a rectangular column of appreciable size, the pressure on the front side *plus* the suction on the rear side (roughly equal to each other, in most cases, and both always present) is about 1.5 times the "velocity pressure," or "impact pressure." That is, the formula for calculating is as follows:

Pressure on Front Side + Suction on Rear Side (P):
$$P = 1.5 \times (\tfrac{1}{2} \times d \times V^2)$$
where d = density of dry air = 0.001293 grams per cubic centimeter
and V = actual wind speed in meters per second
If we convert to English units (lbs./cu.ft., ft./sec^2, mph),
we can then reduce our formula to:
$$P = 0.004V^2, \text{ roughly,}$$

in which P = pressure *plus* suction in pounds per square foot of flat surface normal to (at 90 degrees to) the wind, and V = the *actual* (*not* the average) wind speed in miles per hour.

From figure 2-34 we see that a 50-mph wind exerts an impact pressure of 10 lbs./sq.ft., a 100-mph wind exerts an impact pressure of 40 lbs./sq.ft., and a 200-mph wind exerts an impact pressure of 160 lbs./sq.ft.

In the case of cylindrical objects, such as masts, smokestacks, etc., the toppling force due to the wind is much less, perhaps one-half the value that the formula gives, on the assumption that the virtual area perpendicular to the wind is the maximum vertical cross-section. But if the masts support sails, electronic equipment, etc., that's another problem.

Unfortunately, like so many things in life, there is no universally applicable coefficient of wind pressure. It varies widely with the shape and size of the object or obstacle. Also, for certain angles of incidence of the wind, the negative pressure—the suction—may be considerably larger than the pressure on the front side. But at least figure 2-34 will provide a ballpark figure for preliminary (and precautionary) planning.

Pressure

The central low pressure (or pressure falls), per se, of hurricanes and typhoons is normally not considered to be a problem. However, a word of caution. The author still remembers vividly the night of 11–12 November 1962 when the eye of killer Typhoon Karen passed over the island of Guam. Two days before the (predicted, fortunately) arrival of the typhoon, the Navy Seabees on Guam had efficiently and expertly packed and stowed their delicate and expensive instruments and tools in their assigned quonset hut. Upon completion of the task, they carefully sealed the structure to prevent water damage to the instruments. *But*, the structure could not "breathe."

When Karen's eye passed over Guam, the extreme atmospheric pressure drop of almost 100 millibars (2.953 inches) in a period of less than four hours caused the building to literally "explode like a bomb." All that remained was the concrete slab on which the quonset hut had once stood. And to the author's knowledge, none of the instruments and equipment were ever found. They probably ended up in the Philippine Sea.

At first, some scientists thought that a tornado may have been associated with the quonset hut's "explosion," but no evidence was ever found of this.

One should always leave a "vent" for "breathing" on ships, boats, buildings, etc., whenever large atmospheric pressure changes (in a relatively short period of time) are anticipated.

Waves, Swell, and Tides

First, we should distinguish between waves and swell. Waves are generated by the wind, and as these wind-generated waves tend to move out of—or ahead of—the generation area and into regions of weaker winds, they decrease in

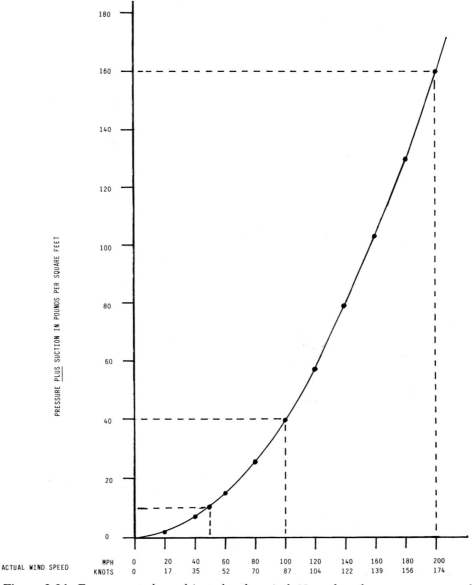

Figure 2-34. Force exerted on objects by the wind. Note that the pressure exerted by the wind increases with the *square* of the velocity. Doubling the wind velocity results in four times the force. (A 50-mph wind exerts 10 lbs./sq. ft; a 100-mph wind exerts 40 lbs./sq.ft.; a 200-mph wind exerts 160 lbs./sq.ft.)

height and increase in period. These decaying waves, which may persist for a long, long time and travel great distances, are termed "swell."

The great wind stress exerted on the ocean's surface in hurricanes and typhoons produces huge waves with extreme heights. Some have been reported as high as 66 feet. Figure 2-35 shows schematically how these swells travel outward in all directions from the center of an intense tropical cyclone. They are observed as a long swell, as much as 2,000 miles distant from the storm center. And the speed of propagation is as high as 1,000 miles per day. Since the average hurricane or typhoon movement prior to recurvature is only 330 miles per day, these swells provide an early warning of an impending hurricane or typhoon.

Referring, again, to figure 2-35, the waves generated in the right rear quadrant (in the Northern Hemisphere) and the left rear quadrant in the Southern Hemisphere, travel in the direction of the storm's movement. Thus, they propagate under the influence of winds having relatively little change in direction for a much longer time than the waves in any other quadrant. Consequently, the highest waves (and later, swells) are produced in these parts of the storm.

When these swells arrive at a distant ship or coastline, the normal wave frequency of 10–15 per minute will have decreased to about 2–5 per minute. And the direction of the swell indicates the position of the storm's center at the time the swell was generated. If this direction remains constant, the hurricane or typhoon is approaching the ship (or area) directly. If it changes counterclockwise (in the Northern Hemisphere), as seen by the observer facing the storm, the center will pass from right to left. If the swell changes direction in a clockwise fashion, the center of the hurricane or typhoon will pass from left to right.

In the Southern Hemisphere, if the swell changes in a counterclockwise

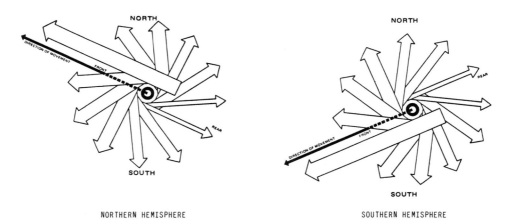

NORTHERN HEMISPHERE   SOUTHERN HEMISPHERE

Figure 2-35. Schematic diagrams of the swells generated by intense tropical cyclones in each hemisphere. Arrows indicate the direction of movement of the swells. The width of the arrows indicates the relative height of the swells.

fashion, as seen by an observer facing the storm, the center will pass from left to right. If the swell changes in a clockwise fashion, the center will pass from right to left.

The damage and erosion caused by waves, swell, and storm-generated surf through the years has caused extensive damage along coastlines all over the world. One must remember that a cubic yard of water weighs three-fourths of a ton, and a breaking wave moving toward shore at speeds of more than 50 knots is one of the most destructive elements connected with hurricanes and typhoons. The erosive power of storm-driven waves is tremendous, for these waves can scour out 100 feet of beach in just a few hours. Perhaps a few definitions would help at this point:

- *Water Level*—The mean height that the water would reach if there were no waves (i.e., the average elevation between wave crests and troughs); the "still water" level.
- *Meteorological Tides*—Departures from normal astronomical tides because of the abnormal action of weather elements.
- *Forerunner*—The slow rise of the tide produced by swells from a hurricane or typhoon while it is still a long distance away.
- *Storm Surge*—A rapid rise in the water level produced by onshore hurricane and typhoon winds and falling atmospheric pressure. More about this in the following section.

The forerunner, alone, may produce tides 4–5 feet above normal, the exact amount depending upon the strength of the wind that produced the swells, the angle between the hurricane's path and the shore line, and the shapes of both the coast and continental shelf, etc. It usually causes rises in the water level along hundreds of miles of coastline, whereas the more rapid and much greater rise associated with the storm surge is restricted to a relatively small section of coastline.

The storm surge normally occurs just to the right (in the Northern Hemisphere) and just to the left (in the Southern Hemisphere) of the cyclone's center, and either shortly precedes or accompanies the arrival of the center. When the surge moves into a long channel, however, the rise in the water at the end of the channel may reach its peak several hours after the storm winds have passed. A hurricane or typhoon moving toward or crossing a coastline will always be accompanied by above-normal tides, particularly near and to the right (in the Northern Hemisphere) of the center (left, in the Southern Hemisphere). These high tides frequently occur at a considerable distance ahead of the advancing center, providing another excellent warning sign.

The Storm Surge

The two major forces that drive the storm surge are the wind stress and the atmospheric pressure gradient. Storms moving parallel to coastlines generally produce smaller storm surges than those crossing the coast, because the time of exposure to onshore winds for water parcels and waves is less. Nevertheless, history has shown that storm surges associated with intense storms moving parallel to coastlines can still be substantial. Storm surge varies significantly with storm intensity and, to a lesser extent, with storm size.

The storm surge causes most of the damage associated with intense tropical cyclones in coastal and low-lying areas. The actual storm surge experienced at any particular locality is a very complicated function of the coastal topography, the size of the storm, the intensity of the storm, the speed of the storm, and the direction of approach of the storm to the coast. Storm surge numerical computer models have been developed that are capable of predicting accurately the storm surge—*provided* that accurate hurricane and typhoon data are available from the analysts and forecasters.

Since extreme storm surges as high as 30 feet can occur, it is imperative that accurate forecasts of hurricane/typhoon track, size, and intensity be "cranked" into the storm surge equations and models to enable accurate surge predictions and minimize the loss of life.

"Hidden" Tornadoes

Another very important aspect of a hurricane or typhoon making a landfall is the strong probability of the formation of tornadoes if the storm is intense. Roughly 25 percent of the hurricanes that make landfall over the United States give birth to devastating tornadoes, according to Drs. D.J. Novlan, W.M. Gray, and E.L. Hill, who have accomplished excellent research on this subject. These scientists have shown that most tornadoes occur in connection with *intense* hurricanes. Also, the tropical cyclones that produce tornadoes are the ones that have *strong vertical wind shear* (variation of the wind vector or any of its components in a vertical direction) in the lowest 6,000 feet of the earth's atmosphere.

Figure 2-36, a schematic plan view based on the research of Drs. Novlan and Gray, shows where one might expect tornadoes to develop within the circulation of intense hurricanes and typhoons. Although tornadoes have been observed in all quadrants and out to a radius of 300 miles from the storm center, the shaded areas show where one can expect the highest occurrence, relative to the direction of the storm's movement.

WATCH OUT FOR FUJIWHARA

In the field of hydrodynamics, the interaction between vortex pairs has long been a favorite subject of analysis. Vortices either attract or repel each other. They rotate about a center of gravity located on the straight line—or great circle—connecting them, and the position of this center depends upon the relative mass of the vortices. If they are of equal strength, they rotate about a point situated midway between them. If they are not of equal strength, the ratio of the two masses determines the location of the point. Also, in addition to mass, the relative intensity of the circulation within each vortex influences the position of the center of rotation.

The interaction of atmospheric vortices has been studied in great detail by Dr. S. Fujiwhara of Japan; hence, the phrase "Fujiwhara effect." Figures 2-37, 2-38, and 2-39 illustrate this principle. In figure 2-37, the northernmost typhoon ("Y") experiences a force acting toward the west from the southernmost typhoon ("X"). In turn, the southernmost typhoon ("X") is subjected to an eastward-directed force. Thus, the axis that may be drawn between the two typhoon centers will rotate counterclockwise with time.

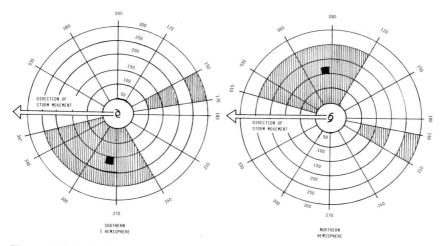

Figure 2-36. A schematic plan view of where the highest occurrence of tornadoes may be expected (shaded areas) within the circulation of a severe hurricane or typhoon. Although tornadoes have occurred in all quadrants and out to a radius of 300 nautical miles from the center, the areas of greatest occurrence are indicated by the shaded areas. The large arrow indicates the direction of movement of the hurricane/typhoon center. The black square is the centroid of all tornadoes. The concentric circles are at 50-n.mi. intervals. Based on the excellent research of Drs. D. J. Novlan and W. M. Gray.

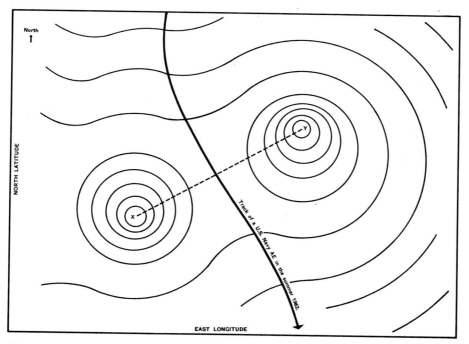

Figure 2-37. Schematic of a typical example of a surface weather map with two typhoons that will undergo the "Fujiwhara effect" (i.e., rotating about each other), with typhoon "Y" forced to move toward the west and typhoon "X" forced to move toward the east.

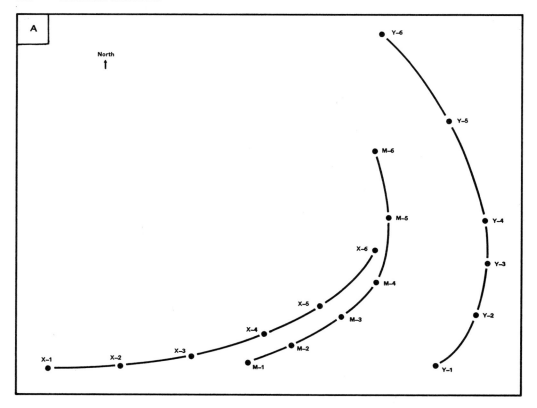

Figure 2-38. The "Fujiwhara effect," showing the tracks of the two typhoons "X" and "Y" and of the mid-point, or center of rotation, for 12-hour intervals.

It was precisely this phenomenon that occurred to the south of Japan in late August of 1945, and necessarily delayed urgent diplomatic negotiations.

Since the midpoint itself moves, outside weather systems obviously influence the typhoon pair. If the displacement of the midpoint is subtracted from the tracks of the typhoons, we obtain the *relative* movement of the two typhoons, and the interaction becomes quite clear. This is shown in figures 2-38 and 2-39. The typhoons rotate about each other and are mutually attracted. As they come closer together, their influence on each other grows, and the relative rotation increases.

It is the Fujiwhara effect that turns the hair of operational meteorologists and forecasters gray in a hurry and causes an anxiety attack among ships' skippers. Yet in 1962, the captain of a U.S. Navy ammunition ship (AE)—en

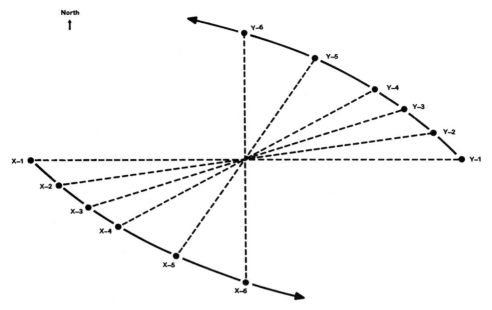

Figure 2-39. The "Fujiwhara effect," showing the displacement of the mid-point subtracted from the tracks, and obtaining the *relative* movement of the two typhoons.

route from Yokosuka, Japan, to Guam—steamed safely through the midpoint between just such a typhoon pair, with no storm damage whatever. However, because of the uncertainties associated with the rotation of typhoon pairs, this course of action is *not* recommended for general practice.

The Fujiwhara effect will occur whenever *any* two strong vortices are in the vicinity of each other, not just with typhoons in the western North Pacific.

SHIP DAMAGE CAUSED BY HEAVY WEATHER

As a result of personal experiences and the news media, many people are familiar with the extensive damage wrought by hurricanes and typhoons on coastlines, public utilities, roads and highways, bridges, houses, and other structures, etc. But only those individuals associated with the sea who have experienced the full fury of these atmospheric monsters can fully appreciate the enormous power of the storm-driven waves and swell and what they can do to the maritime and naval metallic behemoths that ply the oceans of the world. The agonizing wrenching of the metal, the fierce battering of water against the hull and superstructure, the shudders and vibrations of the ship, the screaming of the wind around the superstructure, and the crashing of items and equipment on metal decks and against bulkheads are sounds not soon forgotten. As these huge marvels of architectural design, displacing many thousands of tons, roll, pitch, heave, yaw, and disappear temporarily behind huge waves and swells, one can only be in complete awe of the forces of nature.

Figure 2-40 shows a U.S. Navy destroyer's bow nearly buried in heavy seas during a typhoon in the China Sea in December 1944, as seen from the USS *New Jersey* (BB-62). And figure 2-41 shows the USS *Langley* (CVL-27) rolling sharply as she is pounded by waves during a severe storm in the western Pacific on 13 January 1945, as seen from the USS *Essex* (CV-9).

Figure 2-40. Destroyer's bow is nearly buried in heavy seas in December 1944 during typhoon in China Sea. Seen from USS *New Jersey* (BB 62).

Figure 2-41. The USS *Langley* (CVL 27) rolls sharply as it is pounded by waves during the December 1944 typhoon in the Pacific, seen from the USS *Essex* (CV 9).

The case of the USS *Pittsburgh's* (CA-72) encounter with a typhoon on 5–6 June 1945 has become a classic in world maritime and naval circles. Figure 2-42 shows the ship carrying out her battle assignment with the U.S Third Fleet as she rides out a howling 120-knot typhoon that snapped off 100 feet of her bow. Under her own power, the ship made her way 900 miles back to Guam. This view depicts the awesome seas whipped up by a raging wind. Figure 2-43 is a view of the USS *Pittsburgh minus* her bow, en route to Guam for repairs. And figure 2-44 shows the ship at Guam on 13 July 1945, awaiting repairs. The USS *Duluth* (CL-77), tied up alongside the damaged ship, gives an idea of what is missing from the USS *Pittsburgh*. Figure 2-45 is a close-up view of the ship showing how the mountainous typhoon-generated seas literally "snapped off" the ship's bow.

Figures 2-46 and 2-47 are good examples of what storm-driven seas can do to the flight decks of large aircraft carriers. And figures 2-48 and 2-49 show the extensive internal damage to ship and aircraft (even though thoroughly tied down) wrought by the heavy typhoon seas.

These photos clearly demonstrate why experienced mariners have such a healthy and deep respect for the awesome power of the wind and the sea. And so should you.

Figure 2-42. USS *Pittsburgh* (CA 72) carrying out battle assignment with the 3rd Fleet rides out a howling 120-knot typhoon that snapped off 100 feet of her bow. Under her own power, the ship made her way 900 miles back to Guam. View depicts the awesome seas whipped up by a raging wind.

Figure 2-43. The heavy cruiser USS *Pittsburgh* (CA 72) with bow missing because of damage caused by a typhoon.

MODIFICATION BY MAN

Scientists have attempted many ambitious and difficult projects. But one of the most ambitious projects ever attempted is the modification of intense tropical cyclones. In 1962, Project STORMFURY was organized as a joint project by the then-U.S. Weather Bureau (now the National Weather Service) and the U.S. Navy. Project STORMFURY, under the brilliant scientific direction of Dr. R. Cecil Gentry, was designed to investigate the hypothesis that initiating the freezing of supercooled water in hurricane clouds near the eye could induce a weakening of the storm's intensity.

Hurricane and typhoon damage is caused by wind, rain, waves, and flood, but principally by the wind-driven storm surge that catapults the sea onto the land as a veritable "wall of water, sometimes as high as 30 feet." If the wind speed, and consequently the pressure + suction force, and the height of the storm surge could be significantly reduced, both the death toll and structural damage could be reduced to an appreciable degree.

Preliminary Project STORMFURY results were very encouraging. The modification experiments on Hurricane Debbie in 1969 were the first ever to "seed" a hurricane more than once per day. Debbie was seeded five times in an 8-hour period on both 18 and 20 August. On 18 August, Debbie was a mature hurricane with maximum sustained winds exceeding 100 knots. She was located about 650 nautical miles ENE of Puerto Rico, moving toward the WNW. The seeding aircraft—flying at an altitude of 33,000 feet—penetrated the hurricane eyewall to the area of maximum winds before starting to seed. Then 208 silver iodide generators were dropped on a line extending across the outer wall of the hurricane eye and into the adjacent rainbands that help to "fuel" the hurricane. This was repeated five times, at two-hour intervals. Each seeding run lasted two to three minutes over a path 14–20 nautical miles in length.

Figure 2-44. The USS *Pittsburgh* (CA 72) at Guam in mid-June after riding out a howling 120-knot typhoon in the Pacific. The ship is awaiting repairs.

Figure 2-45. A close-up view of the heavy cruiser USS *Pittsburgh* at Guam. The bow of the ship was later recovered by a tug and towed to Guam.

Figure 2-46. Damage to the bow of the USS *Hornet* (CV 12) from a typhoon in the western Pacific in June 1945.

Before the first seeding on 18 August, maximum winds at 12,000 feet were 98 knots. Five hours after the fifth seeding, these winds decreased to 68 knots—a reduction of 31 percent in the maximum wind speed.

On 20 August, the hurricane had a double eye, an unusual structure for Atlantic hurricanes, but not for Pacific typhoons. This was a complicated situation to handle with the seeding techniques available at the time. However, maximum wind speeds at 12,000 feet before the first seeding were 99 knots. After the final seeding that day, the maximum winds dropped to 84 knots—a reduction of 15 percent. The fact that the hurricane's winds were substantially decreased on both days strongly suggests that at least some changes were caused by the Project STORMFURY experiment.

In the opinion of Dr. R. Cecil Gentry, former Director of the NWS National Hurricane Research Laboratory: "While actual modification of hurricanes may still be some years away, the rapid increase in knowledge in recent years lends support to those who believe that man will be able to exert at least some control on 'the greatest storm on earth.'"

The STORMFURY project was recently reviewed by a panel functioning under the auspices of the U.S. National Academy of Sciences. The following

Figure 2-47. The end of her flight deck buckled and draped itself over the bow of the USS *Bennington* (CV 21) during a typhoon in the western Pacific in June 1945.

quotations from the report of this panel of outside experts are well worth reading:

> The Panel concluded unanimously that the STORMFURY project can now produce more information about the physical characteristics and behavior of hurricanes than ever previously available. The instrumented aircraft now available are superior to any platform or instrumentation that has ever been flown into hurricanes. The STORMFURY group has developed an excellent plan and schedule for the examination and treatment of hurricanes and for evaluation of the results. . . . Evaluation of the STORMFURY project should be based on the fundamental new knowledge acquired on subsequent flights. New information on the characteristics and internal dynamics of hurricanes will lead to improvements in the prediction of the formation, development, and movement of hurricanes.

Since the force exerted by the wind is proportional to the *square* of its speed, if the maximum wind speeds in a hurricane can be reduced by as little as 15 percent, as now appears possible, the destructive force of the wind would be reduced by at least 30 percent. The resultant dollar *savings* for an "average" hurricane striking the United States would be approximately $100 million. And similar savings would result in other areas of the world. Obviously, one

Figure 2-48. A view of a damaged aircraft on board the small aircraft carrier USS *Monterey* (CVL 26) following a typhoon in 1944.

Figure 2-49. Another view of damage to the small aircraft carrier USS *Monterey* (CVL 26) and her aircraft following her encounter with a typhoon in 1944.

cannot put a dollar value on the many thousands of lives that would be saved. The benefit-to-cost ratio is so large that Project STORMFURY should not only be supported on a priority basis, but research and operational funds should be increased substantially and the research effort should be accelerated.

THE APERIODICALLY HYPERACTIVE "EL NIÑO"

The ocean currents of the world are divided into three groups: (1) currents related to the distribution of density in the sea, (2) currents caused directly by the stress the wind exerts on the sea surface, and (3) tidal currents and currents associated with internal waves.

Type (3), currents that are associated with tides and internal waves, run alternately in opposite directions or rotate. Although such currents may attain high velocities, they are not of direct importance to the circulations of the oceans nor to the interaction between the ocean and the atmosphere.

In type (2), if the wind blows for long periods of time from approximately the same direction, the wind drift transports water in the same direction over large areas.

Type (1) currents are the well-known, large-scale ocean currents such as the Gulf Stream off the East Coast of the United States, the Kuroshio running northward from Taiwan to Ryukyu and then close to the coast of Japan as far as latitude 35°N, the Benguela Current, which flows north along the west coast of South Africa, the Equatorial Currents flowing eastward, the Equatorial Countercurrent flowing from west to east, and several others.

The oceanographic occasional juvenile delinquent of the group, causing almost worldwide oceanographic *and* meteorological catastrophic events about once every 18 years (on average), is called "El Niño," so named by South American fishermen. The expression means "the Christ child," or "the child," because the current *usually* starts about Christmastime (and normally lasts until about March). Most of the time, El Niño is not particularly harmful. But in 1891, 1925, 1941, 1972, and 1982–83, the extreme development of the current was associated with disastrous catastrophes of *both* oceanographic and meteorological character.

During the Northern Hemisphere summer, the Peru (Humboldt) Current, flowing northward along the west coast of South America, extends just beyond the equator where it converges with the Equatorial Countercurrent, the waters of which turn mostly toward the north in summer. During the Northern Hemisphere winter, the Equatorial Countercurrent is displaced farther to the south, and part of the warm, but low-salinity, water of the Countercurrent turns south along the coast of Ecuador, crossing the equator before converging with the Peru (Humboldt) Current. This warm, south-flowing current along the South American coast is known as "El Niño." Usually, the southern limit of this current is only about 3–4 degrees south of the equator. In extreme cases, however, El Niño extends much farther south along the coast of Peru, past the city of Callao, as shown schematically in figure 2-50, almost to latitude 15°S. When this happens, oceanographic and meteorological catastrophes occur in many parts of the world—some caused by, and some associated with, El Niño.

The decrease of the temperature of El Niño toward the south shows that

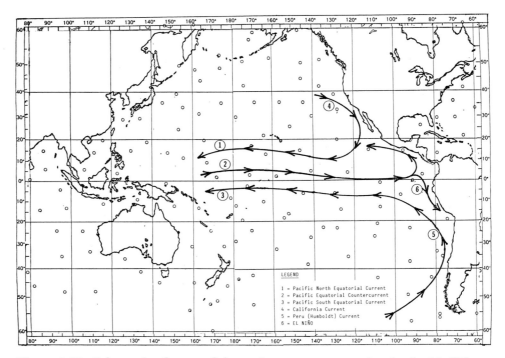

Figure 2-50. Schematic of some of the major ocean currents involved with "El Niño."

these waters are mixed with the cold coastal waters, and during this mixing process, the organisms in the coastal current (from plankton to fish) are destroyed on a *huge* scale. Dead fish cover the beaches, where they decompose and pollute both the air and the coastal waters. So much hydrogen sulfide is released that the paint of ships is blackened—a phenomenon known as the "Callao Painter."

Much more serious is the loss of fish and thus the loss of food to the birds, many of which die of disease or starvation or leave their nests, abandoning their young so that the young birds perish. And no less severe are the meteorological phenomena that accompany extreme El Niño conditions.

In 1982–83, almost all of the 17 million adult birds on Christmas Island in the mid-Pacific died or fled, abandoning their nestlings to starvation and death. This is the largest bird "population crash" of its kind ever recorded. It wasn't storms that drove the birds away. It was because El Niño's ocean currents forced the bird's food supply into deeper water or pushed it far away from the island. Of the 19 species of birds that were on the island, 18 are now gone.

In 1972, El Niño storms destroyed almost 90 percent of the anchovy fishing industry along the west coast of South America. The fishing industry there has still not recovered.

El Niño is a little-understood phenomenon that drastically changes one of the aspects—a very important one—of the earth's general circulation. During conditions of extreme El Niño, three of the atmosphere's strong regions of convergence (one off Australia and Indonesia, another over southern Africa, and the third over the Amazon basin) are shifted in location. The one near Australia and Indonesia breaks down because of its instability and re-forms thousands of miles to the eastward toward South America. And this is thought to be one source of the strange El Niño weather patterns.

The current (at this writing) extreme El Niño conditions, which began in

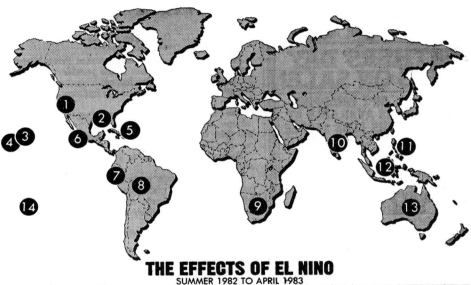

THE EFFECTS OF EL NINO
SUMMER 1982 TO APRIL 1983

Phenomena	Location	Period	Victims	Damage*
UNITED STATES				
1. Storms	Mountain & Pacific States	9/82-present	45+ dead	$1 billion
2. Flooding	Gulf States	12/82-present	50+ dead	$1 billion
3. Hurricane	Hawaiian Islands	11/82	1 dead	$200 million
4. Drought	Hawaiian Islands	12/82-present	—	—
FOREIGN				
5. Flooding	Cuba	1/83-3/83	8 dead	$170 million
6. Drought	Mexico	6/82-present	—	$600 million
7. Flooding	Ecuador, Northern Peru	12/82-present	300 dead	$640 million
8. Flooding	Bolivia	3/83	50+ dead	$70 million
9. Drought	Southern Africa	12/82-4/83	disease & starvation	$1 billion
10. Drought	Southern India & Sri Lanka	9/82-present	—	$220 million
11. Drought	Philippines	11/82-4/83	—	$100 million
12. Drought	Indonesia	2/82-11/82	340 dead	$500 million
13. Drought/Fires	Australia	4/82-3/83	71 dead/8,000 homeless	$3 billion
14. Hurricane	Tahiti	4/83	1 dead	$50 million

* PROPERTY & AGRICULTURAL DAMAGE   SOURCE: National Oceanic and Atmospheric Administration

Figure 2-51. The effects of El Niño felt around the world from the summer of 1982 to April 1983. (Courtesy of the *Washington Post*)

June 1982, are probably the most severe in the last 100 years. The SE trade winds of the Southern Hemisphere have become "stalled." And the warm water normally transported westward toward Asia stopped, reversed, and stagnated off the west coast of South America. The interaction of the warmer water and the wind somehow reversed the direction of the trade winds. And that reversal brought torrential rains to Peru, droughts to Australia, heavy rains and mudslides to southern California, floods to the U.S. Gulf States, unusual hurricanes to Tahiti and the Hawaiian Islands, and other disasters to many parts of the world.

In his excellent article titled "'El Niño' Weather Disasters Continue," which appeared in *The Washington Post*, June 14, 1983, Philip J. Hilts had a compact summary of the effects of El Niño during the period June 1982 to April 1983. This appears as figure 2-51.

One of the many reasons that extreme El Niño conditions are so important to seafarers is that during these conditions, the "habits" of intense tropical cyclones (hurricanes and typhoons) are significantly altered. And every mariner should be prepared for the highly unusual formation, development, and movement of hurricanes and typhoons and other storms.

3

Hurricanes

The storm was terrible and on that night the
ships were parted from me. Each one of them
was reduced to an extremity, expecting nothing
save death; each one of them was certain the
others were lost.

—Admiral Christopher Columbus,
describing the experience of his
four-ship fleet with a Caribbean
hurricane the night of 10 July
1502. (Source: *Early American
Hurricanes, 1492–1870*, by
David M. Ludlum, American
Meteorological Society, 1963.)

AREAS OF FORMATION

The Atlantic Basin (North Atlantic Ocean, Caribbean Sea, and Gulf of Mexico)

The Azores-Bermuda high-pressure area is normally the "center of action" for
the Atlantic basin and the eastern United States during the summer months
and early autumn. The central pressure of this anticyclone averages about
1,026 millibars (30.30 inches) during this time of year. Figure 3-1 shows the
mean position of this anticyclone during the month of August. The center is
located to the SW of the Azores, but the entire system extends from the Iberian
Peninsula across the North Atlantic basin to the southeastern United States.
During the summer and early fall (the "normal" hurricane season in the North
Atlantic), this center of action oscillates north and south with varying degrees
of intensity. And the so-called "departures from normal" in strength and/or
position of the center have a profound influence on the frequency and tracks of
hurricanes in this part of the world. The intertropical convergence zone (ITCZ)
usually reaches its northernmost position in the Cape Verde region in August
and early September, and then, as a rule, begins to recede southward about
the latter part of September.

Figure 3-2 depicts the normal sea-level pressure over the North Atlantic
during the month of February. Note that the mean position of the Azores-
Bermuda anticyclone is much farther south (about 7° of latitude—420 nautical miles) during winter, and that the central pressure is lower (by about 3
millibars). These factors effectively reduce both the N-S and the vertical
extent of the trade winds to the south of the region of high pressure. And all this
has an impact on the migration of the regions of most frequent occurrence of

hurricanes in the North Atlantic, and the lack of hurricanes during the winter and spring months.

In the Atlantic basin, the principal areas of tropical cyclone formation shift eastward and westward seasonally. Early season (May–early June) tropical cyclones occur almost exclusively in the western Caribbean and the Gulf of

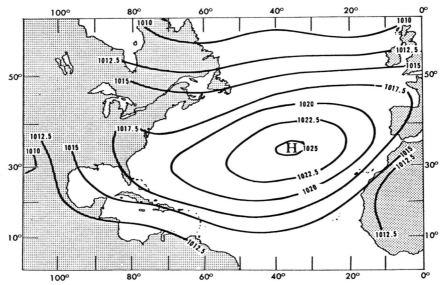

Figure 3-1. Mean sea-level pressure (millibars) over the North Atlantic during August. (Source: *Atlantic Hurricanes*, by Dunn and Miller, Louisiana State University Press, 1960.)

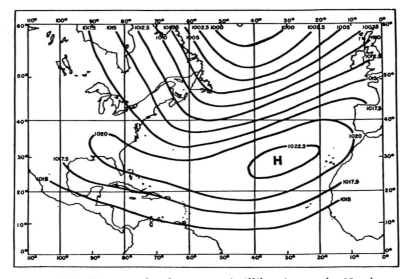

Figure 3-2. Mean sea-level pressure (millibars) over the North Atlantic during February (Source: *Atlantic Hurricanes*, by Dunn and Miller, Louisiana State University Press, 1960.)

Mexico. By the end of June and early July, however, the area of formation gradually shifts eastward, with a small decline in the overall frequency of tropical storms. By late July, the frequency gradually increases, and the primary area of formation shifts even farther eastward.

By late August, tropical cyclones form over a broad area that extends all the way eastward to near the Cape Verde Islands, located about 360 nautical miles off the west coast of North Africa.

The period from about 20 August through about 15 September encompasses the maximum of the "Cape Verde"-type tropical cyclones. Many of these storms traverse the entire Atlantic Ocean in their movement westward.

After about 15 September, the frequency begins to decline and the area of formation retreats westward. By early October, the formative area is generally confined to longitudes west of 60° W, and the area of maximum occurrence is again the western Caribbean Sea. In November, the frequency of tropical cyclones declines further.

Figures 3-14 through 3-21, inclusive, in the section titled "Tracks" in this chapter, show the areas of formation (beginning of tracks) and the paths of tropical cyclones in the Atlantic basin by month (May through December) for the period 1886–1980, inclusive. By leafing quickly through these figures in order, one can easily see the seasonal eastward and westward shift of the areas of formation of tropical cyclones in the Atlantic basin.

Eastern North Pacific (East of 180°) Basin

In much of the literature, the area from the west coast of the United States westward to longitude 140°W is considered the Eastern North Pacific. And the area from 140°W westward to 180° is considered the Central North Pacific. For our purposes, we will consider the area east of 180° as the Eastern North Pacific, and the area west of 180° as the Western North Pacific.

The Eastern North Pacific ranks as the second most active area of the world for tropical cyclone formation. It is surpassed only by the Western North Pacific (west of 180° longitude) region. This fact was not known, however, until the advent of operational weather satellites in the area in 1961. And it wasn't until 1966 that full operational satellite coverage became a reality. Consequently, a scientifically representative tropical cyclone climatology for the Eastern North Pacific could not begin until 1966.

Prior to the operational weather satellite era, information pertaining to tropical cyclones (and other weather phenomena) in the Eastern North Pacific was largely dependent upon merchant marine and naval ship reports. As a result, the areas of formation, positions of first detection, and the "deduced" storm tracks in this area were confined mainly to areas along and between the principal shipping lanes and routes.

The launching of the first meteorological satellite, TIROS I, in April 1960 heralded a new era of tropical cyclone awareness, detection, forecasting, and statistics in the Eastern North Pacific, east of 180° longitude. And one of the facts that has been learned in recent years is the location of the area of formation of these vortices. This is shown schematically by the irregular-shaped "target area," in figure 3-3, which is based on the research of Drs. R.J. Renard and W.N. Bowman at the U.S. Naval Postgraduate School.

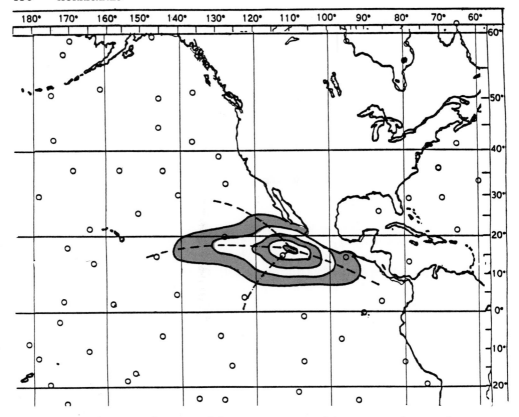

Figure 3-3. Schematic diagram of the primary area of formation of tropical cyclones in the Eastern North Pacific. Note the irregular shape of the "target" formation area, centered about 360 miles due south of the southern tip of Baja, California. (After R. J. Renard and W. N. Bowman, 1976.)

All Other Basins and Areas

For the regions of tropical cyclone and hurricane formation in the North Indian Ocean, the Southwest Indian Ocean, and the Southwest Pacific Ocean and Australian area, the reader is referred to figure 2-23 in chapter 2. Areas of typhoon formation in the Western North Pacific will be addressed separately in chapter 4.

SEASON AND FREQUENCY

The Atlantic Basin

Based on the 95-year record (from 1886 through 1980) of all Atlantic tropical cyclone tracks, the average duration of a tropical cyclone in this basin is about eight days but, as shown in figure 3-4, it may vary from less than two days to as many as 30 days. The most frequently occurring duration is six days. Hurricanes of much longer duration are usually the ones that form in the eastern Atlantic, travel westward, meander slowly, recurve just before reaching the

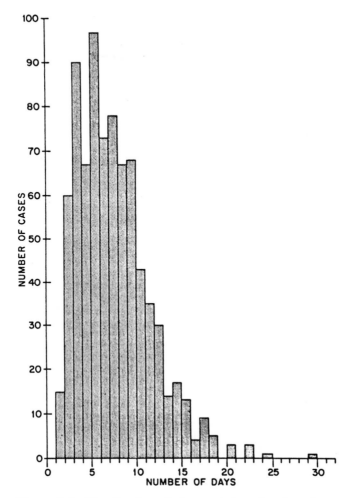

Figure 3-4. Distribution of observed duration (number of days, including the depression stage) of Atlantic tropical cyclones, 1886 through 1980. (Courtesy of NOAA National Weather Service)

United States, and then travel northeastward across the open, unresisting Atlantic.

The hurricane season in the Atlantic basin is considered to be from 1 June through 30 November, although through the years a few tropical cyclones have occurred in other months. The number of tropical storms occurring in any given year varies widely. In 1890 and 1914, for example, only one tropical storm (that we know about) occurred in each year. In 1933, on the other hand, there were 21 tropical storms and hurricanes. And in 1969, there were 12 full-fledged hurricanes. The frequency distributions (1886–1980, inclusive) are shown in figures 3-5 and 3-6.

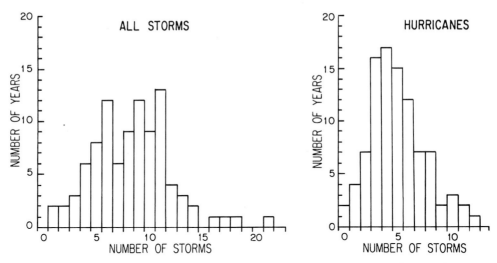

Figure 3-5. Distribution of annual number of tropical cyclones reaching at least tropical storm (34–63 knots) intensity (left) and hurricane (64 knots or higher) intensity (right), 1886 through 1980. The average number is 8.4 tropical storms and 4.9 hurricanes. (Courtesy of NOAA National Weather Service)

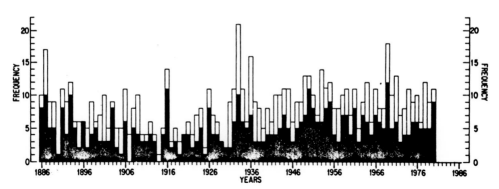

Figure 3-6. Annual distribution of the 793 recorded North Atlantic tropical cyclones reaching at least tropical storm (34–63 knots) strength (open bar) and the 468 reaching hurricane (64 knots or higher) strength (solid bar), 1886 through 1980. The average number is 8.4 tropical storms and 4.9 hurricanes. (Courtesy of NOAA National Weather Service)

Admittedly, the minutiae of tropical cyclone frequency data are questioned by the meteorological purists and the statisticians. And rightly so. Before the advent of regular aircraft weather reconnaissance (mid-40s) and operational weather satellites (early 60s), many tropical cyclones undoubtedly went undetected. And many were probably misclassified as to intensity. Also, in addition to observational problems, other natural trends (such as the effect of large-scale sea-surface temperature anomalies—El Niño, for example) exist in the frequency of tropical cyclones. For our "operational guide" and "non-pure-

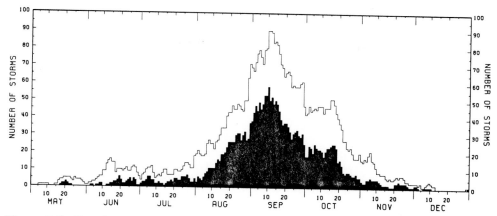

Figure 3-7. Number of tropical storms and hurricanes (open bar) and hurricanes (solid bar) observed on each day, 1 May–31 December, 1886 through 1980. (Courtesy of NOAA National Weather Service)

science" approach, the validity of the tropical storm/hurricane frequencies is acceptable. We want to know primarily, with reasonable accuracy, where, when, and how often these threats to safety afloat and ashore exist, and how and where they travel.

Figure 3-7 shows the incidence of tropical cyclones over the North Atlantic basin on a daily basis for the 8-month period constituting the principal season. It shows the number of tropical storms and hurricanes observed each day, 1 May–31 December, from 1886 through 1980. An examination of figure 3-7 shows a slight maximum around mid-June, followed by a slight decline until mid-July, and a gradual increase in frequency until just before mid-September. An irregular decline in frequency then occurs, interrupted by a slight increase in mid-October.

The so-called "official" Atlantic hurricane season begins on 1 June and ends 30 November. However, Mother Nature occasionally begins and ends the "season" outside of this period.

Eastern North Pacific (East of 180°) Basin

The "official" hurricane season in the area extending geographically from the west coast of the United States to 140°W is from 1 June through 15 November. In the area from 140°W to 180°, it is from 1 June through 31 October. Table 3-1,

Table 3-1. Monthly and annual frequency of tropical storms and hurricanes for the Eastern North Pacific and the North Atlantic tropical cyclone basins. Courtesy of NOAA National Weather Service.

	MAY	JUN	JUL	AUG	SEP	OCT	NOV	ANNUAL
Eastern North Pacific (1966–1976)	0.4	1.7	3.6	4.4	2.9	1.7	0.4	15.1
North Atlantic (1946–1976)	0.2	0.6	0.8	2.4	3.6	1.7	0.4	9.8

which is taken from the excellent research by E.B. Gunther in 1977, shows the average monthly and annual frequencies for the period 1966–1976, and compares them to the North Atlantic basin for the period 1946–1976. Note the variations and differences between the two oceanic basins.

Hurricane IWA and El Niño. Many scientists consider the off-season Hurricane IWA which struck the Hawaiian Islands on 23–24 November 1982 to be associated with the phenomenon of extreme El Niño conditions (see the final section of chapter 2). Of the eight main islands of Hawaii, Kauai (the "Garden Isle") and Oahu (where Honolulu and Waikiki are located)—two of the largest islands in the NW part of the island chain—suffered the greatest damage from the 96-knot (110-mph, 177-kph) winds and the 40-foot waves. More than a week later, most parts of these islands were still without public utilities. This was Hawaii's first *major* hurricane in 23 years. And damage was estimated to exceed $200 million.

On 27 November 1982, President Reagan declared Hawaii a disaster area. And the U.S. Navy dispatched the nuclear-powered submarine *USS Indianapolis* to Kauai to serve as a "floating electric generator" for the 39,000+ power-less inhabitants.

As luck would have it, the geostationary weather satellite (GOES WEST) that monitors the Eastern North Pacific basin—and other areas—blinked shut on 25 November 1982. This left weather analysts and forecasters with a blind eye in this region where Hurricane IWA was conceived, born, traveled, transformed, and died. But, being the resourceful people that they are, the meteorologists of the U.S. National Weather Service availed themselves of other data sources.

Figure 3-8 shows the track of Hurricane IWA during the period 20–26 November 1982. And figures 3-9, 3-10, and 3-11 are the NOAA-7 polar-orbiting weather satellite views of Hurricane IWA on 23, 24, and 25 November 1982. The island of Oahu is at the tip of the arrow in each photograph.

At this writing (hurrah!) a new geostationary GOES WEST satellite is in place.

TRACKS

As mentioned in chapter 2, forecasting the future tracks and speeds of movement (and stalls) of hurricanes and typhoons is one of the most challenging—and difficult—tasks that an operational meteorologist has to face. So much hinges on these forecasts, including human lives. So, it is small wonder that many hurricane and typhoon forecasters feel the great pressure of prediction responsibility, and insist that the "pucker factor" exceed 0.95 on many of these forecasts.

Of the many thousands of hurricanes and typhoons through the centuries, the fact that no two recorded severe tropical cyclone tracks have ever been *exactly* the same in any ocean attests to the infinite variety of tracks. Nevertheless, one can establish and accept the 15 different "basic" tracks of hurricanes and typhoons illustrated in figure 2-24. One must keep in mind, however, that even these 15 basic tracks (in each hemisphere) have many minor variations.

Figure 3-12 shows the track of destructive Hurricane BEULAH, in Septem-

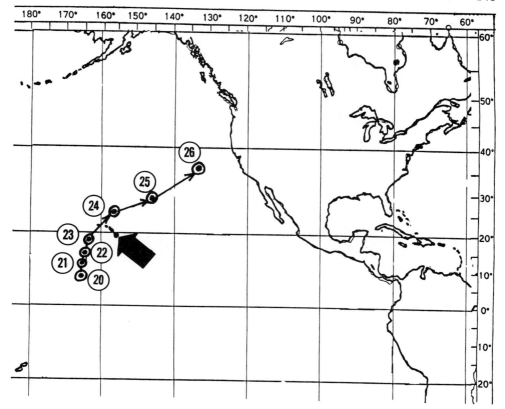

Figure 3-8. Track of off-season Hurricane Iwa during the period 20–26 November 1982. The Hawaiian Islands are at tip of arrow. Hurricane positions are for 1200 GMT. During the night of 23–24 November, 96-knot winds and 40-foot waves caused over $200 million in damage on the islands of Kauai and Oahu.

ber 1967, which took many lives in the Caribbean and caused several hundred million dollars in property damage, expecially in the state of Texas. And figure 3-13 shows one of the longest (21 days) and most erratic North Atlantic hurricane tracks—a forecaster's nightmare—on record. This was Hurricane GINGER from 10–30 September, inclusive, 1971.

Figures 3-14 to 3-21, inclusive, are the track charts (by month) of the 793 tropical cyclones in the North Atlantic basin during the 95-year period from 1886–1980, inclusive. The track charts appear as follows:

- Figure 3-14—May, 1886–1980
- Figure 3-15—June, 1886–1980
- Figure 3-16—July, 1886–1980
- Figure 3-17—Aug., 1886–1980
- Figure 3-18—Sept., 1886–1980
- Figure 3-19—Oct., 1886–1980
- Figure 3-20—Nov., 1886–1980
- Figure 3-21—Dec., 1886–1980

Figure 3-9. NOAA-7 polar-orbiting weather satellite view of Hurricane Iwa on 23 November 1982. The island of Oahu is at tip of arrow. Kauai lies approx. 90 miles to the WNW of Oahu. At this time, the eye of Hurricane Iwa is 420 nautical miles SW of Oahu. (Courtesy of National Air Survey Center Corp.)

These charts are reproduced with the kind permission of the NOAA National Weather Service (NWS), the Environmental Data and Information Service (EDIS), the National Climatic Center (NCC), the National Hurricane Center (NHC), and the National Hurricane Research Laboratory (NHRL). These charts have been derived from the outstanding publication, *Tropical Cyclones of the North Atlantic Ocean, 1871–1980, Revised July 1981*.

Figure 3-22 is a computer plot showing the tracks of the 313 recorded Eastern North Pacific tropical cyclones during the 28-year period 1949–1976, inclusive. And figures 3-23 to 3-27, inclusive, show the tracks of tropical cyclones in the Central North Pacific, as follows:

- Figure 3-23—1832–1949
- Figure 3-24—1950–1959
- Figure 3-25—1960–1969
- Figure 3-26—1970–1977
- Figure 3-27—Hawaiian Hurricane Season, 1978

These charts are derived from the excellent publication, *A History of Tropical Cyclones in the Central North Pacific and the Hawaiian Islands, 1832–1979*, and are reproduced with the kind permission of the NOAA National Weather Service.

Figure 3-10. NOAA-7 polar-orbiting weather satellite view of Hurricane Iwa on 24 November 1982. The island of Oahu is at tip of arrow. Kauai lies approx. 90 miles to the WNW of Oahu. At this time, the eye of Hurricane Iwa is almost directly over Kauai. (Courtesy of National Air Survey Center Corp.)

One older theory of hurricane movement and tracks, first expressed (to the author's knowledge) by meteorologist O.L. Fassig over 70 years ago (in 1913), still deserves consideration. Fassig stated that in a *general* way, hurricanes are carried around the outer periphery of oceanic semi-permanent anticyclones, skirting the southern edge of the anticyclone and turning northward and NE'ward around the western edge, and that the hurricane center would follow—*approximately*—the outer isobar of the anticyclone with the speed of the wind system then prevalent. Figure 3-28 shows that Fassig's theory isn't at all bad, *if one is dealing with averages*. In the complete absence of all data and information and services, this is not a bad rule to follow. *But*, when dealing with individual hurricane tracks and movement, it is quite a different—and frequently vexing—story, as seen from the hurricane and typhoon track charts in chapters 2, 3, and 4.

THE HURRICANE WARNING SYSTEM

Human beings, geostationary satellites, polar-orbiting satellites, reconnaissance aircraft, ships at sea, land stations, radars, environmental data buoys, high-speed computers, and complex (but efficient) communications networks are all integral parts of both the hurricane and typhoon warning systems.

Figure 3-11. NOAA-7 polar-orbiting weather satellite view of Hurricane Iwa on 25 November 1982. The island of Oahu is at tip of arrow. Kauai lies approx. 90 miles to the WNW of Oahu. At this time, the eye of Hurricane Iwa is 470 nautical miles to the NE of Oahu. (Courtesy of National Air Survey Center Corp.)

Figure 3-29 illustrates the technical advances in systems for observing tropical cyclones, 1871 through 1980.

To provide timely and accurate information and warnings regarding hurricanes and typhoons, the oceans have been divided into geographical areas of responsibility as shown in figure 3-30. The "stars" show the locations of the U.S. Department of Defense Centers, and the "circles" show the locations of the U.S. National Weather Service Forecast Centers and Offices.

The U.S. Department of Defense Centers are the Naval Eastern Oceanography Center, Norfolk, Virginia (NavEastOceanCen, Norfolk); the Naval Western Oceanography Center, Pearl Harbor, Hawaii (NavWestOceanCen, Pearl Harbor); and the Naval Oceanographic Command Center/Joint Typhoon Warning Center, Guam, Marianas Islands (NavOceanComCen/JTWC, Guam), in the Western North Pacific.

The major Hurricane Warning Offices (HWOs) of the U.S. National Weather Service (NWS) are located at San Juan, Puerto Rico; New Orleans, Louisiana; Washington, D.C.; Boston, Massachusetts; San Francisco (Redwood City), California; and Honolulu, Hawaii. The NWS National Hurricane Center (NHC) is located in Miami (Coral Gables), Florida. While the responsibilities of NOAA's National Weather Service are to the general public and other in-

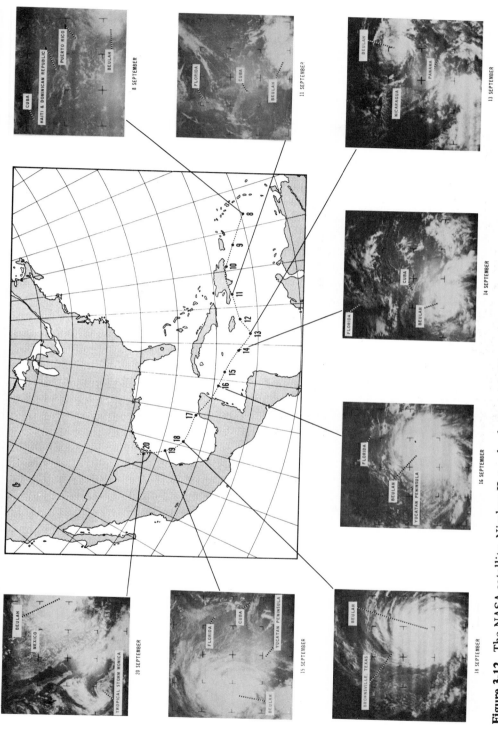

Figure 3-12. The NASA satellite, Nimbus II, tracks destructive Hurricane Beulah across the Caribbean Sea, Gulf of Mexico, and into Texas for two weeks in mid-September 1967. This series of photographs is representative of pictures received by apt stations located in the U.S., Mexico, and Caribbean area as Nimbus II orbited over these regions daily. (Courtesy of NASA Goddard Space Flight Center)

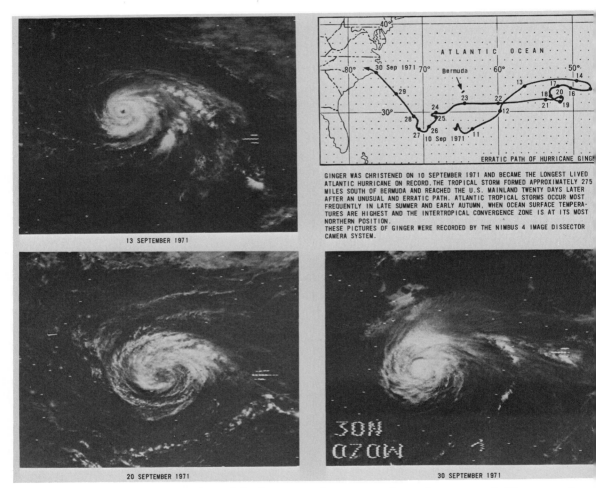

GINGER WAS CHRISTENED ON 10 SEPTEMBER 1971 AND BECAME THE LONGEST LIVED ATLANTIC HURRICANE ON RECORD. THE TROPICAL STORM FORMED APPROXIMATELY 275 MILES SOUTH OF BERMUDA AND REACHED THE U.S. MAINLAND TWENTY DAYS LATER AFTER AN UNUSUAL AND ERRATIC PATH. ATLANTIC TROPICAL STORMS OCCUR MOST FREQUENTLY IN LATE SUMMER AND EARLY AUTUMN, WHEN OCEAN SURFACE TEMPERATURES ARE HIGHEST AND THE INTERTROPICAL CONVERGENCE ZONE IS AT ITS MOST NORTHERN POSITION.
THESE PICTURES OF GINGER WERE RECORDED BY THE NIMBUS 4 IMAGE DISSECTOR CAMERA SYSTEM.

Figure 3-13. Hurricane Ginger. One of the longest and most erratic tracks on record. (Courtesy of NASA Goddard Space Flight Center)

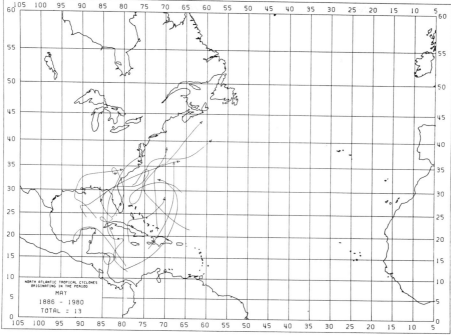

Figure 3-14. North Atlantic tropical cyclones originating in the month of May from 1886–1980. (Courtesy of NOAA National Weather Service, et al.)

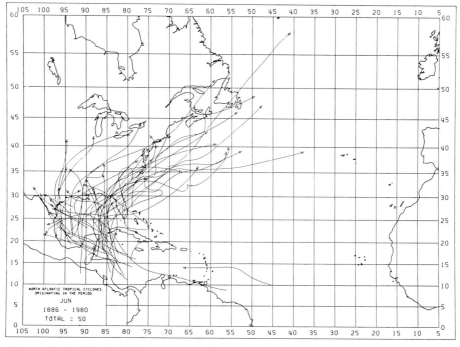

Figure 3-15. North Atlantic tropical cyclones originating in the month of June from 1886–1980. (Courtesy of NOAA National Weather Service, et al.)

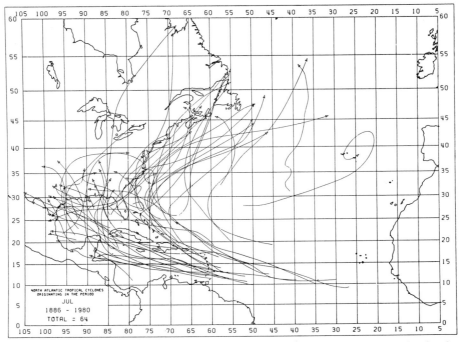

Figure 3-16. North Atlantic tropical cyclones originating in the month of July from 1886–1980. (Courtesy of NOAA National Weather Service, et al.)

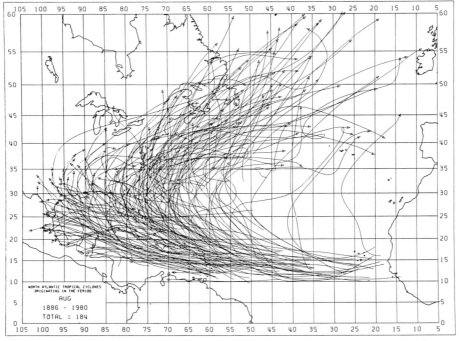

Figure 3-17. North Atlantic tropical cyclones originating in the month of August from 1886–1980. (Courtesy of NOAA National Weather Service, et al.)

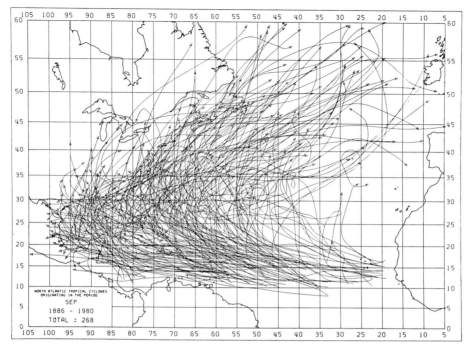

Figure 3-18. North Atlantic tropical cyclones originating in the month of September from 1886–1980. (Courtesy of NOAA National Weather Service, et al.)

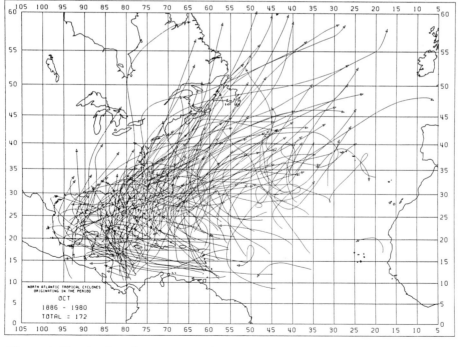

Figure 3-19. North Atlantic tropical cyclones originating in the month of October from 1886–1980. (Courtesy of NOAA National Weather Service, et al.)

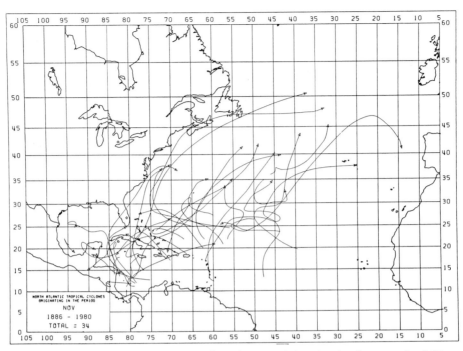

Figure 3-20. North Atlantic tropical cyclones originating in the month of November from 1886–1980. (Courtesy of NOAA National Weather Service, et al.)

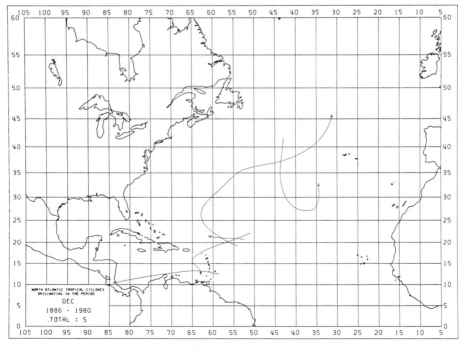

Figure 3-21. North Atlantic tropical cyclones originating in the month of December from 1886–1980. (Courtesy of NOAA National Weather Service, et al.)

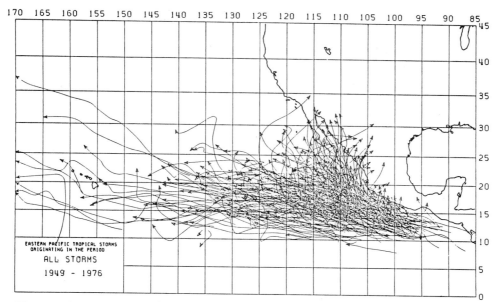

Figure 3-22. Computer plot showing tracks of the 313 recorded eastern North Pacific tropical cyclones, 1949–1976. (Courtesy of NOAA National Weather Service)

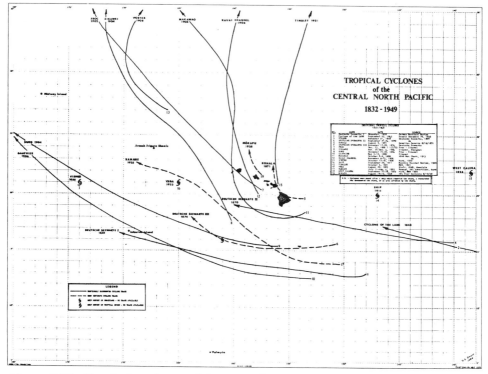

Figure 3-23. Tropical cyclones of the central North Pacific, 1832–1949. (Courtesy of NOAA National Weather Service)

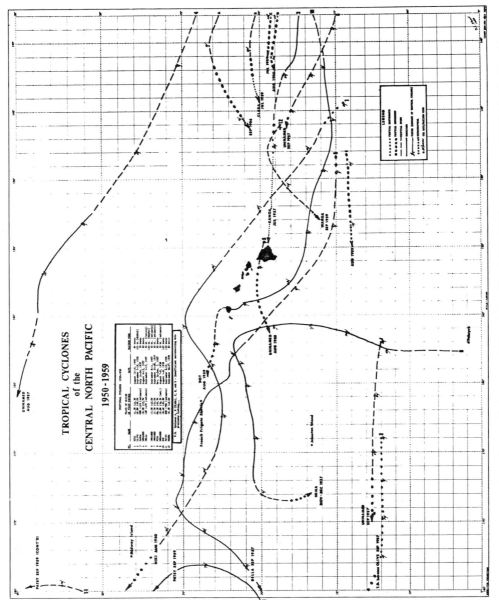

Figure 3-24. Tropical cyclones of the central North Pacific, 1950–1959. (Courtesy of NOAA National Weather Service)

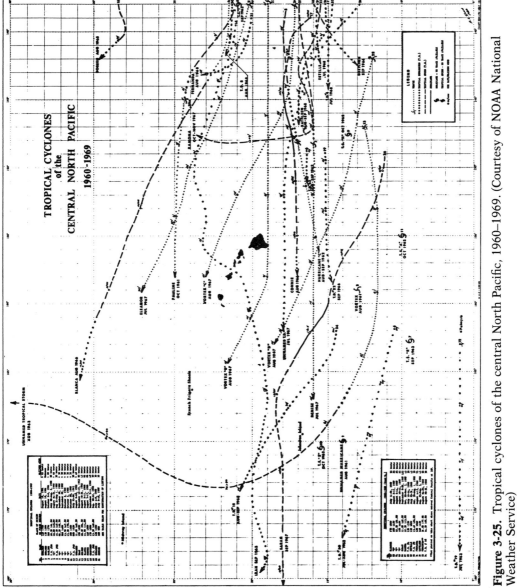

Figure 3-25. Tropical cyclones of the central North Pacific, 1960–1969. (Courtesy of NOAA National Weather Service)

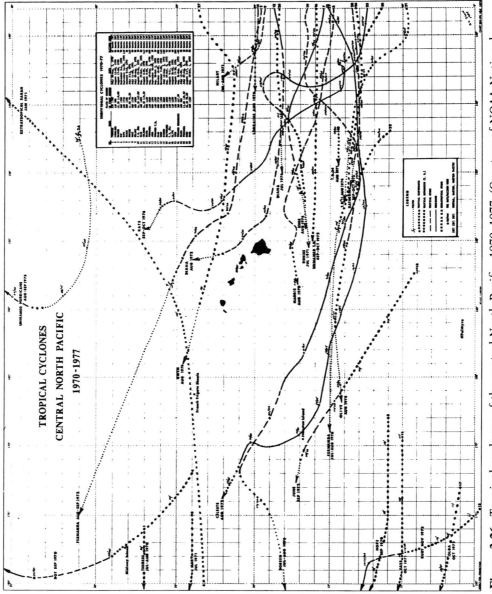

Figure 3-26. Tropical cyclones of the central North Pacific, 1970–1977. (Courtesy of NOAA National Weather Service)

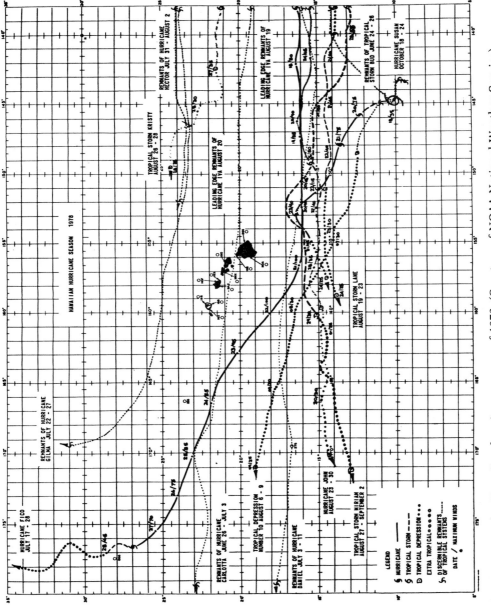

Figure 3-27. The Hawaiian hurricane season of 1978. (Courtesy of NOAA National Weather Service)

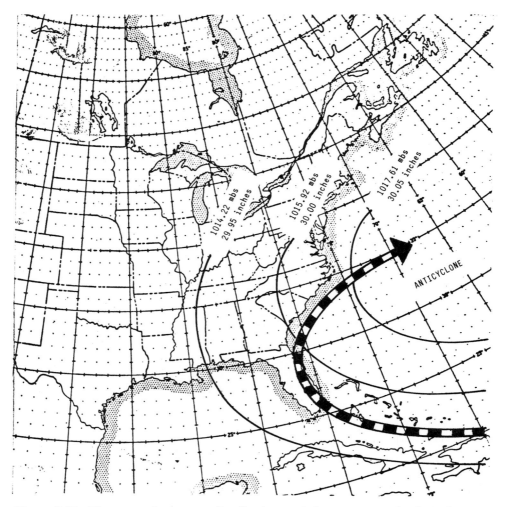

Figure 3-28. The normal pressure distribution and the average path of 130 hurricanes. Solid lines are isobars. Dashed arrow is average path of 130 hurricanes. (After O.L. Fassig)

terests, those of the Department of Defense are to meet the diverse and unique requirements of the U.S. military establishment. In the Western Pacific Ocean areas, in both hemispheres, and in the North and South Indian Oceans, the NavOceanComCen/JTWC, Guam provides forecasts and warnings to all who desire this information (both military and civilian, in accordance with international agreements).

Extremely thorough and complete coordination in all facets of this work is effected amongst the civilian and military meteorological organizations of the United States. And this same cooperation and coordination is extended to foreign countries as well.

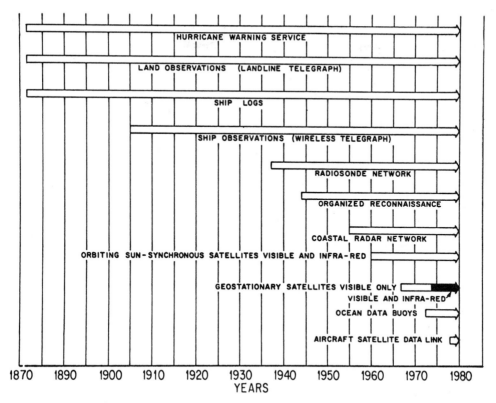

Figure 3-29. Technical advances in systems for observing tropical cyclones, 1871 through 1980. (Courtesy of NOAA National Weather Service)

The geographical areas of responsibility for tropical cyclone/hurricane forecasting and warning are assigned to the National Weather Service (NWS) Hurricane Warning Offices (HWOs) and Hurricane Centers (HCs) as follows.

Caribbean Sea, Gulf of Mexico, and Atlantic Ocean

- HWO San Juan, P.R.: Caribbean Sea, islands, and ocean areas south of latitude 20°N and longitudes 70°W to 55°W (warning responsibility only);
- HWO New Orleans, La.; Gulf of Mexico and its coasts west of longitude 85°W and north of latitude 25°N (warning responsibility only);
- HWO Washington, D.C.: Coastal and ocean areas from latitude 35°N to 41°N and eastward to longitude 65°W (warning responsibility only);
- HWO Boston, Mass.: Coastal and ocean areas north of latitude 41°N and west of longitude 65°W (warning responsibility only);
- NHC Miami (Coral Gables), Fla.: *Forecast responsibility* for all coastal and ocean areas. Also, *warning responsibility* for all areas in the Gulf of Mexico and Caribbean Sea not assigned to HWO New Orleans or HWO San Juan, and those areas in the Atlantic Ocean not assigned to HWO Boston or HWO Washington.

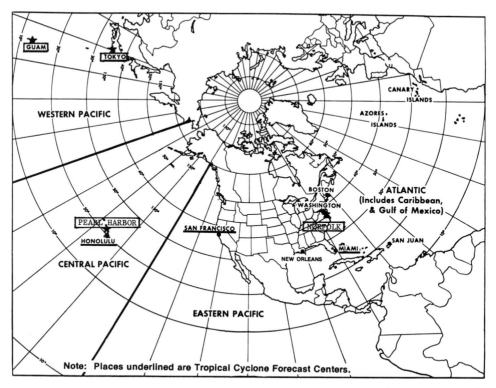

Figure 3-30. The U.S. National Weather Service tropical cyclone forecast areas of responsibility around the world. (Source: *U.S. National Hurricane Operations Plan, 1983.*) U.S. Department of Defense Forecast Centers are indicated by "stars."

Eastern Pacific

The Eastern Pacific Hurricane Center (EPHC) at San Francisco (Redwood City), California, has the *hurricane forecasting and warning* responsibility for the eastern North Pacific Ocean east of longitude 140°W and north of the equator.

Central Pacific

The Central Pacific Hurricane Center (CPHC) at Honolulu, Hawaii, has the *hurricane forecasting and warning* responsibility for the Central Pacific Ocean from longitude 140°W westward to the 180th meridian, and north of the equator.

Note from the preceding paragraphs that the NWS "Centers" have *both* forecasting and warning responsibilities, while the "Offices" have only warning responsibilities. See, again, figure 3-30.

Within the Department of Defense, the NavEastOceanCen, Norfolk, has the forecast and warning responsibilities for the entire Atlantic Ocean, the Caribbean, and the Gulf of Mexico areas for naval units. For both the Eastern and Central Pacific areas, the NavWestOceanCen, Pearl Harbor, is assigned with forecast and warning responsibilities for U.S. ships.

The area forecast and warning responsibilities of the NavOceanCom-Cen/JTWC, Guam will be covered in chapter 4 (Typhoons).

The Numbering System Used by Meteorologists

Tropical depressions are assigned a number that is retained throughout the life of the cyclone. This depression number is not, however, disseminated on advisories after the depression has increased to tropical storm or hurricane intensity and is given a name, or is numbered as a sub-tropical storm. For each Hurricane Center's area, numbering begins with "01" at the start of each calendar year. When forecast responsibility is passed from one Warning Center to another as the depression travels along its route, the assigned number is retained.

For the Atlantic, Caribbean, and Gulf of Mexico, depression numbers are assigned by the NHC, Miami (Coral Gables) after advising the NavEastOcean-Cen, Norfolk.

For the Pacific area east of longitude 140°W, depression numbers (with the suffix "E," i.e., 1E, 2E, 3E, etc.) will be assigned by the EPHC, San Francisco (Redwood City), after advising the NavWestOceanCen, Pearl Harbor.

For the Pacific area west of longitude 140°W and east of 180°, depression numbers (with the suffix "C," i.e., 1C, 2C, 3C, etc.) are assigned by the CPHC Honolulu after advising the NavWestOceanCen, Pearl Harbor.

For the Pacific area west of longitude 180°, depression numbers are assigned by the Joint Typhoon Warning Center (JTWC) of the NavOceanCom-Cen/JTWC, Guam, in the Western Pacific. This will be covered in chapter 4.

The Numbering of Sub-Tropical Storms. When a system becomes a sub-tropical storm, it is assigned a storm number to indicate its sequence of occurrence among sub-tropical storms for that area. Numbering begins with "01" and is consecutive, returning to "01" each new year.

Advisories

In the Atlantic Ocean, tropical storm and hurricane advisories for marine interests (Marine Advisories) are prepared by the NHC, Miami, at 0400, 1000, 1600, and 2200 Greenwich Mean Time (GMT). The Marine Advisories are edited by the Weather Service Forecast Office (WSFO) Washington, and are then included in Part I (Warnings) of the weather broadcasts for high-seas shipping. Coastal radio stations also transmit warnings and forecasts for offshore and coastal waters.

In the Pacific Ocean, Marine Advisories are prepared by the EPHC San Francisco (Redwood City) and the CPHC Honolulu at 0300, 0900, 1500, and 2100 GMT.

Complete details of all these broadcasts are contained in the publication, *Worldwide Marine Weather Broadcasts*, outlined in chapter 1.

THE PERMANENT LISTS OF TROPICAL STORM AND HURRICANE NAMES

When a tropical depression (maximum sustained wind speed less than 33 knots, or 38 mph, or 61 kph) increases to tropical storm intensity (maximum sustained wind speed 34–63 knots, or 39–73 mph, or 63–117 kph) or to hurricane intensity (maximum sustained winds 64 knots, or 74 mph, or 119 kph), the depression number is discontinued and the number is replaced by an appropriate—and sometimes rather imaginative—name. Different lists of names are used for the Atlantic basin, the Eastern Pacific, the Central Pacific, and the Western Pacific.

The names for the Atlantic basin are assigned by the NHC, Miami. For the Eastern Pacific (from the west coast of the U.S. westward to 140°W) by the EPHC, San Francisco (Redwood City). For the Central Pacific (from 140°W to westward to the 180th meridian) by the CPHC, Honolulu. And for the Western Pacific (west of the 180th meridian) by the NavOceanComCen/JTWC, Guam.

In the Atlantic and Eastern Pacific areas, a separate set of names is used each calendar year, beginning with the first name in the set. After all the sets have been used, the same sets are used again.

In the Central Pacific, the system is somewhat different. Here, *all* of the names listed in each column, beginning with column 1, are used before going to the next column.

The tropical storm and typhoon-naming system in the Western Pacific will be covered in chapter 4 (Typhoons).

The following pages contain the lists (sets) of names for the Atlantic, Eastern Pacific, and Central Pacific areas.

Atlantic, Caribbean, and Gulf of Mexico

1983 and 1989	1984 and 1990	1985 and 1991	1986 and 1992	1987 and 1993	1988 and 1994
Alicia	Arthur	Ana	Allen	Arlene	Alberto
Barry	Bertha	Bob	Bonnie	Bret	Beryl
Chantal	Cesar	Claudette	Charley	Cindy	Chris
Dean	Diana	Danny	Danielle	Dennis	Debby
Erin	Edouard	Elena	Earl	Emily	Ernesto
Felix	Fran	Fabian	Frances	Floyd	Florence
Gabrielle	Gustav	Gloria	Georges	Gert	Gilbert
Hugo	Hortense	Henri	Hermine	Harvey	Helene
Iris	Isidore	Isabel	Ivan	Irene	Isaac
Jerry	Josephine	Juan	Jeanne	Jose	Joan
Karen	Klaus	Kate	Karl	Katrina	Keith
Luis	Lili	Larry	Lisa	Lenny	Leslie
Marilyn	Marco	Mindy	Mitch	Maria	Michael
Noel	Nana	Nicholas	Nicole	Nate	Nadine
Opal	Omar	Odette	Otto	Ophelia	Oscar
Pablo	Paloma	Peter	Paula	Philippe	Patty
Roxanne	Rene	Rose	Richard	Rita	Rafael
Sebastien	Sally	Sam	Shary	Stan	Sandy
Tanya	Teddy	Teresa	Tomas	Tammy	Tony
Van	Vicky	Victor	Virginie	Vince	Valerie
Wendy	Wilfred	Wanda	Walter	Wilma	William

Eastern North Pacific (East of longitude 140° West)

1983 and 1989	1984 and 1990	1985 and 1991	1986 and 1992	1987 and 1993	1988 and 1994
Adolph	Alma	Andres	Agatha	Adrian	Aletta
Barbara	Boris	Blanca	Blas	Beatriz	Bud
Cosme	Cristina	Carlos	Celia	Calvin	Carlotta
Dalilia	Douglas	Dolores	Darby	Dora	Daniel
Erick	Elida	Enrique	Estelle	Eugene	Emilia
Flossie	Fausto	Fefa	Frank	Fernanda	Fabio
Gil	Genevieve	Guillermo	Georgette	Greg	Gilma
Henriette	Hernan	Hilda	Howard	Hilary	Hector
Ismael	Iselle	Ignacio	Isis	Irwin	Iva
Juliette	Julio	Jimena	Javier	Jova	John
Kiko	Kenna	Kevin	Kay	Knut	Kristy
Lorena	Lowell	Linda	Lester	Lidia	Lane
Miriam	Manuel	Marie	Marty	Madeline	Max
Narda	Norbert	Nora	Newton	Norma	Norman
Octave	Odile	Olaf	Orlene	Otis	Olivia
Priscilla	Polo	Pauline	Paine	Pilar	Paul
Raymond	Rachel	Rick	Roslyn	Ramon	Rosa
Sonia	Simon	Sandra	Seymour	Selma	Sergio
Tico	Trudy	Terry	Tina	Todd	Tara
Velma	Vance	Vivian	Virgil	Veronica	Vicente
Winnie	Wallis	Waldo	Winifred	Wiley	Willa

Central North Pacific (From longitude 140° West westward to the 180th meridian)

Column 1 Name	Pronunciation	Column 2 Name	Pronunciation	Column 3 Name	Pronunciation	Column 4 Name	Pronunciation
Akoni	ah-KOH-nee	Aka	AH-kah	Alika	ah-LEE-kah	Ana	AH-nah
Ema	EH-mah	Ekeka	eh-KEH-kah	Ele	EH-leh	Ela	EH-lah
Hana	HAH-nah	Hali	HAH-lee	Huko	HOO-koh	Halola	hah-LOH-lah
Iwa	EE-vah	Iniki	ee-NEE-kee	Ioke	ee-OH-keh	Iune	ee-OO-neh
Keli	KEH-lee	Keoni	keh-OH-nee	Kika	KEE-kah	Kimo	KEE-moh
Laka	LAH-kah	Li	LEE	Lana	LAH-nah	Loke	LOH-keh
Moke	MOH-keh	Mele	MEH-leh	Maka	MAH-kah	Malia	mah-LEE-ah
Nele	NEH-leh	Nona	NOH-nah	Neki	NEH-kee	Niala	nee-AH-lah
Oka	OH-kah	Oliwa	oh-LEE-vah	Oleka	oh-LEH-kah	Oko	OH-koh
Peke	PEH-keh	Paka	PAH-kah	Peni	PEH-nee	Pali	PAH-lee
Uleki	oo-LEH-kee	Upana	oo-PAH-nah	Ulia	oo-LEE-ah	Ulika	oo-LEE-kah
Wila	VEE-lah	Wene	WEH-neh	Wali	WAH-lee	Walaka	wah-LAH-kah

Note: All names in Column 1 are used before going on to Column 2. All names in Column 2 are used before going on to Column 3, etc.

HURRICANE HAVENS

It goes without saying that hurricanes are a very formidable and dangerous foe, both at sea and in port. Storm damage degrades a naval ship of the line's ability to fight, results in expensive repairs, and may inflict large personnel casualties. The heavy weather produced by hurricanes can cause severe damage to cargo and hull of merchant ships, take its toll in personnel casualties, and split supertankers in two, causing tremendous environmental clean-up and other problems ashore. *Prudent and early action* by naval captains and force/fleet commanders, merchant marine masters, and pleasure boat skippers in response to tropical storm and hurricane warnings *is essential.*

The classical doctrine held by most mariners, both naval and merchant marine, is that oceangoing ships should leave ports that are threatened by a hurricane or typhoon. Still, despite this natural caution on the part of seasoned skippers, many ships continue to be damaged in port, or after leaving port, as the result of an encounter with a hurricane or typhoon. This is not necessarily the result of poor judgement, poor seamanship, or indecisiveness. It could stem mainly from the relative unpredictability of hurricane and typhoon movement. The average forecast position errors escalate rapidly as the forecast interval increases:

Forecast Interval: (hours)	12	24	48	72
Average Forecast Position Error: (nautical miles)	51	109	244	377

(These statistics, which appeared in the *Monthly Weather Review*, volume 109, 1981, published by the American/Meteorological Society, are based on the research of C.J. Neumann and J.M. Pelissier.) The average 24-hour movement forecast error represents more than half of the average actual movement of these phenomena during the 24-hour period.

Figures 3-31 and 3-32 show the geographical variation in the average 24-hour and 48-hour tropical cyclone forecast errors, respectively.

Under these circumstances of forecast errors, even the most seasoned and experienced mariners must come to terms with the "forecast error factor" in their "decision process equation." Every mariner must assess the relative risks of remaining in port or putting to sea in accordance with: (1) the circumstances of the threat, (2) the facilities of the port, and (3) the capabilities of his ship and crew. In the case of naval ships, the military situation may well supersede other considerations. In any case, the sortie/stay decision is often a very difficult one.

The U.S. Navy's Environmental Prediction Research Facility in Monterey, California, has published an excellent book entitled, *Hurricane Havens for the North Atlantic Ocean*, June 1982, by Lieutenant Commander Roger J.B. Tur-

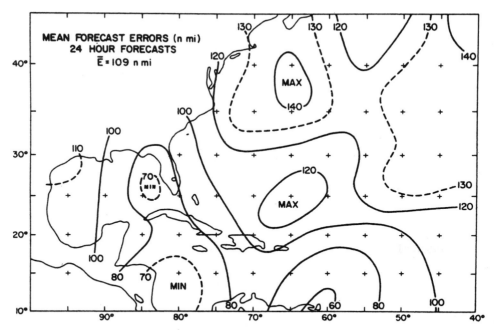

Figure 3-31. Geographical variation in the average 24-hour tropical cyclone forecast error. Ē is the average error for all 24-hour forecasts. Errors are relative to storm's initial position. (From Neumann and Pelissier, 1981.)

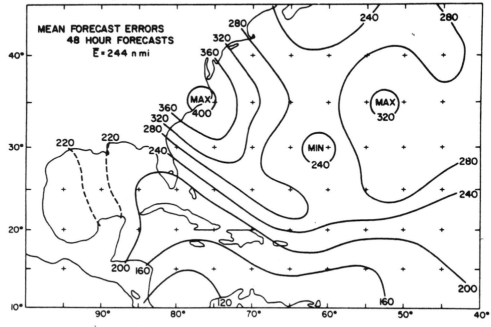

Figure 3-32. Geographical variation in the average 48-hour tropical cyclone forecast error. Ē is the average error for all 48-hour forecasts. Errors are relative to storm's initial position. (From Neumann and Pellissier, 1981.)

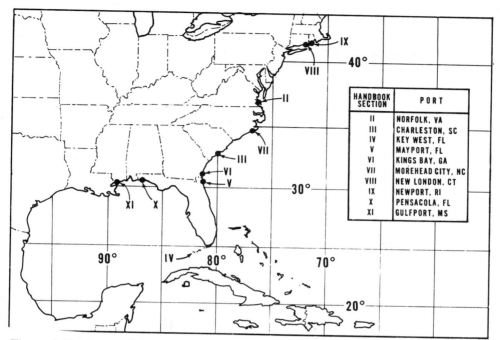

HANDBOOK SECTION	PORT
II	NORFOLK, VA
III	CHARLESTON, SC
IV	KEY WEST, FL
V	MAYPORT, FL
VI	KINGS BAY, GA
VII	MOREHEAD CITY, NC
VIII	NEW LONDON, CT
IX	NEWPORT, RI
X	PENSACOLA, FL
XI	GULFPORT, MS

Figure 3-33. Some of the ports evaluated in the *Hurricane Havens Handbook*.

pin, R.N. and Samson Brand. It is strongly recommended that captains, masters, and skippers who sail the Atlantic, Caribbean, and/or Gulf of Mexico have a copy on board. This book contains an evaluation of many ports and harbors in this area as hurricane havens, and contains much worthwhile information for input in the stay-in-port/sortie decision. Figure 3-33 shows some of the ports evaluated in the *Hurricane Havens Handbook*.

4

Typhoons

... The time for taking all measures
for a ship's safety is while still able
to do so. Nothing is more dangerous
than for a seaman to be grudging in
taking precautions lest they turn out
to have been unnecessary. Safety at
sea for a thousand years has depended
on exactly the opposite philosophy.
        —Admiral C.W. Nimitz, USN
Commander in Chief, U.S. Pacific Fleet

December 1944

Typhoons demand respect! They are all-powerful, destructive, indiscriminate—and sometimes unpredictable. They are nature's second most intense phenomenon, exceeded only by the tornado in local violence. Typhoons have caused the sinking of many ships at sea and in port, during peace and war. Their storm surges have inundated many coastal and low-lying areas, costing many hundreds of thousands of human lives. Typhoons played important roles in the disposition of large battle fleets in World War II, at the time of the first H-bomb "shot" in November 1952, during Astronaut Wally Schirra's orbital flight in October 1962, and on many other occasions.

Nevertheless, many years ago when the author was a young and impressionable commanding officer on the island of Guam, the comments and questions of innumerable captains of naval ships and masters of merchant vessels were as relevant as they were startling. For these were men of authority, with great responsibilities. But somewhere along the line they had missed a lecture. Or perhaps time had erased or eroded the "typhoon memory bank."

"The truth is, I didn't even know that there was a typhoon in the area until my ship was hit by 70-knot beam winds—right after I got into San Bernardino Strait! I guess we were lucky to get out of that one." Thus spoke a captain of the (then) Military Sea Transportation Service (MSTS).

The master of a commercial vessel en route from Guam to Yokohama related that his ship managed to work its way into the eye of an intense typhoon. Cargo damage alone was estimated in excess of $85,000. Damage to the ship could not be estimated at the time. His explanation: "I knew I could outrun that d----d typhoon. But I forgot how fast those huge swells move 'way ahead of those storms. Once those swells hit the ship, my SOA [speed of advance] was cut to four and a half knots. I was a sitting duck, and the eye passed right over me!" He had used up his "nine lives" in that one incident.

The skipper of a U.S. Navy oiler (AO) asked: "How do the winds blow around these typhoons out here? Is it clockwise or counterclockwise?"

And the comment of a seasoned merchant mariner was equally disturbing: "Typhoons, monsoons; they're all the same—just different names."

Many statements such as these made it painfully obvious that a large percentage of military and civilian personnel in positions of command or authority knew little about their greatest nonpolitical peacetime threat in the Western North Pacific—the typhoon.

In his wonderful book, *Typhoon*, Joseph Conrad said it so well: "Had he [Captain MacWhirr] been informed by an indisputable authority that the end of the world was to be finally accomplished by a catastrophic disturbance of the atmosphere, he would have assimilated the information under the simple idea of dirty weather, and no other, because he had no experience of cataclysms, and *belief does not necessarily imply comprehension.* [Author's italics.] The wisdom of his county had pronounced by means of an Act of Parliament that before he could be considered as fit to take charge of a ship he should be able to answer certain simple questions on the subject of circular storms such as hurricanes, cyclones, typhoons, . . ."

What is the origin of the word *typhoon*? That's hard to say. The word is either derived from the Cantonese *t'ai fung* (a great wind), from the Arabic *tufan* (smoke), or from the Greek *typhon* (a monster). Even Aristotle used the word *typhon* for a wind-containing cloud. One thing we do know. This phenomenon should be avoided whenever possible. See figure 4-1 for a satellite's view of a super typhoon packing winds in excess of 135 knots. Gusts (extreme) to 200 knots can be expected.

AREAS OF FORMATION

Just as the Azores-Bermuda high-pressure area is the "center of action" in the Atlantic basin, the Pacific anticyclone, oriented WSW-ENE along latitude 30°–35°N, is the "center of action" for the Pacific region. See, again, figure 2-2b. Normally, this high-pressure area in the Pacific is made up of two individual anticyclonic cells, rather than one cell extending across the entire width of the Pacific from Asia to the United States. During the summer months, the central pressure averages about 1,029 millibars (30.386 inches).

During the period July–November, inclusive—the period of greatest typhoon occurrence—this center, as in the Atlantic, oscillates north and south with varying degrees of intensity. And again, the so-called "departures from normal" in strength and/or position of the high-pressure center have a profound influence on the frequency and tracks of typhoons in the western North Pacific region.

The Intertropical Convergence Zone (ITCZ) usually reaches its northernmost position in late August in the western North Pacific, near latitude 30°N (Ningpo, People's Republic of China). See, again, figure 2-8. Then, it begins to recede southward into the Southern Hemisphere. See, again, figures 2-7 and 2-9.

Figure 4-1. A satellite's view of Super Typhoon Tip in the western North Pacific on 11 October 1979, packing maximum sustained winds in excess of 135 knots. Extreme gusts as high as 200 knots could be expected from this monster. Note the almost perfect circular "eye." (Department of Defense photo)

The position and strength of the western cell of the North Pacific anticyclone, the north-south latitudinal and the vertical extent of the trade winds to the south of the anticyclone, the position and strength of the ITCZ, and the presence of atmospheric waves in the tropical easterlies, all have an impact on the migration of the regions of most frequent occurrence of typhoons in the western North Pacific, and on the decrease in frequency of typhoon occurences during the winter and spring months.

While in the Atlantic basin the principal areas of tropical cyclone formation shift eastward and westward seasonally, the situation in the western North Pacific is somewhat different. Here, the principal areas of tropical cyclone formation shift primarily northward and southward seasonally. There is some east-west seasonal shifting, but it is small compared to the north-south migration.

Figure 4-2 shows the "breeding ground" of the western North Pacific area's typhoons. It extends from 3°N to almost 25°N, and from 110°E to the 180th meridian, although most typhoons form west of 165°E. This is a tremendous area of approximately 6.3 million square miles, and an area that a Western Pacific sailor or yachtsman can hardly avoid. During the 10-year period 1952–1961, inclusive, there were 184 typhoons. This is about par for the course. The triangles in figure 4-2 show the locations in which typhoons began to form. In each 4-digit group, the last two digits indicate the calendar year in which that particular typhoon formed. And the first two digits indicate the typhoon's sequence number for that year. Thus, "0452" means "the fourth typhoon of 1952," "2061" means "the 20th typhoon of 1961," and so on.

Note that approximately 34 percent of the typhoons formed within 500 nautical miles of the island of Guam. A good reason for the local inhabitants and military/civilian personnel stationed there to be ever on the alert.

Figure 4-3 shows where these tropical cyclones first reached typhoon intensity (maximum sustained winds 64 knots, or 74 mph, or 119 kph) or higher.

On average, the north-south seasonal migration of the primary areas of typhoon formation is as follows:
- Jan., Feb., Mar., Apr.—between latitudes 3°–10°N
- May–June—between latitudes 4°–12°N
- July, Aug.—between latitudes 9°–25°
- Sep.–15 Oct.—between latitudes 10°–20°N
- 16 Oct.–15 Nov.—between latitudes 5°–17°N
- 16 Nov.–Dec.—between latitudes 3°–12°N

Figures 4-8 to 4-21, inclusive, in the section titled "Tracks" in this chapter, show the general migration of the areas of typhoon formation (beginning of tracks) and their paths for the period 1950–1959, inclusive. By leafing quickly through these figures in order, one can see the seasonal northward and southward shift of the primary areas of typhoon formation in the western North Pacific.

SEASON AND FREQUENCY

In the western North Pacific, there is no *true* so-called typhoon season. Typhoons can—*and do*—occur in every month of the year. Figure 4-4 shows the number of full-blown typhoons that occurred in each month during the 11-year period 1952–1962, inclusive. This period is typical of almost any 11-year period in the region.

Atlantic sailors are somewhat more fortunate in this regard. They experience a reasonable hurricane "season," from about May 1st to November 30th. Eastern Pacific sailors from June 1st through November 15th. And Central Pacific sailors from June 1st through October 31st. In calendar year 1962, for example, the Atlantic was subjected to only three hurricanes, while the western North Pacific suffered the brunt of 24 monstrous typhoons, similar to

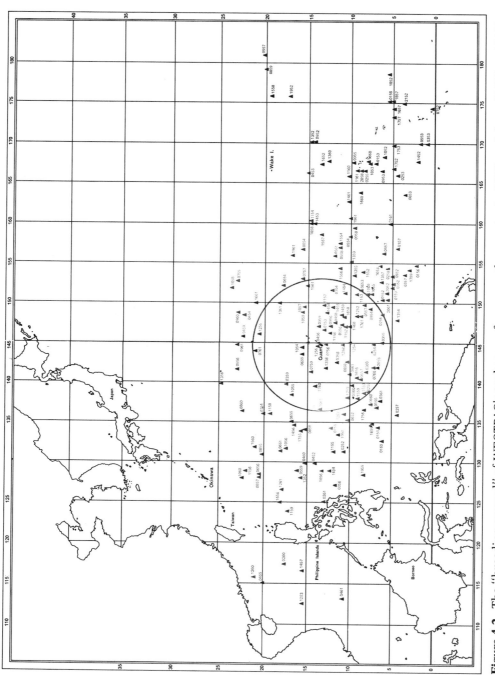

Figure 4-2. The "breeding ground" of WESTPAC's typhoons—from near the equator to 25°N, and from 110°E to 180°E. Triangles show where the 184 typhoons between 1952–61, inclusive, began to form. The last two digits indicate the calendar year typhoon formed. The first two digits indicate the typhoon's sequence number for that year. 0452 means "4th typhoon in 1952," 2061 means "20th typhoon in 1961," etc. Note that 34 percent of typhoons begin to form within 500 N.M. of Guam.

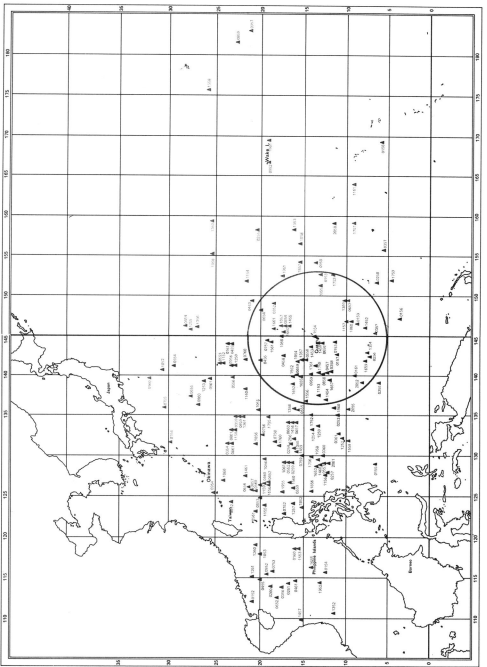

Figure 4-3. Locations in WESTPAC where the 184 tropical disturbances between 1952–61, inclusive, first reached typhoon intensity (maximum sustained winds 64 knots or higher). Note the slight shift in the triangles to the north and west from those of figure 4-2. The 4-digit groups have the same connotation as in the previous figure.

Typhoons	Jan.	Feb.	Mar.	Apr.	May	Jun.	Jul.	Aug.	Sep.	Oct.	Nov.	Dec.	Total
1952	—	—	—	—	—	3	1	3	3	5	3	3	21
1953	—	1	—	—	1	1	1	5	2	4	1	1	17
1954	—	—	—	—	1	—	1	4	4	2	3	—	15
1955	1	—	1	1	—	1	5	3	3	2	1	1	19
1956	—	—	1	1	—	—	2	4	5	1	3	1	18
1957	1	—	—	1	1	1	1	2	5	3	3	—	18
1958	1	—	—	—	1	2	5	3	3	3	1	1	20
1959	—	—	—	1	—	—	1	5	3	3	2	2	17
1960	—	—	—	1	—	2	2	8	—	4	1	1	19
1961	—	—	1	—	2	1	3	3	5	3	1	1	20
1962	—	—	—	1	2	—	5	7	2	4	3	—	24
11-Year Average	0.27	0.09	0.27	0.55	0.73	1.00	2.45	4.27	3.18	3.09	2.00	1.00	18.92
Frequency	3	1	3	6	8	11	27	47	35	34	22	11	208
Per cent Frequency	1.4	0.6	1.4	2.9	3.8	5.3	13:0	22.6	16.8	16.3	10.6	5.3	100

Figure 4-4. Frequency of typhoons in the western North Pacific area. Note that there is no true typhoon season. Typhoons can—and do—occur in every month of the year. However, 90 percent of typhoons occur between early June and late December. Maximum of 22.6 percent in August, and minimum of 0.6 percent in February.

Typhoon CLARA in figure 4-5, which devastated Northern Luzon and parts of the coast of the People's Republic of China.

Although no true typhoon season exists, one can see from figure 4-4 that 90 percent of the typhoons in the western North Pacific occur between early June and late December, with maximum occurrence (22.6 percent) in August and minimum occurrence (0.6 percent) in February. These data include only full-fledged typhoons (maximum sustained winds 64 knots, or 74 mph, or 119 kph, or higher). Tropical storms (maximum sustained winds 63 knots or less) have not been included, although they themselves constitute quite a blow, and are accompanied by torrential rains, heavy seas, and high tides.

On average, one should expect about 19 full-fledged typhoons in the western North Pacific in any calendar year, and at least an additional eight tropical storms whose maximum sustained winds do not quite reach 64 knots, but whose extreme gusts could reach as high as 90 knots.

The above statistics could be slightly on the low side when one considers that before the relatively recent advent of operational weather satellites in the area, the average number of reliable weather reports in the region was only one report per 226,000 square miles! Many tropical cyclones undoubtedly went undetected for days at a time—or perhaps for their entire life span—if they were not on major surface shipping lanes or commercial aircraft flight routes.

As with hurricanes in the Atlantic basin, the duration of typhoons in the Western Pacific extends from a day or two to over a month. The average duration seems to be about 9–10 days. The duration (and intensity) of a typhoon depends on several factors, among them: the track of the typhoon, the ocean temperatures over which the typhoon travels, meteorological conditions near the earth's surface and at high levels in the atmosphere, and so on.

For information in capsulated form on the season and frequency of intense tropical cyclones in the Southwest Pacific and Australian area, the North Indian Ocean (Bay of Bengal and Arabian Sea), and the Southwest Indian Ocean, the reader is referred to table 2-3 on page 96 (Tropical Cyclones).

Figure 4-5. Typhoon Clara at 190521Z September 1981. Intensity at this time was 115 kts. Clara developed northwest of Truk around the 13th and moved west-northwest for four days before reaching tropical storm strength approx. 450 N.M. east of the Philippines. Within 36 hours, she reached typhoon strength and continued to move northwest towards the northern tip of Luzon. Her max. intensity was 120 kts with a sea-level pressure of 924 MBS. She maintained typhoon strength 'til she slammed into the coast of China on the 21st. She then dissipated rapidly as she moved into the hilly terrain. Clara was a devastating storm causing widespread damage to northern Luzon. (Department of Defense photo)

TRACKS

Forecasting the future tracks and speeds of movement (and stalls) of typhoons is no less difficult than forecasting the future tracks of hurricanes. And the forecast responsibilities weigh just as heavily. Additionally, reliable weather reports are much more sparse in the Pacific than in the Atlantic basin.

Individual tracks of typhoons exhibit the same idiosyncrasies as hurricanes in the Atlantic and Eastern Pacific, cyclones in the Indian Ocean, or intense tropical vortices anywhere else in the world. It is suggested that the reader again take a quick look at figure 2-24 in chapter 2, which shows the 15 "basic" tracks of intense tropical cyclones in each hemisphere. Again, one must remember that there are innumerable minor variations to these basic tracks.

Figure 4-6 shows the forecastable track of typhoon ROSE during the period 10–17 August 1971. This satellite view shows Typhoon ROSE when the "eye" was located only 115 nautical miles to the SSW of Hong Kong. Needless to say, damage to property ashore and to ships at sea was excessive, and loss of life was high. The eye passed within 60 miles of Hong Kong, and on the *"wrong"* side (to the west of the Colony). As a result, Hong Kong experienced the highest sustained winds, the highest gusts, and the storm surge.

Figure 4-7 shows the unusual, almost "straight line" track of Typhoon PATSY during the period 14–22 November 1970. This typhoon kept forecasters guessing as to when the center would recurve northward and eastward. It was like "waiting for the other shoe to drop." The eye of Typhoon PATSY moved right over the city of Manila, where it caused considerable damage and loss of life. The two satellite views show the typhoon when the eye was centered directly over Manila on 19 November 1970. The eye later moved into Vietnam late on November 21st.

Figures 4-8 through 4-21 are a 10-year record of typhoon tracks from 1950–1959, inclusive. These charts give a good idea of what a Western Pacific sailor can expect in the way of typhoon tracks at different times of the year. The track charts appear as follows:

- Figure 4-8—Jan., Feb., Mar., Apr., 1950–1959
- Figure 4-9—May, 1950–1959
- Figure 4-10—June, 1950–1959
- Figure 4-11—01–15 July, 1950–1959
- Figure 4-12—16–31 July, 1950–1959
- Figure 4-13—01–15 Aug., 1950–1959
- Figure 4-14—16–31 Aug., 1950–1959
- Figure 4-15—01–15 Sep., 1950–1959
- Figure 4-16—16–30 Sep., 1950–1959
- Figure 4-17—01–15 Oct., 1950–1959
- Figure 4-18—16–31 Oct., 1950–1959
- Figure 4-19—01–15 Nov., 1950–1959
- Figure 4-20—16–30 Nov., 1950–1959
- Figure 4-21—Dec., 1950–1959

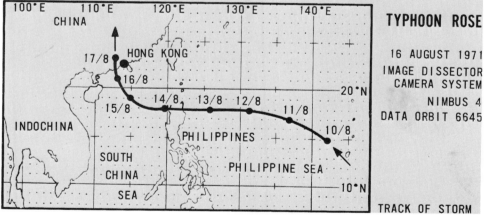

Figure 4-6. The forecastable track of Typhoon Rose during the period 10–17 August 1971. The eye of the typhoon was only 115 nautical miles to the SSW of Hong Kong at the time of the satellite image. (Courtesy of NASA Goddard Space Flight Center)

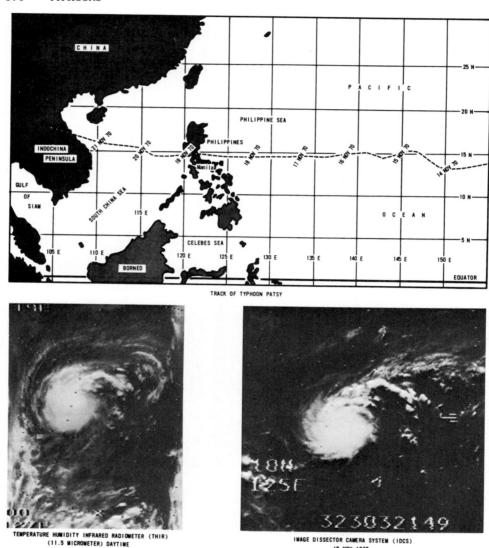

TRACK OF TYPHOON PATSY

TEMPERATURE HUMIDITY INFRARED RADIOMETER (THIR)
(11.5 MICROMETER) DAYTIME
19 NOV 1970

IMAGE DISSECTOR CAMERA SYSTEM (IDCS)
19 NOV 1970

NIMBUS 4 VIEWS TYPHOON PATSY

THESE IMAGES WERE RECORDED AS THE STORM, WITH REPORTED WIND SPEEDS OF 115 MILES PER HOUR, WAS CENTERED OVER MANILA, WHERE IT CAUSED CONSIDERABLE DAMAGE AND LOSS OF LIFE. NIMBUS SENSORS MONITORED THE STORM'S DEVELOPMENT, DAILY MOVEMENT AND DISSIPATION, AS THE STORM MOVED ACROSS THE PACIFIC INTO VIETNAM.

Figure 4-7. The unusual, almost "straight-line" track of Typhoon Patsy during the period 14–22 November 1970. The eye of this typhoon passed right over the city of Manila on 19 November, as shown in the two satellite images, causing extensive damage and large loss of life. (Courtesy of NASA Goddard Space Flight Center)

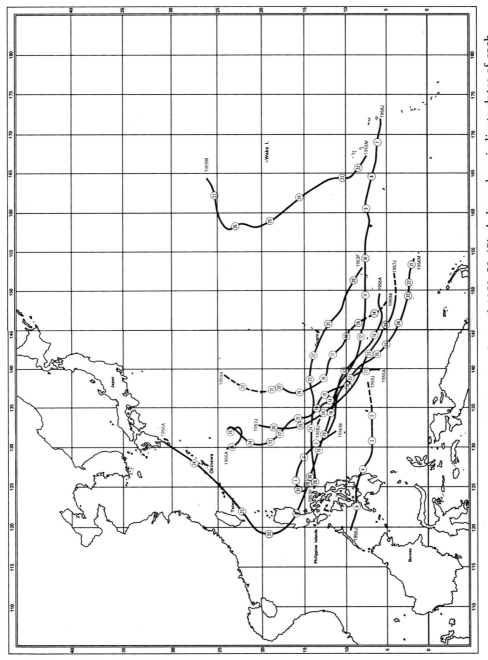

Figure 4-8. Typhoon tracks—January, February, March, April 1950–59. (Circled numbers indicate dates of each month.)

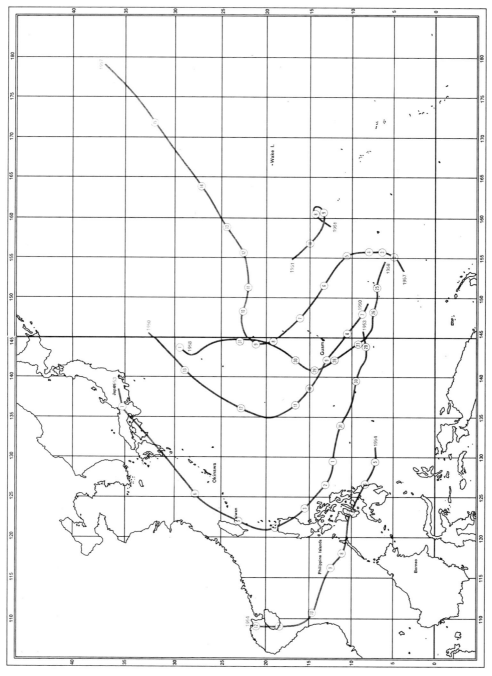

Figure 4-9. Typhoon tracks—May 1950–59. (Circled numbers indicate dates of the month.)

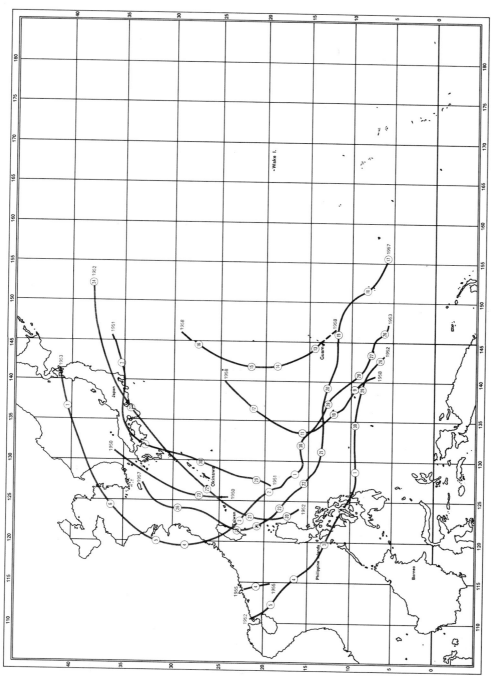

Figure 4-10. Typhoon tracks—June 1950–59. (Circled numbers indicate dates of the month.)

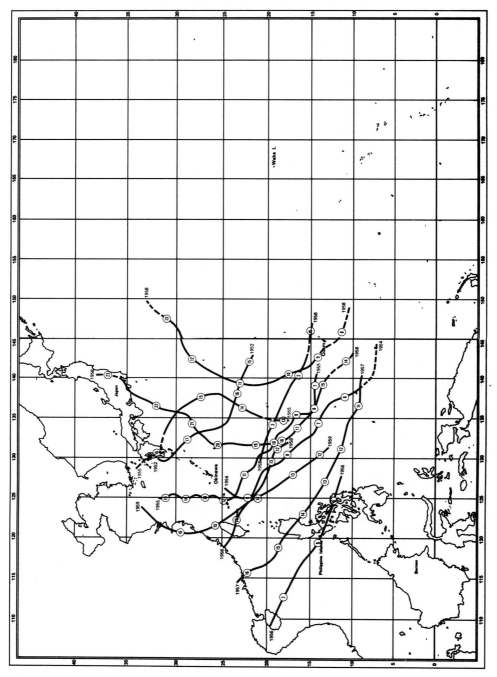

Figure 4-11. Typhoon Tracks—1–15 July 1950–59. (Circled numbers indicate dates of the month.)

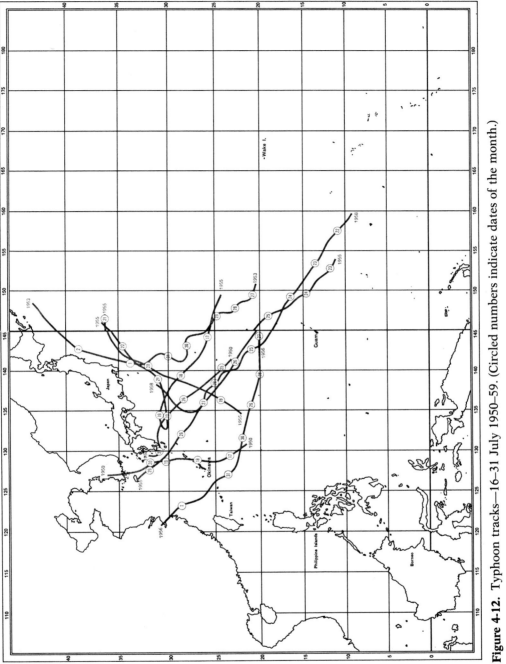

Figure 4-12. Typhoon tracks—16–31 July 1950–59. (Circled numbers indicate dates of the month.)

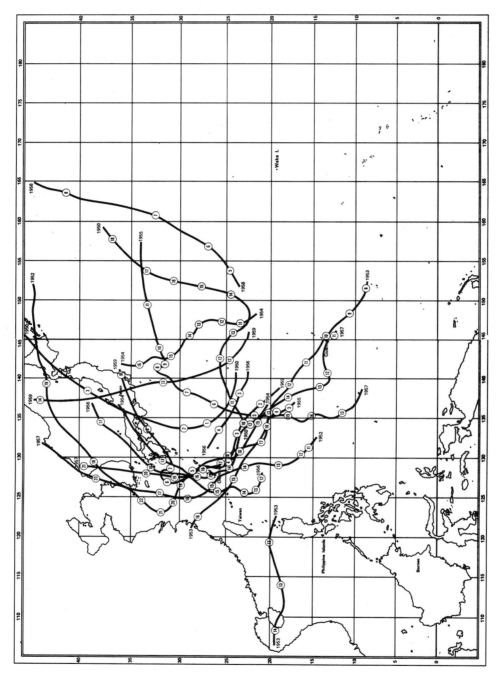

Figure 4-13. Typhoon tracks—1–15 August 1950–59. (Circled numbers indicate dates of the month.)

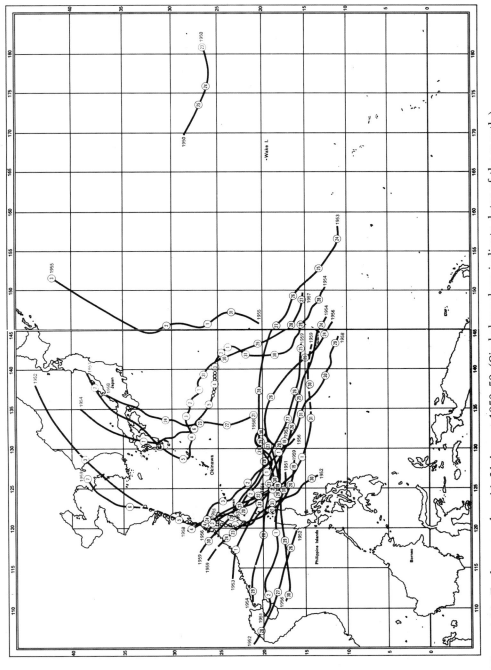

Figure 4-14. Typhoon tracks—16–31 August 1950–59. (Circled numbers indicate dates of the month.)

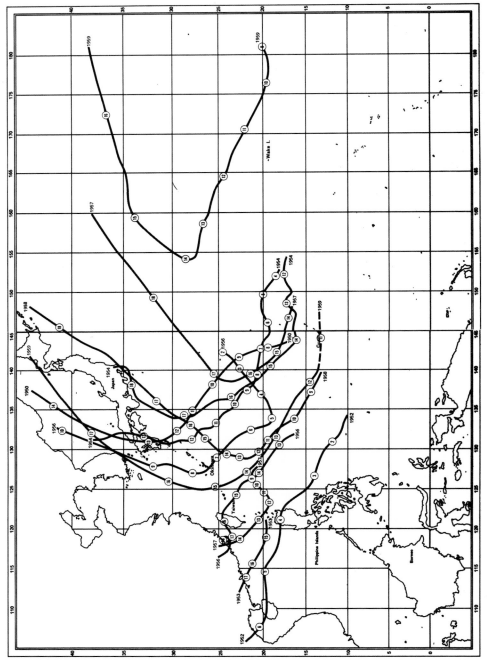

Figure 4-15. Typhoon tracks—1–15 September 1950–59. (Circled numbers indicate the dates of the month.)

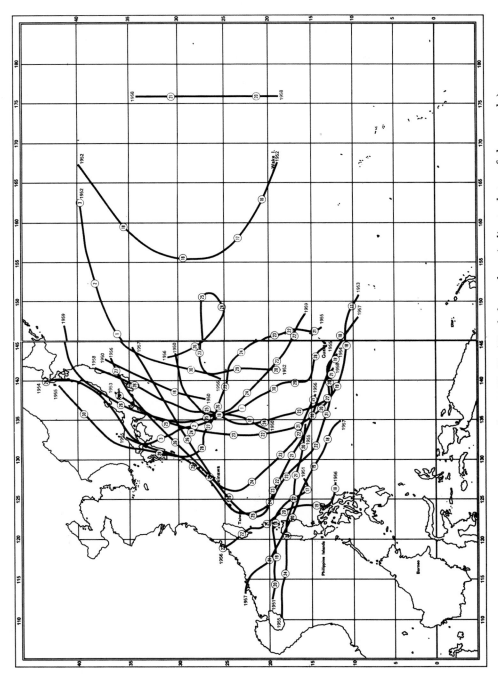

Figure 4-16. Typhoon tracks—16–30 September 1950–59. (Circled numbers indicate dates of the month.)

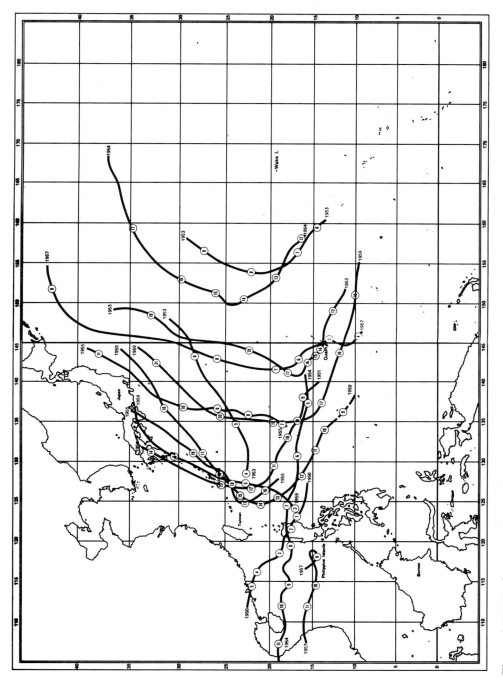

Figure 4-17. Typhoon tracks—1–15 October 1950–59. (Circled numbers indicate dates of the month.)

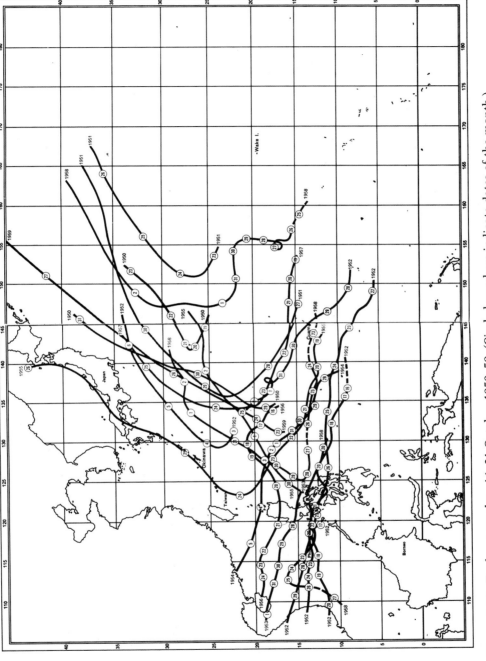

Figure 4-18. Typhoon tracks—16–31 October 1950–59. (Circled numbers indicate dates of the month.)

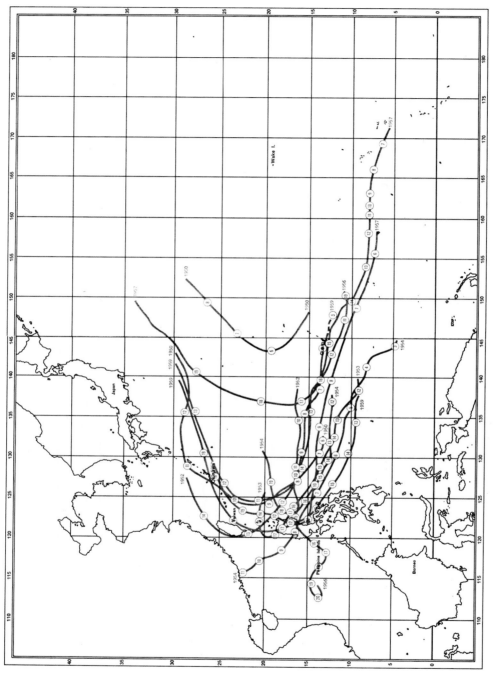

Figure 4-19. Typhoon tracks—1–15 November 1950–59. (Circled numbers indicate dates of the month.)

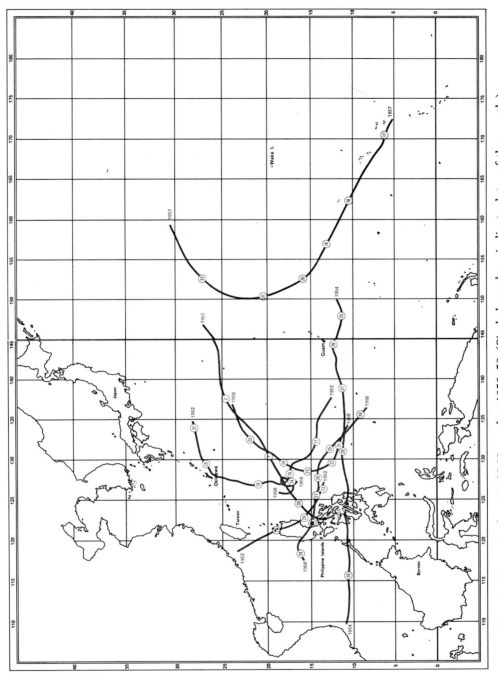

Figure 4-20. Typhoon tracks—16–30 November 1950–59. (Circled numbers indicate dates of the month.)

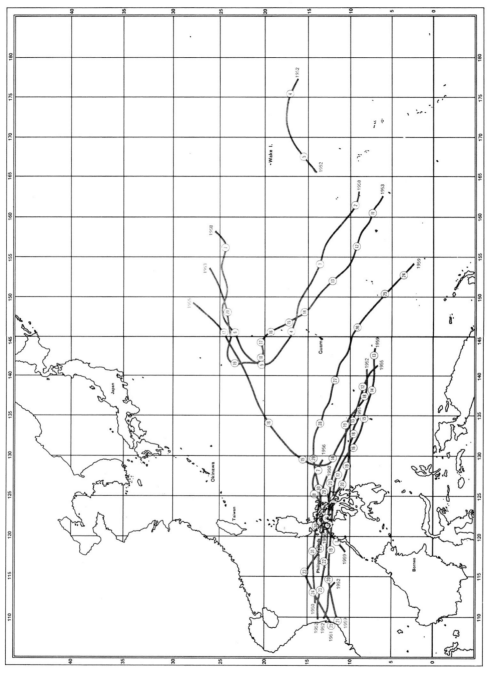

Figure 4-21. Typhoon tracks—December 1950–59. (Circled numbers indicate dates of the month.)

For the principal tracks of intense tropical cyclones (hurricanes, etc.) in the Southwest Pacific and Australian area, the North Indian Ocean (Bay of Bengal and Arabian Sea), and the Southwest Indian Ocean, the reader is referred to figure 2-26 in chapter 2 (Tropical Cyclones).

THE TYPHOON WARNING SYSTEM

As directed by the Commander in Chief, Pacific, the Commander in Chief, U.S. Pacific Fleet established the Joint Typhoon Warning Center (JTWC) as a component of the (then) U.S. Fleet Weather Central, Guam (now the U.S. Naval Oceanography Command Center/JTWC, Guam) on 1 May 1959. Since its establishment, the mission of the JTWC (staffed by both U.S. Navy and U.S. Air Force personnel) has been to: (1) Provide tropical cyclone and typhoon warnings west of the 180th meridian, (2) Determine tropical cyclone aircraft reconnaissance requirements and priorities, (3) Conduct investigative and post-analysis programs, (4) Conduct forecast and detection research, as practicable, and (5) Prepare and disseminate an Annual Tropical Cyclone Report.

Situated atop Nimitz Hill on the beautiful island of Guam (13.5°N–145°E) is the "nerve center" of the weather and oceanographic operation west of the 180th meridian (in both hemispheres)—the NavOceanComCen/JTWC, Guam.

In earlier years, the area of responsibility of this command encompassed only the western North Pacific, westward from the 180th meridian to the Malay Peninsula. Today, however, that area of responsibility has been increased tremendously. It now includes all oceanic areas in *both* hemispheres, from the 180th meridian westward to longitude 20°E (the southern tip of Africa), and from latitude 60°S northward, as shown in figure 4-22. If you are in this area, be sure to copy the Guam broadcasts as listed in the publication *Worldwide Marine Weather Broadcasts* to stay out of trouble. In the event of incapacitation of the NavOceanComCen/JTWC, Guam, the NavWestOcean-Cen, Pearl Harbor has been designated as the Alternate Joint Typhoon Warning Center (AJTWC).

Figure 4-23 shows the infinite variety of weather patterns and weather systems in a portion of the NavOceanComCen/JTWC, Guam's area of responsibility on 4 September 1981 (early fall in the Northern Hemisphere, and early spring in the Southern Hemisphere). The meteorologists stationed here must always be on their toes.

The efficiency of any system is directly proportional to the accuracy and amount of data and information supplied to the system. Consequently, the great importance of each individual surface and upper-air weather report, sea-condition report, radar report, etc.—from weather satellites, land stations, naval and merchant ships, military and commercial aircraft, and pleasure craft cannot be overemphasized. The typhoon warning system can only be as good as the data and information fed into the system. So, if you are operating in or transiting the area, be sure to make and transmit your weather, sea condition, and radar reports.

The competent and dedicated team of Navy and Air Force meteorologists at the NavOceanComCen/JTWC, Guam really have to be "ambidextrous." They

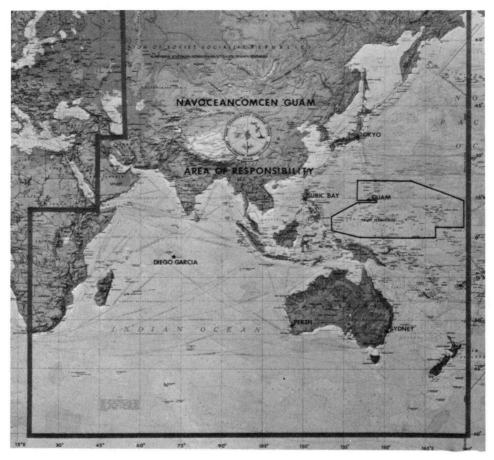

Figure 4-22. The tremendous area of forecast and warning responsibility of the NavOceanComCen/JTWC, Guam—extending from the 180th meridian westward to longitude 20°E, and from latitude 60°S northward, as shown.

must analyze, draw, and forecast the counterclockwise-rotating typhoons of the Northern Hemisphere (as shown in figure 4-24), and with equal dexterity and accuracy, the clockwise-rotating hurricanes of the Southern Hemisphere (as shown in figure 4-25). This takes considerable skill and constant readjustment.

When a tropical cyclone crosses the 180th meridian traveling from west to east, the NavOceanComCen/JTWC, Guam appends to the last warning issued in its area the statement that "Next warning by the CPHC, Honolulu." When a tropical cyclone crosses the 180th meridian traveling from east to west, the CPHC, Honolulu—through the NavWestOceanCen, Pearl Harbor—passes forecast responsibility to the NavOceanComCen/JTWC, Guam.

The Numbering System

North Pacific Area. Tropical cyclones originating west of the 180th meridian and east of the Malay Peninsula (100°E) will be assigned numbers and names by the JTWC, Guam. Systems of tropical depression strength (maximum sustained winds 33 knots or less—remember?) will be numbered serially, 01 through 99, beginning with the first designated tropical depression

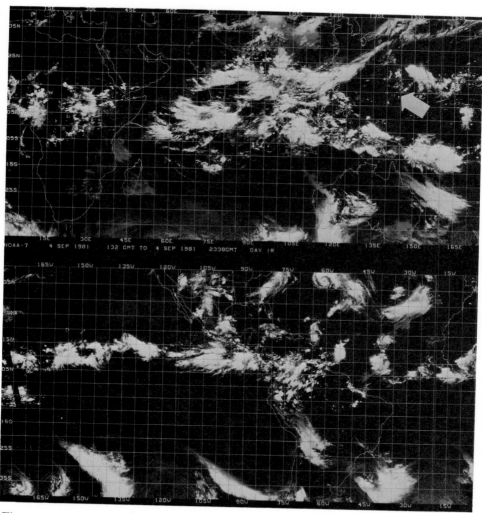

Figure 4-23. The NOAA-7 polar-orbiting weather satellite's view of the different types of weather patterns and weather systems in a portion of the NavOceanCom-Cen/JTWC, Guam area of forecast and warning responsibility (upper image) on 4 September 1981 (early autumn in the Northern Hemisphere and early spring in the Southern Hemisphere. The island of Guam is at tip of arrow. (Courtesy of National Air Survey Center, Corp.)

Figure 4-24. Satellite's view of Typhoon Gay on 20 October 1981, when the "eye" was 775 nautical miles ENE of Taipei, Taiwan (at tip of arrow). Note the perfect *counterclockwise* circulation around the center as shown by the clouds and cloud "feeder bands." Compare this to figure 4-25. (Department of Defense Photo)

(TD) of each calendar year. The JTWC assigns names to tropical storms and typhoons in accordance with the permanent lists of names in this chapter. The names are assigned when the vortex sustained maximum winds reach 34 knots or higher. Numbered and/or named systems crossing the 180th meridian traveling from east to west retain their numbers and/or names, but hurricanes are redesignated as typhoons.

North Indian Ocean. Tropical cyclones originating west of the Malay Peninsula (100°E) and east of the coast of Africa are assigned a number-year identifier (i.e., 1-84, 2-84, etc.) from a sequence controlled by the JTWC, Guam. Tropical systems originating east of the Malay Peninsula and subsequently

Figure 4-25. TIROS-N polar-orbiting weather satellite's view of an intense hurricane in the South Indian Ocean at lat. 15.0°S, long. 70.0°E, 1,150 miles east of Madagascar (Malagasy). Note the perfect *clockwise* circulation around the center as shown by the clouds and cloud "feeder bands." Compare this figure to figure 4-24. (Courtesy of National Air Survey Center, Corp.)

moving into this area, carry the original JTWC, Guam–assigned number or name in parentheses following the newly assigned number-year identifier.

Southern Hemisphere. Tropical cyclones developing in the South Indian Ocean or the South Pacific Ocean are identified by a number-year designator assigned from a sequence controlled by the JTWC, Guam. For those systems originating in the South Pacific east of the 180th meridian, the NavWest-OceanCen, Pearl Harbor contacts the JTWC, Guam for the appropriate number designator.

Foreign meteorological organizations frequently assign names to tropical cyclones in this area. When this name is known, it is included in parentheses after the number-year designator—e.g., 01S-84 (Alice)—on subsequent warnings to avoid possible confusion on the part of seafarers.

Tropical Cyclone Warnings

Warnings are numbered serially beginning with the first warning issued on each cyclone and continued throughout the life cycle of the cyclone, irrespective of a change in intensity classification or area of responsibility. The initial warning is issued when the existence of a tropical depression has been established and the decision is made to designate the vortex. Each warning normally pertains to a single cyclone system. Should a system contain more than one center of circulation (vortex), the multiple centers are reported in the same warning.

Warnings are amended or revised as required by the receipt of new information. Amendments and/or corrections have a letter serially assigned to the original warning number and the abbreviation "AMD" or "COR" will immediately follow the Date/Time Group of the message heading.

Times of Warnings

North Pacific Area. Warnings are issued within two hours of 0000 GMT, 0600 GMT, 1200 GMT, and 1800 GMT. No two consecutive warnings are more than seven hours apart.

North Indian Ocean. Warnings are issued within two hours of 0200 GMT, 0800 GMT, 1400 GMT, and 2000 GMT. No two consecutive warnings are more than seven hours apart.

Southern Hemisphere. Warnings are issued within two hours of either 0600 GMT and 1800 GMT, or within two hours of 0000 GMT and 1200 GMT. This determination is made based upon satellite data availability and the number of tropical cyclones in warning status. This will not change during the life of the particular tropical cyclone. No two warnings are made more than 14 hours apart.

Southern Hemisphere East of 180th Meridan. Warnings are issued at 0300 GMT and 1500 GMT.

Detailed Content of Warnings

A wealth of information (current and forecast) is included in each warning, enabling skippers to make crucial decisions and/or take corrective or evasive measures. These warnings include the following:

- Type of tropical cyclone
- Time and forecast position of the center
- Accuracy (estimated) of the warning positon of the center
- Method of "fixing" the center
- Present movement of the cyclone
- Speed and location of the maximum surface winds and peak gusts
- Radius of the area with surface winds greater than 100 knots
- Radius of the area with surface winds greater than 50 knots
- Radius of the area with surface winds greater than 30 knots
- Repeat of the forecast position

- Twelve-hour forecast position and intensity (including gusts) and radius of area with surface winds greater than 50 knots
- Twenty-four hour forecast position and intensity (including gusts), radius of area with surface winds greater than 100 knots, radius of area with surface winds greater than 50 knots, and radius of area with surface winds greater than 30 knots
- Forty-eight hour outlook position and intensity (including gusts), and radius of area with surface winds greater than 50 knots
- Seventy-two hour outlook position, intensity, including gusts, and radius of area with surface winds greater than 50 knots
- Aircraft reconnaissance plans for the next 24 hours
- Scheduled issuance time of the next four (two) warning messages in the Northern (Southern) Hemisphere areas
- Special and pertinent remarks

Brief Note on the Accuracy of Forecasts

Considering the paucity of data and reports in this tremendous area of responsibility, the meteorologists of the NavOceanComCen/JTWC, Guam do exceedingly well in forecasting the future tracks and intensities of intense tropical cyclones. Figure 4-26 illustrates the method used to determine the vector error and the right-angle error of predicted tropical cyclone positions. Figure 4-27 is a plot of yearly mean forecast errors in the western North Pacific (1972–1981). And figure 4-28 is a plot of the yearly mean forecast errors in the North Indian Ocean (1972–1981).

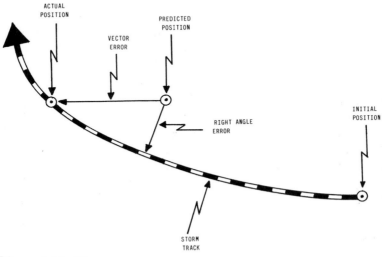

Figure 4-26. Illustration of the method used to determine the vector error and the right-angle error of predicted tropical cyclone positions.

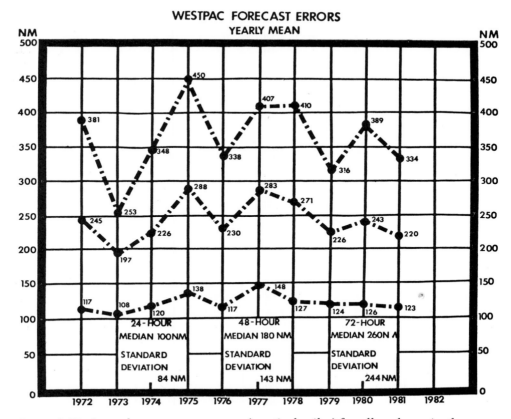

Figure 4-27. Annual mean vector errors (nautical miles) for all cyclones in the western North Pacific (1972–1981).

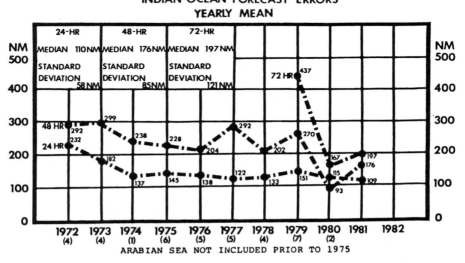

Figure 4-28. Annual mean vector errors (nautical miles) for all cyclones in the North Indian Ocean (1972–1981).

THE PERMANENT LISTS OF TROPICAL STORM AND TYPHOON NAMES

As is the case in the Atlantic basin and the eastern North Pacific, when a tropical depression (maximum sustained winds of 33 knots, or 38 mph, or 61 kph) in the western North Pacific (west of the 180th meridian) increases to tropical storm intensity (maximum sustained winds 34–63 knots, or 39–73 mph, or 63–117 kph) or to typhoon intensity (64 knots, or 74 mph, or 119 kph, or higher), the depression number is discontinued and the number is replaced by an appropriate name.

The names in the western North Pacific—from the 180th meridian westward to the Malay Peninsula (100°E)—are assigned by the Joint Typhoon Warning Center (JTWC), Guam. *But*, there is one exception. Hurricanes that form to the east of the 180th meridian, travel westward, and cross the 180th meridian heading west, retain the original name assigned by the CPHC, Honolulu, but the hurricanes are redesignated as typhoons.

Four columns, or lists, of tropical storm and typhoon names are used in the Western North Pacific area. These appear below.

Western North Pacific (West of the 180th meridian)

Column 1	Column 2	Column 3	Column 4
Andy	Abby	Alex	Agnes
Bess	Ben	Betty	Bill
Cecil	Carmen	Cary	Clara
Dot	Dom	Dinah	Doyle
Ellis	Ellen	Ed	Elsie
Faye	Forrest	Freda	Fabian
Gordon	Georgia	Gerald	Gay
Hope	Herbert	Holly	Hazen
Irving	Ida	Ike	Irma
Judy	Joe	June	Jeff
Ken	Kim	Kelly	Kit
Lola	Lex	Lynn	Lee
Mac	Marge	Maury	Mamie
Nancy	Norris	Nina	Nelson
Owen	Orchid	Ogden	Odessa
Pamela	Percy	Phyllis	Pat
Roger	Ruth	Roy	Ruby
Sarah	Sperry	Susan	Skip
Tip	Thelma	Thad	Tess
Vera	Vernon	Vanessa	Val
Wayne	Wynne	Warren	Winona

Note: Names are assigned in rotation, alphabetically. When the last name ("Winona") has been used, the sequence begins again with "Andy."

TYPHOON HAVENS

Severe tropical cyclones (hurricanes and typhoons) are among the most destructive weather phenomena that a ship or smaller craft may encounter, regardless of whether the ship or craft is in port or at sea. When faced with an approaching typhoon or hurricane, a ship's captain or master, and the skipper of a pleasure craft, must make vital decisions regarding the method of evasion. And these decisions must be reached *at an early stage*—not after the ship has been caught in the full fury of the typhoon.

Fundamentally, the questions are: (1) Should the ship remain in port, (2) Should the ship sortie from port and evade the typhoon at sea, or (3) If at sea, should the ship seek shelter offered by the harbor?

This decision should not be based on expected or forecast weather conditions alone. The decision should also be based on the loading and characteristics of the ship itself, as well as the characteristics of the harbor. And these harbor characteristics include: (1) the natural shelter provided by the harbor, (2) the port congestion, and (3) the port support facilities (both normal and emergency) available.

The U.S. Navy's Environmental Prediction Research Facility in Monterey, California, has published an excellent book on this subject, entitled *Typhoon Havens Handbook for the Western Pacific and Indian Oceans*, by Samson Brand and Jack W. Blelloch, June 1976. It is highly recommended that all who steam and sail these waters have a copy of this publication on board.

It is a gross oversimplification to label a harbor as merely "good" or "bad." It isn't that simple. Consequently, this publication presents a great deal of information about selected harbors in the area to aid commanding officers and masters of ships, and skippers of smaller craft, in reaching sound decisions with respect to their commands. The book also contains a wealth of information about particular geographical areas, including the details of individual ports and harbors, local topographical influences on tropical cyclones, and helpful guidelines for the decision maker as to whether to sortie and evade, or remain in port.

Fourteen ports have been evaluated and rated in the *Typhoon Havens Handbook*. These include Apra Harbor, Guam; Kaohsiung, Chilung (Keelung), Taiwan; Hong Kong; Yokosuka, Numazu, Iwakuni, Kure, Sasebo, Kagoshima, Japan; Buckner Bay, Naha, Okinawa; Subic Bay, Manila, Cebu, Philippines; Pusan, Inchon, Chinhae, South Korea; Diego Garcia, Chagos Islands; Columbo, Sri Lanka; Karachi, Pakistan; Auckland, New Zealand; and Sattahip, Thailand. Figure 4-29 is a locator map of the Western Pacific and Indian Oceans to assist readers with foggy memories, or those who are new to the area.

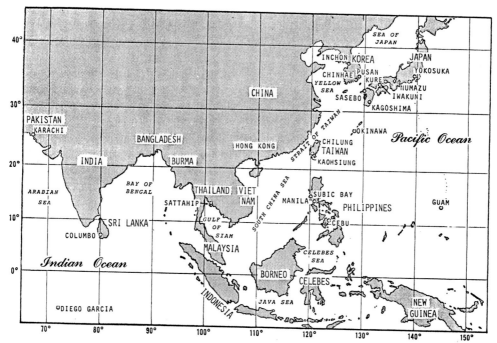

Figure 4-29. Locator map of Western Pacific and Indian Ocean area typhoon havens. For a detailed evaluation of each port/harbor, the reader is referred to the publication, *Typhoon Havens Handbook for the Western Pacific and Indian Oceans*, by Samson Brand and Jack W. Blelloch, June 1976, published by the U.S. Naval Environmental Research Facility, Monterey, California 93940.

5

Extratropical (Cold-Core) Lows and Storms

How little do the landsmen know
Of what we sailors feel,
When waves do mount and winds do blow!
But we have hearts of steel.
                    —The Sailor's Resolution,
                            Eighteenth Century

The words "hurricane!" and "typhoon!" have struck fear into the hearts of many a sailor and landlubber, alike. And justifiably so. These are dangerous phenomena to be reckoned with, and should be circumnavigated or avoided whenever possible. *But*, a temperate (or higher) latitude (cold-core) intense low-pressure system (cyclone) or storm at sea is also a potential danger to the most seasoned skipper. For, a 65-knot wind blowing undisturbed over the ocean for 10 hours will produce waves in excess of 40 feet in height with about a 9-second period, *regardless* of whether this wind was generated by a warm-core hurricane or typhoon, or by a cold-core extratropical storm. The tremendous force exerted by winds and waves does not discriminate between warm-core and cold-core cyclones. Great amounts of damage and life-threatening situations are caused by both phenomena. A mariner must be knowledgeable concerning both types of storm systems, for both produce heavy weather at sea.

CHARACTERISTICS

Compared to tropical cyclones (hurricanes and typhoons), extratropical cyclones are much more complex atmospheric phenomena.

There are several differences between tropical and extratropical cyclones. Some of the most important differences are the lack of symmetry of wind circulation, temperature and temperature distribution, pressure distribution, cloudiness, and precipitation in extratropical cyclones. Another important difference is that although the maximum winds associated with extratropical cyclones usually do not reach the maximum speeds of hurricanes and typhoons (115–180 knots), the high winds associated with extratropical cyclones cover a much larger geographical area. Also, the "eye" observed in hurricanes and typhoons is not found in extratropical cyclones. And rains are not as torrential in extratropical cyclones.

Whereas the "average" diameter of hurricanes and typhoons is of the order of 300–450 nautical miles, intense extratropical cyclones frequently have a diameter of almost 2,000 miles, sometimes extending from one side of the Atlantic (New England or Newfoundland) eastward to the British Isles.

Another very important difference is the distribution of maximum wind speeds around the center. In tropical cyclones, the maximum winds exist in the area immediately surrounding the center, decreasing in speed as one goes outward from the center. But in extratropical cyclones, the regions of maximum winds almost always exist in various shapes and patterns at some distance from the center—in the periphery, to the right of the direction of movement in the Northern Hemisphere, and to the left of the direction of movement in the Southern Hemisphere. Figure 5-1 is a schematic diagram illustrating the different distribution of hurricane-force winds (64 knots, or 74 mph, or 119 kph, or higher) around tropical and extratropical cyclones. The shaded areas represent the regions of hurricane-force winds.

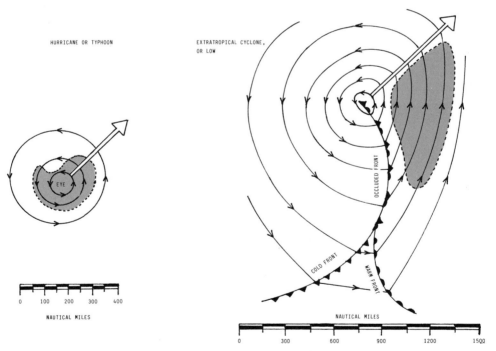

Figure 5-1. Schematic diagrams of the general distribution of hurricane-force winds (64 knots, 74 mph, 119 kph, or higher) around tropical (warm-core) and extratropical (cold-core) cyclones in the Northern Hemisphere. The shaded areas represent the regions of hurricane-force (or higher) winds. Large arrows indicate direction of storm movement. Hurricane "eye" not drawn to scale.

Extratropical cyclones are more numerous and most intense during the winter months, whereas tropical cyclones are characteristic of the summer season in each hemisphere.

Because of the high winds and the wind-generated high waves and seas created by extratropical cyclones—resulting in hazardous marine conditions—all mariners and pleasure boaters should know something about the characteristics, formation, tracks and movement, and decay of these atmospheric systems. Table 5-1 is a brief summary of extratropical (cold-core) cyclone characteristics. And figure 5-2 is a schematic diagram of some of the horizontal and vertical features of extratropical cyclones.

FORMATION

The fact that extratropical cyclones do not have the symmetry of tropical cyclones indicates that these cold-core storms are much involved with different types of air masses. Also, that these air masses are distributed unevenly around the center. As a matter of fact, it was through a comprehensive study of extratropical cyclones that the "air-mass concept" of modern meteorology was formulated over 50 years ago at the Geophysical Institute in Bergen, Norway.

As is the case with tropical cyclones, there are several theories (convection, thermal, eddy, frontal, etc.) which attempt to explain the formation of extratropical cyclones. But the formation of these phenomena is so complex that no single theory adequately answers *all* of the questions. For our purposes, however, perfect and infallible theory is not necessary. An elementary understanding of where and when extratropical cyclones (cold-core low-pressure systems) are likely to form, and an idea of the "danger signs," will serve our purpose.

Low-pressure systems, or simply lows, that develop over deserts (such as

Table 5-1. Brief summary of some of the more important characteristics of extratropical (cold-core) cyclones.

Weather:	Usually moderate to heavy rain or snow, depending upon temperature. *Stormy*.
Clouds:	Almost all types, ranging from low clouds to high clouds.
Circulation:	Winds spiraling inward in a counterclockwise fashion in the Northern Hemisphere. Winds spiraling inward in a clockwise fashion in the Southern Hemisphere.
Wind speeds:	Strong everywhere, except in the very center. Maximum winds are at some distance from the center.
Temperature:	Usually cold, or warm changing to cold.
Average movement:	In winter: 25 knots. In summer: 18 knots.
Size:	From 200 to 2,000 nautical miles.
Shape:	Circular or elliptical, and in between.
Marine threat:	Yes, definitely. Strong winds and wind-generated high waves and high seas.

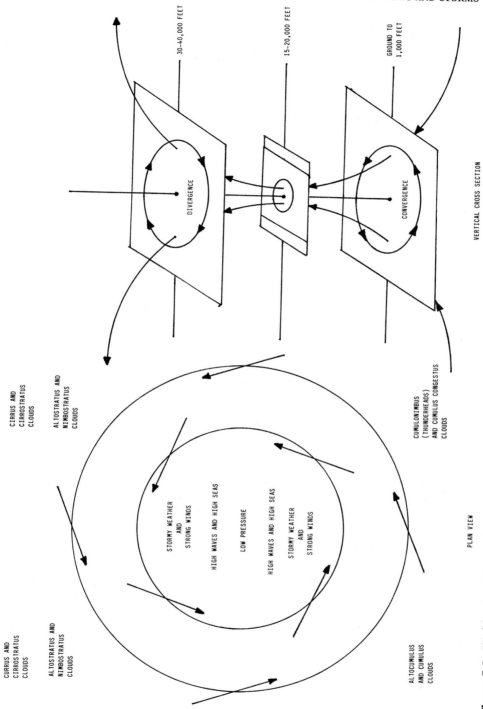

Figure 5-2. Highly simplified schematic diagram of some of the features of extratropical (cold-core) cyclones in the Northern Hemisphere.

"dust devils") are not of great interest to seafarers unless one is cruising in the Red Sea, the Persian Gulf, or similar waters.

Extratropical cyclones frequently form along weather fronts, and these lows *are* of great interest to mariners. Low-pressure systems that form on the leeward side of mountain ranges situated near the east coasts of continents are also of great interest to mariners, because these lows will soon move eastward over the sea. And extratropical low-pressure systems generated by the combination of irregular coastlines (such as the east coast of China and the Cape Hatteras area of the United States), and warm ocean currents (such as the Kuro Current in the western North Pacific and the Gulf Stream in the western North Atlantic) are of equal—and perhaps, greater—interest to mariners, as we shall discuss later in this chapter in connection with the development of "secondary" lows.

Since extratropical cyclones frequently form along weather fronts, they occur with greatest frequency in the higher mid-latitudes where the cold air masses and warm air masses meet along the polar and the arctic weather fronts. In the Northern Hemisphere, there is a maximum frequency of lows near 50°N in winter, and near 60°N in summer.

In the Atlantic, one of the most favored regions for the development of extratropical cyclones is off the Virginia coast and in the general area to the east of the southern Appalachian Mountains. These lows sometimes undergo almost explosive intensification and are often called "Hatteras Lows or Storms." They travel northeasterly along the Gulf Stream. Sometimes they eventually stagnate near Iceland or in the waters between Greenland and Labrador. Other times they produce dangerous storm conditions around the British Isles after having crossed the North Atlantic.

In the North Pacific, there is a broad band of frequent extratropical cyclone activity extending all the way from Southeast Asia northeastward to the Gulf of Alaska. Some storms, which form on the mid-Pacific polar front, take a more southerly track and eventually reach the west coast of the North American continent as far south as Southern California.

Figures 5-3a, b, c and figures 5-4a, b, c illustrate the early and late stages of development and decay of an extratropical cyclone along a weather front. Figure 5-3a shows a cold easterly air current north of a weather front, and a warm westerly air current to the south of the front. Because of a perturbation in atmospheric flow, a "wave" along the weather front begins to form, as shown in figure 5-3b. Since the atmospheric wave along the front is unstable, the amplitude increases with time and soon reaches the stage as shown in figure 5-3c, which is the so-called "cyclone model," after Professors J. Bjerknes and H. Solberg. According to the wave theory of cyclones, atmospheric waves are unstable only within a certain range of wave lengths. Waves shorter than about 400 miles are stable waves and do not develop. And waves longer than about 2,000 miles also do not develop. Atmospheric waves whose lengths lie between about 400 and 2,000 miles are unstable when there is sufficient wind shear along the weather front. Thus, *only unstable atmospheric waves develop into extratropical cyclones and storms.* And that's why these atmospheric waves are called cyclone waves.

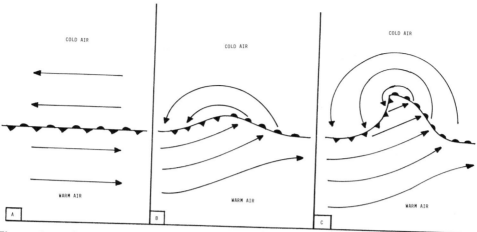

Figure 5-3. The development of an atmospheric extratropical wave cyclone up to the stage of the "cyclone model." (After Prof. S. Petterssen)

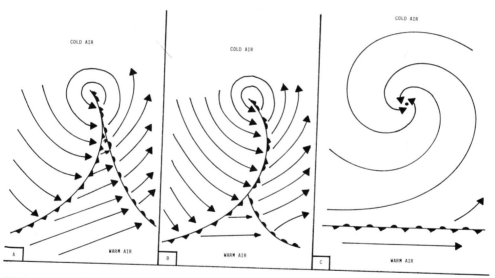

Figure 5-4. The later stages in the development and decay (dissipation) of an extratropical wave cyclone. (After Prof. S. Petterssen)

As shown in figures 5-3a and b, the extratropical wave continues to develop after it has reached the "cyclone-model" stage. After the amplitude of the wave continues to increase, the cold front overtakes the warm front, forming an occluded front (figure 5-4a). As the occlusion process continues, the occluded front increases in length (figure 5-4b). Finally, the occluded front dissolves (figure 5-4c), and the cyclone becomes a large whirl of more-or-less homogeneous air, to the north of a quasi-stationary (for the time being) weather front. And we're almost back to where we started.

Barometric pressure at the earth's surface varies by only a few percent (rarely more than 3 percent in 24 hours). Pressure changes in the vertical are *much* larger. Consequently, air converging (flowing together) in one layer of the atmosphere must be nearly compensated by air diverging (flowing apart) in another layer. Otherwise, barometric pressure at the earth's surface would rise or fall almost without limit.

Because the *mass* of the air is conserved, the air must travel vertically from layers of convergence to layers of divergence. When the air spirals inward toward the center of an extratropical cyclone, producing a strongly convergent flow, it is forced to rise vertically upward through the atmosphere. As the air rises, it is cooled adiabatically (no gain or loss of heat; cooled by expansion), the water vapor in the air condenses, clouds form, and precipitation in the form of rain or snow (depending upon temperature) results.

To compensate for the air spiralling rapidly inward (converging) toward the center of the cyclone at lower levels in the atmosphere, the air at high levels in the atmosphere must be spiralling outward (diverging) at an equal or faster rate. See, again, figure 5-2, vertical cross section. If this were not the case, the cyclone would "fill"—pressure could no longer be lower at the center of the cyclone than in its periphery—and the low-pressure system would disappear. Admittedly, this is an oversimplification. Any theory concerning the formation of cyclones must account for the innumerable details of convergence, divergence, the conservation of energy and mass, and many other factors.

The major extratropical cyclones affecting seafaring men (and women) are those associated with weather fronts, along which air masses of differing temperatures and densities collide and the warmer (lighter) air is forced to rise. When the convergence at lower levels and vertical currents (and the divergence aloft) are strong enough, a storm is born.

Intense extratropical cyclones are characterized by many types of clouds (as shown schematically in figure 5-2, plan view), ranging from high clouds to low clouds, moderate to heavy precipitation in the form of rain or snow (depending upon temperature), high winds that sometimes shift abruptly with strong gusts, high waves and confused high seas, and generally stormy conditions.

Whenever you experience the combination of a rapidly falling barometer, a steadily increasing wind, increasing waves and/or swell, and increasing middle and low clouds, *check immediately* with your local National Weather Service Office and/or the nearest U.S. Coast Guard Office. If you are under way, get on that radiotelephone! It doesn't pay to be overconfident.

TRACKS AND MOVEMENT, "SECONDARY" LOWS, AND METEOROLOGICAL "BOMBS"

Tracks and Movement

Extratropical cyclones travel at varying speeds in each hemisphere. And sometimes they remain stationary for a day or two. During the summer months, these lows travel about 432 nautical miles per day (an average speed of about 18 knots). And during the winter months, they travel about 600 nautical miles per day (an average speed of about 25 knots). In general, these lows are much more stormy and much more sharply defined in winter than in summer.

North of latitude 30°N and south of latitude 30°S, extratropical cyclones generally move from west to east. Consequently, a low-pressure system located to the west of your position will probably envelop you at some near-future time, depending on the speed and exact direction of movement of the system, your distance from the low-pressure system, and your own course and speed. Sometimes, however, these systems do not "follow the rule." They *may* "dissolve" before reaching your position. They *may* remain stationary for a short time or a long period of time. They *may* travel in primarily a north-south direction (instead of eastward). Or, they *may* even retrograde toward the west. One should use the "easterly movement rule" with a certain caution and a great deal of prudence.

Extratropical cyclones do have favorite tracks around the world in each hemisphere. These tracks are illustrated in figure 5-5. The solid arrows show the principal tracks. And the dashed arrows show the secondary tracks. All tracks are for the winter season in each hemisphere (Dec., Jan., Feb. in the Northern Hemisphere, and June, July, Aug. in the Southern Hemisphere).

"Secondary" Lows

Cyclogenesis—a new term in our vocabulary—simply means the development of a new cyclone (or low-pressure system), or the strengthening of an older cyclonic circulation in the atmosphere. It is applied to the development of a cyclonic circulation where previously one did not exist, as well as to the intensification of existing cyclonic flow. While cyclogenesis usually occurs together with *deepening* (a decrease in atmospheric pressure), the two terms should not be used synonymously.

Secondary cyclones (or lows) are cyclones that form near, or in association with, primary cyclones. For example, secondary cyclones often form along the east coast of the United States, especially in the vicinity of Cape Hatteras, North Carolina—becoming a hazard to east coast sailors—when a primary cyclone is present over the Great Lakes region. Across the Atlantic, secondary cyclones frequently form to the SW of Ireland when there is a strong primary cyclone in the vicinity of Iceland. And secondary cyclones frequently form in the Baltic area when a primary cyclone is present near the coast of Norway.

Center jump is another term frequently used by meteorologists. It means the formation of a second pressure center within a well-developed low-pressure system. The original low-pressure center diminishes in magnitude as the new center deepens. And the center of the cyclone appears to "jump" from the first to the second point of low pressure.

There are several features to look for on a weather map in determining future areas of possible cyclogenesis (and marine threat). These may be kinematic (motion) symptoms, dynamic (force in relation to motion or equilibrium) symptoms, or a combination of both.

In scientific circles, the word *tendency* means the local rate of change of a

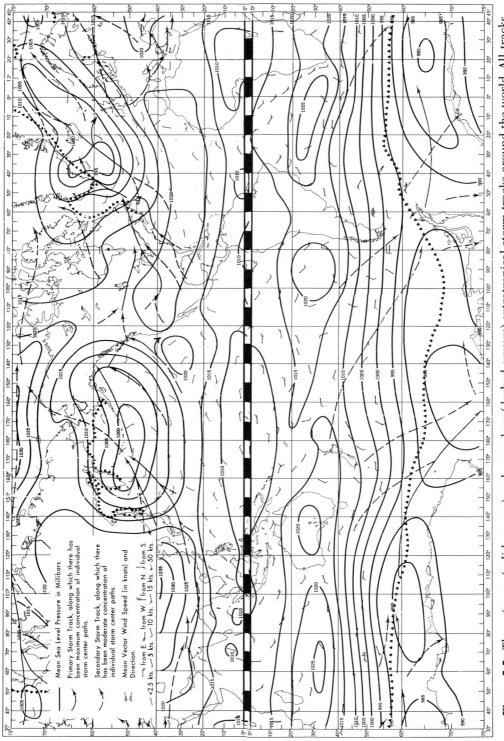

Figure 5-5. The primary (solid arrows) and secondary (dashed arrows) extratropical storm tracks around the world. All tracks are average tracks for the winter season in each hemisphere (Dec., Jan., Feb. in the Northern Hemisphere and June, July, Aug. in the Southern Hemisphere). (Source: *U.S. Navy Marine Climatic Atlas of the World*, vol. 8, 1969)

vector or scalar quantity with time at a given point in space. And as used by meteorologists, the term *pressure tendency* (or *barometric tendency*) means the atmospheric *pressure change* for a three-hour (or other specified) period, ending at the time of observation.

One good way of determining where cyclogenesis, or the development of a secondary cyclone, is likely to occur, is to examine the pressure tendencies along a weather front. An ordinary, steadily advancing cold front will usually have the strongest rising pressure tendencies behind it in its northeast portion. The tendencies then decrease in magnitude fairly regularly as one proceeds toward the SW along the front, as shown in figure 5-6. If, however, instead of this "normal" distribution of pressure tendencies behind a cold front, a secondary maximum of pressure tendency occurs behind the front, as shown in figure 5-7, a new frontal wave development, or secondary cyclone development (cyclogenesis), is probably imminent.

Another feature to look for on a weather map is the component of the wind normal to (at 90° to) the weather front. Along one section of the front, it may be

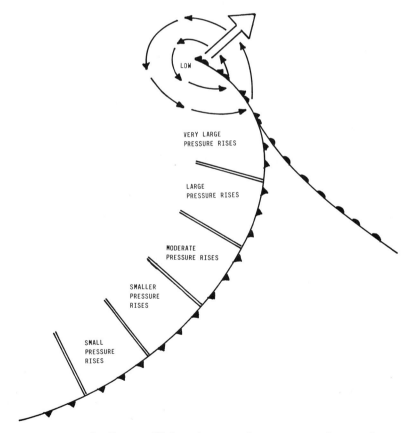

Figure 5-6. The "normal" distribution of pressure tendencies behind an ordinary, steadily advancing cold front.

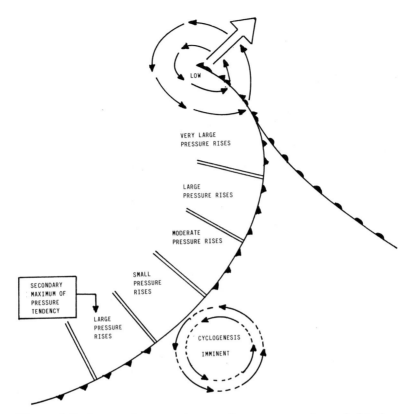

Figure 5-7. A secondary maximum of pressure tendency behind an advancing cold front usually means that cyclogenesis, or a new secondary low-pressure system, is imminent.

stronger than along another section, as shown in figure 5-8. This will cause the front to move more rapidly where the wind component normal to the front is stronger, and retard it where the wind component is lighter. A wave then develops along the weather front, and if other conditions are favorable, a secondary low develops and deepens.

Dynamic considerations such as the effect of atmospheric perturbations in the vicinity, the intrusion of a deep, cold air mass, and the effects of mountain barriers all contribute to cyclogenesis and the formation of secondary low-pressure systems. The difference in the coefficient of friction of air blowing over a land surface and of air blowing over a water surface must also be taken into account. Friction is less over water, and the air blowing over the water accelerates relative to the air blowing over land.

The reason that cyclogenesis and the development of secondary lows is so important to seafarers is that these processes in the atmosphere can—and frequently do—occur with such explosive development (especially off Cape Hatteras

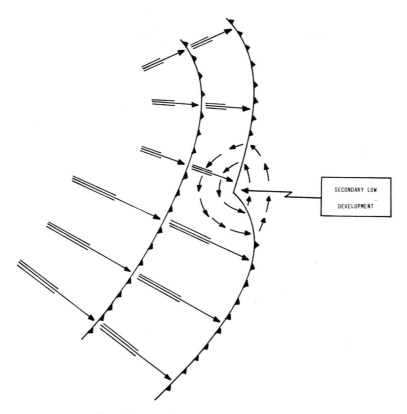

Figure 5-8. When the wind component normal (at 90°) to a weather front is stronger along one section than along another section, this will cause the front to move more rapidly where the wind component is stronger. A wave development or secondary low will result.

and off the SW coast of Ireland) that many sailors (and even meteorologists) have been caught completely off guard. Sometimes with disastrous results.

Secondary lows in each hemisphere almost always develop on the equatorial side of the primary low, and circulate around it in the general air flow—but at the same time, participating in the general movement of the system as a whole. It is unusual for the secondary low to complete more than half a revolution around the primary low because the primary low is usually then decreasing in intensity as the secondary increases in intensity. In this case, the secondary low becomes the dominating circulation. Under these circumstances, the secondary may absorb the primary, or the primary may remain as a shallow and relatively weak area of low pressure—only a large bulge in the isobars of the secondary low.

When a secondary low attains the appropriate size, depth, and intensity of the primary low, the centers then rotate counterclockwise (in the Northern Hemisphere) or clockwise (in the Southern Hemisphere) around the point midway between them, at the same time both advancing with the speed and direction of motion of the system as a whole. Remember our discussion of the "Fujiwhara effect" in chapter 2?

The region *between* a primary low and a secondary low is frequently one of weak pressure gradients and, consequently, light and variable winds. On the equatorial side of the secondary low, strong pressure gradients are the rule. This results in gale- or storm-force winds (and sometimes hurricane-force winds) at much greater distances from the primary low than originally forecast, while only light winds may occur in the vicinity of the primary low where gale- or storm-force winds were originally predicted.

Intense secondary low-pressure systems are accompanied by a rapidly falling barometer (in advance of the system), high winds, low clouds, heavy precipitation, only fair to poor visibility, and high waves and seas. And because of their potential for unexpected and "explosive" development, they constitute a particular threat to mariners.

Figures 5-9 through 5-17 are a magnificent sequence of GOES weather satellite views of the process of strong cyclogenesis and the subsequent explosive development of an intense secondary cyclone between the peninsula of Florida and Cape Hatteras, North Carolina. The sequence shows the rapid development and intensification of the extratropical low as it meanders and travels northeastward along the Gulf Stream, and its eventual merging with another low-pressure system that later swept northeastward from the vicinity of Cape Hatteras. The arrows indicate the center of this intense secondary low-pressure system.

Meteorological "Bombs"

Meteorologists have known for decades that many extratropical cyclones "deepen" (a decrease in central pressure) very rapidly—almost "explosively." But it wasn't until about 1979 that such a descriptive term as "bomb" was applied to the process.

In an excellent paper entitled "Synoptic-Dynamic Climatology of the 'Bomb,'" published in the *Monthly Weather Review*, volume 108, October 1980, by the American Meteorological Society, Professors Frederick Sanders and John R. Gyakum of M.I.T. defined a meteorological "bomb" as an extratropical surface cyclone whose central pressure fall averages at least one millibar per hour for 24 hours.

Professors Sanders and Gyakum studied this explosive cyclogenesis in the Northern Hemisphere during the period September 1976–May 1979. They found meteorological bombs to be primarily maritime, cold-season events. They also found that bombs most usually occur about 400 nautical miles downstream from a moving trough of low pressure at about 18,000–20,000 feet in the atmosphere, within or on the poleward side of the maximum westerly winds aloft, and within or ahead of the planetary-scale troughs of low pressure.

Professors Sanders and Gyakum found further that this explosive development occurs over a wide range of sea-surface temperature, but that it occurs preferentially near the strongest sea-surface temperature *gradients* (where the

Figure 5-9. GOES weather satellite view of strong cyclogenesis taking place between the peninsula of Florida and Cape Hatteras, North Carolina, on 11 November 1981. (Courtesy of National Air Survey Center Corp.)

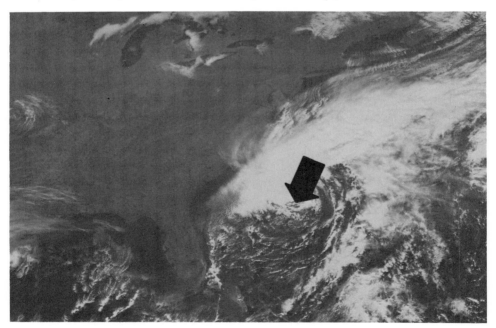

Figure 5-10. GOES weather satellite view on 12 November 1981 of conditions shortly after the explosive development of the extratropical cyclone to the SE of Cape Hatteras, North Carolina. Center is at tip of arrow (Courtesy of National Air Survey Center Corp.)

Figure 5-11. GOES weather satellite view on 13 November 1981 shows that as the center of the low (at tip of arrow) moved northeastward along the Gulf Stream, it continued to intensify. (Courtesy of National Air Survey Center Corp.)

Figure 5-12. GOES weather satellite view on 14 November 1981 shows the low-pressure center (at tip of arrow) continuing to intensify as it oscillates very slowly in almost the same location for the past 24 hours. (Courtesy of National Air Survey Corp.)

Figure 5-13. GOES weather satellite on 15 November 1981 shows that the extratropical cyclone center (at tip of arrow) has moved only a very short distance toward the NE in the last 24 hours as it continues to intensify. Cold air from the Canadian Provinces now begins to inject itself into the vortex. Another weather system in the central United States begins to intensify as it moves eastward. (Courtesy of National Air Survey Center Corp.)

Figure 5-14. GOES weather satellite view on 16 November 1981 shows that the intense extratropical low center (at tip of arrow) has traveled very slowly northeastward in the last 24 hours as it expands laterally. The intensifying weather system from the central United States continues to move eastward. (Courtesy of National Air Survey Center Corp.)

Figure 5-15. GOES weather satellite view on 17 November 1981 shows that the center of the extratropical low-pressure system (at tip of arrow) has accelerated its movement toward the NE in the last 24 hours. The second intensifying low-pressure system, which the day before was located to the south of the Great Lakes region, has moved rapidly ESE'ward and is now located in the vicinity of Cape Hatteras. (Courtesy of National Air Survey Center Corp.)

Figure 5-16. GOES weather satellite view on 18 November 1981 shows the two extratropical low-pressure systems merging into one huge cyclonic circulation off the New England and Canadian coasts in the northwestern Atlantic. (Courtesy of National Air Survey Center Corp.)

Figure 5-17. GOES weather satellite view on 19 November 1981 shows that the two individual low-pressure centers are now indistinguishable, and a huge cyclonic circulation now dominates the entire western North Atlantic Ocean area. (Courtesy of National Air Survey Center Corp.)

temperature changes the greatest amount in the shortest distance). Interestingly, they found that these storms develop along the leading edge of an outbreak of bitterly cold air over the western Atlantic, but that the cold air does not actually penetrate to the very center of the low.

Obviously, this phenomenon should be of great interest to naval captains, merchant marine masters, and the skippers of pleasure craft, for it poses considerable hazard and threat to all. The tragic loss of life in the Fastnet Yacht Race off the British Isles, 11–14 August 1979, was attributable to a rare summer meteorological "bomb." This will be discussed in the following section.

Sanders and Gyakum also found that pronounced frequency maxima of meteorological bombs occur north of latitude 25°N in the westernmost portions of both the Atlantic and Pacific oceans, within or just to the north of the warm waters of the Gulf Stream in the Atlantic and the Kuroshio in the Pacific. They suggest that there is a second area of bomb generation in the Pacific between longitudes 160°W and 170°W. They also found that in the Atlantic there are extensions of modest bomb frequency north of latitude 50°N to the east of Labrador, and also in an extended region from the western approaches to Ireland and the United Kingdom to the Barents Sea. Figure 5-18 shows the approximate geographical areas of meteorological bomb events for the Atlantic and Pacific basins in 1978–1979.

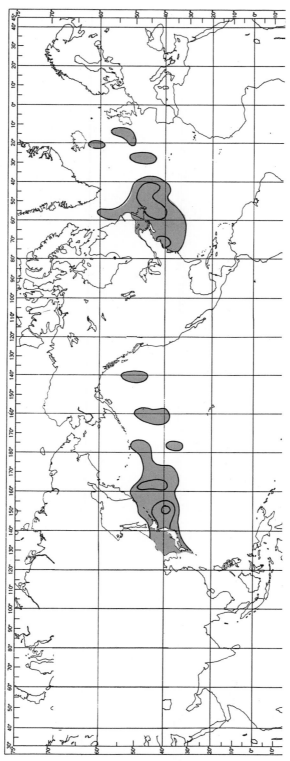

Figure 5-18. Approximate major geographical areas of meteorological "bomb" events for the Atlantic and Pacific basins in 1978–79. (After Sanders and Gyakum)

Professors Sanders and Gyakum found further that there is a notable lack of explosive cyclogenesis in the Aleutians and in the Greenland-Iceland area, where mean winter atmospheric pressure is lowest and cyclone frequency is highest. Their data confirm the prevailing view of meteorologists that these regions are the graveyards, or resting places, of migratory cyclones, rather than areas of meteorological bomb development. According to Sanders and Gyakum, bomb frequency in the Northern Hemisphere peaks during the month of January, when about two bombs occur each three days.

All mariners must be on their guard against the threat of meteorological bombs. During the Atlantic bomb of 10 September 1978, the central pressure of the storm fell to 955 millibars (28.2 inches) with a deepening of 50 millibars (1.48 inches) in 24 hours—a rate of 2.083 millibars per hour for 24 hours! In this storm, the dragger *Captain Cosmo* was lost, and the luxury liner *Queen Elizabeth II* was damaged.

It is interesting to note that Professors Sanders and Gyakum found that although bomb frequency is about half again larger in the Pacific than in the Atlantic, more than twice as many *extreme* bombs occur in the Atlantic.

A further word of caution. Sanders and Gyakum conclude that their study sample underestimates both the frequency and intensity of intense oceanic cyclogenesis. This means that every skipper should keep a very close weather eye on *pressure changes*, wind, seas, and cloud formations to avoid (or at least minimize) the threat of meteorological bombs.

METEOROLOGICAL ASPECTS OF THE FASTNET YACHT RACE DISASTER
11–14 August 1979

For centuries, British history and tradition have been strongly linked with the sea. And the biennial Fastnet Yacht Race (conducted to the south of the British Isles) is an integral part of this tradition. This race is also a real test of seamanship and diverse nautical skills, and " a supreme challenge to ocean racing yachtsmen in British waters."

The course of the Fastnet Race is from Cowes, Isle of Wight, direct as safe navigation permits to the Fastnet Rock, then back to Plymouth, passing to the south of the Isles of Scilly and Bishop Rock, a course distance of approximately 605 nautical miles. The course of the Fastnet Race is shown in figure 5-19.

During the 1979 Fastnet Race, a "meteorological bomb" detonated in the midst of the racing fleet on the night of 13–14 August. Maximum wind gusts as high as 68–80 knots and steep maximum wave heights of 50+ feet were estimated by competitors and search-and-rescue aircraft crews. At the height of the storm, most competitors were scattered between Land's End and Fastnet Rock. Ships and especially smaller craft in this area are vulnerable to high winds and seas from directions of about SSE through SW to NW. There is no barrier (land mass) protection from the wind, and converging deep-ocean wave and/or swell trains can be drastically steepened under certain conditions of wave/swell period and by the shallowing of bottom contours as one approaches the land masses.

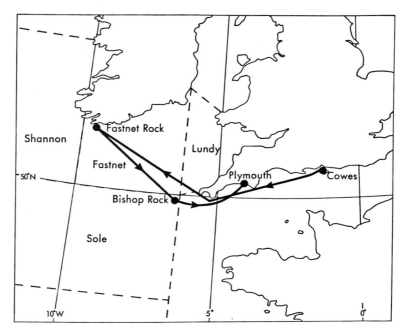

Figure 5-19. The course of the Fastnet Race. (Source: "The Fastnet Race—A Forecaster's Viewpoint," by A. Woodroffe, *Meteorological Magazine*, vol. 110, 1981) (Reproduced with permission of
the Controller of Her Britannic Majesty's Stationery Office)

Extreme weather and sea conditions the night of 13–14 August 1979 resulted in the tragic loss of 15 lives. Of the 303 yachts which started the race,
only 85 finished. And 24 yachts were abandoned to the elements.

The first race over this course was sailed in 1925, and races have been sailed
every other year with the exception of the period of World War II (1939–1945).
Through the years, a number of Fastnet Races have been sailed in gale force
winds, but none with such tragic consequences as occurred in 1979.

The meteorological bomb that burst in the midst of the Fastnet competitors
the night of 13–14 August began as a weak low-pressure system in the United
States on 9 August, traveling eastward. At this time, no forecaster could
possibly have guessed or predicted the marine tragedies and deaths that this
low would cause within four days. And no computer, regardless of how finely
"tuned," could do any better.

Saturday, 11 August

At 1230 Greenwich Mean Time (GMT), a total of 303 yachts sailed from Cowes
on the Isle of Wight at the start of the Fastnet Race. This race is organized by
the Royal Ocean Racing Club (RORC) and is part of the series of international
yacht races that count toward the Admiral's Cup trophy. Figure 5-20 shows the
locations and central pressures of the major highs and lows and the weather
fronts. At this time, the weak low-pressure system that would become the
"meteorological bomb" of 13–14 August was located over Nova Scotia. The

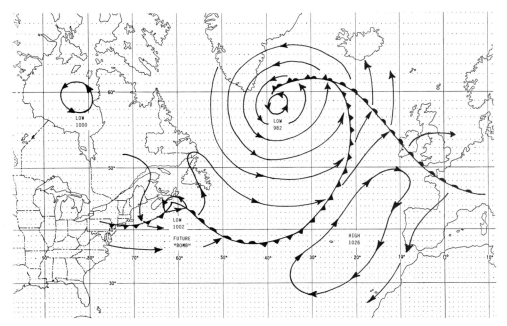

Figure 5-20. Locations of major surface weather fronts and high- and low-pressure systems (central pressures in millibars) at 1200 GMT, Saturday 11 August 1979, near starting time of the Fastnet Race.

central pressure was 1002 millibars (29.589 in.). A major low-pressure system with a central pressure of 982 millibars (28.998 in.) was located 220 N.M. to the SE of the southern tip of Greenland, and was moving NE'ward at 13 knots. A third vortex with a central pressure of 1000 millibars (29.530 in.) was almost stationary over Hudson Bay. The ridge of the Azores high-pressure cell (anticyclone), oriented NE-SW and with a central pressure of 1026 millibars (30.298 in.), was inching its way toward the British Isles. Figure 5-21 is a weather satellite's view of the NE'ern Atlantic near the time of the start of the 1979 Fastnet Race.

Most ironically, the primary worries of the racing competitors at the start of the race were the possible future lack of wind and the increasing possibility of sea fog.

At high levels in the atmosphere, westerly winds of 130 knots were propagating over the central North Atlantic region. The future meteorological bomb was situated about 175 N.M. to the south of the jet stream.

Sunday, 12 August

Meteorological and oceanographic conditions developed almost as expected (and predicted) by the forecasters. As shown in figure 5-22, the major low-pressure system located the previous day to the SE of Greenland drifted NE'ward and split into two individual cells with central pressures of 986 millibars (29.117 in.). A cold front was approaching the Fastnet course from

Figure 5-21. TIROS-N weather satellite image of the NE'ern Atlantic area on Saturday, 11 August 1979, 3½ hours after the start of the Fastnet Race. (Courtesy of National Air Survey Center Corp.)

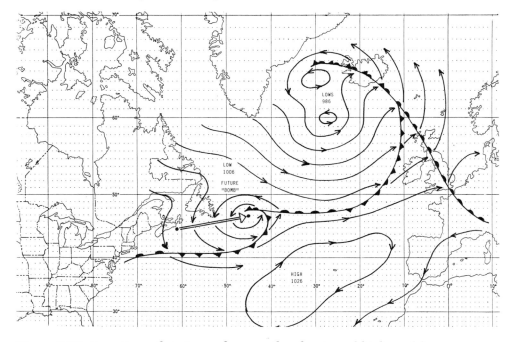

Figure 5-22. Locations of major surface weather fronts and high- and low-pressure systems (central pressures in millibars) at 1200 GMT, Sunday 12 August 1979.

the west. The future bomb was now traveling eastward at about 30–40 knots, and was located approximately 300 N.M. east of Newfoundland. But the central pressure had *risen* by four millibars in the last 24 hours as the eastward movement of the low accelerated. The ridge of the Azores high-pressure cell that had been approaching the Fastnet course receded 450 N.M. toward the SW in the last 24 hours. *But*, the track of the future bomb was moving closer under the main axis of the jet stream at high levels in the atmosphere. Figures 5-23 and 5-24 show the TIROS-N weather satellite's views of the eastern and western North Atlantic regions, respectively, on 12 August 1979.

Monday, 13 August

0000–1200 GMT. This was a very difficult situation for the weather and oceanographic forecasters. A complete dearth of information within a 350-N.M. radius of the low-pressure system destined to become a meteorological bomb in the future confronted the forecasters when they relieved the watch in the early morning hours. The nearest weather/oceanographic observation was from the Ocean Station Weather Ship "Charlie" (52.7°N-35.5°W), which was well outside the circulation of the potential bomb. The weather ship's report gave no clue as to the central pressure or intensity of the low-pressure system.

A post-analysis of the situation, as illustrated in figure 5-25, shows that by 1200 GMT, the now rapidly developing low-pressure system was located a mere 250 N.M. west of Fastnet Rock. The central pressure had fallen to 997 millibars (29.441 in.), a pressure drop of 9 millibars in the last 24 hours, and a drop of 5 millibars in the last 6 hours. The bottom was now just beginning to drop out of things. Also, the jet stream at higher levels in the atmosphere near 33,000 feet had increased to over 150 knots along latitude 50°N. The mean E'ward translational speed of the surface low-pressure system during the period 12/1800 GMT – 13/0600 GMT was approximately 51 knots!

1200-1800 GMT. About noon, the pressure tendency at Ocean Station Weather Ship "Romeo" (47.0°N-16.9°W), approximately 240 N.M. SSE of the potential bomb, experienced an accelerated fall of 5 millibars/3 hours, accompanied by an increase in surface wind from 20 to 32 knots. But again, meteorologists were uncertain about the exact position and the central pressure of the potential bomb because there were no ship weather reports within about a 200-N.M. radius of the estimated position of the center.

As the winds at Ocean Station Weather Ship "Romeo" continued to increase to 40 knots, it was clear to the forecasters that the potential bomb was beginning to decelerate in E'ward translational speed and that the pressure falls in the center of the low were increasing (i.e., the low was beginning to "deepen" rapidly). Figure 5-26 shows the surface weather situation at 1800 GMT, with the detonating meteorological bomb now located approximately 180 N.M. WSW of Fastnet Rock. Figure 5-27, the TIROS-N weather satellite view of the afternoon situation, shows that the low is definitely "deepening." The cloud system had developed a marked "comma" shape, indicating that the circulation was increasing rapidly. Compare this cloud configuration with figure 5-24.

During the period from 12/1800–13/1800 GMT, the central pressure of the

Figure 5-23. TIROS-N weather satellite image of the NE'ern Atlantic area on Sunday, 12 August 1979, approximately 27½ hours after the start of the Fastnet Race. (Courtesy of National Air Survey Center Corp.)

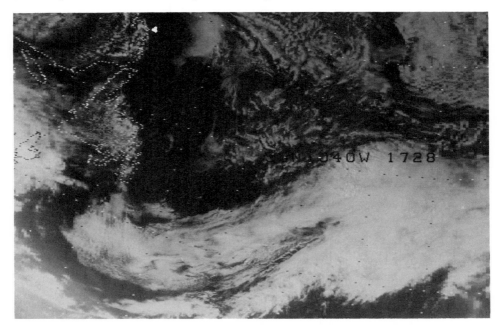

Figure 5-24. TIROS-N weather satellite image of NW'ern Atlantic area on Sunday, 12 August 1979. The future "meteorological bomb" is in the lower right of the picture. (Courtesy of National Air Survey Center Corp.)

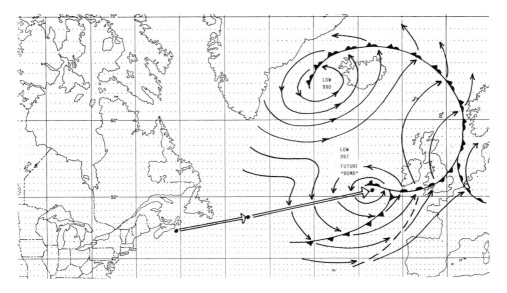

Figure 5-25. Locations of major surface weather fronts and low-pressure systems (central pressures in millibars) at 1200 GMT, Monday 13 August 1979.

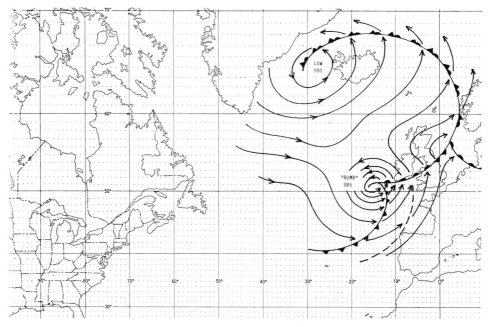

Figure 5-26. Locations of major surface weather fronts and low-pressure systems (central pressures in millibars) at 1800 GMT, Monday 13 August 1979.

Figure 5-27. TIROS-N weather satellite image of the developing "meteorological bomb" to the west of Ireland on the afternoon of Monday, 13 August 1979. Note in particular the "comma" shape of the cloud system, indicating that the low-pressure system is "deepening" and that the circulation is increasing. (Courtesy of National Air Survey Center Corp.)

low decreased from 1006 millibars to 985 millibars, a drop of 21 millibars in 24 hours (0.88 mb/hr). In the last 12 hours, the central pressure fell from 1002 millibars to 985 millibars, a drop of 17 millibars in 12 hours (1.42 mb/hr). And in the last 6 hours, the pressure fell from 997 millibars to 985 millibars, a drop of 12 millibars (2.0 mb/hr).

At 1625 GMT, the British Meteorological Office issued a FORCE 8 GALE WARNING (34–40 knots) for the Fastnet Race course area. And at 1705 GMT, the warning was upgraded to SOUTHWEST GALE FORCE 9 (41-47 knots).

1800–2400 GMT. Steadily accelerating pressure falls in SW Ireland confirmed that a meteorological bomb was about to envelop the valiant Fastnet racing fleet. But unfortunately, as luck would have it, three ship reports that were nearest to the low-pressure center reported pressures that were wrong or incorrectly encoded. Again, a degree of uncertainty was thrust upon the forecasters.

Figure 5-28 shows the surface weather situation at 13/2400 GMT (or 14/0000 GMT), with the meteorological bomb centered approximately 90 N.M. NW of Fastnet Rock and adjacent to the SW coast of Ireland. The central pressure of the low-pressure system had dropped from 985 millibars (29.087 in.) to 978 millibars (28.880 in.) in the last 6 hours, an additional 7 millibars.

At 2145 GMT, the British Meteorological Office issued a new warning of

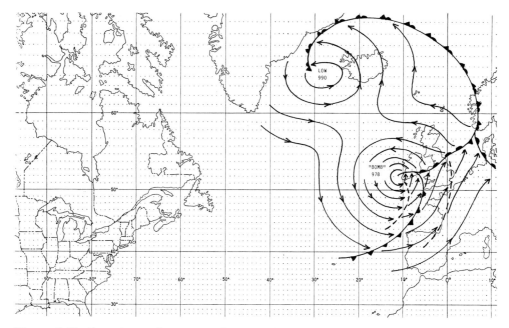

Figure 5-28. Locations of major surface weather fronts and the "meteorological bomb" with a central pressure of 978 millibars (28.880 in.) at 0000 GMT, Tuesday 14 August 1979.

SOUTHWEST GALE FORCE 9 (41–47 knots) INCREASING TO FORCE 10 (48–55 knots).

Between 13/1800 GMT and 14/0000 GMT, the cold front accelerated E'ward out of the primary trough of low pressure. This is not unusual in explosively developing low-pressure systems.

Tuesday, 14 August

0000–1200 GMT. At 0250 GMT, an additional warning was issued, indicating that the worst was yet to come, and that surface winds would shift abruptly from SW to NW within the next six hours. Mean wind speeds of 55 knots with maximum gusts as high as 80 knots, and steep maximum wave heights of 50 + feet, are considered entirely realistic in a situation such as this.

The rapid wind shift from SW to NW as the trough of low pressure swept across the Fastnet Course from west to east during the night resulted in the strong, gusty winds and the very high waves and swells coming from different directions. This made conditions especially difficult, particularly during hours of darkness. Many highly experienced competitors stated later that although wind conditions were somewhat difficult, it was the chaotic and unusual sea conditions that provided the greatest hazard and were the most dangerous they had ever experienced.

Figures 5-29 and 5-30 show the surface weather situations at 0600 GMT and 1200 GMT, respectively. The central pressure of the storm steadied at 980

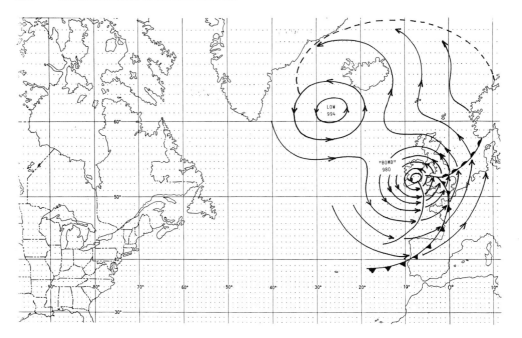

Figure 5-29. Locations of major surface weather fronts and the "meteorological bomb" with a central pressure of 980 millibars (28.939 in.) at 0600 GMT, Tuesday 14 August 1979.

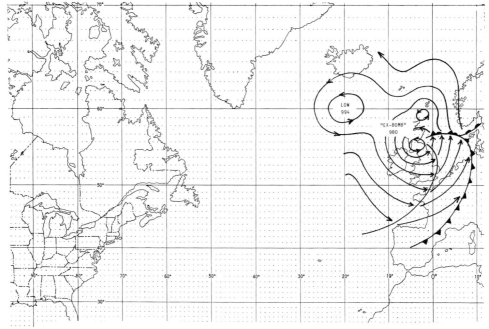

Figure 5-30. Locations of major surface weather fronts and the "meteorological ex-bomb" with a central pressure of 980 millibars (28.939 in.) at 1200 GMT, Tuesday 14 August 1979.

millibars (28.939 in.) as it moved NE'ward across Ireland and into eastern Scotland, causing considerable damage en route in Wales and the western Midlands.

Note the Fujiwhara effect of the two lows upon each other from figures 5-26, 5-28, 5-29, and 5-30. As the original low in the vicinity of Iceland moves SE'ward, the meteorological bomb moves NE'ward, the two lows rotating about a point between them.

At 1200 GMT, the storm continued its NE'ward movement, increasing its distance from the Fastnet course and allowing weather and sea conditions to subside slowly. Figure 5-31 shows the TIROS-N weather satellite view of the area in mid-afternoon. Conditions are beginning to improve. And figure 5-32 shows the TIROS-N weather satellite view of much-improved conditions over the British Isles on the afternoon of Wednesday, 15 August. *But,* look at what is approaching from the west!

Figure 5-33 is a continuity plot of the track and central pressure of the meteorological bomb from 0000 GMT, Saturday 11 August 1979 to 1200 GMT, Tuesday 14 August 1979.

In Retrospect

Because of explosively developing meteorological and oceanographic conditions, the 1979 Fastnet Race demanded special knowledge, skill, and courage on the part of all competitors, which they exhibited.

At the most crucial times meteorological and oceanographic reports and

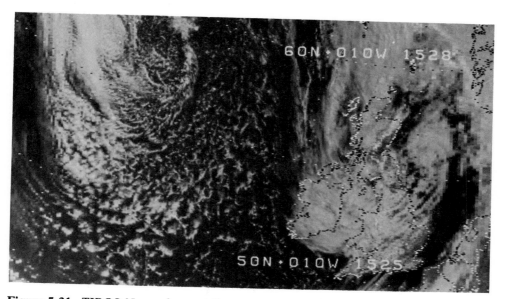

Figure 5-31. TIROS-N weather satellite image of the NE'ward moving "ex-bomb" blanketing the British Isles at mid-afternoon on Tuesday, 14 August 1979. (Courtesy of National Air Survey Center Corp.)

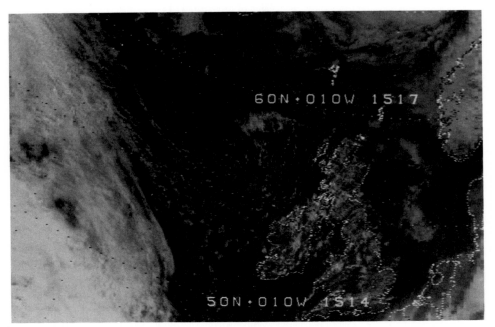

Figure 5-32. TIROS-N weather satellite image of greatly improved weather conditions over the British Isles after the storm headed for the Norwegian Sea in the afternoon of Wednesday, 15 August 1979. But is that another threat approaching from the west? (Courtesy of National Air Survey Center Corp.)

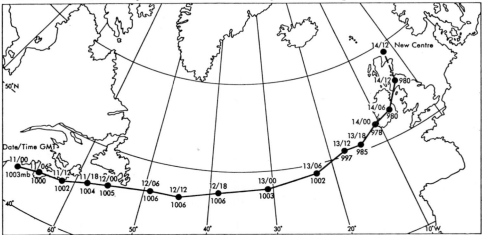

Figure 5-33. Continuity plot of the track and central pressures (millibars) of the "meteorological bomb" from 0000 GMT, Saturday 11 August 1979 to 1200 GMT, Tuesday 14 August 1979. (Source: "The Fastnet Race—A Forecaster's Viewpoint," by A. Woodroffe, *Meteorological Magazine*, vol. 110, 1981) (Reproduced with permission of the Controller of Her Britannic Majesty's Stationery Office.)

information from the ships at sea pertaining to the meteorological bomb were not available to analysts and forecasters. These dedicated individuals did all (and more) that could be expected of them.

Controversy will probably persist as to the nature of the greatest threat (i.e., strong winds and high seas coming from different directions, or the extreme steepness of the huge waves before winds and waves differed in direction— also, the exact cause of the excessive steepness of the waves).

For readers who desire detailed information on the 1979 Fastnet Race, the following literature is highly recommended:

The 1979 Fastnet Race Inquiry Report of the Royal Yachting Association (RYA) and the Royal Ocean Racing Club (RORC), by Sir Hugh Forbes, Sir Maurice Laing, and Lieutenant Colonel James Myatt, 1979.

"The Storm," by Alan Watts, which appeared in *Yachting World*, October, 1979.

"Tracking a Killer Storm," by Robert B. Rice, which appeared in *Sail*, October 1979.

"The Fastnet Storm—A Forecaster's Viewpoint," by A. Woodroffe, which appeared in the *Meteorological Magazine*, volume 110, 1981.

6

Yacht and Vessel Design for Heavy Weather

That splendour of fine bows which could
stand the shock of rollers never checked
by land.
  —*Ships*, John Masefield, 1916

Aside from the meteorology associated with the 1979 Fastnet Race, there are
obviously other important aspects of the tragic event needing careful study to
help avoid any repeat occurrences. These aspects include a reexamination of
the risks involved in ocean racing, further thought about heavy-weather seamanship and how small yachts should be handled in survival conditions,
reevaluation of safety gear, and investigations into the seaworthiness of the
type of yachts participating in the race. Studies have already been made of
these matters, and they will most probably continue for some time to come.
Although it seems unlikely that there will ever be any standard or pat solution
to the problems involved, a lot has been learned or relearned already, and it is
not too early to draw a number of valid conclusions.

WHOLESOME CHARACTERISTICS FOR SAILING YACHTS

Regarding sailing yacht design, it seems fair to say that over the last few
decades there have been many boats designed for ocean racing that are a far
cry from wholesome types suitable for the worst kind of weather offshore. In
fact, there has been a gradual trend toward pure racing boats with a number of
unseaworthy characteristics, which have been encouraged by some of the
handicap measurement rating rules. In the opinion of many knowledgeable
yachtsmen, a particular culprit has been the International Offshore Rule
(IOR) under which the 1979 Fastnet racers were competing and to which rule
the vast majority of the participating boats were designed. By no means are all
IOR designs unseaworthy, but there is little doubt that many of the smaller,
more extreme types have some unwholesome, even dangerous features for
very heavy weather offshore. These include extremely broad beam, very light

displacement, shallow underbody, high center of gravity, too much flare or flam, and excessively high freeboard, all of which increase vulnerability to capsizing. Other features such as an exceedingly tall rig; a very fine entrance together with lack of sheer and a sharp, knuckle forefoot; lack of overhangs; and an extremely short fin keel contribute to burying and/or handling and directional control difficulties. Extremely light displacement; flat areas of the hull; fins and skegs that are not faired into or integrated with the hull; and very tall, lightly constructed masts may also result in scantlings that are far from adequate for the worst weather at sea.

Susceptibility to capsize can be estimated most readily from hydrostatic analysis, and indeed this is a long-accepted practice in naval architecture. This analysis is normally derived from lines plans and an inclining test (often required along with dimensional measurements to obtain a racing yacht's handicap rating), from which a value for metacentric height and vertical center of gravity is calculated. Under the relatively new MHS (Measurement Handicap System), which provides a complete description of the underwater hull shape, the range of positive stability is figured, and this gives a close approximation of the angle of heel at which the yacht will capsize in static conditions.

Figure 6-1 shows an example of a sailing yacht's stability curves as calculated by the MHS. This particular boat is a 1967 pre-IOR design, an Ohlson 38A sloop, measuring 36 feet 8 inches overall and 26 feet 7 inches on the waterline with a 10-foot, 3-inch beam and a draft of 5 feet 6 inches. Resistance to capsize, shown by the righting arm (righting moment divided by displacement), is greatest at 75 degrees heel, and the upper curve indicates that the

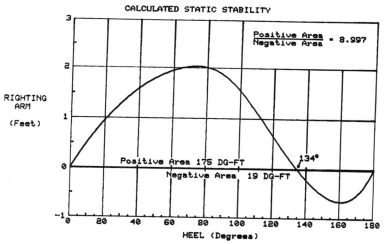

Figure 6-1. Stability curve for an Ohlson 38A as calculated under the MHS. Above the base line the curve shows positive stability and below the line, negative stability. The ratio of positive to negative is shown in the upper right corner. (Courtesy of the USYRU)

boat will capsize (lose positive stability) at 134 degrees heel. It is interesting that a sister hull with a thousand pounds of ballast added to the bottom of her keel water tank loses positive stability at 140 degrees. In figure 6-1, the curve under the heavy base line indicates negative stability or the boat's resistance to righting after she has capsized. The area under the positive stability curve is proportional to the amount of energy required to capsize the hull, while the area above the negative stability curve is proportional to the energy needed to right it. The ratio of positive to negative area is shown in the upper right hand corner. For this particular boat the ratio suggests that about nine times as much energy is needed to capsize her as to right her. By contrast, figure 6-3 shows a modern IOR boat with a stability range of 110 degrees and a ratio of

Figure 6-2. The Ohlson 38A *Kelpie*, whose static stability curve is shown in figure 6-1.

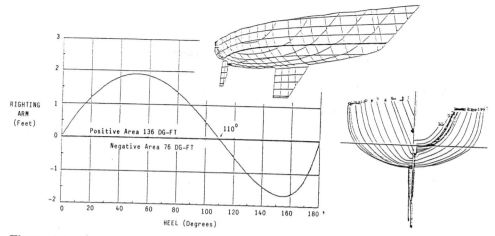

Figure 6-3. The stability curve of a typical IOR boat with a stability range of only 110 degrees and ratio of only 1.79. (Courtesy of Karl L. Kirkman)

positive to negative area of 1.79, indicating much greater vulnerability to capsize.

Bar charts of the MHS fleet's distribution of static stability characteristics are shown in figure 6-4. Important with regard to capsizing and righting, the two parameters charted are the limit of positive stability and the stability ratio. The MHS fleet shown in the charts includes a variety of boats ranging from IOR types (but not the most extreme) to conservative fast cruisers. The MHS states that "no specific limits for safety have been set. Probably none can be." But it warns "if you have a modern racy flat-bottomed boat and if its limit of positive stability is close to 90 degrees, it will be better not to sail it in dangerous seas." This admonition is gentle but definitely sincere.

It can be seen that the Ohlson 38A is considerably better than the average MHS boat in both stability range and ratio, which indicates that, in considering resistance to capsize and tendency to right in static conditions, this boat is relatively safe. It is interesting, but certainly not conclusive, that one of these boats went through the worst of the 1979 Fastnet storm with few difficulties. (She kept sailing, beating and then broad reaching, under storm jib alone, and according to her skipper, she suffered damage amounting only to "approximately one dollar and 25 cents for a new sail batten and a whistle for the kettle"!) Astonishingly, one recent study of yacht capsizing has predicted that a boat such as the Ohlson 38 with the 140-degree stability range is 38 times safer with respect to capsize than a similar-size boat of the type shown in figure 6-3 with the 110-degree stability range.

As has been emphasized, we have been discussing static stability, and that is only part, perhaps a small part, of the capsize picture. The other consideration is dynamic stability, which is the behavior of the yacht when she is struck more or less broadside by steep breaking seas. This is the real world, where it is difficult to account for many of the factors that effect a capsize. In some cases certain design characteristics of the yacht may have a beneficial effect on her

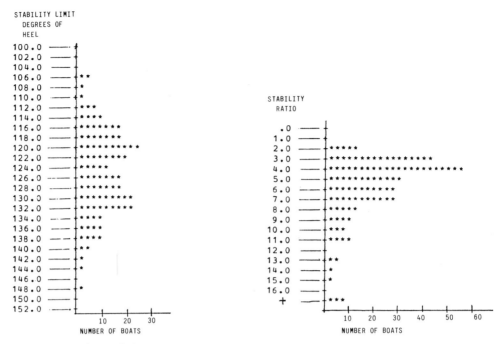

Figure 6-4. The stability range and ratio of the MHS fleet reveals that most of these boats have less than desirable resistance to capsize and ability to self-right. The more extreme IOR boats are far worse. (Courtesy of the USYRU)

static stability but an adverse effect on her dynamically or vice versa. An outstanding example of this is a tall, heavy mast. It raises the boat's center of gravity (CG), but the mast favorably affects her roll inertia, which greatly increases the boat's resistance to capsize.

Since the Fastnet disaster, a number of scientific studies of capsizing have been made. Some of these have been carried out by J.O. Salsich at the U.S. Naval Academy Hydromechanics Laboratory, by the Wolfson Unit at the University of Southampton, by J.A. Keuning at Delft University of Technology, by G. Visinean at Berkeley, by E.D. Cokelet at the Pacific Marine Environmental Laboratory, by P.G. Spens at the Stephens Institute of Technology, by T. Nagel at the David Taylor Naval Research and Development Center, and so forth. With respect to dynamic stability of yachts, a particularly important tank-testing program is being carried out at Hydronautics Ship Model Basin by Karl L. Kirkman, one of the four directors of the Committee on Safety from Capsizing, which is jointly sponsored by USYRU (the United States Yacht Racing Union) and SNAME (the Society of Naval Architects and Marine Engineers). As a result of such studies and other information gleaned from observations and reasonable theory, we are better able to understand the effect of hull design characteristics on both static and dynamic stability and to evaluate the net result.

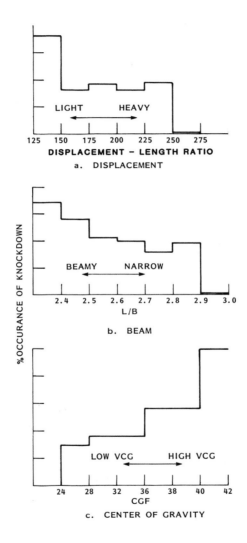

Figure 6-5. Relation of Fastnet capsize to vessel characteristics. It can be seen that light, beamy boats, with high centers of gravity were far more susceptible to capsizing, although these graphs do not consider size, which is an extremely important factor. (Courtesy of SNAME and the Sixth Chesapeake Sailing Yacht Symposium—authors Karl L. Kirkman, Toby Jean Nagle, and Joseph O. Salsich)

Dealing with one characteristic at a time, let us first consider beam. Wide hulls have great initial static stability, but they tend to reach the point of capsize at a relatively low angle of heel. From a dynamic standpoint their great waterline plane tends to keep them level with the wave slope when a steep wave is taken on the beam. This not only increases heel, but it also exposes a lot of the topsides to the breaking wave top. Furthermore, if thrown over on her side, the beamy boat will expose a great expanse of bottom area to the wind and seas, and she may deeply bury the lee deck edge, thereby increasing susceptibility to capsize.

Between the inception of the IOR in 1968 and the Fastnet disaster, there had been a general trend towards gaining sail-carrying power through broad beam rather than with ballast. In a 1981 technical paper entitled *Sailing Yacht Capsize*, authors Olin J. Stephens, Karl L. Kirkman, and Robert S. Peterson wrote: "... the fastest boats for their rating (IOR) often combine great beam and consequent initial stability with a high center of gravity, thus in effect obtaining a double bonus under the IOR. This direction was particularly effective for small boats where the weight of the crew on the weather rail offered another bonus in stability. Thus the modern small IOR racing boat has more than a little in common with the sandbaggers of almost one hundred years ago." As every old-time sailor knows, the sandbagger could easily capsize.

Perhaps the most serious aspect of broad beam, especially beam at the deck level due to flam or flare of the topsides, is the increase in stability when the boat turns upside down. In other words, if the boat should happen to capsize and turn turtle, she will not easily right. In the case of one 1976 half-ton IOR design (not the most extreme design), it was calculated that the capsized boat would have to be rolled to 63 degrees before she could self-right. During actual capsizes some beamy boats have remained upside down for as long as twelve minutes. A centerboard IOR quarter-ton design racing off the coast of Japan in 1978 capsized and could not be righted until she became so full of water that she could not be kept afloat. Fortunately, her crew were able to extricate a life raft stowed under the cockpit just before the boat sank. In several cases slow-righting boats have drowned (or nearly drowned) crew, who were secured in the cockpit with safety lines.

Thus, it seems obvious that enormous beam is undesirable. Karl Kirkman has mentioned a simple rule of thumb for ideal beam for the offshore sailing yacht as being ¼ waterline length plus 2 feet. This formula allows for the fact that small boats are proportionally beamier than large boats. By no means does Kirkman suggest this rule as a hard and fast dictum but only as a rough guide for safety at sea. By this standard it can be seen that most modern boats, especially the extreme IOR and MORC (Midget Ocean Racing Club) racers, are much too beamy for the worst conditions offshore.

Displacement is another characteristic that has an effect on resistance to capsize and also seaworthiness in general. A vessel's weight affects static stability, because this is multiplied by the heeled boat's righting arm (the distance between vertical lines through her centers of buoyancy and gravity) to determine her righting moment. Then considering the dynamics of the situation, a light boat is more easily thrown about by steep waves. These facts indicate that very light displacement is undesirable from a safety standpoint in heavy weather, and certainly a reasonably heavy hull has a more comfortable motion. It is also true that very light displacement boats normally have shallow, flat underbodies that tend to pound and expose flat areas to the force of the seas. Light construction may (or may not) be sufficiently well engineered to accept the stress of continuing heavy weather, but quite often extremely light boats, even those with adequate structural strength, have skins of insufficient thickness to resist puncture from floating objects or broken masts. On the other hand, displacement should not be tremendously heavy or the boat may lack sufficient buoyancy and "ship it green." Solid water on deck is not just uncomfortable; it can be seriously destructive and even wash crew overboard. Displacement, therefore, should not be extremely light or heavy.

Moderation is also the key to ideal freeboard. High topsides are detrimental because they raise the center of gravity while exposing a great area to the waves and wind. On the other hand, they extend the range of static initial stability, delaying the submerging of the deck as the boat heels. When freeboard is too low the rail is submerged at a relatively low angle of heel, and when the hull is thrown by a breaking sea, it can trip on its deck edge and be rolled. Incidentally, another safety consideration worthy of some thought is that very high freeboard makes it difficult to recover a man overboard.

A low center of gravity (CG) is, of course, essential to a high range of static stability. It is not always realized, however, that in one respect a low CG can detract from ultimate dynamic stability. The reason for this is that when the boat is struck beam-on by a sea, the lever arm that rolls her runs from a central point on her side where she is struck to her axis of roll. As Thomas C. Gillmer, the author of *Modern Ship Design* has written, "It may be assumed without appreciable error that the axis of roll is longitudinally through G in most ships." This means that a low CG will lengthen the roll moment arm. Nevertheless, the net effect of a low CG will be beneficial, and this has been borne out in tank tests at Hydronautics by Karl Kirkman. He has found that merely adding ballast to the bilge may not be helpful and may actually be harmful, since the roll moment arm overcomes the benefits of inertia at the relatively high ballast location. But if the ballast is lowered well below the waterline, the inertia overwhelms the moment arm. Not surprisingly, the best place for ballast to work most effectively in resisting a capsize is at the very bottom of the keel. This location will not only increase static stability with a longer righting arm, but more importantly from a dynamic standpoint, it will increase the moment of inertia to slow a roll and help prevent the boat from turning turtle. Those IOR racers that have all their ballast in the bilge and none on the keel might be considered dangerous in the worst weather offshore. The same could be said of early cruisers that carried all their ballast "inside."

The most dramatic results of the tests at Hydronautics and the Naval Academy have been the effect of a tall, heavy mast on the roll inertia. Boats without masts are very much more subject to being rolled over than those with masts, and this fact can clearly be seen in the accompanying graphs prepared by Kirkman. He explains in simple terms that the rolling of a boat around her

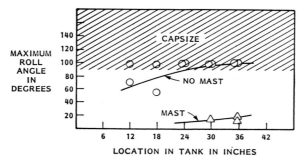

Figure 6-6. The effect of a mast on models capsized in the model tank. The shaded area shows the roll angles at which the model capsizes, while the right to left positions show the model's location relative to the cresting of the wave. It can be seen that the boat with no mast is very much more likely to capsize. (Courtesy of SNAME and the Sixth Chesapeake Sailing Yacht Symposium—authors Kirkman, Nagle and Salsich)

longitudinal axis is similar to the spinning of an ice skater turning about his vertical axis. With arms outstretched the skater spins relatively slowly, but with arms lowered against his sides, he decreases the moment of inertia and spins rapidly. A sailboat with her mast down will behave in a similar manner and can easily be rolled through 360 degrees. Thus we might observe that the old-time seamen, who recommended chopping down the mast during a survival storm, were often giving the wrong advice.

Considering its favorable effect on the roll inertia, the tall IOR rig is desirable, but such masts may more easily break, while they raise the boat's CG and, of course, the center of effort of her sails, thereby making the boat more vulnerable to knockdowns and perhaps directional control problems under full sail. It would seem far safer to have a somewhat shorter rig with heavier scantlings, and for any net loss in moment of inertia due to the shorter masts, to compensate with extra keel ballast. This will not only increase the inertia but also lower the CG. On the other hand, the mast should not be too low, as the moment of inertia is weight times the square of its distance from the axis of rotation, so the height of the mast has a much greater effect on resistance to rolling than weight on the keel, which is only a short distance from the axis. Thus the old argument for the superiority of the gaff rig because of the reduction of tophamper when the sail is down is not really valid in regard to rolling over in a storm.

The Committee on Safety from Capsizing has recommended requirements for heavier mast scantlings, and a USYRU technical committee has developed a screening test to determine minimum moments of inertia for masts. This formula considers such factors as the boat's righting moment at 40 degrees, mast panel length, distance from chainplates to the boat's centerline, whether the mast is keel or deck-stepped, and the modulus of elasticity of the mast material. There will also be certain restrictions on rigging that needs constant adjustment while under way, such as multiple backstays, baby stays, chicken stays (to counteract spinnaker pole thrust), or any other rigging that requires a lot of attention from a skilled mast tuner to keep the mast and rig intact.

The committee feels that it is vital to stop mast breakage at sea, and although at least one prominent designer doesn't agree, Kirkman and company think that it is perfectly possible to design masts that have a good chance of surviving a capsizing. Certainly it is true that some existing cruisers and even a few racers have been rolled without being dismasted, and therefore improved mast scantlings with heavier, more sensible rigging should afford reasonable rig survivability during a capsize. Needless to say, the mast and rig should not be too heavy, as this will raise the CG to the point where it could dangerously affect the boat's static stability, and of course, she would lack sail-carrying power.

Lateral plane does not seem to be a very significant factor judging from capsize tests thus far performed on models in the tank. One would think that the deeper the draft and the greater the lateral plane, the more apt a boat is to trip on her keel and be rolled over when struck on the beam by a breaking sea. Kirkman explains that this does not show up in tank tests, because the well-heeled model is dragging her keel in the turbulent wake of her hull as it moves sideways, and therefore there is very little lateral resistance. The tank tests tend to reinforce the widely held belief that deep-keel boats are more resistant to capsize than centerboarders, because susceptibility to tripping is a less important consideration than having a low center of gravity (the deep-keel boat normally has a lower CG).

Nevertheless, common sense would indicate that the tripping problem should not be dismissed altogether as a result of these tank tests. Lightweight models may be thrown more easily by waves, and their keels do not go as deep into dense water as do those of full-size boats. Furthermore, the deep-draft boat with a lot of lateral plane is initially heeled more easily than the shoal-draft boat, which tends to skid sideways rather than heel. Experienced offshore centerboard sailors usually advise pulling up the board in extremely heavy weather to avoid tripping. There is also the logical theory that boats with very short (but deep) fin keels are less resistant to tripping, because such keels are subject to stalling and loss of lateral resistance at low speeds. This may indeed be true, although the short fin creates other problems such as lack of structural integrity and directional control. Again moderation seems the best policy, and the ideal seagoer would do well with (1) modest lateral plane, as a balance between good directional stability and resistance to tripping, and (2) reasonably deep draft for low placement of ballast and, incidentally, to afford sufficient windward ability to "claw off" if caught on a lee shore.

In extremely heavy weather, of course, boats can be capsized not only by being rolled over in beam seas but also by being pitch-poled (turned stern over bow) by following seas or capsizing diagonally (a simultaneous combination of rolling and pitch-poling). Boats with very fine bows and full quarters, characteristic of some of the smaller, more extreme IOR racers, are especially subject to the latter type of capsizing. Daniel Strohmeier, one of the four directors of the previously mentioned Committee on Safety from Capsizing, has called this particular vulnerability to capsizing "tricycle stability." In

Figure 6-7. A model of a 44-foot Luders-designed Navy yawl being capsized in the Rickover Towing Tank at the U.S. Naval Academy. A lot can and has been learned from such testing. (Photographers John Hoyte and Audrey Greenhill)

other words, he is comparing the diagonal capsizing of a boat having an extremely asymmetrical hull with the turning over of a cycle having one wheel forward and two aft. From the standpoint of safety at sea it certainly seems desirable to have a hull moderately symmetrical, with the bow full enough to prevent burying and the stern full enough for reasonable buoyancy but not sufficiently buoyant to drive the bow under or to cause poor helm balance when the boat is heeled. Complete symmetry (identical bow and stern lines) is not at all ideal, however, because of the boat's resistance to head seas, and a probable tendency toward hobby-horsing (violent pitching).

What is the effect of size on boat behavior in heavy weather at sea? From time to time one hears a small-boat sailor opine, perhaps rationalize, that his boat is the safest size for offshore sailing. The argument is that the very small craft rides over seas that would slam into a much larger boat and that a tiny fragile bottle can survive any kind of storm at sea. There is a degree of truth to this theory, and it may be argued that a small boat, as compared with a larger one, has greater proportional strength for a given construction. However, the type of seas most devastating to a vessel will sooner and more often be encountered by a small boat in the open sea, and she will be subject to the possibility of such conditions for a longer period of time. The steep tops of small breaking waves that may not be a problem for a vessel of medium or large size will be relatively larger and thus more dangerous to a small boat, while the normal short crested seas commonly seen offshore may have peaks that extend the entire length of a short boat but perhaps only half the length of a large boat.

Aside from the relativity of boat and wave size, the scaling laws such as those pioneered by William Froude must be considered, and these indicate that the large vessel has the greater roll inertia to help her resist a capsize. Scaling laws also help the large boat in regard to wind velocity and initial stability. For a given wind velocity the small boat feels a stronger wind, and also she has a more tender hull form if it is geometrically similar to the large boat. This is an important reason why small craft are given greater proportional beam, yet this broad beam gives them the ultimate stability disadvantages previously discussed. Thus, it is not surprising that the vast majority of the boats that came to grief in the Fastnet storm were the smaller ones, those in the 30- to 35-foot range of overall length. Their size and shape combined to increase their vulnerability.

Although oceans have been crossed by undecked or partially decked boats, the safest craft for offshore work are those that are capable of being made completely watertight. When this is not possible, flotation is highly advisable. Even when the open boat is unsinkable, she should have enough flotation to enable her to float fairly high when swamped, otherwise bailing her out may be exceedingly difficult if not impossible. Complete watertightness means that all deck openings can be closed and that their covers are reasonably leak proof.

Cabin houses are very vulnerable to seas breaking aboard, and they are often not as strong as they should be for rugged conditions offshore. The safest kind are low, well rounded or with sloped sides, and crowned as much as possible without compromising safe footing for the crew. They should have ample support from bulkheads, knees, and/or posts below, and wood trunks need tie rods or the equivalent securing them to the deck. Windows should be small with heavy frames and with generous space between them.

Problem areas in regard to watertightness are cockpits and companionways. Deep cockpits give a certain amount of security to the crew, but they should be in the form of watertight wells fitted with large scuppers that allow rapid draining overboard, and cockpit soles should be sufficiently high above the waterline to allow good drainage under all conditions. Large wells with slow drainage can be dangerous, because a large sea breaking aboard can fill the cockpit and weight down the stern, increasing susceptibility to being pooped and adversely affecting stability. More importantly, unless the companionway sill is high above the cockpit sole, which is often not the case, water from a boarding sea will rush below and flood the cabin. The higher the companionway sill the better, unless it is so high and exposed that it affects crew security when entering and exiting the cabin. It is absolutely essential that all seagoing boats, especially sailboats that are subject to knockdowns, have a sturdy and secure lower companionway storm slide when the sill is low. More will be said about this later when details of vessel inspections and modifications are discussed. All companionways, hatches, and ventilators on sailboats should be as close as possible to the centerline to minimize the risk of flooding during an unexpected knockdown (as might occur during a white squall, for example) when these openings are not closed.

SAFETY FEATURES FOR OTHER CRAFT

Problems for the powerboat in heavy weather offshore are obviously quite different from those of the sailboat in similar conditions. The normal small powerboat has considerable beam, a short, lightweight mast (if she has one at all), and little if any ballast. This means that she has a relatively high center of gravity and high waterplane inertia maximizing wave slope response. The skipper of such a craft should be especially careful not to get broadside to any steep breaking seas, for his boat could be rolled over, and she could remain inverted or even sink without watertight integrity and flotation.

Another problem, aside from that of limited stability, is lack of hull balance. A fast powerboat normally has an extremely asymmetrical hull with a sharp, fine bow and full, flat sections aft to promote planing in smooth water. This kind of hull is often difficult to handle in heavy seas, because at low speeds, when the sharp bow is not lifted, it may tend to dig in or root. At the same time, any wave lifting the extremely buoyant stern will force the bow farther down. This causes a loss of directional control, and when driving into head seas a lot of water comes over the bow. Then too, if the broad stern comes out of the water, the boat will lose a lot of initial stability, and this will increase her vulnerability to capsizing. Should the boat be run off before the seas, the lack of directional control makes her subject to broaching to or turning inadvertently so that she is beam to the seas. As the noted British naval architect Uffa

Fox has written, ". . . high-speed powerboats are of necessity more liable to broach than almost any other kind of vessel."

Two means by which the planing boat designer can combat this problem are with some variation of the cathedral hull form or else a constant deadrise deep V form (see figure 6-8). A successful version of the latter hull was developed by designer Raymond Hunt, and it has been used effectively on offshore powerboat racers. With this type of hull the deadrise, at an angle of about 24 degrees, is kept more or less constant from far forward to the stern. Although this boat cannot plane as quickly as one with flatter sections aft, the ride is softer, and there is less buoyancy aft and thus less tendency for the stern to depress the bow at low speeds in a seaway. This hull form may also be given

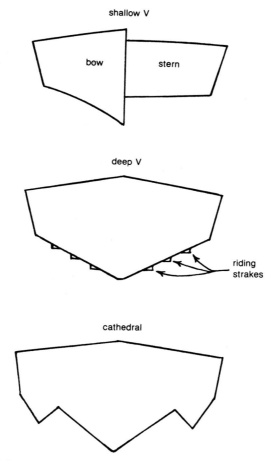

Figure 6-8. Variations of the V hull. The top section is the most common form for the protected-water planing hull. The middle section is the constant deadrise form often found on fast offshore powerboats, while the lower section shows a means of increasing initial stability and adding some buoyancy forward.

riding strakes or longitudinal steps (see the illustration) to promote directional stability and to lift the hull slightly and thus reduce the wetted surface. The disadvantage of the deep V configuration is that the boat tends to porpoise in head seas and may list more during turns. Trim tabs are often used to overcome these difficulties.

The cathedral hull (derived from the word cat-hedral) has added buoyancy in the chine area, quite often in the form of small V'd chine sections (see figure 6-5), and this buoyancy is brought well forward. There are a number of variations on this design, one successful form being credited to designer Richard Cole. Some of these designs increase wetted surface, and one would think they might pound in head seas; but there is often an air-cushioning effect under the chines to soften the ride, and the extra buoyancy at the sides increases initial stability.

When flat after V sections are used, it is important that the boat be provided with a substantial skeg aft for steering control in following seas. Without this the stern can skid sideways, especially if she has a fine, deep forefoot. The tiny rudders used on high-speed boats make the problem much worse. It is often helpful if the steeply V'd bow sections are slightly convex rather than concave, as this will provide more buoyancy forward, and mitigate pounding in head seas, although the boat might throw more spray at high speeds and will probably need a spray rail at the chine. The convex curve also has the advantage of greater inherent strength.

Other forms such as scow types or variations on the so-called sea sled with wide, flat, or inverted V sections forward can be successful, if somewhat wet, in fair weather. With adequate flotation such designs are reasonably safe in fairly rough waters when not far offshore. However, they have very little reserve stability (despite having great initial stability), and of course, the vast majority of fast boats have a very small range of operation. Small open craft with a short cruising range are obviously not seaboats and should only be taken a limited distance offshore in fair weather. Incidentally, any outboard motorboat that has a low or cutout transom for a short shaft motor needs a high watertight well just forward of the transom (see figure 6-9).

Large V-bottom, long-range cruisers can be safe enough offshore in all but the most violent kind of weather, and they have good resistance to initial roll as compared with round-bottom designs, but the lines of any offshore boat should not be extremely asymmetrical. The stern and quarters might have to be narrowed or fined somewhat to minimize the risk of broaching, even if there is some sacrifice to planing ability. Designer Edward S. Brewer has criticized some stock V-bottomed cruisers as having their chine too low in an attempt to obtain more interior space. He writes, "Such boats can pound like the devil and push a wall of water ahead of them at low speeds." The chines, he advises, should be fairly high at the bow and enter the water well aft.

For extended offshore cruising, the moderately heavy displacement, round bottom, semi-fisherman type is generally regarded by knowledgeable seamen to be the safest type of yacht. Sometimes described as a modified trawler yacht, this kind of boat has a fairly deep, heavy hull that is sturdily constructed; fairly high freeboard with generous sheer; a long keel, usually with a

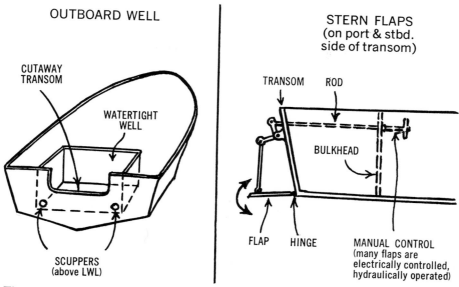

Figure 6-9. An outboard motor well should be used when the transom of a small boat must be cut down to accommodate a short shaft outboard motor.

large, well-protected single propeller at the keel's after end, and an ample rudder abaft the screw; some sail for steadying or riding purposes and emergency propulsion; some deeply located ballast; and sufficient tankage for extended range.

The forefoot may be well rounded for steering control, but it should be sufficiently deep to prevent the bow from lifting out when pitching. Those boats having too little forefoot can pound in head seas and/or have their bows knocked to leeward when they are lifted out. Not all trawler yachts have balanced hulls; in fact, a fine entrance is an asset for making progress against head seas and to prevent throwing a lot of spray. However, there should be ample flare and at least a little overhang forward, and as with seagoing V-bottom craft, there should be reasonable fore-and-aft symmetry to inhibit any tendency to broach. The late designer/design critic Robert Henry wrote, "The powerboats that seem to perform well at sea are the round bilge displacement type with a narrow stern to prevent broaching in a following sea." The importance of such a stern is to limit volume and therefore excessive buoyancy aft, and a similar result can be achieved by fining the lower waterlines aft, even if the stern is fairly broad high above the water. Indeed, this may be desirable for some reserve buoyancy in seas that threaten to poop. Maximum beam amidships should be moderate to avoid uncomfortably jerky rolling; a possible dangerous waterplane responsiveness to beam seas; and even to alleviate any tendency to pitch-pole when running off before large following seas.

The commercial fishing trawlers, designed for year-'round operation in some of the roughest waters, are often thought to be the last word in seaworthiness, and they are generally well designed for their purpose. It should be kept in mind, however, that their purpose is different from that of a yacht, and when the designer does not have to be concerned with ability to tend fishing gear and great load-carrying capacity, certain improvements can be made. For instance, extremely heavy trawlers can have their displacements decreased for better performance under power and greater buoyancy in rough waters. The offshore powerboat designer and author of *Voyaging Under Power*, Robert Beebe, feels that a displacement length ratio (displacement in long tons divided by the cube of load waterline length divided by 100) can be as low as 270 for a 50-foot LOA, normally proportioned, ocean-crossing motor yacht. A fishing trawler of that size might have a D/L of 400 or more.

The trawler yacht might also have a lower prismatic coefficient or be less full at her ends for less resistance in head seas, dryness, and better engine efficiency at moderate cruising speeds. The yacht also should have more freeboard amidships and aft, which will extend her range of stability (provided it doesn't raise her center of gravity too much), and the height will keep more water off the decks. The bow should have considerable height for dryness in head seas, and most trawlers have this feature. Captain Beebe confesses that his nearly perfect offshore powerboat *Passagemaker* falls a little short in this particular respect, for he wrote, "We often wished our bow was higher by a foot or so, . . ." On the other hand, the bow should not be so high as to block visibility from the helm and require an excessively tall pilothouse.

Many commercial fishing trawlers are underballasted as a result, perhaps, of attempting to carry the largest possible payload. This has led to capsizings in heavy weather, quite often after the vessels are loaded with catch and/or when their rigging and superstructures have become coated with ice in freezing weather. It was mentioned in the publication *Fishing Boats of the World* that Swedish trawlers have had a relatively good record in resisting capsizes, because they are generally well ballasted.

Just about any round-bottom offshore powerboat needs one or two means to stabilize against rolling, and a well-accepted means is to carry a steadying sail. Its mast can also be used to support riding and emergency propulsion sails, but these require extra ballast to counteract their heeling force. Reasonably tall masts can favorably affect the roll moment of inertia, as explained earlier, and this gives the vessel a slower, more comfortable rolling motion. However, allowances must be made, especially when there is a lot of rigging, for icing, which may raise the center of gravity to a dangerous height.

Superstructures should be kept to a reasonable height not only because of windage and their effect on the vessel's center of gravity, but also because lofty pilothouses and the like are vulnerable to the force of seas breaking aboard. It is also important that windows be conservative in size. Obviously, they need not be as small as a sailboat's, partly because they aren't subject to striking the water during a beam ends knockdown. Nevertheless, an offshore powerboat's windows and ports can be severely battered by hard spray, so all glass should be specified with this in mind (more will be said on this subject later).

On account of their large size, ships do not have the same motion and stability problems as smaller craft. This was brought home to me recently when I talked to a veteran ship's captain, who has commanded a variety of large merchant vessels all over the globe since World War II. Every now and then there is a report of a small yacht having been capsized by a so-called "rogue sea," a huge freak wave much larger than the seas surrounding it; but this ship's captain said that in all his years of sailing the oceans in every kind of weather, including hurricanes, he had never seen a huge rogue sea. Of course,

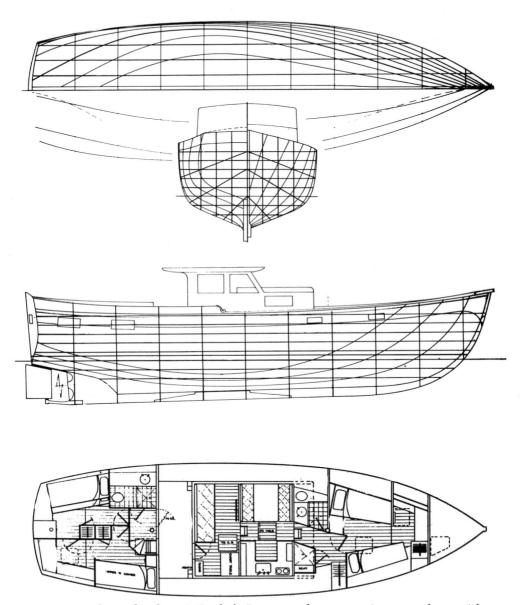

Figure 6-10. Plans of Robert P. Beebe's *Passagemaker*, a seagoing powerboat with an outstanding record of successful offshore passages.

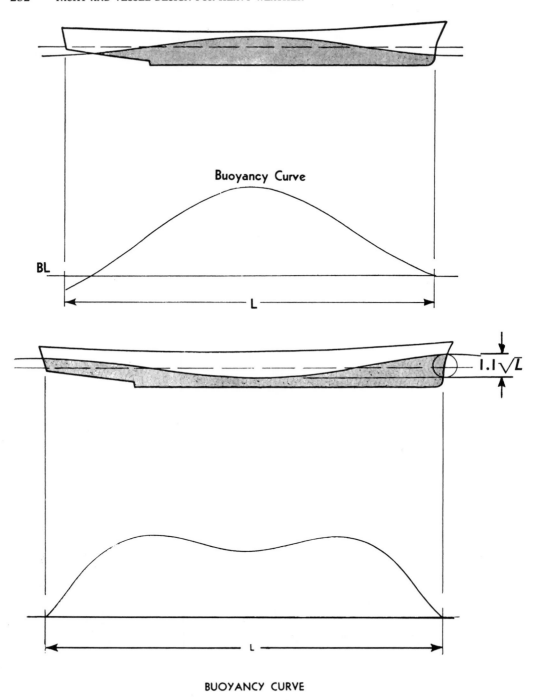

BUOYANCY CURVE

Figure 6-11. The buoyancy curves in typical hogging and sagging conditions (from *Modern Ship Design* by Thomas C. Gillmer)

he recognized that such waves exist, and he felt fortunate to have avoided them. His good fortune, however, made me wonder whether the captain might have encountered at least a few such seas had he commanded smaller vessels. A rogue sea for a boat is not necessarily a rogue for a ship.

Of course, large ships can and do capsize on rare occasions, but the main cause is generally not from steep waves alone. It is usually a result of groundings, collisions, hull cracking, perhaps as a result of hogging and sagging stresses, (see figure 6-11) lack of watertight integrity on deck, cargo shifting, free-surface effect, and dangerous shortening of the vessel's metacenter.

Groundings or collisions with other vessels, icebergs, or other heavy objects can cause skin punctures or splits that result in flooding and a complete change in stability characteristics. Watertight bulkheading may guard against sinking, but the vessel's stability will change all the same, so her undamaged stability should take into account the possibility of flooding, and whenever possible the bulkheading should run longitudinally as well as transversely.

Fatigue cracking may possibly occur on very long ships exposed to repeated bending and twisting stresses as a result of the ends and middle of the ship being exposed to entirely different wave forces. When the buoyant forces of waves are working at the bow and stern while the ship is relatively unsupported amidships, she is sagging; but when a large wave is amidships and there is little buoyancy at the ends, she is being hogged. These forces, trying to bend the entire hull, create stresses that act alternately on the deck as well as the bottom, and when the latter is in tension, the former is in compression or vice versa. Thus, longitudinal stiffening of the hull is important even at the deck level, and reasonable continuity of deck stringers must be considered when cargo hatches are designed. Incidentally, there have been a number of failures of deck plating as a result of stress concentration at hatch corners, and many modern hatches are now designed with rounded corners. Watertight

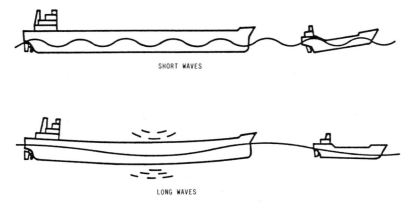

SHORT WAVES

LONG WAVES

Figure 6-12. The effect of wave length on ship size. The figure illustrates the stress on short and long vessels in short and long seas. (Courtesy of Det Norske Veritas and Kåre Lindemann)

integrity of the deck is important even on a large vessel, not only to preserve the cargo, but also for the sake of maintaining proper buoyancy and stability. In a few rare cases vessels have foundered after having been pooped by large following seas that flooded the interior through faulty hatches, ventilators, low blower intakes, or other openings.

A major cause of merchant ship capsizings is from the shifting of cargo. This most often results from improperly securing the cargo and/or allowing the ship to take substantial rolls. Violent synchronous rolling, where the ship's period of roll coincides with wave period, can be alleviated with cargo loading that has a favorable effect on the roll inertia, and more will be said about this presently in the brief discussion of metacentric height. When the ship is caught in conditions that cause heavy rolling, a change in heading will often take care of the problem. A turn that brings the vessel more nearly end-on rather than beam-to will normally ease the motion, but obviously, from the standpoint of meeting a schedule or staying in a formation, it is desirable to stay on course. In the interest of comfort and to allow a vessel to keep to her course and to minimize off-the-track storm avoidance courses, many ships are fitted with anti-roll devices. These vary from sophisticated gyrostabilizers and activated fin stabilizers (see figure 6-13), to anti-roll tanks, to fixed exterior appendages such as keel end plates and bilge keels. The latter, especially the long fin-like bilge keels at the turn of the bilge, are relatively simple and are among the more effective devices for roll dampening when the ship is under way. In small vessels, such as commercial fishermen, paravane stabilizers (publicized by Robert Beebe as "flopper-stoppers"), suspended from outrigger booms, are very effective if somewhat troublesome to handle (see figure 6-14).

Free-surface effect is the effect on stability of a liquid shifting within a vessel. As the ship rolls or lists, any loose internal liquid, attempting to keep its surface horizontal, moves its weight suddenly to leeward, creating a capsizing force. This occurs not only with bilge water but with fuel, water, and other liquids within tanks. The broader the tank, the more pronounced the effect unless the tank has been topped off. Although many skippers are reluctant to put salt water in their fuel tanks for obvious reasons, standard preparations for the heaviest weather that include filling slack fuel tanks with seawater illustrate the concern for free surface. All tanks, especially those with great breadth, should have baffle plates or swash bulkheads, and these should generally run transversely as well as longitudinally. Fish tanks are a problem on certain fishing vessels, and these tanks should be subdivided to keep the boat properly trimmed and minimize free surface.

A most important consideration regarding a vessel's initial stability and susceptibility to rolling is her metacentric height or GM, the distance from the hull's center of gravity to a point above it (in seaworthy vessels) called the metacenter. A simple means of showing the metacenter's location is to find the center of buoyancy (center of immersed volume) of the slightly heeled hull and to draw a vertical line through the CB and extend it until it intersects the vessel's centerline (see figure 6-15). The point of intersection is the metacenter (M). The position of the metacenter is determined by the designer, and normally it is calculated for different conditions of loading. The GM can also be found from an inclining experiment during which the vessel is heeled slightly with weights. A simple method for the master at sea to determine the approximate GM is to time the period of roll and then use the formula $T = .44B/\sqrt{GM}$, where T is the full rolling period in seconds and B is beam. Timing the roll should be done repeatedly at different times of the day and the results averaged for greater accuracy. On modern ships, stability tables and computers such as the Stabilogauge are often used to solve stability problems such as the change in GM resulting from changes in cargo.

A high GM makes the vessel stiff, giving her great initial stability and a quick, jerky roll; while a low GM produces just the opposite, low initial stability with a slow, easy roll. The latter condition, within reason, is desirable

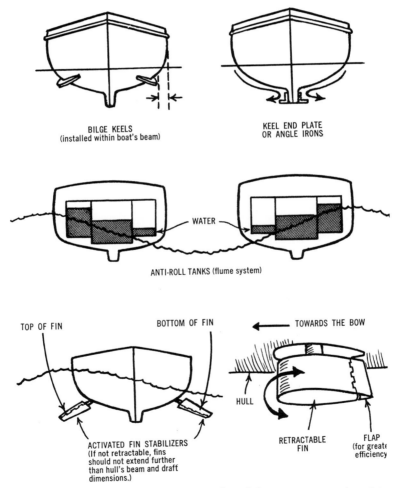

BILGE KEELS
(installed within boat's beam)

KEEL END PLATE
OR ANGLE IRONS

WATER

ANTI-ROLL TANKS (flume system)

TOP OF FIN

BOTTOM OF FIN

TOWARDS THE BOW

HULL

ACTIVATED FIN STABILIZERS
(If not retractable, fins
should not extend further
than hull's beam and draft
dimensions.)

RETRACTABLE
FIN

FLAP
(for greate
efficiency

Figure 6-13. Permanent power vessel stabilizers. Activated stabilizers have little effect unless the vessel is moving ahead.

not only for comfort but also to reduce racking stresses, vulnerability to cargo or ballast shifting, and susceptibility to synchronous rolling. Passenger ships concerned with minimizing seasickness and maximizing comfort are nearly always given short GMs. On the other hand, the metacentric height should not be extremely small on any vessel, or she may lack a safe margin of reserve stability in the event of flooding or the shifting of cargo. Furthermore, if synchronization does occur between the period of the seas and the ship's roll a small GM could produce a dangerous motion. La Dage and Van Gemert, authors of *Stability and Trim for the Ship's Officer*, recommend a moderately small GM, perhaps between two and three feet for a loaded freighter of medium size. Naval vessels often have relatively long GMs to ensure adequate

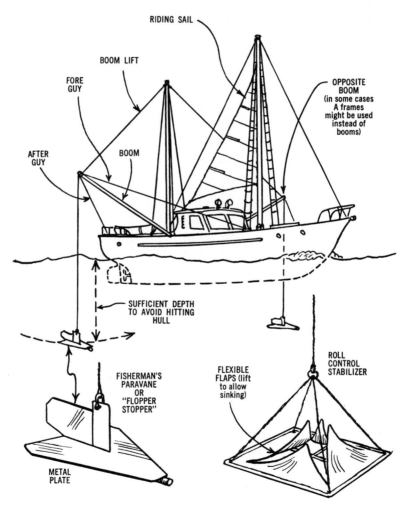

Figure 6-14. Removable roll stabilizers, sometimes called fisherman's paravanes or flopper stoppers.

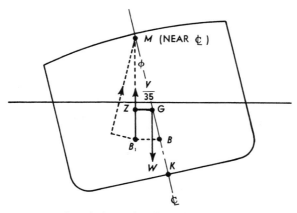

Figure 6-15. Initial stability of a ship showing the centers of buoyancy and gravity and the metacenter. (From *Modern Ship Design* by Thomas C. Gillmer)

stability under damaged conditions, for high-speed turns, and so forth. On the other hand, the GM cannot be too long when the ship must act as a reasonably steady gun platform.

Metacentric height can be adjusted by varying the distribution of cargo and/or ballast. Upper and lower 'tween-deck spaces are used for cargo stowage to help keep the center of gravity high. Wing ballast tanks are an effective means of dampening violent rolling, because, being near the ship's sides, far from the centerline, they favorably affect the mass moment of inertia without raising the CG too high. It is a dangerous practice to raise G above M, for then the ship would have unstable equilibrium and perhaps take on a substantial list. If the attempt were made to correct the list by moving cargo or ballast to the high side, the ship could capsize. This has happened. Examples of recommended GMs are: 1.6 feet for a passenger vessel with a beam of 80 feet, 3 feet for a freighter with a beam of 60 feet, and 5.6 feet for a tanker with beam of 70 feet. GMs for small power cruisers are roughly from 2 to 2.5 feet and 3 to 3.5 feet for a sailing vessel.

VESSEL INSPECTIONS AND MODIFICATIONS

A number of important lessons were learned from the 1979 Fastnet Race about preparing a small yacht for heavy weather at sea. Perhaps the most serious problem for the competitors was the lack of security in the cabin. Heavy gear was often thrown around down below when the boats were rolled over or knocked down. As a result, the crew were injured, and many felt it necessary to go on deck where they were subject to being washed overboard. In a number of cases, the crew took to life rafts, because they could not stay below and were afraid to stay on deck for fear of the boat rolling over. This proved to be a fatal mistake in some instances where life rafts capsized or were torn apart. There seems to be little doubt that the cabin of a boat with complete watertight integrity is the safest place to be, *provided* all heavy gear and stores are well secured and there are means of securing the crew in their bunks.

Before the Fastnet disaster, few if any ocean racers had their equipment installed or gear and stores stowed in such a way that they would remain in place during a capsize. Even now there are probably few boats that could turn completely upside down without a lot of heavy gear coming loose. Time and again one hears stories of damage or injuries from heavy storm anchors shifting, batteries falling, canned goods and cooking utensils or tools becoming projectiles, large floor boards being tossed about, lockers full of heavy gear spilling their contents, and gimballed stoves coming loose. In one case, a small-boat sailor in a storm offshore became so concerned about gear flying around his cabin during knockdowns that he nailed all nailable loose objects to his screwed-down wooden cabin sole.

Particular care must be taken to see that inside ballast cannot possibly move at any angle of heel. It must be fastened or fiberglassed in place, not merely wedged. All lockers should have substantial latches and not the ludicrous magnetic fasteners found on some boats. Drawers and sliding berths need to be safetied with locking pins or some other means. There should be ample eye straps for lashing lines, and bunks need belts or lashings to hold in crew members at any angle of heel. Shelves must be provided with nets or sea rails that will contain their contents, and stoves need locking devices. How many boats have bolts for their ice box lids to prevent heavy blocks of ice from falling out during an inversion?

It is also important, of course, that all loose gear and movable equipment on deck is well secured, especially safety items such as life rafts and buoys and

Figure 6-16. A high companionway on a yacht that has made numerous Atlantic crossings.

fittings necessary to operate the vessel. One boat in the Fastnet Race lost nearly all her winch handles when they fell overboard after a 120-degree knockdown. Another competitor repeatedly had her compass fall out of the binnacle.

More than a few stock boats do not have latches on their cockpit seat lockers, and the lids are subject to falling or washing open during beam ends knockdown. Normally, those lockers are open to the bilge, so an open lid could allow massive flooding and possibly lead to sinking. Then too, it is possible for companionway slides to fall out during a knockdown or roll over, and indeed this happened during the Fastnet Race. The companionways most subject to losing their slides are those with slanted sides (with the vertical portion of the hatch wide at the top and narrow at the bottom). Such a configuration means that the slides need only lift a short distance before they are loose. Slots that hold the slides must be deep, and the slides should be capable of being locked into position with bar bolts or some other arrangement. Ocean racing rules now require that companionway securing arrangements be "operable from above and below." Standard slides provided for stock boats are seldom satis-

Figure 6-17. Sturdy storm slides with a small latching plexiglass window and locks to hold the slides in.

factory for storm conditions, because they are often lightly constructed and usually fitted with ventilating slots that can admit a lot of water.

Windows on many stock boats are improperly glazed. Glass should be the safety type that is used for the windshields of American automobiles. This is laminated glass that is shatterproof. In some cases on semiprotected waters perhaps, tempered glass might suffice, but this kind can shatter even though it is very strong. Plexiglass and even Lexan can get scratched, but they are safe provided they are thick enough to resist significant flexing. Large windows need storm shutters, normally plexiglass sheets bolted on from the outside; while frames should be substantial and generously overlap the glass so that it can't pop out.

Other safety-related fixtures that should be carefully checked before going offshore where heavy weather could be encountered are: life lines and pulpits, handrails, all scuppers and valves, stuffing boxes, bilge pumps, piping and wiring, skid proofing of deck surfaces, strong points for safety line attachments, all rigging, and all parts of the steering assembly including the rudder.

Life lines and pulpits are required for most ocean races, and indeed, they should be considered essential on any offshore boat. Common failings on stock boats are weak life-line installations of insufficient height. The life-line stanchion sockets should be substantial, either welded or through-bolted to the deck, and spaced no more than seven feet apart. Beware of triangular-shaped socket bases with sharp corners, as they can puncture the deck if the stanchions are forced away from being vertical. There should be upper and lower life lines carried taut, and the former should be above knee level, otherwise it may trip a person and be more of a hazard than a safeguard. Life lines need toggles (universal joints) to prevent fatigue of terminal fittings, and any pelican hooks in the assembly should be safetied with lashings, tape, or some other means to prevent them from opening inadvertently. Pulpits must be sturdy, and if a gap is necessary between the bow pulpit and the life lines to allow the passage of a low-cut jib, the space should be minimal, and a means of closing the gap should be provided for offshore work.

Hand rails are essential above and below decks. Very seldom are there enough on stock boats, especially below, and quite often they are inadequately secured. A former Coast Guard Chief of Boating Safety once told me he inspected a power yacht that had her hand rails merely glued on; there were no fastenings whatsoever! Needless to say, hand rails should be secured as though the crew's life depended on them, and that means heavy construction with through bolts and large washers under the nuts. On large boats, where shrouds are difficult to reach when working at the mast, pipe rails (sometimes called "sissy bars") are needed in way of the mast so that the crew can attach themselves to them and lean against them when handling halyards or sails. Another place where sturdy pipe rails are needed is on either side of an elevated or exposed companionway. Below decks there should be hand rails or grabs in way of the companionway ladder, along all passageways, and in the galley. Vertical posts afford great personal security, and they also strengthen the cabin top.

Figure 6-18. When there is considerable distance between a boat's mast and her shrouds, it makes sense to have pipe rails near her mast.

Toe rails are often too low or even omitted on racing boats, but this is a dangerous practice, especially when boats sail offshore or even on protected inland waters at night. These rails should run entirely around the edge of the deck and be high enough to act as a foot brace. They are quite often varnished, but this makes them slippery. Raw teak is about the most satisfactory surface for skid proofing without unduly compromising appearance. It is not advisable to varnish any surface that will be walked on, and needless to say, all smooth decks such as those of fiberglass or aluminum need skid proofing. This may be done with abrasive paint, molded in rough patterns, or adhesive deck tread. A particular area that often needs to be made less slippery is the companionway ladder.

An offshore boat needs ample strong points, perhaps heavy bolted eye straps, to which safety lines can be attached. Sailors often hook on to the life lines, but this can be a risky practice in the heaviest weather, because of the outboard location and because life lines can break under severe shock loading. Strong points are particularly needed at the helm, of course, and also near the companionway, in such a place that one can hook on before coming on deck, as crew have been lost overboard when leaving the cabin before they have had a chance to secure themselves.

One of the most essential requirements for heavy weather is an efficient means of clearing the bilge of water, because boats can work and open seams or leak through small deck openings that cannot be made absolutely watertight. In just about every offshore boat there should be at least two large-capacity bilge pumps, one on deck, preferably near the helmsman, and one down below in the cabin. The deck pump should not be installed, as is often the case, in a cockpit seat locker in such a way that the locker lid must be opened before the pump can be operated. Discharge lines need a high loop to prevent back syphoning, and through-hull outlets should be as high as possible above the waterline. The intake line usually needs a strainer to guard against the pump becoming jammed from chips of wood, paper labels, or the like. There should be reliable valves, preferably seacocks, on all through-hull fittings, even those above the waterline that could be submerged when the vessel heels. It is important to carry tapered wooden plugs to fit all holes through the hull, and it is sometimes recommended that the plugs be taped to the hoses that lead to the holes. Pump handles must be sturdy, and when they are removable, they should be secured with a lanyard. Never rely entirely on mechanical or electric pumps—carry at least a few large-capacity manual pumps and several hefty buckets. It is seldom a good idea to have a bilge pump discharge into the cockpit, unless perhaps there is ample drainage.

A particularly vulnerable part of almost any boat is the rudder, and a number of them broke during the Fastnet race. On that occasion the main cause of failure was due to weight-saving construction using carbon fiber. It has been said that builders at that time were not completely familiar with certain properties of the relatively new material, such as those of molecular alignment, and as a result scantlings were deficient for the conditions met. Regardless of weight, rudders and all parts of the steering assembly should be over-engineered to have a large margin of safety, because extended exposure to heavy weather imposes abrasion, fatigue, and torsional stress, all of which are difficult to calculate. Areas to examine before a long cruise or race offshore are fastenings, rudder straps, pintles, the heel fitting, bearings, bushings, cables, sheaves, rudder quadrant, rudder head fitting, stuffing box, worm gearing, and so forth. Check for excessive play or looseness in the steering system, and vibration, binding, or jamming when the helm is put hard over.

Parts of the rigging to check before putting to sea are: the spreaders, threads on turnbuckles, wire cables (especially where they enter terminal fittings) to see that no strands are broken; all pins for wear and to ensure that they are properly cottered; rivets and other fastenings to make sure they are tight and in good condition; swages to see that they are not distorted or cracked, tangs and chainplates to make sure they are not corroded or have not shifted, etc. See that there is no evidence of chafe, that fittings are not bent or worn or cracked, that there are toggles wherever there could be bending in more than one direction, and that wire and fittings are properly aligned to avoid bending stresses. Remember that the loss of a mast not only endangers the crew, subjects the hull to holing, and takes away motivating power, it also has an adverse effect on the roll moment of inertia.

Most of the foregoing remarks have been intended primarily for offshore sailboats, but they also apply to other kinds of seagoing vessels, although in some cases not to the same degree. For instance, the windows of a power boat do not have to withstand the enormous stress of a slap from solid water during a knockdown, yet her windows are usually quite large, and they can be subjected to extremely hard jets of heavy spray. Thus, glass should be heavy, *at least* ¼ inch thick, and tempered, while storm shutters or screens ought to be provided for particularly vulnerable windows for use in the roughest conditions when, for one reason or another, the vessel must be driven into head seas. In certain cases on passenger vessels, the Coast Guard requires wire-inserted glass.

Obviously, the rigging on power vessels is not subject to the same stresses as that on sailboats, particularly ocean racers. Nevertheless, offshore power boat masts often support riding sails that are exposed to heavy winds, and booms lift heavy cargo or other gear such as nets, boats, or stabilizers. It is therefore important that the rigging on all seagoing vessels be periodically inspected and that any questionable parts be replaced at once. Actually, there are federal regulations that control cargo gear, including rigging, on American ships.

As a matter of fact, most U.S.-registered commercial ships, such as cargo vessels, tankers, and passenger ships, have strict construction, equipment, and inspection requirements that are set forth in the *Code of Federal Regulations*, Title 46—*Shipping*. Vessels subject to these regulations must be inspected by the Coast Guard every one or two years and must carry a number of Certificates of Inspection. No attempt will be made here to discuss Title 46, which is composed of eleven volumes, but a few more points in regard to heavy-weather requirements should be mentioned.

Many ships deeply loaded and with little freeboard, especially tankers, will "ship it green" and have their decks swept by seas. This results in three major concerns, superstructure damage, watertight integrity, and crew security. In regard to the latter, cable travelers are rigged on low decks in other than protected waters. These are equivalent to yacht jacklines often seen on offshore yachts. The Coast Guard requires that a traveler be stretched between deckhouses when they are more than 150 feet apart, but prudence might dictate that a cable be rigged when deckhouses are much closer if seas are coming aboard. Vessels that have properly constructed catwalks or raised bridges or below-decks passageways are exempt from the cable requirement. Incidentally, all passageways need continuous hand holds.

High bulwarks are a great aid to crew security, but if there aren't enough freeing ports or other drains, they could create a stability hazard. A slow-draining deck full of water not only raises the vessel's center of gravity but also subjects her to the dangerous effects of free surface. This is particularly a problem with some trawlers, as the decks may contain fish or loose gear that can clog the scuppers or freeing ports. Some boats have the entire bulwarks or rail raised above the deck so that there is a generous space all around through which water can flow. At any rate, freeing ports should be large, and if there is danger of any objects on deck being swept through them, a grating or network of lines can be used.

Watertight integrity of all deck openings is not always easy to ensure, since doors and even hatch covers are occasionally left open when they should be closed. Normally, heavy cargo hatch covers should be permanently battened

Figure 6-19. This photograph illustrates the value of cable travelers and hand rails on low decks of ships.

down when at sea, and they are made watertight with tarpaulins, threaded dogs and gaskets, or similar devices. When holds must be entered from deck, some hatch covers can be fitted with screw-down manholes for easy access. Lazarette hatches on some fishing vessels are a problem because they often lack high coamings, and they are sometimes not dogged. Seas can wash aboard, especially when the boat is down by the stern, and dislodge the hatch. Incidentally, it is not uncommon to see dogs rusted in the open position. They should be used and kept well lubricated.

Whenever possible, doors leading to the accommodations should be in the after ends of superstructures (never in the forward ends). If side doors are necessary they should be hinged on the forward side so that the door will afford some protection against spray blowing aft even when it is open. Dogs for watertight doors are not always easy to operate, but they should be operable

Figure 6-20. A destroyer shipping it green. Solid water taken over the bow can sweep the forward decks and damage the superstructures of many vessels.

with one hand so that a crewman can use his other hand to hold on. It is hardly ever wise to have side entrances on sailing vessels, since there is always the possibility of an unexpected knockdown. There should always be an alternate exit for every below-decks, manned compartment to allow escape in an emergency, and the exits should be large enough to permit the passage of a person wearing a life jacket. Ventilators must be as high as possible and provided with flaps or covers for heavy weather. Frequently air intakes to engine rooms are too low.

Of course, a safeguard against being swept by heavy seas is adequate freeboard, but cargo vessels are loaded as deeply as possible for obvious reasons. Merchant ships are required by law to limit loading in accordance with their Plimsoll markings, which are marks not to be submerged, painted on each side of the vessel (see figure 6–21). Minimum allowable freeboard depends on the location of the voyage and the time of year. Load markings, standardized by an international convention in 1930, show lines for: tropical fresh water, marked TF; fresh water, marked F; tropical, marked T; summer, marked S; winter, marked W; and winter North Atlantic, marked WNA. Most cargo vessels trim level when beginning a voyage, as this generally allows maximum cargo. As the voyage progresses, fuel is used from forward tanks first to allow the bow to gradually lift, thereby improving freeboard forward and producing some keel drag aft, which usually improves the ship's handling characteristics.

Although Coast Guard inspections are required periodically, it is customary for merchant ships to be privately inspected by independent survey organizations such as the National Cargo Bureau before each voyage. This procedure gives reasonable assurance to the owners, crew, and insurance agents,

Figure 6-21. Plimsoll marks that regulate the loading of a cargo ship. (Photo by David Q. Scott)

from an impartial observer, that the vessel is ready for sea. Surveyors are generally highly experienced former ships' captains. They check such items as Plimsoll marks, deck lashings, hatches, loading with respect to stability, fuel capacity, ullage readings on tankers, settlers and strainers, stowage of volatile cargos, dunnage and measures taken to prevent cargo from shifting, jumbo gear, and so forth.

Periodic surveys would not be out of order for fishing vessels, because these craft have minimal legal requirements for equipment and inspections, yet they are exposed to some of the heaviest weather. The master of a fisherman must shoulder even more of the responsibility for sea fitness than most skippers. About the same could be said of yacht masters, although there are usually inspection requirements for long-distance ocean races. At any rate, anyone in command of an offshore vessel should fully realize that he has a responsibility not only to his crew and owners (if he is not the owner), but also to those who might come to his rescue in the event that he gets into serious trouble.

7

Safety Gear and Storm Preparation

It will be no time to look for what
is missing or out of place when a
storm comes up at sea.
—An ancient Phoenician seaman,
        more than 2,300 years ago

Inadequacies of safety gear on the disastrous Fastnet Race strongly suggest
that such equipment is far from adequate on many other vessels. The Fastnet
racers, after all, had equipment requirements, and they were subject to spot
checking. But many individual yachts that put to sea—commercial fishermen,
and ships of foreign registry, exempt from Coast Guard inspections—have
minimal safety requirements.

MISCELLANEOUS SAFETY EQUIPMENT

Certain safety equipment such as life lines, pulpits, and bilge pumps, which
are more or less fixed to the boat, have already been discussed. In this chapter
the most basic equipment that is for the most part portable will be covered.
This gear is only related to heavy weather, and it doesn't include such equipment as that intended for fire fighting or medical emergencies.

One item that could be considered as either fixed or portable, depending on
its design, is the boarding ladder. Any boat that sails with a small crew,
especially one with high freeboard, should have some means by which a
person in the water can climb back aboard. Fixed ladders are usually mounted
on a vessel's stern where they don't cause drag and are least vulnerable to
damage. This location also facilitates boarding when the boat has a sizable,
nearly vertical transom. The bottom of these ladders usually fold down so that
when they are to be used, the bottom rungs will extend well below the surface.
A line is normally attached to the folding part so that it may be reached and the
ladder pulled down by a person in the water. It is highly advisable to have the
lower rung deep enough for a man overboard to easily reach it with his foot,
and there should be enough distance from his foot to his hands (where they

grip the ladder) for adequate leverage so that he can haul himself up without undue strain.

The owner who doesn't want to mount a fixed ladder on the stern may carry a conveniently stowed portable ladder, but this will be less secure and take time to break out. A better but still not perfect arrangement is to use a rope ladder with wooden rungs that is firmly made fast to the stern pulpit and is rolled up when not in use. The ladder can be held in a roll with light lashings that can be broken by a line hanging overboard that is easily reached by a person in the water. The bottom rung should be weighted to make it sink when the ladder is hanging down.

When a person in the water is exhausted or weighed down with heavy clothing, he may have difficulty climbing aboard even with a ladder, so there should always be a tackle such as a handybilly that can be rigged from a boom to lift the victim and swing him aboard. On the conventional sailboat, a vang rigged to the middle of the main boom will often suffice, while davits will be most helpful on vessels that have them. Powerboats with large vertical transoms can have low boarding platforms aft, and these will assist not only the victim but also the crew who are helping him aboard.

Figure 7-1. This stern view of a modern ocean racer shows her transom-mounted boarding ladder. The hole in the transom is a well for a man-overboard pole. (Photo by Sally Henderson)

On large vessels a cargo net hung over the side may be more helpful than a Jacob's ladder. In cold waters, however, it could be dangerous for a man overboard to climb either a net or ladder, as he could be suffering from a newly discovered affliction known as "pressure collapse." This discovery, made by Surgeon Commander Frank Golden, senior medical officer at England's Institute of Naval Medicine, shows that some deaths, occurring after emergence from cold water, result from a kind of collapse thought to be caused by the change from water pressure on the body to air pressure when the effects of cold make it difficult for the body to adjust. Dr. Golden compares the effect of this ailment to a sudden hemorrhage, and he says "the blood rushes to the feet." He recommends that a victim who has fallen from a ship be rescued by lowering a lifeboat and lifting the victim into the boat in a seated or fetal position.

Some recent test trials for a man-overboard study have shown that a rescue mat (a floating mat normally made of closed-cell PVC) towed with a floating line behind the boat returning to pick up the victim is highly effective. Easily stowable rescue mats may be marketed after the conclusion of this man-overboard study.

Under new SOLAS (Safety of Life at Sea) regulations, ships will be required to carry one or more rescue boats. These are designed to facilitate man-overboard pickups and other rescues. Rubber boats similar to those used on Coast Guard cutters or other boats specifically designed for rescue purposes are suitable. Even a properly designed non-enclosed life boat can qualify as a rescue boat.

Whenever there is any risk of falling overboard in heavy weather, it is obviously prudent to don some kind of life preserver. Every American vessel is subject to federal regulations regarding personal flotation devices (PFDs).

Figure 7-2. A boom vang similar to the one shown in this photograph is handy for lifting and swinging aboard an exhausted man-overboard. (Photo by Rip Henderson)

Requirements depend on the size and type of boat, and details can be obtained from the U.S. Coast Guard or Coast Guard Auxiliary. Under federal regulations PFDs are categorized into five different types in order of effectiveness, with Type I being considered the most effective. Types I, II, and III are wearable kinds such as jackets or vests, and Type V is also wearable, but is approved only for restricted use. Type IV, however, is the non-wearable kind that is thrown from the boat to a person overboard. The best of these are ring or horseshoe buoys of closed-cell foam covered with orange or yellow plastic-coated cloth, but buoyant seat cushions with handles also qualify. The latter afford minimal flotation and must be grasped, but they are necessary, in my opinion, for they are nearly always immediately available and can be thrown to a person overboard at once, while he is still close to the boat.

For offshore use in heavy weather many sailors prefer flotation coats that qualify as Type III PFDs. Although these may not provide the same degree of safety as Types I and II, they are less bulky and awkward to wear, are more likely to be worn, afford greater protection against the cold, and reduce the risk of hypothermia. Many of the newer types, developed after the Fastnet disaster, also have permanently attached safety harnesses and well-designed pockets for safety lights and whistles. More will be said about these when personal equipment is discussed in the next section.

Anyone who sails shorthanded in remote waters during heavy weather or who is on deck alone at night should wear a PFD. In addition, if the boat is rigged for self-steering, it makes sense to tow a tripping line astern that may be grabbed by a person falling overboard. If the line is long enough and it is floating, there is a fairly good chance that it can be grabbed and pulled hard enough to disengage the self-steering. The boat should be balanced to luff up into the wind when the steering gear is tripped, and this will give the man overboard a fighting chance of reaching the boat, or at least the luffing sails should awake the watch below. A simple tripping system using a spring-leaded piston shackle is illustrated in figure 7-3.

The Offshore Racing Council (ORC) requires horseshoe lifebuoys attached to man-overboard poles on yachts racing at sea. Fitted with an orange or yellow flag, a pole is ballasted so that the flag flies *at least* six feet above the water, and it should be capable of remaining this high in strong winds. The purpose of this is to facilitate locating the buoy in rough seas. It can be exceedingly difficult finding any floating object when it is in the trough between waves. A self-igniting water light must also be attached to the horseshoe buoy, and this should be a strobe flasher bright enough to be visible in broad daylight. Most man-overboard lights are hung upside down on deck, and they are ballasted to float upright. This self-righting action activates the strobe. Certain makes of man-overboard lights have rubber caps that have allowed water to leak inside when they are hung upside down. This problem can be overcome by putting a hose clamp around the bottom of the rubber cap and tightening it enough to keep water out. Serious leakage can short-circuit the light and render it useless. Other ORC requirements for a horseshoe lifebuoy are that the pole be attached with 25 feet of floating line and that the buoy be equipped with a drogue, dye maker, and a whistle.

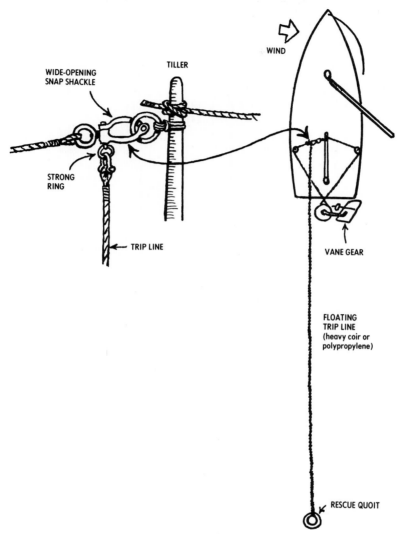

Figure 7-3. A simple arrangement allowing a man-overboard to trip the self-steering gear. This or a similar arrangement is recommended for a singlehander or when only one person is in the cockpit.

For some sailors, including myself, part of the incentive for cruising is to get away from communication with the shore. Nevertheless, it is undoubtedly true that a two-way radio provides a considerable measure of safety. You need a long-distance receiver for weather reports and a transmitter, of course, to call for help if you need it. Currently, the ORC requires only that there be a transmitter and receiver and that an emergency antenna be provided if the regular antenna depends on the mast. Certain long-distance ocean races such as the Bermuda Race, however, specify that two radiotelephones be carried:

Figure 7-4. A man-overboard pole with horseshoe life ring. The coiled line attaching them is made free to run when the boat puts to sea. (Photo by Rip Henderson)

(1) a VHF (very high frequency) and (2) a marine single sideband or marine double sideband or amateur (ham) radio capable of operation on 7085 KHz SSB.

The VHF radio is short ranged (little more than line of sight, depending on antenna height and power of the set), and it is really only handy at sea for communicating with nearby ships or other yachts if one is ocean racing or cruising in company. The United States VHF monitored emergency frequency is channel 16, 156.8 MHz, and the ORC recommends installing VHF channel 72, 156.625 MHz Simplex, which is an international ship-to-ship channel. An important lesson learned after several sinkings of fishing vessels is that any fixed radio should have its battery located in a high position so that it will not soon be drowned as the boat fills with water.

Whether or not a boat has a transmitting radio, she should have portable EPIRBs (emergency position-indicating radio beacons). These are small portable units that send out distress signals over the aircraft emergency frequencies 121.5 and 243 MHz. There is also a slightly larger type such as the Safety Link and Callbuoy that not only emits a sound signal but allows voice transmission on the marine emergency frequency 2182 KHz. The advantage of these portable types is that they need not be continously manned, and they can be carried into a lifeboat or raft. The aircraft frequencies are more likely to be heard far offshore unless one is in a shipping lane or near other vessels. One survivor of a sudden sinking on an ocean race told me that he felt he would have been rescued much sooner from his life raft had he had a portable VHF, since competitors nearby were monitoring channel 16. There is now a "coastal type" EPIRB (for use when no farther than 20 miles offshore) which operates on VHF-FM and sends out a brief alerting signal on channel 16 and then switches to channel 15 to send a direction-finding signal. Portable EPIRBs are designated as Class B by the Coast Guard. Class A types are float-free devices that are mounted on vessels externally and actuate automatically. These types are required on inspected commercial vessels. In the near future, there will be Type C EPIRBs, which will operate on 406.025 MHz, and these will be monitored by SARSAT (search-and-rescue satellite aided tracking) space satellites.

Figure 7-5. EPIRBs carried on the author's boat. The small one, a Narco, transmits a distress signal on 121.5 and 243 MHz, while the larger one, a Callbuoy, transmits voice as well as a signal on 2182 kHz. (Photo by Sally Henderson)

Visual distress signals are also needed, and there are minimum federal requirements that may be obtained from the Coast Guard. All recreational boats over 16 feet must carry both night- and day-signaling devices. Those intended for use in the day only are floating or hand-held orange smoke signals and the distress flag, a three-foot square flag with a black square and ball on an orange background. Remember, too, that the national flag hoisted upside down is an ancient signal of distress. A mirror is not required, but it can be highly effective on a sunny day. Relatively unbreakable, a signal mirror has rounded edges and a sighting hole. Operating instructions are often printed on the back.

Distress signals for both day and night are various red flares. Some are hand-held, others are shot from launchers such as Very pistols, and still others are hand-held rocket-propelled flares. Of the launched signals, the parachute flares have by far the longest burning time, since the parachute naturally slows descent. Red flares are the signal of distress, while white flares are for the purpose of attracting attention. The latter type has about twice the brightness of the former, thus it is often a wise plan to use the white before the red to be sure your distress signal is seen. Plenty of extra flares should be carried, because even new ones don't always function properly.

Two other distress signals are the mast strobe flasher and electric distress light. The latter is simply a powerful flashlight that can be used to flash SOS in Morse code, which is . . . - - - . . . flashed four to six times each minute. The Coast Guard approves the distress light for night use only and requires that the light flash automatically. Permanent masthead strobe lights or even man-overboard strobes hoisted up the mast can be effective even in bright daylight or fog. However, the use of these lights has been abused, and the Coast Guard has recently ruled that they may be used for distress only. They are not to be used for anti-collision purposes, but I would not hesitate to use the masthead strobe on my 37-foot sloop if I were about to be run down by a steamer on a dark, stormy night.

Sound signals are not only required by the rules of the road, but they are also important for distress situations. Continuously blowing a horn or firing a gun is obviously an effective means of attracting attention. Particularly audible are freon air horns and the shrill sound-makers on electric bull horns. These devices are portable and are advantageous in that they can be taken in a life boat or raft.

A high degree of self-sufficiency is needed offshore, thus every seagoing vessel should have a wide selection of tools and spare parts for jury rigging and repairing damage. Needless to say a wide assortment of screw drivers, pliers, and wrenches is needed. Regarding the latter, be sure there is an adjustable end wrench that will fit the largest nut on the vessel. On my boat this happens to be the packing gland nut on the propeller shaft stuffing box, and, of course, it is essential that there be a means of tightening this nut. As a matter of fact, all nuts such as those for keel bolts and through-bolted fittings must be kept tight. Neglecting to do this has caused fittings to pull off in heavy weather, and I know of a boat that was dismasted because of loose nuts on her stem head fitting.

Essential tools for sailing vessels are rigging cutters, because after a dismasting, a broken spar hanging over the side in rough seas could punch a hole in the vessel's side. Before purchasing a rigging cutter it is a good idea to try cutting a piece of the largest rigging on your boat, because some small cutters are inadequate and will only mash the wire. Some ocean-racing regulations drawn up after the Fastnet disaster require two hack saws plus six blades and two drift punches capable of driving out all standing rigging clevis pins. Two handy tools for making rigging repairs are a press for clamping compression sleeves on wire rigging when a loop is desired and a banding instrument or large adjustable metal hose clamps that can be used for fishing broken spars.

There should also be tools and materials for repairing punctures to hull, decks, or superstructures. Fairly large sheets of plywood should be carried unless there are locker doors or trap doors under bunks or elsewhere of similar material that can be used for patching large holes. Of course, hammers, saws, drills, wood files, nails, screws, bolts, etc., are necessary, and an essential item is a wrecking bar to pry off inner ceilings that might block access to a hole in the hull. It is also prudent to carry sheets of copper and/or lead for patching, and caulking material and putty that can be used under water. Although seldom carried, a collision mat or at least a square of canvas with grommets and lashings should be aboard every offshore boat so that a hole in the hull can be covered from the outside.

A safety item that ought to be aboard most large vessels is a line-throwing apparatus. This is normally a rocket-launching gun that can propel a line well over 200 yards. The advantage of the device is obviously for use in rescue operations when it is necessary to put a line aboard another vessel or to the shore when the distressed boat is grounded.

Last, but far from least of the safety equipment mentioned in this section, is weather-predicting equipment. This may take the form of sophisticated instruments such as weather facsimiles, which supply up-to-date synoptic charts, or the simplest devices such as a weather radio and a barometer. In my opinion the latter two items should be aboard every cruising boat. The use of a barometer in forming tropical storm strategy will be mentioned in chapter 8. Weather can be obtained from other stations listed in the publication *World Wide Marine Weather Broadcasts*, published by the Department of Commerce. Hourly high-seas storm reports are available on the time signal stations WWV and WWVH. (See chapter 1.)

PERSONAL EQUIPMENT

This section includes wearable or personal portable safety gear that has not yet been covered. Its purpose from a safety standpoint is to keep you aboard or, failing that, to keep you afloat, to prevent hypothermia, and to make you conspicuous.

Considering all kinds of weather, perhaps the most important personal gear for keeping you on board is proper footwear. Even with the best skid-proofing, decks can be slippery when wet, and this can be aggravated on heeled sailboats, especially if you are to leeward and there is a lot of deck crown. There are a number of shoes, such as Sperry Topsiders, that are made specifically for the sailor and have treads that afford good grip in wet weather. Boots are made with the same kind of soles. Anyone going offshore should be certain that his soles are a skid-proof type and that the treads are not overly worn. Incidentally, foam-lined boots may very well have positive buoyancy, and it is very often best to leave them on when overboard, unless it is perhaps necessary to swim any distance. Boots provide warmth, and struggling to remove them can be exhausting.

Undoubtedly the most valuable piece of gear for keeping the crew aboard in heavy weather is the safety harness. This is basically a heavy belt with shoulder straps and a short safety line that can be clipped onto the rigging or the strong points discussed in chapter 6. A number of safety-harness failures occurred during the Fastnet Race, and as a result new recommendations have

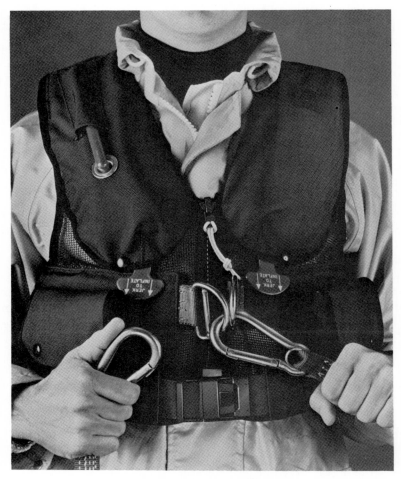

Figure 7-6. The Fastnet safety harness by Switlik. Notice the double snap hooks to allow escape if held under and the air tube for mouth inflation to provide buoyancy. (Courtesy of Switlik Co.)

been made by the ORC. These call for webbing straps of nylon with a minimum breaking strength of 1,000 kg per 25-mm width, a safety line no longer than 2 meters made of nylon rope or webbing with a breaking load of 2,080 kg, and self-closing hooks large enough to fully close around a metal cylinder 12.7-mm in diameter and able to withstand a load of at least 1,500 kg. If castings are used, they must be made by the investment (sometimes called "lost wax") casting process. All metal parts must be nonmagnetic.

It is interesting that the U.S. Navy specifications for harnesses are even more demanding in most respects. For instance, the harness must have a tensile strength in excess of 5,000 lbs, while the safety line and webbing must exceed 6,000 lbs of tensile strength. Both the ORC and Navy also require stringent drop tests, whereby a dummy is dropped six feet or more to test for shock loading.

Although the ORC allows a choice of having the safety line permanently attached or readily detachable from the harness with a hook, the latter arrangement allows the wearer a better chance of escape if he should happen to be held underwater by his safety line. Hooks should be the interlocking carabiner kind or preferably the safety type such as that made by Gibb, which prevents accidental opening. Lines should be spliced rather than tied, because knots such as the bowline can weaken a line by almost 50 percent. The ORC calls for four full tucks and two tapered tucks for each splice. Some sailors prefer two safety lines so that when moving about they never need to be unhooked. Recently, Ronstan Marine of Clearwater, Florida, has introduced the Ronstan-Viking-Latchway (RVL) system, which avoids the need to unhook and rehook when sliding a safety hook along a wire that passes a stanchion or rigging obstacle. The RVL is a small, cylindrical turnstile (accepting the harness hook) that slides past obstacles along a special heavy wire attached to the life-line stanchions. Ronstan's installation looks strong, but beware of hooking onto ordinary lifelines, as quite often they are not strong enough for extreme shock loading.

Whether wearing a safety harness or not, there is always the possibility of your falling or being thrown overboard, so you need some form of personal flotation. It has been mentioned that there are excellent flotation jackets that meet PFD Type III requirements, and many of these have the safety harness integrated with the jacket. This makes a lot of sense for heavy weather conditions, because a flotation jacket can keep you warm and dry, it does not overly restrict movement or make it awkward to board a canopy-covered life raft, and it has plenty of pockets in which you can carry such articles as a knife and signaling devices. Furthermore, it can help prevent hypothermia, which in cold weather is a greater danger than the threat of drowning. Disadvantages of a flotation jacket are that it may not be as buoyant as a PHD Type I or II, and it may not float you face up if you should lose consciousness. Not all jackets have crotch straps, but they are necessary to prevent the garment from riding up under the wearer's chin.

Signaling equipment that should be carried in pockets or on straps include a small strobe light and a loud whistle. It is not often suggested that a dye marker be carried on one's person, but it is easily carried and could be a real help to rescuers in finding a man overboard. There are a number of pocket-size personal man-overboard lights on the market, but some of them are not strobes. The Xenon strobes, however, are by far more visible than conventional lights. Be sure these devices are thoroughly waterproofed with O-rings and well-seated rubber caps that fit over switches. Whistles should be a referee or equally loud type made of noncorrosive material. There are also air horns that are small enough to be carried.

About the last word in personal protection are survival suits, and these should be carried on all boats that operate in cold waters, especially fishing craft used during winter months and/or in northern waters. U.S. federal

Figure 7-7. An exposure suit such as this one by Bayley is often indispensable for vessels operating in cold waters. It is not as cumbersome or expensive as it appears to be. (Courtesy of Bayley Suit, Inc.)

regulations now propose that ships operating in waters north of 35°N latitude or south of 35°S latitude must carry "exposure" suits. These are normally made of neoprene foam sandwiched between nylon, but under international SOLAS (Safety of Life at Sea) regulations, there are exemptions for large ships with life boats that allow "thermal protective aids," bag-like garments made of space blanket material. The main value of a survival or exposure suit is that it helps prevent hypothermia, chilling of the body core, which can kill a man overboard in a matter of minutes when he is inadequately protected with insulation. Another function of the suit is to afford flotation, and the more elaborate types are inflatable, normally through an oral tube. There are a variety of flotation garments affording thermal protection, but it is generally agreed that the foam-insulated dry suit covering the whole body is the most effective in reducing heat loss. These suits can be donned surprisingly fast with practice, because they are fairly flexible and can be opened wide with waterproof zippers. If possible they should be donned before going into the water. These zippers must be kept well lubricated with paraffin or wax. Fitted divers' wetsuits are also effective in retaining body heat. As with PFDs, all survival or exposure suits should be generously fitted with reflective tape on the above-water parts so that they will be highly visible to a searchlight at night. A very effective tape is the "ResQ" type with innumerable microscopic beads of glass on wide sheets, which can be applied to almost any surface. Of course, exposure suits should be equipped with personal strobe lights and whistles.

LIFE RAFTS

It is the safest policy to envision life rafts as last-resort equipment that should not be used in heavy weather unless the mother vessel has almost completely filled with water and is in imminent danger of sinking. Although a large ship's life boats may need to be launched early, before the ship takes on a pronounced list, abandoning a vessel prematurely for the apparent safety of a life raft may be like jumping from the frying pan into the fire, as a number of the 1979 Fastnet Race sailors discovered when their rafts were capsized or torn apart by the seas. Aside from offering more security, the mother ship will more often than not provide superior shelter and protection against hypothermia. Furthermore, she will be better equipped in every way and usually will have a more tolerable motion for greater protection against chronic seasickness. Also, there can be some risk in boarding a raft. In many cases, however, vessels have been abandoned needlessly. Time and again derelicts have been found floating high and often without really serious damage many days after the abatement of the heavy weather that caused their abandonment. Some crews might be alive today had they stayed with their ships.

Nevertheless, when a vessel at sea is really sinking (or burning uncontrollably) there is no denying that an escape vehicle is an absolute necessity. It is what a parachute is to an aviator when his plane catches on fire or comes apart. Thus, every offshore vessel should be equipped with quality rafts or boats sufficient to take off the entire crew. Certain vessels, such as some tankships, are even required by law to carry a sufficient number of life boats on

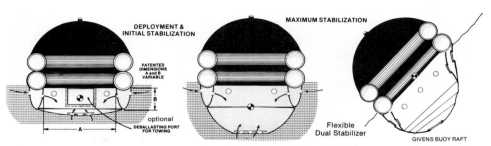

Figure 7-8. This inflatable life raft, a Givens, has a huge water ballast bag, and it is the most stable, but not the most mobile, type.

each side to accommodate all persons on board. (Legal requirements for shipping can be found in the *Code of Federal Regulations*, Title 46.)

Just what determines quality in an inflatable raft may be open to some debate. At the least, there is disagreement about stability requirements. There is one school of thought contending that stability is the major concern, and rafts should be provided with large water-filled stability bags attached to their bottoms to prevent capsizing. On the other hand, there is the argument that huge water bags inhibit the raft from yielding to a breaking sea, thereby subjecting it to greater risk of damage. This school also contends that a large bag takes a relatively long time to fill with water, thus affording little stability during the crucial boarding period, and once the bag is filled the raft is relatively immobile when it may be necessary to move it quickly away from the sinking ship. At least one raft manufacturer believes in high mobility for rafts and even supplies a sail. This type is oblong in shape, and the stability pockets are designed to minimize resistance to forward motion. Another argument for this type is that it resists spinning. The philosophy behind mobile rafts is that there are times when you should not wait for rescue but should try to save yourself. This makes sense under certain circumstances, but one should usually not leave the scene of the disaster when rescuers know its position. Then too, the boat-shaped raft nearly always trades off some stability for locomotion.

As with any boat design, life raft design involves some compromises. The crew of a vessel operating in cold stormy waters where dangerous seas are frequently encountered might want the emphasis on raft stability, but the crew of a vessel in warm regions off the beaten track and far from shore or shipping lanes might opt for locomotion at some expense to stability. Although it is true that many rafts used in the Fastnet storm lacked adequate stability, there is a feeling among some experienced seamen that the huge ballast bag is an "overkill" solution to the problem. Since the Fastnet experience, most raft manufacturers have increased the size of their underwater stability pockets, and this approach represents a middle-of-the-road solution.

There seems to be little argument that raft canopies are needed, especially in cold waters, but unless carefully designed these can contribute to capsizing from wind pressure, and in some cases the entrances are too small for a large man in a bulky life jacket. A complaint heard from some Fastnet racers was that the entrance covers could not be adequately closed. Other raft problems during the Fastnet storm, aside from capsizings, were: canopies tearing and the arch tubes (supporting the canopy) bending and losing air, insufficient hand grips inside and on the bottom, the splitting apart of the two large buoyancy rings, lack of security of supplies, weak attachment of drogue line and/or painter, the painter being too far from the canopy entrance, and lack of insulation in the bottom. Incidentally, Maurice Bailey, who spent 117 days in an inflatable raft, told me that he felt a double inflatable bottom is essential. He also thinks that for lengthy periods in a life raft there should be a double canopy, larger than normal apertures, and more interior pockets and attachment points. Another problem sometimes encountered is failure of CO_2 cylinders to properly inflate, but this may be due to lack of care and inspections. Since the Fastnet experience, a number of raft improvements have been made on most models.

About the best one can do to ensure that he has proper rafts is to buy those that are Coast Guard approved and have them inspected every year or two by an approved inspector. Don't try to economize on size or by purchasing cheap makes, and keep the rafts well protected, preferably in well-sealed fiberglass canisters. These containers usually lack handles, but quite often they are needed. Normally, the canister is strapped to the deck with lashings using quick releases such as pull-pin snap shackles, and its painter, which controls inflation, is firmly secured to the vessel. When a raft is needed, the canister is thrown overboard, the painter is pulled, and the inflating raft breaks open the canister. Boarding can be effected by climbing or jumping into an entrance or jumping into the water next to the raft or even onto the canopy of some makes. There should be a sturdy life line around the buoyancy rings, boarding ladders, and righting straps on the bottom in case the raft inflates upside down or is capsized. Water-level boarding platforms on life rafts will be required for ships subject to the new SOLAS regulations. Large ships (with freeboards over 15 feet) have their rafts launched from davits. Most raft manufacturers provide an optional hydrostatic release that can either be operated manually or automatically by water pressure if the vessel should happen to sink suddenly.

The use of a life raft drogue (small sea anchor) is also somewhat controversial. It is generally agreed that a drogue will stabilize the raft, and certainly it minimizes drift, as the accompanying graph (figure 7-9) clearly illustrates. During the Fastnet disaster, however, some rafts seemed to fare better without drogues. In one case, it was reported that use of the drogue held the raft too firmly and allowed waves to break against and over the canopy. The raft occupants decided, therefore, to haul in the drogue, and when this was done the freely drifting raft yielded to the waves and behaved much better. Later, the raft manufacturer agreed that this was the proper tactic. Nevertheless, there certainly are times when a drogue may be needed, and these include occasions when it is necessary or desirable to hold an oblong raft end-to the seas, to keep a circular raft from spinning, to better position stability pockets, and to keep the access door away from the seas. Furthermore, excessive drift may make the raft hard to find or possibly allow it to pass an island refuge.

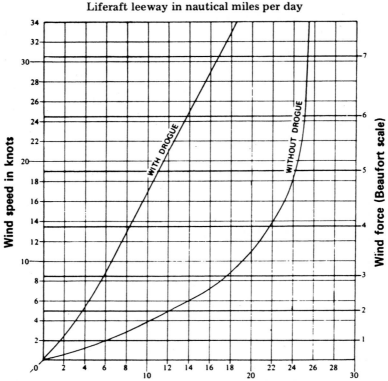

Figure 7-9. A graph resulting from U.S. Coast Guard studies showing life raft drift with and without a drogue. These are average figures, and they don't include the effect of current. Actual drift will be more or less than the graph shows depending on the raft's load, degree of inflation, the type of ballast, and windage. (Courtesy of U.S. Coast Guard)

Although figure 7-9 shows that average drift without a drogue is less than 26 miles per day in Force 7 winds, the Coast Guard has written that drift has been so much as 80 miles per day in lightly loaded, fully inflated rafts in Force 10 winds.

Offshore Racing Council standards for life raft equipment include: one buoyant rescue quoit attached to at least 30 meters of buoyant line, one safety knife, one bailer, two sponges, one sea anchor permanently attached to the raft, two paddles, one repair kit, one topping-up pump or bellows, one waterproof flashlight, three hand-held red distress flares, six anti-seasickness tablets for each person aboard, survival instructions on a plastic sheet, gas inflation, and a grab bag containing a second sea anchor, two safety can openers, a first aid kit, a rust-proof graduated drinking vessel, two "cyalume" sticks or two throwable floating lamps, one daylight signaling mirror, one whistle, two red parachute flares, three red hand flares, non-thirst-provoking food rations and barley sugar or the equivalent, watertight receptacles containing fresh water (at least one-half liter per person), one copy of the illustrated table of life-saving signals, nylon string, and polyethylene bags. It is certainly prudent to have an additional emergency kit kept in a locker near the raft that contains some other gear such as an EPIRB, a strobe flasher, a dye marker, screw-type wood plugs to repair punctures, a portable VHF radio, a jerry jug of water, an air horn, a space blanket or warm garments, a small compass, and a solar still (designed for life rafts or boats). Requirements for escape vessels on board ships are found in the aforementioned *Code of Federal Regulations*, Title 46. New SOLAS regulations will require that an EPIRB be carried on each side of a ship and stowed in a manner that allows it to be readily placed in a life boat or raft, and open life boats will be required to carry exposure suits for three of the crew and space blankets (or thermal protective aids) for the rest of the crew.

PREPARING FOR HEAVY WEATHER

Lack of preparation for heavy weather very often results from procrastination. Even when the vessel is well equipped, her skipper may delay taking protective action until the last minute, when some thorough preparations are exceedingly difficult to achieve. Reasons for procrastination perhaps are the attempt to maintain a schedule, the competitive urge to continue driving a boat in a race, reluctance to rouse the off watch, or simply wishful thinking that bad weather will never materialize. These are fairly normal reactions when a storm is brewing, and no skipper wants to be overly cautious or an alarmist, but it is his responsibility to be prepared. The best seamanship requires a trace of pessimism.

One of the first preparations when heavy weather is expected is the taking of seasickness pills. There is nothing that can debilitate a crew like seasickness, and it usually takes some time for remedies to work, so don't put off taking them. If pills are swallowed after a person is sick, they often can't be kept down. Of course, many sailors are not prone to seasickness, and they may refuse to take certain remedies such as antihistamines that can produce drowsiness. Should such a sailor find himself unexpectedly nauseated in severely rough weather, there is at least one simple remedy, and I have learned this from first-hand experience. Although not well known, a prescription medicine called Bucladin is obtainable in the form of small yellowish pills that are held under the tongue and thus absorbed into the body without swallowing. A fairly recent development is the Transderm, a small medicated disc (also requiring a prescription) that is stuck behind the ear, where it delivers a gradual dose of scopolamine through the skin. This system, too, avoids the need to swallow, but it may take two or three hours to work, and there can be deleterious side effects, so it should not be used without consulting a doctor and carefully following directions. A completely different remedy, recently revealed by Dr. Daniel Choy, is the wearing of wrist bands that apply pressure to the Nei-Kuan points on the wrists. This method is related to acupuncture, and it is said to be highly effective in many cases. Information about the wrist bands can be obtained from Ulmer Sails at City Island, New York.

Another ounce of prevention worth a pound of cure is donning foul weather gear well ahead of time and keeping your clothes and bedding dry. Once you get wet in the ocean it takes almost forever to dry out, because the salt in your clothing absorbs moisture from the air even on a relatively dry day. A thorough soaking in heavy weather is not just uncomfortable; it can be demoralizing over a long period of time and lead to hypothermia even when the weather is not extremely cold. Obtain high-quality foul weather gear, including boots, and use it. If your boat is subject to leaks below, keep your clothes and bedding in waterproof bags.

Other morale boosters during heavy weather are food and hot drinks, and these are also helpful to the crew's strength and endurance. But the galley may be difficult, if not impossible, to use in the roughest seaway, especially on board a small boat; thus food and hot drinks should be prepared well in advance of the heavy weather. Of course, food cannot always be kept hot, but certainly drinks such as boullion, chocolate-flavored mixes, coffee, and tea can be kept at least warm in thermos jugs over extended periods.

When the seas grow rough, the crew should not delay donning flotation gear (PFDs or flotation jackets) and safety harnesses, because it will be necessary to move about the deck securing equipment, battening down, and shortening sail. Jack lines or cable travelers should be rigged if they are not already, and the crew should use their safety lines when performing the various chores on deck. If really severe weather is anticipated, it is often a wise plan to rig a number of taut (but not exceedingly so) grab lines around the cockpit, but it is important to see that they are not rigged in such a way as to seriously impair movement or trip the crew.

Other preparations for a blow include securing all gear below and stowing in lockers all loose equipment on deck. When this is being done, any gear that might be needed during the heavy weather should be hauled out and put in a convenient location. These items would include heavy lines that might be needed for rodes or drags, anchors and drogues, storms sails, lashing lines, sheets and tackles, portable bilge pump, bucket, flares, flashlights, and so forth. The lower storm slide in the companionway should be bolted in place early in the game, and additional vertical slides will be needed as the weather deteriorates. All portholes and hatches, including cockpit seat lockers, should be dogged. Vulnerable ventilators need to be covered or closed, even *Dorade* types in survival conditions. When possible, engine control panels on deck should be protected with covers. Close all seacocks except those for scuppers, and shut off the engine exhaust valve if the engine is not being used. Put extra lashings on all heavy objects on deck such as anchors and the dinghy. Pad any sharp corners below or projections against which a person could be thrown. Check the bilge and pump it dry. See that there are lashings or belts on the bunks to prevent the crew from being thrown around in the cabin, and put the first aid kit in a convenient location. Commercial vessels additionally need security checks for their cargo, booms, and large hatch covers. Conditions of ballasting and free surface must be known. All lashings should be snugged up, particularly when they are of rope, and all machinery should be checked to see that it is operating properly. The engine might need to be kept warm even if a power vessel lies ahull. More will be said about preparing ships for heavy weather in chapter 8.

On sailing vessels, the reduction of canvas must be commensurate with wind strength whether racing or not, because safety and controllability can be lessened when a boat is laboring from being overburdened. In shortening down, the main considerations are reducing the sail area to minimize pronounced heeling and violent pounding, to use sails sufficiently strong and small to prevent damage to them or the rig, to raise them high enough to keep solid water from breaking against them, and to maintain steering control and proper balance for the tactic that will be used. Regarding the latter point, when reaching or heaving to, the sails' total center of effort should be nearly amidships, but when running off, the center of effort should be far forward. If the boat can lie to a sea anchor off the bow, a riding sail is set far aft. (Much more will be said about storm tactics in the next chapter.) Check the rigging to see that it is taut and protected from chafe as much as possible. Secure unused booms with lashings if they are not in gallows frames. In some cases an unused boom might be lowered and secured to the cabin top or deck to prevent it from swinging from side to side.

A final thought on preparing for a storm is to be sure you know your position before the weather deteriorates, because visibility can be very limited in a blow, and your tactics might depend to a large extent on your proximity to shore. Obviously you want to get as much sea room as possible, and you never want to run with any speed toward a lee shore when there is any possibility of reaching it before the storm abates. Even if that shore has a harbor, it can be risky going through a narrow entrance during heavy weather in poor visibility, and high tides associated with the storm could very much detract from the harbor's protection. Navigating during a hard chance can be exceedingly difficult, so it certainly makes sense to know where you are before the blow commences.

8

Tactics and Vessel Handling in Heavy Weather

It is a seaman who shortens sail
in time, but a lubber who cracks on
till all's blue.
　　　—Captain A. J. Kenealy, 1905

There can be no hard and fast rules for heavy weather tactics, because too many variables exist in the weather, sea state, type and design of vessel, condition of vessel and her crew, geographic location, and other factors that affect the course of action. Nevertheless, alternative strategies and the behavior characteristics of representative vessels in typical heavy weather conditions can be discussed in very general terms.

RECOMMENDED COURSES IN TROPICAL STORMS

About the firmest rules one can present in regard to conduct in tropical cyclones would be those in accordance with the so-called "law of storms" often associated with Henry Piddington and other early authorities. It should be borne in mind, however, that there are plenty of exceptions to these rules and that standard advice is of a very general nature.

Let us assume that a vessel at sea in the Northern Hemisphere has received warning by radio of an approaching hurricane. The forecast probably gives the storm's whereabouts a number of hours earlier, its estimated course, wind strength near the center, and approximate speed of travel. Obviously, the vessel's master should do his utmost to avoid the storm, but this is not always easy to do, especially in a slow-moving small sailboat, since hurricanes can change course drastically and suddenly speed up or slow down. If the vessel is close to shore and near a well-protected harbor she might seek shelter if the storm is far away, otherwise she should head offshore and try to get all possible sea room. Remember that some harbors that are protected in most conditions may turn into death traps in a hurricane due to extreme wind shifts and tremendously high tides. For this reason large seagoing vessels often leave harbors in advance of a tropical storm to ride it out at sea.

In accordance with the law of storms, a vessel far offshore should first determine where she is in relation to the storm center. This can be done by carefully and constantly observing the wind while hove to. Ballot's law tells us that if you face the wind in the Northern Hemisphere, the center of the low pressure is about 115 degrees to your right. Should the wind direction remain constant and increase in velocity, you are directly in the storm's path, and if it keeps on course, the eye will pass right over you. The barometer would be steadily falling as the eye approaches. A backing wind (shifting counterclockwise) indicates that you are in the so-called "navigable semicircle" of the storm, which is its left side (to your left if you were in the eye facing the direction to which the storm is moving). Seas are generally less violent, and the wind strength is diminished by the forward movement of the storm in this semicircle. A veering wind (shifting clockwise) shows that you are in the "dangerous semicircle," the right-hand side of the storm. The right front quadrant has the most dangerous seas, while the winds immediately behind that quadrant tend to be the strongest, because they are reinforced by the storm's forward moment. There could be much higher winds in the front quadrant if tornadoes are present. A rising barometer and diminishing winds indicate that you are at the rear of the storm and it is moving away from you.

Standard advice for a vessel in the path of an approaching tropical cyclone is to run as fast as conditions permit at right angles to the storm track. If you are or will be in the left-hand, navigable semicircle, you should run off with the wind more or less broad on the starboard quarter. Sailboats, of course, would be on the starboard tack. The same advice is given to a vessel directly ahead of the storm track; she should be headed at right angles to the track toward the navigable side. A sailboat would be running on the starboard tack with the wind between her quarter and stern. The unfortunate vessel ahead of the hurricane in its dangerous semicircle would normally head in the opposite direction, as much as possible at right angles to the track of the eye and away from it.

Even if the vessel in the right front quadrant is a fast powerboat or a large ship, it is very dangerous to try to outrun the hurricane or pass across its track to the navigable semicircle, because the heavy swells preceding the storm will severely hamper the vessel's speed, and the eye could very well pass right over her. A sailing vessel under sail will not be able to head at right angles to the storm track, but she should sail close-hauled as far as possible away from the track. If she is so close to the storm that she cannot carry on under sail, the usual recommendation is for her to heave to on the starboard tack. What headway she makes will take her mostly away from the eye's track, and the shifting wind will draw aft, thus minimizing the risk of getting caught aback (having her sails fill from the wrong side as the wind shifts across her bow).

When a sailboat in the navigable semicircle must be hove to, oft-repeated advice is for her to lie on the port tack in the Northern Hemisphere. This is in conformance with an ancient generalized rule that a sailing vessel should heave to on the tack that allows the wind to draw aft. The reason for this advice is to minimize the risk of getting caught aback. There was probably greater risk in getting caught aback for the old time square rigger than for a modern, wholesome type of fore-and-aft rigged boat.

As said before, many of the rules associated with the law of storms can have exceptions, and one of these might be heaving to on the port tack when in the navigable semicircle. Such a practice would take the boat more or less toward the eye, and although she should not be forereaching to any great extent when hove to, she might be making at least some headway and considerable leeway, which would put her closer to the storm center. About the last place a vessel wants to be is in the eye, as the seas there will be tremendously steep and chaotic with no wind to flatten or control them. Another factor is how the sailboat lies with respect to the seas in the navigable semicircle. If she lies nearly beam to them when hove to and the seas have dangerous breaking tops, the boat could be rolled over. When the wind is too strong to run under sail away from the eye, then she might run before the seas under bare poles, perhaps towing drags astern.

Obviously, none of the standard rules should be followed when doing so heads the vessel toward a lee shore, other ships, or any object with which she could collide. Also, in some circumstances, it might be inadvisable to head toward a strong current or a shoal that could cause steeper seas. Then, too, the course of action would depend on how well the vessel is behaving with respect to the seas. If she were repeatedly being pooped by following seas or in danger of broaching to or being rolled down by waves on the beam, then her attitude and tactics should be changed or at least modified.

A minor modification of the standard advice is suggested by the comments of Robert H. Simpson, a former associate director of the U.S. Weather Bureau and chief of the National Hurricane Warning Center in Miami, who is also an experienced yachtsman. Simpson, who has flown through a great many hurricanes, has written about the danger of a small boat being in the navigable semicircle of a severe hurricane. He feels that a safer location for small craft is in the right rear quadrant where the seas are longer and less confused. This could mean that if the boat were in (or almost in) the left rear quadrant, she might run off under reduced sail or bare poles perhaps (rather than heave to) in order to head for the rear right quadrant. An important consideration before deciding on such a heading is whether or not the boat would be exposed to dangerous beam seas that could capsize her.

When planning tactics to avoid the storm center, the general tendency for a storm to recurve discussed in chapter 2 should be carefully considered (see figure 8-1). Bear in mind that in the Northern Hemisphere the storm track turns to the right and the recurving will be greatest in the middle latitudes, although storm tracks are extremely varied and often highly erratic.

Remember that the rules discussed here apply to the Northern Hemisphere, and that cyclones revolve in the opposite direction (clockwise) in the Southern Hemisphere. In the latter location a vessel directly in front of a tropical storm has the dangerous semicircle on her right hand and the navigable semicircle on her left. Of course, the storm will track from low to high latitudes and recurving will be to the left.

SAILING YACHT TACTICS

Heavy weather tactics for sailing yachts might be divided into two general categories—active and passive. The former means continuing to sail under drastically reduced canvas. The active category would include the boat that is continuing toward her destination or the proper side of a storm (either at slow

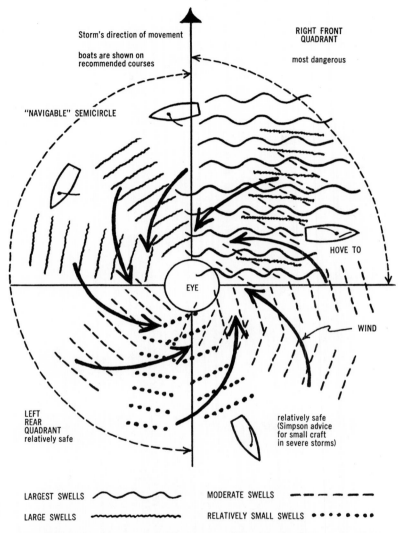

Figure 8-1. Tropical storm strategy. Although the boats are shown on generally recommended courses, the exact headings will depend on how the vessel lies when hove to or behaves when running off and the direction and nature of the seas. It could be very dangerous taking steep breaking seas of the plunging variety on the beam. (From *Sea Sense* by Richard Henderson)

or fast speeds, depending on wind and sea conditions) and also the boat that has given up trying to go where she wants, but is running off before the storm at considerable speed.

Passive tactics are inactive ones, where the boat has either stopped headway or is running off slowly or is drifting freely, stripped of all sail. In effect, she has given up trying to fight the elements and is yielding to them, simply waiting for the bad weather to pass by. With such tactics it is usually not necessary to man the helm.

Actively pressing on under sail involves progressive reduction of sail, and this requires a variety of well-made heavy-weather sails and an efficient means of shortening down. Such tactics also require a strong boat and a reasonably sound crew, who are not devastated by fatigue or seasickness and are able to make frequent sail changes and can steer efficiently. The particular

Figure 8-2. The author's boat with her storm sails hoisted. Both the storm staysail with an area of 42 square feet and the storm trysail with an area of 70 square feet are close to the Rod Stephen's rule of thumb for size.

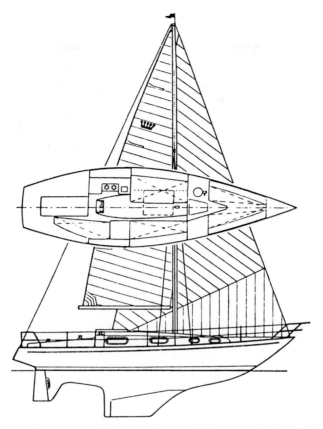

Figure 8-3. The Contessa 32, a wholesome boat with long stability range, was the only boat in her class of 58 starters to finish the 1979 Fastnet Race.

sail combinations carried will, of course, depend on the direction as well as velocity of the wind and also on the sea conditions.

For beating to windward and also running off, you need a small storm jib or staysail, and there should be a means of holding the sail's luff to its stay with hanks or some means other than a bolt rope that fits into a groove. Slotted luff foils often used on racing boats can allow the jib's luff to escape or jam in a real blow. Several rows of reef points or eyelets and reef cringles are needed for mainsails, and every sailboat that goes to sea should have a storm trysail. A number of boats in the Fastnet storm might have fared better with proper trysails. Rod Stephens, the well known expert on rigging and seamanship, puts it much more strongly. In regard to the lack of storm trysails on board the racers, he said, "That's why there was so much trouble in the Fastnet." Another failing during that race was that storm sails were oversized. Rod Stephen's rule of thumb for storm trysail size is .05P squared and .025P_2 squared for the storm headsail, P being the height of the mainsail and P_2 the height of the foretriangle. Whatever sail combination is used, it is of the utmost importance that the sails be kept filled and are not allowed to flog a great deal, for they will not last long if permitted to flap in a really strong wind.

Some boats, especially the very light ones, successfully ran off before the wind and seas at relatively fast speeds in the Fastnet Race. Despite their success, I am not always enthusiastic about this tactic, particularly in modern IOR boats. It can be done if there are plenty of highly competent helmsmen aboard who can take turns steering, because the boat has enough speed for good steering control and she can be headed away from or between dangerous breaking seas. Make one mistake, however, and she could be pooped (have a following sea break over her stern), as the stern may be sucked down to some extent, even that of a light boat, and the high stern wave can reinforce the following sea, making it more apt to break aboard. I have known several yachts (not Fastnet racers) that were seriously pooped when running off, and although the vessels survived, the crew on deck were badly injured, one with a broken rib that punctured his lung. In one case the helmsman was thrown with such a force against the wooden steering wheel that it shattered, and incidentally, he feels that the old-fashioned wheel that was designed to break at the hub prevented him from being impaled on the spoke. Needless to say, every boat with wheel steering needs a strong emergency tiller.

Perhaps an even greater risk for a modern light boat is the possibility of broaching to. With her fine bow and full body abaft amidships as well as her short fin keel, the extreme type of IOR racer is apt to root and turn uncontrollably broadside to the seas unless she is very skillfully handled. An inadvertent turn at high speed adds a lot of centrifugal force to the power of the offending sea, and the boat could be rolled over. The risk of a broach or even pitchpoling (turning end over end) is much greater at night when the helmsman cannot see very far and cannot attempt to avoid large following seas or "holes in the water" ahead. Another consideration concerning high speed running off is that when the boat is moving fast she spends a maximum length of time on the wave's crest in a position of least stability, rather than having the wave pass by more quickly were she moving slower.

Undoubtedly, one of the most successful small boats in the Fastnet storm was a Contessa 32, which was the only boat in her class of 58 to finish the race. She beat to windward during the storm under a storm jib and fully reefed mainsail. During the height of the blow, the head pulled out of the jib and the boat continued to sail close hauled under her reefed main. It is interesting that one of her crew wrote she "continued steadily on her course at 4 knots to windward with a much easier motion following the loss of the jib." The Contessa had no problems except that she took one beam ends knockdown while her jib was still up, but she righted promptly and no serious harm was done.

The success of this boat may be credited partly to tactics and good helmsmanship and perhaps partly to luck, but it should be pointed out that she (and her sisters) were among the most wholesome small yachts in the race. In fact, she was used as the benchmark boat for an investigation of the tragedy by the

Royal Yachting Association. The Contessa 32 is a moderate displacement boat with a relatively long integrated fin keel and separated rudder abaft a sizable skeg. Her beam is generous but not excessive, and she has a healthy ballast to displacement ratio of over 45 percent. Her vertical center of gravity is well below the load waterline and the GM is over 3 feet. Studies showed that she can be heeled to 157 degrees before losing positive stability, and if calculations were accurate, this gives her a far greater range of stability than any boat measured under the MHS (see figure 8-4).

A point that should be emphasized in regard to active tactics is the need for plenty of capable crew. On an ocean race this requirement can usually be met, but a singlehander or a skipper sailing shorthanded with a small, exhausted or unskilled crew may very well have to resort to passive tactics. One occasionally hears of shorthanded boats successfully running off at high speeds, but their success may be due to exceptional helmsmanship and crew endurance, the right conditions of sea and weather, a boat well suited to the tactic, and perhaps a little luck as well.

A classic example of shorthanded scudding is the case of Bernard Moitessier's 40-foot steel ketch *Joshua*, when she ran before tremendous seas in the

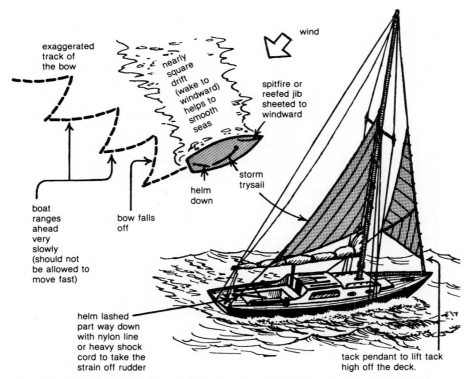

Figure 8-4. A small yacht hove to under a storm trysail and spitfire jib. A larger boat or one with a larger foretriangle would behave better with a storm staysail.

South Pacific in 1965. Moitessier adopted what he called the Dumas technique (named after a famous singlehanded circumnavigator) of running without towing drags astern. Stripped of all sail, *Joshua* was steered so that she took each crest at an angle of from 15 to 20 degrees of being dead astern. With no one to relieve him at the helm except his wife, Moitessier ran off at considerable speed in a gale that lasted for days. This worked well for *Joshua* partly because of the Moitessiers' steering skills; partly because the seas were long and relatively regular, although exceedingly steep; and partly because *Joshua* was well suited for the tactic. Of fairly heavy displacement, she had a long keel but with a moderately cut-away forefoot, a central cockpit that afforded protection for the helmsman in following seas, a large deep rudder well aft, a fairly full bow, and a pointed stern (which some consider the best type for following seas, although that point is debatable).

It should be kept firmly in mind that Moitessier's technique might not work so well for other sailors in different boats and in other conditions. While *Joshua*'s skipper strongly endorsed the tactic for his circumstance, he admitted, "Just because we got away without suffering damage I cannot pretend to talk like an authority on the handling of a yacht in the high latitudes of the South Pacific." Incidentally, *Joshua*'s designer, Jean Knocker, expressed his opinion that in following seas "it is desirable for safety's sake to let the crest pass under the boat as quickly as possible," and this statement suggests slow speed, at least on the crest. He further said that he is filled with admiration for the proficiency of *Joshua*'s crew as helmsmen, and he also thinks the double-ender is a good type of boat for those conditions.

Even Moitessier doesn't advocate running off at exceedingly fast speeds. He recommends a speed of between 5½ and 6 knots for *Joshua*, which is about equal to the square root of her waterline length. There always should be enough speed for the rudder to work efficiently so that you can take the seas at the right angle, steer away from combers, and counteract any tendency to broach. Moitessier is against towing drags because they hamper steering. The problem is, however, that many boats, especially light-displacement racers, get going far too fast, and they can't slow down without towing drags. Sometimes even drags won't slow the boat and she'll begin to surf, but they often will reduce speed if they are small drogues, automobile tires, or other objects that cause a lot of resistance. One trick that will help alleviate the detriment to steering caused by towing drags astern is to secure the towing lines at the rail on both sides of the boat amidships rather than at the stern. Observe that the towing bitt on a tug boat is as far as possible amidships.

Needless to say, a prerequisite for scudding is ample room to leeward. One cannot use this tactic when he is anywhere near a lee shore. Storms can last for many days and a boat running off with any speed can cover a lot of ground before the storm abates.

Before concluding this brief discussion of active tactics, I should mention the use of the auxiliary engine. I know of a few instances where its use has been helpful in heavy weather. In a couple of cases the engine was run to give the boat better steering control when she was scudding, and in other cases it was used to help hold the boat's bow toward the seas to prevent them from hitting her beam on, thus reducing susceptibility to capsize. I have even heard of backing the engine against a sea anchor streamed from the bow to help hold the head up. Of course, it takes a fairly powerful engine and large propeller for any real effectiveness in severe conditions, and unless the prop is deep, it may spend a lot of time out of water. Another consideration is ventilation for the engine without sacrifice to watertight integrity. Also, it could be difficult to keep the exhaust outlet out of water, and incidentally, if the engine is not run, the outlet should be closed if reachable with a plug when there is no shut-off valve. Instrument/control panels located in the cockpit are often vulnerable to flooding and shorting out in heavy weather, and it is a good idea to have a duplicate panel mounted below with a means of disconnecting and covering the one in the cockpit. Obviously, the engine can be valuable when trying to clear a lee shore or entering a harbor to seek shelter, but reduced sail should be available to assist the auxiliary or to take over in the event of engine failure.

Be sure to keep your fuel tanks clean, as any sediment that has collected on their bottoms will be stirred up in a seaway to the great detriment of carburetors and fuel injectors.

Passive tactics consist of three basic alternatives: heaving to, lying ahull, and riding to a drogue. These alternatives are used when the vessel is being damaged through the use of active tactics; or when her safety is being threatened by such action; or, as said earlier, when the crew are sick, fatigued, or unable to effectively man the helm. Another reason for using passive tactics is for the purpose of keeping the boat in a relatively stationary position, without moving any great distance. This would be done when one does not want to get too far off course, when there is concern about obstructions or lee shores, or when awaiting rescue after a call for help. Of course, close proximity to a lee shore or something else you want to avoid, such as a storm center, shoal, or dangerous current, may very well require active tactics taking you away from the danger.

Heaving to means stopping headway, and in sailing vessels this is normally accomplished by backing sails that counteract the thrust of forward-driving sails. The classic means of heaving to in a sloop in heavy weather is with a storm trysail (or a deeply reefed mainsail if there is no trysail) trimmed flat and counteracted with a backed storm headsail sheeted flat to windward. The tactic is illustrated in figure 8-5. This illustration shows a small sloop with a backed storm jib or spitfire; on larger boats and those with cutter rigs, however, it is often more effective to use a backed storm staysail, which brings the two counteracting sails closer together and improves balance. On my boat, a 37-foot sloop, I have a removable staysail running from the middle of the mast (opposite the point where the after lower shrouds secure to the mast) to a point about four feet abaft the stem head.

When hove to with counteracting sails, the standard practice is to lash the helm down (with the rudder to windward). This keeps the boat headed up when the after sail drives her slowly ahead. She slows down as the after sail begins to luff, and the backed headsail forces her head away from the wind.

Figure 8-5. The author at the helm of his boat in the Gulf Stream with a plunging breaker on the quarter. The boat is running off nicely under a storm jib. (Photo by Sally Henderson)

After falling off, the boat gathers way again and the cycle is repeated. Of course, different boats behave differently, so it takes some experimentation to find just the right combination of sails and rudder angle.

Some sailors heave to with the helm manned, but this means that the boat must be allowed to forereach to some extent for any helm control, and I would call this more of an active tactic. The advantage of such an action is the ability to have at least a little maneuverability and thus some capability to avoid dangerous crests, but should you be hit by a crest your forward speed will increase the impact and perhaps cause more solid water to dump aboard. The advantage of passively heaving to (with minimal forereaching) is that the boat will make very little headway but a lot of leeway and yield to the seas, thereby lessening their impact. In addition, the boat will leave a drift wake to windward that may help smooth the seas and possibly cause some of them to break before they reach the boat.

The modern yacht will generally lie anywhere between 75 to 50 degrees off the wind when hove to under storm trysail and a backed headsail. She will not keep to a constant heading but most likely her bow will make a zig zag track as she "backs and fills" and the seas knock her bow to leeward (see figure 8-6). Every attempt must be made to minimize rapid backing because this can put a great strain on the rudder, but the heading should be high enough to hold the bow somewhat up to the seas to lessen the risk of capsize. A yawl or ketch may be able to set a small storm sail on her mizzen mast to help hold up her bow.

When the winds become too strong to carry any sail, the vessel must either run off, lie ahull, or ride to a sea anchor. If storm sails are well made, however, and they are very small and the boat is sturdily rigged, they can be carried in extremely heavy winds. It is interesting that Rod Stephens wrote me he does not consider any wind occurring during the Fastnet storm as being too strong to carry sail. Nevertheless, there may come a time when sails (or rigging) are looking suspect, heavy spray is breaking against them, they are badly shaking the mast, they are causing knockdowns, or the boat cannot be slowed and controlled. Then it is time to remove all sail or at least drastically reduce it.

Lying ahull means that all sail is lowered and the boat is allowed to find her natural position and drift off to leeward, yielding to the force of the seas. Most boats will lie between beam-on and quarter-to the seas, depending on the rig, underwater profile, and freeboard. It is customary to lash the helm down (rudder to windward) to inhibit excessive forereaching. This tactic, also called hulling, is controversial, and some experienced seamen have said they would never use it, since a boat is most susceptible to capsizing and/or having a wave break on the cabin top when lying beam to the seas. On the other hand, a great number of blue-water sailors have lain ahull very successfully in the right conditions.

I have used the tactic on two occasions in the mid North Atlantic, once for 15 hours during a force 10 gale, and our 37-foot sloop behaved beautifully. Advantages of the tactic are that it is easy to do, no one need be on deck, and the boat is presenting maximum buoyancy to the seas (rather than minimum buoyancy if end-on to the seas). The boat may roll quite a lot in the trough, blanketed behind high waves, but out of the trough she will be held reasonably steady by the wind pressure on her rig. From our experience I found that our boat heeled considerably on the crest so that breakers struck the topsides rather than dumping on the cabin top. Furthermore, the square drift caused by the boat's approximate two knots of leeway seemed to make most of the waves break before they hit us.

The greatest danger of lying ahull is in being struck by a rogue wave or steep plunging breakers while the boat lies beam to the seas. This could roll her over, especially if she has a short range of stability. In my opinion, a requirement for hulling is the predominance of spilling-type waves (those that break some-what gradually at the very crest) rather than plunging seas (those with steep faces that rear up and suddenly topple over). The latter type are most often found in a strong current or in shallow water, even over a continental shelf when the wave "feels bottom." Other requirements are a relatively high range of stability, a very strong cabin top, small windows, and absolute watertight integrity with sturdy storm slides that are kept closed.

Lying to a sea anchor is also a controversial tactic. The main purpose of this passive alternative is to hold the vessel's end to the seas, thereby lessening the risk of capsize, and also to minimize drift towards a lee shore. Arguments against the tactic include lack of yield to the impact of seas and the fact that it is often difficult to hold the bow of a modern yacht into the seas. Furthermore, there can be a great deal of strain on the sea anchor gear and certain parts of the boat.

In former times when many a small yacht had a deep forefoot and/or the windage of the rig was fairly far aft, the sea anchor could be streamed success-

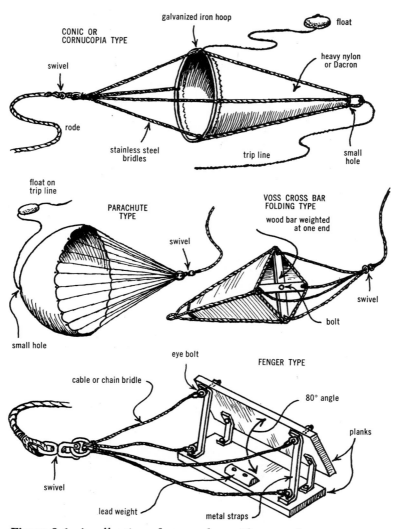

Figure 8-6. A collection of sea anchors. The parachute type causes the most drag, while the Fenger drogue causes the least.

fully from the bow. Most modern yachts, however, are too cutaway under the water forward to lie with their bows up, and they will spend much of the time nearly beam to the seas with or without a sea anchor. Even some old-time boats having great hull depth forward would not hold their bows up with a sea anchor. For a dramatic example of this behavior, read Jack London's *The Cruise of the Snark.* One partial solution to this problem is to get a small, flat riding sail aft that will help hold the head up. Centerboard yawls with their boards up (to avoid tripping) can sometimes use this technique effectively. One such boat of my acquaintance has on several occasions ridden out gales nearly head to wind with the mizzen sheeted flat and without a sea anchor. The helm was loosely lashed with shock cord to reduce the risk of damage to the rudder caused by the boat being thrown backwards.

The other alternative for a modern yacht is to stream the sea anchor astern. This might work well for a boat that lies naturally with her quarter toward the wind, but it requires ample freeboard aft, proper stern cleats and chocks, a small self-bailing cockpit well, a high companionway, and sturdy storm slides. To keep the boat's stern to the seas, a very small storm jib trimmed flat amidships will probably be needed forward. The main drawback of this tactic is that seas will break with real force against the stern when the boat is held too firmly with a large sea anchor, and this will not only increase the probability of seas breaking aboard but also of damage being inflicted on boat and gear.

This strain can be alleviated by using a smaller sea anchor or a drogue that allows some give and a Nylon rode that is fairly stretchy. Figure 8-7 shows several kinds of sea anchors. The parachute type, if sufficiently large, holds a boat most firmly, while the Fenger type allows the most drift. Of course, drogues can be improvised with sails, anchors with boards lashed to them, and so forth. One of the best drags is an automobile tire, especially when it is weighted and towed from a bridle so that it stands on end.

A sailor/engineer, Donald J. Jordan, has recently been experimenting with sea anchors used with model yachts in breaking seas. Originally Jordan made capsize studies in a home-made tank, but now he places models in the wakes of towed boats. He has found that a sea anchor streamed astern can help prevent a boat lying beam to the seas from capsizing. There is one serious hitch to this

Figure 8-7. A model being tested for capsize resistance by Donald Jordan. The wave is created by a boat under way. (Courtesy of Donald Jordan)

Figure 8-8. Running off before large following seas. Note that the insulators on the mizzen shrouds are the fail-safe kind that keep the shroud's integrity even if the insulator should break. The ring buoy is immediately available, although the after horseshoe appears to be lashed to the life line. Buoy lashings may be all right if they are easily breakable.

tactic, however; it requires a nonelastic anchoring system. Should the rode stretch and the anchor move significantly when the boat is struck by a steep beam sea, she can easily be rolled. But if there is very little give to the rode and anchor, the bow will be thrown to leeward while the stern remains relatively stationary, and this turning stern to the seas will very much reduce the probability of capsize. The dilemma is that the shock-loading of a nonelastic system may damage the boat and her gear.

In regard to this problem, Donald Jordan has written me: "I believe that it may be possible to predict the loads with reasonable accuracy. The loads must be of sufficient magnitude to catch the stern of the boat and prevent it from swinging down with the wave. I doubt that the load will go above 5,000 lbs for a boat with a displacement of 10,000 lbs. This, of course, can pull off a cleat or even the transom, but if properly distributed into a modern fiberglass hull it should not be a problem. However, more work is required before I would have any real confidence in making recommendations."

Since the above was written, Jordan has developed and extensively tested, with help from the U.S. Coast Guard, a promising device called the series drogue. This consists of a long Nylon rode (perhaps 150 feet) to which a great many miniature conic sea anchors are attached, evenly spaced along the line. A 25-pound conventional metal anchor is shackled to one end of the rode, and it is towed astern. Advantages of this system are that shock loading is minimized, and there is no danger of the drogue tumbling or collapsing with the passage of a wave. Testing with models and full-sized boats has revealed remarkable ability to prevent capsizing.

It is interesting that Shewmon Incorporated of Dunedin, Florida, advertised as "the sea anchor specialists," claims that "steep violent seas require long ropes with great springing action." This company, which manufactures sturdy cloth sea anchors and drogues of all sizes, warns against an anchoring system that holds a boat too firmly. Although Shewmon recommends a moderately large size to hold the vessel's end to the seas, the company's literature proclaims that "if a sea anchor is too large it will not yield, causing rope and bow hardware overloading. Worse still, as the overstretched rope recovers, it will pull a rapidly rising vessel right off the tops of steep waves." Incidentally, testing by Shewmon has shown that rodes should be braided rather than

Figure 8-9. This sailing vessel appears to be hove to in heavy weather. Even though she probably has fairly short masts as a result of being gaff rigged, there seems to be enough wind to steady her and give her a slight angle of heel.

stranded line, the latter tending to twist the bails or bridle lines. There should also be a swivel where the bridles join the rode, but swivels do not always turn easily when heavily loaded.

Sea anchors seem most appropriate for small shoal-draft boats, any craft with a very low range of stability, and of course, vessels that are drifting toward a dangerous lee shore. Lifeboats, dories, and such have used sea anchors effectively for ages, and larger capsizable boats such as powerboats and multihulls have also had success with this tactic when they can be held end-to the seas.

Parachute sea anchors have been touted, particularly for use with multi-hulls, but world-famous multihull designer Richard C. Newick has written me: "The big parachutes scare me both in deploying/retrieving, strength, durability, and sheer power to almost stop a vessel—which isn't desirable." He also described how a competitor sailing a small Newick trimaran in the 1980 OSTAR (Observer's Singlehanded Transatlantic Race) spent most of his time during a gale "trying to untangle a big parachute while lying ahull," a tactic he considers very dangerous for his multihull designs.

Dick Newick has had success with his 31-foot Val trimaran in very steep seas (produced by a Force 8 Gulfstream gale blowing against the current) by streaming two conic-type sea anchors. A large one was deployed from the bow of the main hull and another smaller sea anchor was streamed from the weather ama on a shorter rode that was weighted. He wrote me that this method "takes care of the odd wave from a different direction that has been known to capsize boats." Newick says that when he has tried the two-sea-anchor solution, his boats were never unstable enough directionally to present the "wrong" side of the boat (the ama without a sea anchor) to the waves. However, he admits "it could happen, which might be a good argument for using one larger sea anchor from either bow or stern." Many of his newer offshore multihulls are designed with consideration for taking heavy seas on the stern, and he writes that he would now lie to a large sea anchor from a bridle off the outer hull sterns on many of his designs that are not vulnerable to breaking seas from aft.

With most passive tactics oil can be used to help calm the seas. Although it will not flatten a steep plunging breaker in really horrendous weather, it will help prevent some crests from breaking. A recommended method is to fill a semiporous cloth bag with rags or oakum soaked in heavy oil and hang this over the windward side or tow it astern. Animal or fish oil is more effective than petroleum, but there may be an abundant supply of the latter.

In real survival conditions, where it is highly probable that a small yacht will be rolled over no matter how she is handled, it may be the safest policy for all crew to hole up below. Of course, this requires complete watertight integrity and that all gear, equipment, and crew are properly secured to resist a 180 degree inversion. All hatches must be dogged, ventilators (even *Dorade* types) closed, and storm slides locked in place. Heavy equipment below must be secured in accordance with advice given in chapter 6, and the crew should be lashed or belted in their bunks. After a six-year capsize testing program by

Figure 8-10. It appears that this destroyer has been pooped and is rounding up and draining her after deck.

Donald Jordan and the U.S. Coast Guard, Jordan concludes that to survive an ultimate storm, use of the series drogue "is the best bet and lying ahull is the next somewhat painful alternative." It is a fact that many derelict yachts (and other vessels), which have been abandoned because their crew thought they were about to sink, have later been found afloat and with little serious damage other than being dismasted. This gives great credence to the theory that the crew should stay with their ship, but obviously they must have a means of securing themselves and their gear to prevent injury.

POWERBOAT & SHIP HANDLING

The main problems faced by powerboats in heavy weather were discussed in chapter 6. Handling techniques must consider the relatively short range of stability and lack of hull balance in the planing type motorboat. Another important consideration, of course, is the distance range under power. In a lengthy storm at sea a boat with limited tankage and a gas-guzzling engine could dangerously deplete her fuel supply if power were used hour after hour.

When the stability range is very limited, a beamy power cruiser with a lot of top hamper or a small open motorboat generally should be held end to the seas in very steep waves. In the interest of reaching shelter or proceeding toward her destination, she might run in the trough, parallel with the crest lines; but she should usually be headed off or else headed up at slow speeds when out of the trough on the wave's face. The small planing boat with very fine bow and full, flat stern should probably be headed up into the wave crests, as she could broach when running off, stern to the seas. Such a boat, especially one with an open cockpit, should not drive into the seas with any more speed than that necessary for steering control. More speed could cause the seas to break aboard with damaging force and possibly cause the boat to swamp. Even a decked-over powerboat could suffer serious stability problems from the filling of a large, wide cockpit.

It will be helpful to play the throttle, keeping the speed generally low but giving the engine a kick ahead when this is needed to hold the bow up and just before bursting through a breaking crest that threatens to throw the boat backwards. Speed up the face of the wave, though, should be no faster than that needed to make the rudder work effectively. Although a crest should usually be met head-on, quite often the face can be climbed at a slight angle, and breaking tops might be avoided by altering speed and steering around them. It is sometimes recommended that powerboats approach the crest line at an angle of up to 30 degrees, but this will depend on the character of the seas and also the behavior of the boat. The 30-degree approach can slightly increase buoyancy or reduce pitching, but the trade off may very well be increased rolling or difficulty in holding the bow up. As a very general rule for small to medium size vessels, the greater the approach angle the more the boat will roll. This is not necessarily true for a ship in short seas because of her enormous beam.

If the bow of a small planing boat cannot be held up to the seas under power without shipping a lot of water, or there is a shortage of fuel, or the propeller cannot be kept submerged, a sea anchor might be used to lie end on. When the boat has some forefoot and little if any keel drag or skeg aft, she might lie to the anchor off the bow. It should be helpful to put some weight forward, provided the boat has an ample foredeck to keep water out of the bilge. Should the boat "lose her head" and tend to lie beam on or quarter to the seas, then the sea anchor could be tried off the stern. This tactic could be risky, however, when the boat has an open cockpit and a low transom, unless perhaps she has a great deal of flotation, because seas could break over the stern and quickly swamp her.

Occasionally one hears recommendations that a fast planing boat should run before heavy seas at high speed. This keeps the bow elevated, and it can work effectively with skillful handling for short periods of time, as, for example, when passing through surf before entering an inlet. But the boat must be able to keep up with the seas and travel at their speed. She can then be positioned in the trough or back of a wave (never on the crest) and ride it into smooth water. The technique can be dangerous, however, for long periods of time in deep water, because storm waves may move too fast for the boat, they may be too irregular, or the boat might quickly run out of fuel. It is even possible for her to go too fast and dig into the back of a wave or fall into a "hole" in certain conditions. Quite often a safer technique for a motorboat without extremely asymmetrical hull lines is to run off at slower speeds towing a drogue, a small sea anchor perhaps. The drag aft will somewhat hinder steering but will hold the stern into the waves, and the slow speed will allow the crest to pass the boat as quickly as possible. When it is desired to speed up momentarily or to allow more responsive steering, a trip line can be rigged to the bottom of a conic sea anchor, and this will also simplify recovery when the anchor is brought back on board.

Heavy-displacement vessels, such as trawler types with relatively narrow sterns and especially double-enders, can usually run off more successfully at slow speeds. Their hulls are better balanced and they have less tendency to broach. They should be run sufficiently fast for good steerageway but rarely pushed to or beyond hull speed, as this could cause the stern to squat and the boat's own wave system to reinforce the following seas, thus creating a risk of being pooped. Depth and size of propeller and size of rudder will have considerable bearing on how fast the vessel should be run for best steering control.

Deep-bodied and heavily ballasted powerboats might even lie ahull when the waves are fairly long and the breakers are spilling types rather than plungers. Another requirement for this tactic would be moderate-sized windows of proper glass as discussed in the last chapter. If the boat has a mast, perhaps a small riding sail could be set aft to hold the bow up a little at least. Should she tend to hold her quarter up with no sail, the riding sail might be set forward to help keep the stern to the seas.

Large ships can also lie ahull with engines shut down. This is the tactic strongly endorsed by Captain Elmer Malanot and expounded in appendix VI of this book. It is interesting that near the beginning of this century Captain J.C. Voss recommended this tactic for steamers, and early editions of Knight's *Modern Seamanship* tell of a number of successful hulling experiences by ships. Of course, Captain Malanot's typhoon doctrine is not universally accepted, as the writings of some other ship masters in the appendixes indicate, but there seems little doubt that hulling can work well under the right circumstances. These depend on the character of the seas, the type of ship, length of GM, condition of ballasting, watertightness, security of cargo, and so forth.

The seas near the center of a typhoon or hurricane can be tremendously confused and seemingly come from all directions, and a dormant drifting ship lying about beam to or quarter to the wind could fare well by hulling, provided she is not heeled to a dangerous angle by the force of the wind. Indeed, this was the strategy that worked so well for Captain Malanot in Typhoon *Ruth*. The British *Admiralty Manual of Seamanship* reports other cases of ships successfully riding through, or very near to, the center of typhoons in the Pacific with engines stopped. A 1965 edition of this manual states: "When near the center of the typhoon, the ships lay with the wind approximately abeam, but the waves approached from all directions." Reportedly, these ships sustained "no damage whatsoever."

On the other hand, when the wind and seas are from the same direction, hulling might not necessarily be the best tactic, especially when there is a

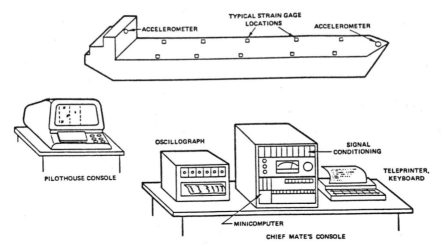

Figure 8-11. Some monitoring instruments on a modern Great Lakes vessel. (Courtesy of Det Norske Veritas and Kåre Lindemann)

coinciding of the wave period and ship's period of roll, causing synchronous rolling. This could be a particular concern for top-heavy men-of-war or vessels with cargo that could shift.

Before lying ahull, or using any other heavy weather tactic for that matter, a ship's master must know the characteristics of his vessel. He should know her degree of stability in loaded or light condition, her GMs in those conditions, her inertial characteristics, her degree of watertightness, possibility of cargo shifting, condition of her tanks with regard to free surface, length of seas most likely to cause synchronous rolling, vulnerability of equipment and hull to racking and bending, etc. Some of this information is often acquired through experience, but some can be estimated by naval architect/marine engineers or surveyors and is available from manuals or monitoring equipment (see figure 8-12). Regarding the latter, some modern ships now have instrumentation such as accelerometers, strain gauges, roll warning devices, and other sophisticated equipment to inform the master of his vessel's behavior. Information about this is included in a manual entitled *Summary of a Course in Shiphandling in Rough Weather*, obtainable from the National Technical Information Center under the U.S. Department of Commerce.

Condition of loading has a considerable effect on the vessel's behavior in heavy weather, but it is not always easy to say exactly how she will react to confused seas. In general, it could be said that a deeply loaded vessel suffers from being most subject to shipping green water, that she has a smaller GM, and she has a shorter range of stability due to the fact that her deck edge will be submerged at a relatively low angle of heel. On the other hand, she benefits by having her propeller and rudder well submerged, and her usual small GM gives her a slower roll and consequently less racking stress and normally less chance of synchronous rolling. It is also true that a deep hull tends to roll less because more of her hull is in the flatter subsurface wave slopes.

Figure 8-12. Slamming into a big one. The photograph illustrates the potential destructive power of head seas when a vessel is driven into them with any speed.

A lightly loaded vessel suffers from greater wave slope near the surface, more windage on the hull, and a greater chance of propeller emersion. The latter drawback may also be aggravated by aeration of the water, which can extend three feet or more below the surface in a severe storm, although the hull will tend to sink deeper. Despite having a relatively high center of gravity, a light ship can and should have a fairly long GM, but when the metacenter is too high, racking is severe and there is more chance of cargo (if she has any) or ballast shifting. According to *Stability and Trim for Ship's Officers*, a lightly loaded Victory ship has a GM of about eight feet, which makes her excessively stiff.

Nevertheless, it is generally most prudent to have a GM slightly longer than normal for extremely heavy weather to minimize shipping water and for additional stability. This could be especially true for certain top-heavy naval vessels and ships that are relatively vulnerable to flooding. Although certainly not conclusive, it would seem, from information in this book's appendixes, that the destroyers lost in the December 1944 Pacific typhoon might have fared better with improved stability. Ships with ballast tanks can have the center of gravity and GM adjusted by ballasting with sea water, and inertia can be optimized when the vessel has wing tanks. In a real emergency certain forms of top hamper can be jettisoned.

A highly experienced merchant ship captain recently told me that when motion becomes severe he waits for a "smooth," when the waves are momentarily flatter, and then he turns and runs dead before the seas. Next, he checks the cargo for security and sees that all deck openings are properly closed. When this is accomplished, he may or may not resume his original course, depending on the weather and other factors. Continuing to run off presupposes that the ship handles well and has no great tendency to yaw or broach to. Regardless of the heading, the engineer should be instructed to stand a strict throttle watch to prevent the propeller from spinning in the event that it emerges.

High speed in an attempt to optimize steerageway when running off could cause enough centrifugal force during an extreme yaw to dangerously augment the capsizing force of a steep beam sea. Another concern when running before it is the risk of being pooped. A wave breaking over the stern may not have as much force as one coming over the bow when the ship is headed into the seas, but it may strike more vulnerable parts of the vessel. There are a few cases of ships having been sunk by pooping seas. Hatches and doors must be well secured, of course, and ventilators closed. Blower intakes are sometimes too low and engine rooms become flooded. It should be kept in mind that when a vessel is on the crest of a large wave she has the least stability, and therefore the sooner the wave passes under her, the better. Advice is usually to run off at the slowest possible speed that will allow reasonable steerageway. Running off at fast speeds will also tend to increase the vessel's quarter waves, which will reinforce following seas and possibly increase their pooping capabilities.

The other alternative for ships in heavy weather is to head into the seas. A destroyer commander of World War II told me that his standard operating procedure was to head up with just enough speed to hold the bow about 30 degrees to the wind when the seas and wind were approximately from the same direction. It can be seen in appendix VII, however, that Lieutenant Commander A.G. Graham disagrees with this advice and thinks that it is better to head more directly into the seas. His argument is that in a gale the wind on only one side of the bow will force the head off and require considerable speed to keep from falling off into the trough. Of course, it is nearly always desirable to slow down as much as possible when "heading into it," because speed causes more seas to break aboard and vastly increases their force. On the other hand, the angular approach may give the bow greater buoyancy, so finding the right technique for the particular situation may take some experimenting. It is worth noting that in the early 1900s, Admiral Austin Knight, author of *Modern Seamanship*, interviewed 40 prominent steamship masters and only seven preferred to lie bow-on in heavy weather. Most advocated lying ahull or steaming slowly before the seas.

Under the S03 project (a research project on rough weather shiphandling sponsored by the Norwegian Maritime Directorate, the U.S. Coast Guard, and participating shipowners), guidance charts resulting from model and full-scale studies have been prepared to aid masters in determining the effect of different headings and speeds. In the aforementioned manual *Summary of a Course in Shiphandling in Rough Weather*, charts are shown for a VLCC (Very Large Crude Carrier) in laden condition. These are graphs that estimate the vessel's behavior at all headings with respect to roll, vertical acceleration of the bow, relative motion of the bow (which considers the probability of shipping green water and slamming), and vertical bending moment (bending stress on the hull). The graphs show behavior at fast speed (17 knots), slow speed (8.5 knots), and no speed (0 knots), and in short seas (less than one quarter of the ship's length), medium seas (between one-quarter and one-half the ship's length), and long seas (greater than one-half the ship's length).

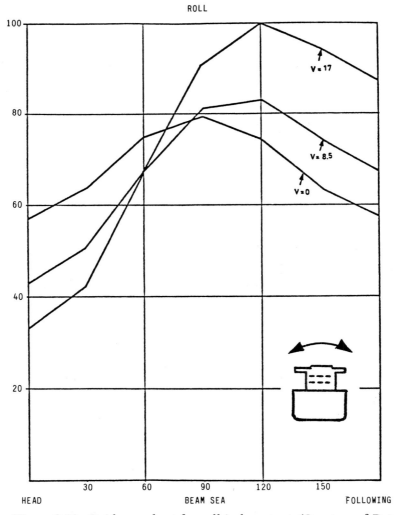

Figure 8-13. Guidance chart for roll in long seas. (Courtesy of Det Norske Veritas and Kåre Lindemann)

A sample chart for rolling in long seas is shown in figure 8-13. For the VLCC, which is 330 meters long, it can be seen that when drifting she rolls most when the seas are on the beam, but she rolls far more in beam seas at fast speed, while her maximum roll is at fast speed headed 120 degrees from the seas. In contrast, on another chart for medium seas (figure 8-14), maximum rolling occurs at fast speed when the vessel is headed at 150 degrees. For the most part, the vessel will tend to roll least in head seas, pitch (actually, vertically accelerate her bow) the least in following seas, ship the least water between quartering and following seas, and bend less in beam seas; but the set of charts show a lot of variations depending on speed and wave length. Needless to say,

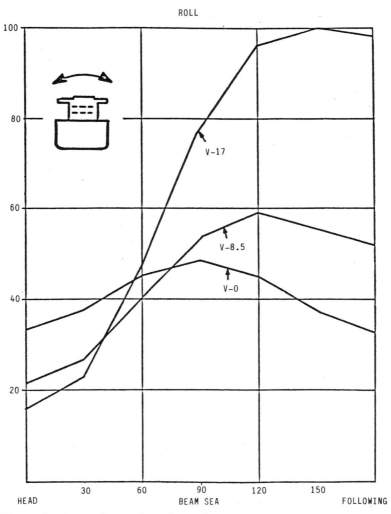

Figure 8-14. Guidance chart for roll in medium seas. (Courtesy of Det Norske Veritas and Kåre Lindemann)

behavior will change with different types of ships, and seas can be extremely irregular and unpredictable, so guidance charts can only give information of a very general nature and show basic principles. They do, however, give some indications of behavior trends, and as the above-mentioned manual puts it, they "will form a fundamental basis for the general understanding on how different wave systems influence the ship's seakeeping qualities."

Heavy-weather shiphandling involves priorities of concern depending on the type of vessel, and this should have an influence on the course of action. For instance, a primary concern for a tanker is shipping water, as this can and has caused damage to the superstructure, thus this vulnerability due to low freeboard would bode against driving into head seas. On the other hand Ro-Ro (roll on and roll off) ships are more vulnerable when rolling, as this imposes great strain on cargo lashings, and this would bode against beam or quartering seas. Passenger ships, of course, are concerned with passenger comfort and minimizing rolling, while some cargo vessels with large deck openings are vulnerable to torsional stress, and ships carrying liquid may be concerned with impact from sloshing. Obviously, tactics must be sought that minimize the stresses to which a particular ship is most vulnerable.

As mentioned at the beginning of this chapter, there can be few if any absolute dictums on handling vessels in heavy weather, because there are so many "all depends on." About the best a master can do is to learn all he can about his vessel and her characteristics, keep well informed of the weather, and thoroughly familiarize himself with all handling options. The essence of heavy weather seamanship is anticipation. This means thinking ahead, considering what might happen, planning a course of action and alternatives, and acting before it is too late. The latter point was succinctly made by Admiral Chester Nimitz when he wrote, "The time for taking all measures for a ship's safety is while still able to do so."

APPENDIXES

I

400 Years of Hurricanes*

By Chief Aerographer's Mate Charles R. Coates, U.S. Navy

Hurricanes, like other weather phenomena, have been in existence since the beginning of time. But on his first trips to the Caribbean, Columbus identified the tropical storms there as being different in some way from the extratropical disturbances of the Mediterranean. On his last trip to the New World, Columbus encountered a severe hurricane which brought to the attention of all concerned the major characteristics of these tropical storms. This storm created widespread damage to the Spanish fleet with a loss of 32 ships and hundreds of lives.

From the time of the bad storm in 1502 until the present day, widespread interest has arisen concerning the action, characteristics, and peculiarities of the tropical storms which occur each year at some location along the Gulf of Mexico, Caribbean, or the Atlantic. Statistics vary as to the average number which may occur in any one year. As many as 20 storms have been tracked within one season from June and through November. During some years there has been no storm of significance.

In the 456 years since Columbus came to the New World, the history of the Caribbean has been punctuated by the action of the tropical storm—the hurricane. Even the name is native, being derived from the Carib god Huracan whose frown makes livid the sky and whose lips, pursed for blowing, create the circular tempest. No resident or frequent traveler to the Caribbean can long count on missing the phenomenon of the hurricane in all its infamous activity.

Santo Domingo, the capital of the Spanish in the island of Española, appeared to be extremely susceptible to hurricanes of the early period. On

* From United States Naval Institute *Proceedings*—May 1949.

August 3, 1508, a severe hurricane visited the city with heavy damage. Again in July, 1509, almost the entire city of Santo Domingo was destroyed by a hurricane. Over half of the observed hurricanes of the sixteenth century were reported in the Santo Domingo vicinity.

A review of the hurricane characteristics will show why the number reported in the sixteenth century was small, and why Santo Domingo seemed to be the center of activity. The storms originate in the doldrums of the Atlantic, a little north of the equator, and are caught up by the easterly trades to be sent spinning into the Caribbean. But because hurricane winds seldom occur more than fifty to one hundred miles from the storm center, many storms pass unnoticed in sparsely settled areas. Often the heavy rainfall on the outer rim of the hurricane is a godsend to the dried up vegetation, and the benefits far outweigh the squally weather over the area.

A true interest in the study of the hurricane had to wait until the Caribbean was more densely settled, about 1550. Roberts, in his book *The Caribbean*, reports in detail the extent of colonization in the year 1542. The report shows the growth of the area during the first fifty years, but what is more important to the student of weather is that it shows the spread of population who may report the occurrence of severe tropical storms.

The census of 1542 shows Española as still the center of cultural and social interests, with the largest part of the Spanish colonial population living here and along the eastern coast of Cuba. Puerto Rico had been settled, but little had been done in colonizing the Lesser Antilles extending from Antigua to Trinidad. Most of the population in South America settled along the coast, with the two centers of population at Panama and Cartagena. Parts of Central America were settled, with the largest colony at Vera Cruz. Florida had only scattered settlements of an intermittent nature, St. Augustine being the more permanent of the group.

Tracing the average path of the hurricanes on the population map even now, it is easy to see that a large number of the storms will still pass outside the populated centers. But in contrast, travel in the area has grown to the point where many of the storms are reported by transients within the area. One such storm which might have influenced history considerably was that encountered by Sir John Hawkins off Dry Tortugas in August, 1568. This severe storm drove the British fleet ahead of it and into the Spanish port of Vera Cruz where Hawkins later seized San Juan de Ulua fort to dominate the harbor.

History shows that the destiny of St. Augustine might have been entirely influenced by the hurricane which moved over the city in 1565. On September 16, the fate of St. Augustine was secured for the Spaniards when a hurricane struck both the French and Spanish fleets; but because most of the Spaniards were ashore, it was to their advantage, even though all of their heavy ships were lost in the blow. This storm, like many of the other hurricanes, came with widespread harbingers of bad weather if only Ribault, the French commander, had been able to recognize the signs of the weather lore.

No scientific study explained in detail the action of the hurricane until the nineteenth century, but many of the early mariners must have been able to correlate the changes in the sky and oppressive weather with the coming of the hurricane. In 1502 Columbus was vindicated as a prophet because he warned the city of Santo Domingo of the coming storm. Even today the prediction of a storm occurring in this part of the Caribbean during the month of June would be called unseasonable, and draw attention to the persons forecasting such a phenomenon.

Probably the earliest extended and accurate description of a tropical storm is found in the narrative of Alvar Nuñez, treasurer and "High Sheriff" of the expedition of Pánfilo de Narváez, which reached the West Indies in the autumn of 1527. Nuñez had been despatched to the port of Trinidad with two ships to take on supplies. There he describes the weather as looking "ominous," and from this beginning proceeds to log in detail the events of the storm with more than a lay knowledge of its action. Each report in part brings out some of the major differences in tropical and extratropical storms.

Through the eighteenth century the library of hurricane reports continued to grow. The descriptive terms were in general the same, and except for the number of lives lost or the location of the storm they were all similar. Many of the storms had very great influence on the social, educational, and military matters of the day. A hurricane period was established in part, for it was noted early in the history of hurricane study that the worst storms occurred during the month of September. The current folk rhyme of the British West Indies summarizes the knowledge available to the population of the Caribbean as early as 1565.

June, too soon
July, stand by
August, don't trust
September, remember
October, all over.

The year 1780 is one that stands out in bold relief from other years in the study of the hurricane. This was the year of the "Great Hurricane," thought to be the most violent of the eighteenth century. Colonel Reid says: "Three great storms occurred nearly at the same time; and these have been confounded together, and considered but as one. The first destroyed the town of Savanna-la-Mar, on October 3, 1780. The second, by far the greater one, passed over Barbados on the 10th and 11th of the same month and year. The third dispersed and disabled the Spanish fleet, under Solano, in the Gulf of Mexico, after it had sailed from Havanah to attack Pensacola."

A report on the "Great Hurricane" describes in detail what might be expected in any great tropical storm. The following account by Elisee Reclus, published in 1874, is given here to review that thought. It is only through the forecasts of impending danger that protection is offered the coastal cities of today.

The most terrible cyclone of modern times is probably that of the 10th of October, 1780, which has been specially named the "great hurricane." Starting from Barbados, where neither trees nor dwellings were left standing, it caused an English fleet anchored off St. Lucia to disappear, and completely ravaged this island, where 6,000 persons were crushed in the ruins. After this, the whirlwinds tended toward Martinique, enveloped a convoy of French transports, and sunk more than 40 ships carrying 4,000 soldiers; on land the towns of St. Pierre and other places were completely razed by the wind, and 9,000 persons perished there. More to the north, Dominique, St. Eustatius, St. Vincent, and Porto Rico were likewise devastated, and most of the vessels which were in the path of the cyclone foundered with all their crews. Beyond Porto Rico the tempest bent to the northeast, toward the Bermudas, and though its violence had gradually diminished, it sank several English warships returning to Europe. At Barbados, where the cyclone had commenced its terrible spiral, the wind was unchained with such fury that the inhabitants hiding in their cellars did not hear their houses falling above their heads; they did not feel the shocks of earthquake which, according to Rodney, accompanied the storm.

The description of this storm was in terms of scientific knowledge accumulated from extended study during the last part of the eighteenth and first part of the nineteenth centuries. Use of the word "cyclone" and the movement of the storm along a track was part of the modern knowledge coming into use at this time. Piddington proposed the name "cyclone" to express the "tendency to circular motion." In his *Sailor's Hornbook*, Mr. Piddington credited Captain Langford with the earliest published statement of the nature of tropical storms appearing in the publication *Philosophical Transactions* in 1698. But nearly fifty years before, a German geographer, Bernhardus Varenious, treated hurricanes as whirlwinds in a book entitled *Geographia Naturalis*.

William Dampier, a master seaman and world voyager, wrote much in detail about the winds within the tropical storms. He describes conditions experienced in a typhoon off the coast of China in the year 1687, at which time he came to the conclusion that there was no difference between the typhoon and the hurricane except in name.

In 1819 Professor H.W. Brades, of the University of Breslau, worked out the idea of the synoptic weather map. Even though he had to use reports that were old and of no value for forecasting, he was able to set up a detailed study of the laws of the storms. From observations taken in 1783 Brades established the circulation of winds in a cyclone. The study was picked up by Heinrich Wilhelm Dove, physicist and meteorologist, to show that cyclones rotate clockwise in the southern hemisphere as compared to counterclockwise in the northern hemisphere.

William C. Redfield was enabled to give a more fundamental account of the phenomena of rotation and translation based upon observations of West Indian hurricanes collected over a ten-year period. In 1831 he defined a cyclone as consisting of a large mass of air with a rapid motion of rotation counterclockwise, a calm center, and a motion of translation. By sequent researches he identified the region between the equator and the Tropic of Cancer as the place of origin of the storms. The scientific study of cyclones and hurricanes was well under way by the middle of the nineteenth century, but still no use of the knowledge had been made in trying to forecast the coming of the storms.

Following the invention of the weather map by Brades, some system of relaying current weather reports had to be improvised before accurate forecasts could be issued on a daily basis. Collection of weather observations was greatly facilitated with the invention of the telegraph in 1843. Ten years later an attempt was made to collect daily weather reports from a network of stations for the sole purpose of issuing weather forecasts to the public.

The science of forecasting had been well developed long before it was possible to collect information from ships at sea. Most of the Caribbean network of stations had to wait until the beginning of the Spanish-American War. Many of the hurricanes which formed in the Caribbean and Atlantic remained unreported until they moved in close to the coast of the United States weather net. An example of this occurred in September, 1874, only a few years after the formation of the weather service under the direction of the Chief Signal Officer of the U.S. Army. The storm of September 25–30 affected Florida, and, after being picked up on the weather chart, developed great force off the Carolina coast.

The first ship report of a hurricane was received by wireless on August 26, 1909, when the S.S. *Cartago* was off the coast of Yucatan. This part of the early system of ship reports was one of the twice-daily messages sent by wireless from all ships so equipped. Provision was soon made for reporting at intervening hours, and during periods of unusual weather. Thus, from the time of the first weather message from a ship at sea in 1909 until the present, the procedure of using ship observations has continued to improve. Ships at sea now take balloon soundings to obtain the direction and velocity of the winds aloft, and the use of radiometeorograph on shipboard is a common form of weather observation.

Between the time of the invention of the weather map and the use of the wireless for reporting weather from ships at sea, much effort was put forward by research meteorologists to determine the exact nature of the hurricane. Reports from the laymen of the Islands were of little value. These reports described in detail the damage done, but during the storm only the approximate wind velocity could be indicated, and after the storm passed every effort went towards the repair of the damage. Some mention in the early reports brought out the fact that many hurricanes were associated with the advancement of definite cloud formations. The winds and temperatures received comment from some of the observers, for it was often calm and the weather was oppressive with the heat.

Roberts, writing in his introduction, gives an excellent lay description of the coming hurricane. This was the only information available to the population prior to 1900, and is the principle rule still used by many. "The signs of what is about to happen are unmistakable. Small cirrus clouds appear, drifting high and fast. They are followed by nimbus clouds, dark and ragged. The tides rise, because far away the advancing storm is whipping the water before it. The first phase may take an hour or two. The world has grown preternaturally still—and then the wind and the rain come roaring."

Father Viñes, of Havana, was one of the early students of tropical meteorology who made a concentrated effort to set up a series of forecast rules for the benefit of the public. He found that often when the hurricane is still at a distance the barometer sometimes rises above its normal heights. Soon thereafter the barometer begins to fall. The amount of fall at any given place depends upon the intensity of the hurricane and the direction of its movement with regard to the points of observation. The success of Father Viñes' system is noted in a letter describing the hurricane of 1928, nearly fifty years after the father went to work on the idea. Part of the letter by Charles R. Hartzell of San Juan follows: "The first indication of the storm was on Tuesday night of the 11th, when my barometer began to feel unusually healthy and went to what was plainly the anticyclone of a disturbance."

With reference to the barometer as an instrument to foretell the coming of the hurricane, it has also been used to determine the intensity of the storm—the common rule being that the lower the barometer, the greater the storm. From actual observations this has not always proven to be the case, but the record of some of the world's lowest pressures still gives rise to an exciting study. Our own country holds the record for the lowest reading of a shore-based barometer, but lower readings have been reported by ships at sea. Some of the low readings often referred to are listed here below:

	Inches
• H.C. Ship *Duke of York*. Kedegree, 1833	26.30
• Havana, Cuba. October 10 to 11, 1846	27.06
• Ship *Favorita*, in harbor, Apia, Samoa, April 6, 1850	27.05
• False Point, India September 22, 1885	27.08
• S.S. *Arethusa*, 13°55'N, 134°30'E. December 16, 1900	26.16
• Basilan, Frank Helm Bay. September 25, 1905	26.85
• S.S. *Sapoeroea*, 460 miles east of Luzon. August 18, 1927	26.18
• Lower Matecumbe Key, Fla. September 2, 1935	26.35

Works by Gray, Dunn, Reid, and others have shown that the pressure is not a definite criterion of the storm intensity. The Miami storm of September, 1926, is generally conceded to be as severe as any storm ever to hit the United States. Studies of this storm are important because most of the record was made by trained Weather Bureau personnel using modern instruments. The barometer at the Weather Bureau office fell to 27.61 inches when the eye of the storm passed over the city. Another severe Florida hurricane passed over West Palm Beach in 1928, when a low reading of 27.43 inches of mercury was recorded.

Charles L. Mitchell, of the U.S. Weather Bureau, carried out an extensive research program to try to establish the average track and origin of the hurricanes which move into the Caribbean and the United States. He replotted the tracks of all storms between 1887 and 1922, inclusive. The daily weather maps of the Weather Bureau were checked to verify details, and ships' logs for the period were studied. Results of his study are still considered to be the best information available on the storm frequency, average tracks, and place of origin during each part of the season. Mr. Mitchell's findings can be summarized:

(1) The advance and decline of the number of storms during the season is definite. A hurricane season can be narrowed down to the three months of August, September, and October.

(2) Majority of the hurricanes developed over the western Caribbean or far to the east of the Lesser Antilles.

(3) The influence of large high pressure areas on the movement of the hurricane is very marked.

(4) A hurricane will recurve to the north and northeast at the first opportunity regardless of the time of the year.

(5) When the hurricane describes a loop it is always to the left.

In recent history the New England hurricane of September, 1938, is still cited in many illustrations used in literature describing tropical storms. This storm, like many of its forerunners, had certain characteristics which make for interesting study. Its speed of movement from Hatteras to Long Island is a case of an unusual condition attending the storm. Other illustrations point up the fact that another storm, but of weaker nature, occurred in 1944; these two storms of 1938 and 1944 are set up for comparison with the two occurring in 1815 and 1821. Any study of hurricanes must then be narrowed somewhat if any approach is to make for intelligent evaluation.

It is not enough to describe the intensity of hurricanes in terms of loss of life, maximum winds, highest tides, lowest pressures, and many other features given to the hurricane. An accurate study of the four hundred year history is hampered because of the changing values of the units often set up for comparison. In most histories the attention is drawn to the loss of life, which can often be attributed to the high winds and tides accompanying the storms. One of the greatest catastrophes of all times is that referred to as the Hooghly disaster of 1737, when a furious cyclone destroyed 20,000 craft of all descriptions, and 300,000 people perished. In our own country the memorable Galveston Hurricane of 1900 is often recalled when a heavy loss of life is spoken of, for 6,000 persons gave up their lives in this storm.

To the mariner, layman, and others the history of the hurricane is only a backdrop to the present-day developments which aid him in protecting life and property from the fury of the hurricane. For this reason the last twenty years are the most important in the hurricane history. Some authors prefer to narrow the time interval down to the last ten years, arguing that it was not until 1935 that scientific study of the upper air was started in the Caribbean area. We might even go farther and say that it was the wartime effort of aircraft weather reconnaissance and microseismic work that began to pay the largest dividends in better hurricane protection.

Regardless of the time interval used in the history of the hurricane, it is necessary that we realize the stage of the present development to know how far the study has come in the last four hundred years. We have progressed from a point where there was no knowledge of the physical nature of the hurricane until the present day when it is possible to track them hourly across the ocean by use of aircraft, electronics, and microseismic devices. From the records of such methods it is possible to determine the size, shape, cross-section, and intensity of the storms. Weathermen are working on the assumption that forewarned is forearmed, and if the population can be warned of the coming storm the public can devise means for its own protection. This system of warning has been extended to all ships at sea, aircraft which may enter the storm area, and others who may see fit to use the information.

A short review of the two major wartime developments in the study of tropical storms is in order to complete the history of the hurricanes. Prior to the war, and extending from about 1935, considerable work had been carried out in the Caribbean area to extend the number of upper air observations. Pilot balloon soundings had increased in number so that a daily chart of the winds at all levels could be worked out to aid the forecaster in predicting the course of any hurricane. Radiometeorograph stations were expanded to give a better cross-section of the atmosphere in the vertical. The study of the upper air over the Caribbean is of major historical importance to the United States and to ships at sea which may be under the hurricane influence. During the hurricane season of 1944 work was started with aircraft observations in and near the hurricanes as they progressed along their track—the idea being that if an airplane could go out and spot the storm center, report the attending winds, and return to base, a running track of the storm could be plotted from each such observation. A flight could normally take off early in the morning from the nearest base to the hurricane, fly through the storm for observation purposes, and proceed to another field for safety. Another flight could carry out a similar procedure during the afternoon to give a minimum of two flights each day. Both the Army and Navy made experimental flights in 1944 which proved this to be a successful way of tracking the hurricanes. These flights were made with a good background of experience gained since the war began.

In 1945 the first tropical weather reconnaissance by the use of aircraft was established on a scheduled basis. For the Atlantic service twelve planes were made available—six from the Army Air Forces, and six Navy patrol bombers. These flights were coordinated in their observation work by the joint staff of Army, Navy, and U.S. Weather Bureau officials. Similar work was also carried out in the Pacific for the benefit of task force units and fleet commanders. . . .

Parallel to the aircraft reconnaissance program was the microseismic program whereby hurricanes would be tracked by the use of microseismographs. Microseisms related to hurricanes are thought to originate at the center of the storm over the sea. Father Macelwane, of St. Louis University, conceived the idea of a tripartite station consisting of three instruments in a triangle to take bearings on the hurricanes as they move over the ocean surface.

The Aerological Section of the Navy activated the Hurricane Microseismic Research Project late in 1943 [No longer in being.—Ed.] upon recommendation of the Joint Meteorological Committee. The first station was put in operation in 1944 at Guantanamo Bay, Cuba. The results of the Guantanamo station were verified by the weather flights in 1944 and 1945, making it possible to expand the work to cover the entire Caribbean, south Florida, and Corpus Christi. This work, too, has expanded into the Pacific as an aid in tracking tropical storms of that area.

To bring the history of the hurricanes up to date we have only to add the work of the hurricane reconnaissance squadrons and the microseismic project to the network of upper air observations. . . . With this close scrutiny of the area of storm formation it is unlikely that ever again will a hurricane breed, move through the ocean area, and affect the population of any Caribbean island, ship at sea, or United States city without adequate warning.

II

A Hurricane in Puerto Rico*†

By Lieutenant Commander O.H. Holtmann, U.S. Navy

Destructive hurricanes are not common in Puerto Rico. True, three have occurred in the past four years, two of these being classed as major disasters, the one of September 13, 1928, known as the San Felipe, after the saint's name of the day, and the one which occurred in 1932 on September 26, known as the San Ciprian. Prior to the San Felipe we must go back twenty-nine years to August 8, 1899, to find another record of a violent hurricane, the San Ciriaco. The great loss of life in that hurricane, three thousand, was due to the lack of facilities for prompt distribution of the warning to the rural population, and not to its particular violence, for winds of only 75 miles an hour were recorded in San Juan, which, however, was about 30 miles from the path of the center. The San Felipe in 1928 was the most destructive hurricane recorded in the West Indies. This storm formed near the Cape Verde Islands off the coast of Africa, and the center moved almost due westward until near Guadeloupe, French West Indies, then changed to west by north, and passed over that island where it caused great destruction. Passing a short distance south of St. Croix, where the lowest barometer reading was 27.50 inches, the wind velocity reached 90 miles per hour in St. Thomas, 50 miles north of the center. It entered Puerto Rico near Guayama (barometer 27.65) on the southeast coast and passed diagonally across the island in a west-northwest direction at an average velocity of translation of about 13 miles per hour. At San Juan an extreme wind velocity of 160 miles per hour was recorded when one cup of the anemometer blew away. The storm, however, increased in intensity for three

*The author wishes to make acknowledgment to Mr. F.E. Hartwell of the U.S. Weather Bureau, who furnished much of the information contained in this paper.
†From United States Naval Institute *Proceedings*—February 1933.

hours after this. Previous to looking up the records I had asked Captain Evans, now in the SS *Borinquen*, what the maximum wind velocity was in the San Felipe. He replied lightly, "Oh, about 200 miles an hour." The sailor's gift of exaggeration, I thought, and discounted this considerably. When one considers, however, that San Juan was about 30 miles north of the center, and that the lowest barometer reading in San Juan was 28.81, compared with 27.65 at Guayama, Captain Evans does not seem far from the truth. In Puerto Rico 300 were killed, and the property damage was estimated at fifty million dollars. This was the same storm which, continuing on to Florida, caused 1,836 deaths there.

Of the nine most destructive hurricanes which have occurred in Puerto Rico during the last hundred years, only one, that in 1867, occurred after the first of October. As September, 1932, drew toward its close, the people here, especially the fruit growers, who had thousands of boxes of fruit on the trees, and needed one hurricane-free year to recover financially, began to lose their anxious expressions. Their hope was disturbed when at 9:00 A.M., on September 26, the Weather Bureau at San Juan issued the following bulletin:

> Tropical disturbance central this morning between St. Kitts and St. Martin. Should reach the Virgin Islands this afternoon and eastern Puerto Rico by midnight.

St. Kitts reported a barometric pressure of 29.68 and wind from southwest force 7. This last report was not in itself alarming, for while it definitely established the fact that a cyclone had formed, and that Puerto Rico would probably lie in its path, it was at that time of only moderate intensity. At Dominica, about 140 miles south-southeast of St. Kitts, the prevailing trade winds were not affected, that place reporting a normal barometer with wind from east, force 2, indicating a very small center. From the estimated center at 9:00 A.M. to San Juan was about 190 miles, and in that distance it could be expected that the intensity would increase greatly. By 9:00 P.M., St. Thomas and St. Croix reported 60 miles an hour gales and the Weather Bureau estimated that the center was somewhere between these two islands. Up to this time there was no indication in San Juan of anything unusual in the weather. At noon there had been a thundershower with heavy rain which lasted about half an hour after which the sky cleared. All "indications of the approach of a tropical hurricane" as described in one of our textbooks were absent, although at dark the center was only about 75 miles away, and no one with whom I talked had any oppressive feeling or "felt it in their bones."

With no land areas lying in its path the intensity rapidly increased until the vortex entered the east coast of Puerto Rico, at 10:00 P.M. of the twenty-sixth probably directly over the harbor of Ensenada Honda, where the steamer *Jean* of the Bull Line and the lighthouse tender *Acacia* had anchored. The *Jean* had both anchors down with 90 fathoms of chain on each in good holding ground, and her engines were turning over before the vortex struck. She dragged almost a mile in a southeasterly direction and went aground before the wind shifted. The bottom was soft and luckily she remained on an even keel. By lightering her cargo she was refloated without any serious damage the next day. The captain reported that the barometer was fascinating to watch, the needle vibrating over the extreme bottom of the scale (27.70 inches). The *Acacia* dragged all the way to the entrance of the harbor and when the wind shifted with the passing of the center, she dragged all the way back again, with her engines going at full speed, and finally went aground in the northern part of the harbor. The barometer on the *Acacia* reached a low of 28.00 inches.

In San Juan at 10:00 P.M., the barometer read 29.73, wind from the north 27 miles an hour. From then on the barometer dropped rapidly, and the wind rose correspondingly fast. At midnight the barometer had dropped to 29.50, wind northeast 62 miles an hour. Shortly thereafter the steel framework at the Weather Bureau, on which the anemometer was mounted, collapsed, but the meteorologist, Mr. F.E. Hartwell, estimated that at 12:50 the wind was blowing not less than 120 miles an hour, the barometer at that time reading 28.95. There was no lull for the exact center passed to the southward, while the wind shifted through east to southeast. Thereafter the wind dropped rapidly and by 4:00 A.M. it was all over, the wind shifting back to the east (normal trade wind direction) with a velocity of only 35 miles an hour, barometer 29.60.

At the height of the storm, the noise could best be described by the sound made by a locomotive starting a heavy train just before the exhaust merges into a continuous roar. The volume of the sound can be inferred from the fact that minor sounds, such as that made by a large limb striking across a wooden shutter, a garage door weighing perhaps 600 pounds being thrown against the back door, or a palm tree 3 feet in diameter at the base being blown onto the roof of the garage, were drowned out. . . . Sand and water were forced into seemingly impossible places. The "watertight" globes around the light fixtures on our front porch, protected by a 2-foot overhang of the porch roof, were full of water although the roof, made of cemented tile, held and did not leak. Water was forced in under doors, through cracks, and around the window casings at such a rate that vigorous work with mops and towels was given up as useless.

Morning showed the extent of the disaster. Men had been at work since daylight clearing the roads of fallen trees, telephone poles, and all sorts of wreckage, and by 11:00 A.M. a car could get through most of the main highways. The island which had been so beautiful before was now in indescribable confusion. There was hardly a leaf left on the trees and shrubs still standing. Winter seemed to have come suddenly during the night. On one vacant lot in the Condado section, I had previously counted eighty-two coconut palms, all of them estimated to be over forty years old. After the hurricane I counted forty-two still standing. Over the countryside familiar landmarks were missing, their place being taken by others whose existence was not guessed before, since they had been hidden by shrubbery. In some sections there was not a building left wholly standing within 10 miles. Casualties were 225 dead, about 3,000 injured. Property damage will reach nearly thirty million dollars. The greatest loss of life was caused by the collapse of buildings which were supposed to be "hurricane-proof." Only the heaviest concrete or masonry buildings with tile roofs escaped undamaged. A peculiar effect of damage caused by air pressure as distinct from that caused by wind velocity was noted in the case of our garage which was of the same heavy construction as the house and, except for the doors, was almost air tight. The doors were torn off, one being thrown against our back door, moving a little north of east, while the other became jammed against a palm tree which had been blown down, and moved about northeast. The only winds of hurricane force were from north and northeast! Pressure inside had blown the doors directly into the wind.

The wind seemed to lose some of its violence as the vortex moved overland, being greatest where it entered the island on the east coast, and decreasing somewhat at the point where it left, on the northwest coast, near Arecibo, although this latter town reported the greatest proportion of deaths. Its total was swelled, however, by twenty-four men who took refuge in a new public garage, all of whom perished.

After leaving Puerto Rico the only report of winds of hurricane force was that from San Pedro de Macoris on the southern coast of Santo Domingo (90 miles per hour). No further report of the storm was received for some days and it finally entered British Honduras south of Belize.

Damage to shipping except small craft was slight. Beside the *Jean* and the *Acacia* previously mentioned, one ship in San Juan Harbor had her bridge and boats blown away, the three-masted schooner *Gaviota* was wrecked in the harbor and several pier buildings were badly damaged.

After a four-hour superficial survey of the affected area on the day after the storm, my reaction was "The San Felipe couldn't have been as bad as this, because it will take more than four years to remove the scars of this one." A month after the hurricane I was not so sure. In the tropics nature heals her wounds quickly. . . . Two weeks later there were new buds and shoots on the trees, the hibiscus was in bloom, and it was spring again.

III

Pitching on a Prayer*

Captain I.F. Wood, *Alcoa Runner*
Alcoa Steamship Company, Inc., Mobile, Alabama

. . . As Master of a freighter I matched wits (unwittingly) with one of those devastating tropical cyclones. It was hurricane Carol of 1954, the one that toppled the steeple on Old North Church in Boston, snuffed out over 68 lives, and caused estimated damage of almost one-half billion dollars.

The ship, my command, is a C-2 type freighter built in 1944 at Wilmington, North Carolina . . . a single screw, turbine vessel, 459 ft. long, 63 ft. wide, and 37 ft. deep, having a raked stem and an elliptical stern. . . . Her normal speed is 16 kt. . . . She can carry a "payload" cargo of approximately 10,500 tons, which is an enormous amount of cargo for any type ship.

Ten thousand tons of bulk phosphate were loaded at Tampa, Florida, on August 26, 1954, destined for one of the fertilizer plants at Norfolk, Virginia. When the ship departed from Tampa, she was loaded to her maximum draft of 28 ft., 6⅞ in.

. . . The pilot left at the Tampa seabuoy on August 26 at noon. A course was set south to pass between Rebecca Shoals and Dry Tortugas, the southwest extremity of the Florida Keys. The sea was smooth and the atmosphere clear.

That evening, the Radio Officer received the first U.S. Weather Bureau storm advisory on hurricane Carol. It read, "A small tropical storm has formed in the Atlantic and at 4:30 P.M. it was near 29.2°N., 76.5°W. or about 275 mi. east of Daytona Beach, Florida, and moving northwest about 12 m.p.h.

This article . . . has been reprinted with the kind permission of Captain Wood. It first appeared in a 1956 issue of *Polaris*, the quarterly magazine of the U.S. Merchant Marine Academy at Kings Point, Long Island.
*Extracted from *Mariners Weather Log* (U.S. Department of Commerce)—November 1963.

Strongest winds estimated 65 to 70 m.p.h. over a small area near the center. It is increasing slowly in intensity and may soon reach hurricane force. Northerly movement indicated for the next 12 to 24 hr."

... It was felt that the storm was so far in advance of the ship that there was only a remote possibility of overtaking it.

The ship passed between Rebecca Shoals and Tortugas at midnight, August 26 and all day August 27 the Keys and lower coast of Florida lay on our port side about 8 mi. off. The mighty Gulf Stream was flowing north with a velocity or strength of 3½ to 4 kt. The ship must have been in the axis of the Gulf Stream. When she was abeam of Miami she was averaging 19½ kt. The sky was blue with a few fleecy clouds, the sea was smooth, the temperature was 85 degrees, and the barometer was normal. There were great expectations for a record passage from Tampa to Norfolk due to the fine weather and the rampaging Gulf Stream.

At noon on August 27 the Radio Officer received Bulletin No. 4 on the hurricane: "Carol has remained almost stationary during the last 6 hr. but is probably moving very slowly 3 to 5 m.p.h. in a northerly direction. At 11 A.M. it was centered near 30°N., 76°W. or 325 mi. east of Jacksonville. Strongest winds estimated by aircraft this morning 70 to 80 m.p.h. extending 40 mi. from center. Gale force winds extend outward 50 to 60 mi. This small hurricane will probably show very slow increase in intensity and size during next 24 hr. Movement will continue in a northerly direction. Shipping should exercise extreme caution from present position northward to the Carolina coast next 36 to 48 hr."

Jupiter Lighthouse, just north of Palm Beach, was abeam at 4:30 P.M. August 27 and speed was reduced to 45 r.p.m. or "Half Ahead." I informed the responsible officers about the reduction in speed and told them that the purpose was to allow Carol to pass on to the northward of us.

From star observations taken early on the morning of August 28 it was found that in spite of the reduced speed, the vessel had traversed considerable distance during the night (with the aid of the Gulf Stream). A Weather Bureau advisory obtained at 5 A.M. located the hurricane about 300 mi. east of Jacksonville with highest winds estimated at 115 m.p.h. near the center and gales extending out 100 mi. The storm was expected to increase slowly in size and take a northerly path. At 6 A.M. the Chief Mate was called out and given orders to prepare the ship for heavy weather by putting storm plugs in all ventilators, extra lashing on the lifeboats, and securing plough steel wires across all hatches to the cargo holds.

At about 6 P.M. on the evening of August 28 the Weather Bureau report still described Carol as practically stationary. At this point the ship was in such a position that an important decision had to be made. She was between the hurricane and the mainland. The Gulf Stream was adding 2 m.p.h. to the engine speed. If the vessel was turned around and headed back for Miami, the hurricane might dally around further and a loss of three or four precious days on an already tight schedule might ensue. If she were pressed on to her destination, she might get caught in the hurricane—a deep loaded ship worth 5 to 6 million dollars, $135,000 worth of cargo, and 46 lives. . . . The ship was experiencing good weather and the barometer was normal, showing no evidence of the storm. A decision was made to proceed. If the estimated position of the hurricane were correct and it stayed stationary for the next 24 hr., the ship could be past Cape Hatteras and almost to Norfolk. . . .

Justification for the decision to proceed and apprehension for the safety of the command kept me on the bridge all that night. At midnight the barometer had dropped slowly from 30.00 to 29.80 in. but there was no alarm over that. By 5 A.M., however, the sea was increasing and the wind and seas were shifting toward the starboard beam. These C-2 ships roll very heavily when the wind and sea are on the beam. In a rough or heavy beam sea they roll severely enough to endanger equipment and fittings. At 6 A.M. the course was gradually changed from 40 to 70 degrees to ease the rolling.

The seas were growing longer and heavier and by 9 A.M. on August 29 they had become so violent that there was no longer any delusion about escaping the hurricane. The ship had been maneuvered into the path of the storm or dangerously near it. Plans were made accordingly to handle the ship with as much care and skill as could be mustered. The Chief Engineer was ordered to start pumping a slow trickle of fuel oil over the side by means of the bilge pumps. . . . There was a 50 gallon drum of so-called "Storm Oil" in the bows with outlets through the stem of the ship but the efficacy of that would have been somewhat equal to the effect of a bucket of water tossed at a house on fire. A steady flow of black fuel oil oozed out of the starboard side of the ship's hull all the time she was in the hurricane. No one will ever know how much that expended fuel oil helped to break the force of the seas encountered during the period of the hurricane.

. . . By "The Law of Storms" the rules and directions for one caught in my position were to put the wind on the starboard quarter and run for it. There are always exceptions to the rule and this was one of them. Had the wind been put on the starboard quarter, the ship would have been heading for the coast between Charleston and Cape Hatteras. . . . However, in addition to the impossibility of doing "what the book said," the deeply laden ship in my judgement would not have taken it safely before those solid walls of water. It was a great consolation at that period to hear a U.S. Coast Guard directive to Diamond Shoals Lightship to hold its position at all costs.

Throughout the storm the ship's bow was kept to the wind favoring the starboard side slightly because of the fuel oil discharge on that side. It was found experimentally that by varying the engine revolutions between 40 and 50 r.p.m., the vessel's bow could be kept into the seas preventing her from broaching broadside. The above mentioned revolutions were sufficient for the required purpose of steering directly at the seas yet seemed to give minimum aid to the destructive waves crashing over the decks.

Saturday August 29 was a wild, fierce day for all hands. The Log Book contained nothing but entries such as "mountainous sea," "heavy rain," "vessel rolling and pitching heavily." "wind force 11–12," etc. Ordinary routine broke down. Meals were only makeshift. Nobody slept. Nobody could. The rolling was too violent. It was a physical impossibility to keep oneself in a bunk. The wind blew so furiously that the spray and wind-driven rain actually beat the paint off the starboard side of the midship house down to the bare metal which is a thing rarely experienced in a lifetime at sea. Waves attained a height of over 40 ft. by the best approximation. Their size was so tremendous that it was frightening even to experienced seamen to look at them.

. . . We almost lost both lifeboats to the fury of the storm. Due to excessive rolling, the boats began to ride up in their davit tracks. All hands—engine, steward, and deck—turned-to to save the boats, and by much work, diligence, and improvisation the boats were kept safely secured in their cradles. It was grand optimism, our battle to save the lifeboats.

When the ship was taken off her normal course of 40 degrees she was put on a course of 70 degrees to ease the rolling. The course was gradually changed to the right as the wind and seas changed in that direction until eventually the ship was on a course of 200 or almost the reverse of her original course. About 30 minutes after midnight on August 29, I noticed that the wind and seas suddenly got into confused conflict. I was keeping a diligent watch on the steering to prevent the ship from getting broadside to those tremendous seas. It was deathly important that the helmsman not lose his vigilance or lapse into inattention. There was a perceptible movement of the wind and seas back to the left. The wind, rain, and spindrift were pelting the ship so unmercifully that it was impossible to see or look ahead except through the protection of the wheel house windows. I was fortunate to grasp the significance of that violent conflict of wind, seas, and rain and to quickly note the shift of the wind and seas back to the left. The ship was directed gradually back around an arc of the compass from 200 through north until eventually she was on a course of 270 or due west.

There was a time during the storm when I doubted the survival of the ship if an abatement of the wind and seas didn't favor us. Those mountainous seas would surge at the bow and it seemed inevitable that they were going to sweep the decks clean and knock the midship house over the stern, but miraculously the ship would raise over the worst of the impact, shaking tons of spray back over the bridge, enveloping it in green water and blinding all vision for seconds.

. . . The ship's radar was kept in continuous operation during the hurricane and the whistle was dutifully blown at 2 minute intervals as required by law in low visibility. However, the rain and spindrift came in solid sheets at times and the whistle and radar were just something to keep us company. Disaster would have been inevitable had an unfortunate ship been on a collision course with us.

The weather began to abate rapidly after noon Monday, August 31. Eventually the ship was on a course of 270, due west toward the Carolina coast. At 6 p.m. on that day when about 25 mi. off the coast heavy fuel oil was pumped over the side to break the force of the tremendous swells and the ship was turned around to a southerly course and away from Carol and the shoals. An inspection of the decks was made for heavy weather damage. No major or heavy damage was found but considerable damage to small deck fittings and electrical cables was discovered. I lay down that night at 10 p.m. after 66 continuous hours of vigilance on the bridge.

Hourly readings of the barometer were recorded in the Log Book from the time the ship was abeam of Jupiter Light. A summary of the readings is:

August 27   6 P.M.   30.06 in.
August 28   Noon   30.00
August 28   4 P.M.   29.91
August 29   4 P.M.   28.74
(Lowest reading during storm)
August 30   8 A.M.   28.81
August 30   Noon   29.24
August 30   4 P.M.   29.60
August 30   6 P.M.   29.78
August 31   8 A.M.   30.02

. . . Captain E. W. Malanot of MSTS recently wrote a very fine article called "Typhoon Doctrine" (see page 000) in which he advocates stopping the ship and letting her ride it out—engines stopped-dead ship. People have asked me why I didn't try the Malanot doctrine. I fear that Capt. Malanot's article will be misleading to some people, especially shoreside workers and inexperienced seamen. He mentions his draft of 12 ft. 2 in. forward and 17 ft. 3 in. aft. I can imagine that such a draft would be favorable in certain types of ships for laying dead in the sea before a storm. But the Malanot plan would be unsuitable for a heavy, deep-loaded ship like mine when loaded to her marks 28 ft. 6⅞ in.—one foot deeper than her builder's maximum draft due to that doubler plate welded to her sheer strake. . . .

IV

Riding Out a Philippine Typhoon*

By Commander R. P. Eyman, U.S. Coast and Geodetic Survey

"It's an ill wind that blows nobody good" is a trite old proverb that has been bandied about through the years and one wonders whether there is any basis of truth in it, especially at such times when you happen to be the "nobody" on whom the elements are venting their full fury. However that may be, I am sure that I can speak for the entire ship's company that thoughts, if any, along that line those of us on the *Pathfinder* may have had while riding out a severe typhoon in the northern Philippines, were most certainly centered on nothing but the forward half of that familiar quotation. In retrospect, of course, having safely weathered the particular storm, the full meaning of the saying began to dawn as the real value of such an experience was recognized—not, mind you, that there has ever been any desire to seek a more liberal "education" by repeating such an experience unnecessarily.

The U.S. Coast and Geodetic Survey ship *Pathfinder*, a flush-deck, coal-burning, steel steamer of 875 tons, had in her time weathered more or less successfully many typhoons. Built in Elizabeth, New Jersey, in 1899, she was sent from duty in Alaska to the Philippines in 1901 where she continued in operation until destroyed in early 1942 as a result of Japanese hostilities. Her triple-expansion engines of 846 horsepower gave her a speed of about 12 knots originally, but this had decreased through the years to a maximum of about 10 knots. The complement consisted of 9 officers (Americans) and a crew of 71 Filipinos.

On being ordered to command of the *Pathfinder* in the spring of 1932 instructions were received to resume hydrographic surveying operations,

*From United States Naval Institute *Proceedings*—March 1945.

initiated several years previously, along the northwestern and northern coasts of Luzon. Work in these areas could, in general, only be carried on from March through October; that is to say, during the period of the tail end of the northeast and the major portion of the southwest monsoons—in short, the typhoon season. Having had, as a junior officer, several rather close brushes with typhoons during a previous three-year hitch in the Philippines and an experience or two with hurricanes while in command of a small vessel in Florida waters, the writer had developed a healthy respect for such storms and realized that no "gravy-train" assignment lay ahead of us for the next few months. Although the general condition of the 33-year old *Pathfinder* was considered fairly good, there was no intention that we take too much for granted or deliberately pit her seagoing qualities against undue weather hazards, if such could be avoided gracefully. Suitable all-weather harbors were few and far between, being limited to that of Port Bolinao, 130 miles to the southward, and Port San Vicente, 100 miles to the eastward of Cape Bojeador on the northwestern tip of Luzon, with the additional possibility of finding fair anchorage in the mouth of the Cagayan River at Aparri, approximately midway along the north coast.

By the end of June work off the northwest coast had been completed. This part of the project had been carried on steadily and without unusual incident. Weather had been generally good and the few times it became necessary, adequate shelter from the northeast could always be obtained by anchoring close under the lee of the shore. In fact, this part of the season might readily have been termed the "milk run." After making a few minor repairs, including the renewal of a number of defective boiler tubes and the installation of two tobin-bronze metal rods as diagonal bracing along the after bulkhead of the wooden pilothouse to stiffen it and remedy a slight "working" which occurred with the roll of the ship, we sailed from Manila on July 11 to take up our assigned work along the north coast of Luzon. By now the Northeast had subsided and typical Southwest conditions had set in with light variable breezes, smooth seas, and good visibility, the latter often exceptionally good just before a storm. There was a rather disturbing element present, however, that caused us to keep a very close watch on the weather. A trough of low pressure extending from the China Sea through the Balintang Channel and far out toward the Ladrone Islands had developed shortly before our arrival and showed no signs of filling up or moving on. As a matter of fact, it persisted for about a month. This trough or path of least resistance offered an enticing invitation to any disturbances that might be forming in the Pacific typhoon breeding grounds to set a course in our direction and hook up full speed ahead.

Except for a survey of the bar and mouth of the Cagayan River, made soon after our arrival, to determine whether access could be had to an anchorage within the river mouth—shoaling was found to preclude this—plans had long since been made to take the best possible advantage of every break in the weather to operate farthest from shelter and to reserve the near-by areas for operations during doubtful or suspicious periods when it might become necessary to seek refuge on rather short notice. In general, local weather conditions continued favorable and work was carried on with but one interruption until

July 25, despite the fact the "lows," disturbances, and typhoons were being reported almost daily in practically all surrounding areas. On the 18th a typhoon had appeared in the Pacific about 300 miles to the eastward of Luzon and by the 20th was crossing that island only about 60 miles to the southward of our anchorage at San Vicente. It did not, however, affect us to any great extent aside from passing squalls with 50- or 60-mile breezes which, coming off the land, did not kick up any seas.

By July 25 a low that had shown up several days previously far out toward the Ladrones had finally graduated and was reported as a typhoon of light intensity some 300 miles to the eastward of central Luzon moving WNW—in our direction. Work was continued throughout the day, but indications of approaching trouble began to be manifest. Although the barometer had been below normal for some time, its diurnal oscillation now disappeared and the trend was definitely downward. The surface wind was a light NE breeze, but the high clouds indicated greater velocities. Clouds became thicker and squalls became more frequent and violent, and the breeze steadily freshened to moderate NE. Anchorage was made that evening in San Vicente outer harbor and a close watch kept on developments. During the night the barometer continued to fall gradually, squalls became somewhat more frequent but only slightly more intense, and the breeze continued to freshen from the NE. Weather reports received at this time did not indicate anything more serious than a low, or very light typhoon, still located about 200 miles out in the Pacific. By early morning of the 26th it was apparent that a typhoon of considerably more severity than previously reported was closing in on us and that it was now time to make all preparations accordingly. The ship was taken into the inner harbor and anchored in the center of the basin with the port anchor to which "false" palms had previously been attached. All awnings, dodgers, and loose gear were removed from above deck; small boats and other deck gear were secured with additional lashings; all rigging and stays were examined and set up taut; hatches not immediately necessary and skylights were covered and battened down; the second set of false palms was attached to the starboard anchor; the spare bower anchor was rigged over the side in readiness for dropping and the end of a coil of 12-inch Manila hawser broken out from the hold and made fast to it for emergency use—needless to add that a full head of steam was maintained and the engines kept warmed up for instant use.

Having completed all the above preparations by 0900, our situation was carefully reviewed. The ship was riding comfortably to one anchor in the center of a landlocked harbor, with swinging room of about 450 yards' diameter; the depth of water within this area was about 4 fathoms with mud bottom (which we hoped would prove of good holding quality—how good, we found out to our entire satisfaction later). Fringing the anchorage basin for an average width of about 400 yards were shoals and coral reefs, permitting a maximum scope of anchor chain of about 75 fathoms providing the mooring held in the center of the basin. The ground tackle consisted of two stock 1500-lb. bower anchors to which the false palms above referred to had been attached. These palms, four in number, were of 1-inch boiler plate about 2 by 3 feet, roughly triangular in shape, curved slightly to fit the regular palms snugly, and held in place by means of four 1-inch steel bolts; this extra equipment added about 250 lb. to each of the 1500-lb. bower anchors. The anchor chains consisted of 94 fathoms of 1⅛ inch on the starboard, and 120 fathoms of 1¼ inch on the port. The spare anchor was a stock type of 2079 lb. Since the *Pathfinder* had tendency to yaw badly when riding to a long mooring, it was decided to limit the scope first to 45 fathoms and later, if necessary, to pay out not more than 60 fathoms. We would ride to one anchor as long as possible, or until the course of travel of the storm could be more definitely determined, and then, when necessary, the second anchor would be dropped where it would serve the best purpose. The wind was still holding NE with no sign of shifting, indicating that we were on or very near the storm path, and latest reports placed the center only some 100 miles off. By noon, with the wind still holding the same direction and having steadily increased to about 50 miles per hour, squalls becoming more frequent and violent, and the barometer dropping steadily about .04 inch per hour, it was decided to delay no longer in dropping the second anchor and so, with the next lull, the starboard anchor was let go not too wide off the port anchor and both chains paid out to 45 fathoms and secured.

Anticipating a wakeful and rather busy night and since there seemed nothing else to be done for the time being, the writer thought a little siesta might come in handy, and so, with a competent watch set, time was taken out after lunch for a rest of about a couple of hours. The storm gradually but steadily grew more violent up to 1600, with practically continuous rain and a NE wind up to about 70 m.p.h. Shortly after 1600 the storm began to break in real earnest with squalls of increasing fury; seas began to pick up in our sheltered anchorage; darkness settled down and visibility became extremely limited. An officer was stationed in the eyes to keep the pilothouse advised of the lead of the moorings; the engines were used frequently to keep the ship's head into the wind and to ease somewhat the strain on the anchor chains, taking due care not to override them; the drift lead of about 15 lb. was soon replaced by another of about 25 lb., but this proved of academic interest only as the force of the wind on the bight of the line was so great that it was impossible to determine the relationship between the drift lead and the vessel; a Quartermaster was detailed to take occasional soundings off the stern to try to detect any incipient dragging. The fury of the storm increased in violence each minute. The gale howled and screamed through the rigging. The torrential rain was carried in horizontal sheets by the force of the wind which continued to rise in violent gusts—upon its reaching 100 m.p.h. the vanes of the anemometer were carried away, thus preventing further recordings. It was impossible to see beyond the bow of the ship. The waves in the harbor were whipped up to a height of 6 to 8 feet and the crests were blown off in a continuous foam of white spray. The pilothouse shuddered with each heavy gust and it was feared that it might be carried away. To face the wind and rain directly was practically impossible. Watching the lead of the moorings was an extremely difficult task. To make one's way about the deck it was necessary to cling to a rail or life line and, wherever possible, crouch below the bulwarks. A cautious turn about deck was taken at intervals to examine the security of gear and several times it was found necessary to break out the crew to strengthen some of the lashings— one of the launches was found partially lifted from its chocks. As the storm mounted in fury the barometer continued its nose dive; with each tapping of the glass the indicator hand dropped a hundredth or two with no sign of leveling off; each time the pilothouse door was opened the barometer needle would drop another point and a small hatch about 20 inches square in the center of the deck leading to a small storage compartment beneath was blown off.

Shortly before 1800 the force of the gale appeared to abate slightly and within a very few minutes rapidly decreased in violence to a moderate NE breeze. This sudden change in the situation called for immediate action as it was now evident that the center or eye of the storm was upon us and that the gale would break anew at any minute, probably from a new quarter. Anchor chains were hove in short in readiness to swing to the new direction when this could be determined, and a close watch was kept for the first signs of the rear half of the storm. The wind dropped to a very light breeze, veering slowly from ENE to NE to N × E and then died out completely. The rain ceased; the heavy clouds began to grow thin and finally broke away entirely revealing a beautiful blue, unclouded sky overhead with the last waning rays of the setting sun pouring through. This "fool's paradise" lasted for only about 20 minutes. The barometer had finally stopped its dive at 28.12". The lull gave us an opportunity to make a quick survey of our situation which appeared to be so far so good; no serious damage was apparent, and the anchors had dragged very little, if any.

Soon, however, thin cloud streamers began racing across the clear blue overhead from an ESE direction—this was the clue we had been awaiting. The ship was quickly swung around to this new heading and maneuvered to a position between the anchors with the engines. Within no time the surface breeze began to pick up from the ESE; the spare anchor was let go and the ship kicked astern to a mooring of 45 fathoms on the chains and with about the same on the Manila hawser—all were equalized as much as possible and secured. It was fortunate that this scope had previously been decided upon as it was now discovered that there was a badly frayed strand in the hawser only a few fathoms inboard when all had been secured. These arrangements had barely been completed before the storm again began to gather real headway— dense clouds had blotted out the blue sky, heavy rain squalls had returned, and the breeze freshened in quickly succeeding gusts. Within less than 10 minutes the gale had mounted to its previous intensity and finally exceeded its former fury. This half of the storm was somewhat more nerve-racking than the first half, what with complete pitch-black darkness except for lightning flashes and with the greater severity and frequency of the gusts which reached an estimated velocity of well over 100 m.p.h.—probably 115 to 125. It was much more difficult to keep a close watch on the lead of the moorings, but the officers assigned to this duty did a magnificent job and as a result of their directions, signaled by flashlight, the ship was kept headed into the gale with fairly uniform tension maintained on the moorings. It was now simply a matter of riding it out and hoping that the anchors would hold and nothing give way, as it seemed that having passed through the forward half of the storm in a matter of a couple of hours, the rear half, although much more intense, should not last too long. The barometer by this time was rising rapidly.

Shortly after 2200 a slight diminution in the strength and frequency of the gusts was detected. By 2230 the decrease was decidedly noticeable and from then on the force of the gale rapidly declined until shortly before midnight when only a very gentle breeze was blowing from the SE. Although the sky remained partly overcast, the rain squalls became infrequent and of no particular violence. We had apparently weathered the storm safely and, although it was too dark to determine whether we had dragged anchors, at least we were afloat and not piled up in the midst of mangrove bushes.

The morning of the 27th broke cloudy, with light southerly to southwesterly breezes and intermittent light rains. It was noted that the ship had dragged not more than 15 or 20 yards during the entire storm, and the answer was soon disclosed. What was thought to be a mere routine job, that of picking up the anchors, was commenced about 0700, but was not completed until about 1130; the windlass lacked power to break them out and it was necessary to heave each one short in turn and steam ahead full speed to accomplish it. When brought to the surface the reason was at once apparent; the anchors had dug well into the bottom and each brought up a load of hard-packed mud weighing probably a half ton or more and requiring the use of shovels and pike poles along with the hosing to remove it and clean the chains and anchors. There remained no further doubt about the holding qualities of this particular anchorage.

A careful examination revealed that except for the pilothouse we had suffered practically no damage. The force of the wind had opened many seams in the tongue-and-grooved framing of the forward part of the pilothouse in a number of places by as much as one-half inch and it is firmly believed that the diagonal bracing, referred to before, was all that saved it from being carried away. Some of the awning stanchions were somewhat awry and a few spreaders were missing, but otherwise everything was intact. The deck was littered with all sort of debris from ashore—small branches, palm fronds, sand, pebbles, etc. During the night we had also captured a large sea bird of the goony family which had been blown in from sea by the gale and had sought refuge on the deck of the ship. On making a turn of inspection one of the officers had suddenly and literally come face to face with this tall, black, strange creature in the dark behind one of the hatches and with the help of several crew members had succeeded in placing it in a large crate; it was liberated the following morning when it appeared to have recovered from its exhaustion.

Although the barometer had leveled off, it still remained below normal and the weather continued unsettled and did not clear as quickly as might be expected once the typhoon had passed. Local conditions, however, were not unfavorable and work was resumed on the 28th and carried on until the afternoon of the 29th, when, fuel and supplies running low, it was necessary to return to port. On rounding Cape Bojeador southbound, somewhat to our surprise we ran into a strong SW gale with rough seas. Despite reports indicating much better weather ahead, conditions became worse the farther south we proceeded and the barometer crept lower. Not caring to subject the gallant old vessel to unnecessary punishment and strain, we eased ahead through heavy head seas and pulled into San Fernando about noon on the 30th and awaited there more favorable weather. On the morning of August 2 our voyage was resumed and arrival at Manila was made on the morning of August 3, completing not-soon-to-be-forgotten experiences with tropical disturbances that had ranged through the full scale within a period of less than one month.

It was with genuine regret that some months later orders of detachment were received and my relief came aboard to take over command, but my tour of duty in the Philippines was finished and it was now time to return to the States and leave the vessel in the hands of my successors, who invariably held the same high regard and feeling of warm attachment for the faithful old ship. The *Pathfinder* continued on surveying duty in various areas of Philippine waters until the advent of the present war. Having recently returned to Manila, she was slightly damaged in one of the first Japanese bombing raids, but was able to proceed to Corregidor with valuable records. Off Corregidor she suffered further damage from bombings during the last days of December, 1941, and had to be beached. The last report, transmitted in March, 1942, indicated that the 43-year-old veteran was among those listed for total demolition to prevent her falling into enemy hands. Although the long career of this vessel had thus come to an inglorious end, her name is perpetuated in a new ship completed that same year. The new *Pathfinder* is a modern all-steel vessel of 1,900 tons, especially built and equipped for surveying work in the most remote regions, and, since her completion, has been steadily engaged on just such duties, frequently in enemy-held territories, the accomplishment of which has had a vital part in the successful operations of our naval and military forces in carrying the war ever closer to total victory.

V

The Typhoon Lady*

By Lieutenant (j.g.) Robert J. Lauer, U.S. Navy

Quite a few naval vessels weathered quite a few typhoons during the recent war in the Pacific, but I feel that very few could approach the record of survivals per typhoons encountered established by the U.S.S. *San Jacinto*.

The little CVL met her first tropical storm west of the Palau group of islands in September of 1944. However, her baptism was mild, and she only skirted the storm, suffering nothing worse than two days of heavy rolling and pitching.

The disdain for typhoons thus engendered in the minds of her ship's company was shattered abruptly in December of that year when, as a unit of Task Force 38 supporting Army operations in the Central Philippines, she became entangled in the worst marine disaster the Navy had known to that time. That infamous typhoon which capsized two destroyers and several smaller craft leaving no survivors, came upon Admiral Halsey's carrier task force at precisely the time when it could not retire to safer waters.† The Army had just landed troops on Mindoro Island and needed every bit of air support the Navy could provide. The decision to remain in the area and assist the invasion until the last moment was, no doubt, a difficult one to make but the success of the operation surely justifies the losses suffered at the hands of the elements.

Having been warned beforehand of the approaching storm the *San Jac* had set her typhoon bill. All moveable gear had been lashed down. Additional lines from aircraft on the flight and hangar decks were made fast to the securing grommets in the deck. Elevators were lowered to increase the GM and the "Little Queen" waited for the blast.

*From United States Naval Institute *Proceedings*—June 1949.
†The author is in error. There were a few survivors.

The intensity of the storm could never have been imagined beforehand. Winds of over 100 knots and seas 70 to 80 feet high lashed at the ships of the formation. To ease the ferocious pounding the course was adjusted to place the ships in the trough of the seas, and speed was reduced to the minimum required to maintain steerageway. All hands stood by their respective spaces to insure their security.

It was a terrifying sight to watch the gigantic breakers on the crest of the seas looming up, sometimes as much as thirty degrees above the horizontal, as the ship slowly rolled through forty degrees or more. It would have been suicide to venture onto the flight deck. It speaks well for the flight deck crews that every plane located there held fast.

However, down on the hangar deck it was another story. The TBMs, the heavier planes, had been struck below. The hangar deck could just hold the ten of them in two rows of fives. They were lashed down with all the manila available, since this took place before the advent of steel cable securing lines. At the peak of the storm the weight of the planes pulling against the lines under the excessive roll proved too much to hold. A plane broke loose and was hurled into the one beside it, breaking it loose from its moorings. With every roll of the ship the two would careen across the deck and smash against the bulkheads, carrying away everything in their paths—spare engines, belly tanks, tractors and other articles of gear.

An heroic effort to harness these murderous missiles and secure them to the bulkheads was led by the air group commander, Commander Gordon Schecter (who was subsequently lost in action over Kyushu), but it soon proved impossible and exceedingly hazardous.

In a very short time other planes had been cut loose by the wreckage of the first two, and within a half hour the entire hangar deck was a mass of flying carnage threatening sure death to anyone who dared enter into it. A spare engine near the port side aft broke its securing lines and, on the starboard roll, flew across the hangar deck and passed through a steel roller curtain as though it were a piece of paper.

Gasoline and oil covered the deck. A spark was struck, and flames leapt up in the middle of the hangar. The hangar deck sprinkling was turned on, and hoses and foam were played on the fire from the openings to the cat walks. This, combined with the torrential rain and sea water from openings punctured in the sides soon produced a virtual flooding of the hangar deck. Then machine gun ammunition from the planes began to go off, fired by the flames and by being struck with the flying debris.

The four uptakes and most of the ventilation piping led through the hangar. These were ruptured and carried away by the hurtling wreckage, and the salt water flowed into the openings, flooding many compartments below and freezing or shorting out much electrical equipment as well as cracking one boiler drum.

Spare steel plates, carried in the elevator pits, slithered back and forth mercilessly gouging the elevator pistons and rendering them inoperative. All ventilation and most lighting was lost. It seemed almost inescapable that if the storm continued the ship herself must soon be abandoned. Then, like a last minute reprieve, the storm began to abate. The fires were extinguished and flooded compartments pumped out.

As the ships re-formed toward sunset of the third day of the storm the *San Jac* seemed but a ghost of her former self. She had power for propulsion and steering, but not much else. The humid air, and the lack of ventilation and light, coupled with the sickening motion as the ship rode over the long swells characteristic of a passed typhoon, made living below unbearable. Meals in the wardroom, with tables and chairs lashed to the deck or bulkhead and with smashed china on the deck, consisted of unsatisfactory rations of cold sandwiches and rancid coffee. Two feet of water stood in the crew's mess and had to be pumped out before meals could be served. Everyone aboard was exhausted.

But then as if by magic morale skyrocketed. The rumor swept the ship in a few minutes. Naturally she would return to the States for repairs! To a crew which has been in the forward area continuously for eight months the news was like manna from Heaven.

The task force retired to Ulithi, where representatives of ComSeron 10 inspected the damage. The scuttlebutt continued. The crew nervously awaited the word that the next port would be San Francisco. But the fates decided otherwise, and a sister ship, the *Monterey*, also badly damaged, was elected to return to the States after being cannibalized by the *San Jacinto*.

The "Little Queen" went alongside a repair ship where she stayed for ten days; the ten days over Christmas. The crew of the repair ship, the *Hector*, worked untiringly during that time, twenty-four hours a day, and did a miraculous job of overhaul. By the first of the year the ship was as good as new and at sea, about to participate in the next operation.

Needless to say the information that the ship would remain in the forward area did very little to help morale, particularly in view of the fact that every man aboard had been quite certain he would soon be home, and because the repairs were affected over Christmas week. It would be difficult to depict the depth of the gloom which settled over the ship Christmas morning when, instead of reveille, *Deck the Halls with Wreaths of Holly* was piped over the P.A. system.

However, it was but a matter of a few days at sea until all hands felt normal again. A week after leaving Ulithi the task force was in the South China Sea where, it was hoped, the remnants of the Jap fleet could be ferreted out and destroyed. Three weeks later the task force steamed through the Balintang Passage, leaving the South China Sea without having seen a major Jap naval vessel, a smooth sea, or the sun.

Operations during the month of February placed the San Jacinto successively off Iwo Jima, Tokyo, Iwo again and Tokyo again, and finally in the Inland Sea, headed for strikes against the Nagoya area. These latter strikes were cancelled, however, for icy winds from the north were churning up such violent seas that aircraft operations were deemed too hazardous to attempt. The task force then retired to Ulithi to prepare for the nightmarish three months of strikes against the Japanese mainland and the Nansei Shoto, including the invasion and securing of Okinawa. The only pleasant feature of that whole affair was, ironically, the weather.

The respite from the fury of the elements terminated in June, however, when the task force, operating southeast of Okinawa, encountered, simultaneously, two typhoons which culminated their northeasterly movement by combining at approximately the same geographical location occupied by Task Force 38.

The task group of which the *San Jacinto* was a unit bore the brunt of the storm and experienced a rare accomplishment in passing through the eye of the westernmost typhoon. At that point the wind and sea moderated considerably, and a patch of blue sky could be seen overhead. The barometer had reached a record low of, I believe, about twenty-seven inches. Of course as the cyclone moved on, its force again built up to a maximum, and then gradually subsided. The violent effects of the storm were felt for approximately forty-eight hours.

During the greater part of the storm the ships were headed so that the wind was on the port bow and the sea on the starboard bow. Turns were made for five knots, but actually the ships barely moved through the water.

The *Pittsburgh*, alongside the *San Jacinto*, was so violently shaken that she lost her bow. The *Duluth* narrowly escaped a like fate, but suffered such severe pounding that she was forced to retire to Guam to have her bow strength members repaired. The *Bennington* and *Hornet*, the CVs of the group, suffered identical casualties when both of their flight decks forward collapsed over their forecastles after the supporting members had been carried away by the seas. It was interesting a few days later to watch them launch aircraft off the after end of their flight decks. Practically all scouting planes topside on the battleships and cruisers were either carried away or hopelessly battered.

The *San Jacinto* rode out this typhoon with a minimum of damage, having suffered nothing worse than several buckled deck plates and cracked seams, and a number of slightly bent deck stringers. However, the personnel experiences were quite harrowing. For a period of about five hours as the ship rode out the mountainous seas the effect was as though some titanic crane were lifting the bow higher and higher, until it seemed the ship would surely break her back, and would then release it and permit it to drop with a frightening crash and shudder.

After the storm had passed the *San Jac* found herself, with the exception of the 20 mm sponsons forward, in full operating condition. She had learned from experience how to conquer a typhoon.

As the Japanese envoys were signing the terms of surrender aboard the *Missouri* on September 2, 1945, the U.S.S. *San Jacinto* was headed for San Francisco, after seventeen months of uninterrupted operations against the enemy, for which she later received the Presidential Unit Citation.

It seemed that even in peacetime the little CVL could not escape the violence of the sea. In December of 1945, while engaged in the Magic Carpet operations, she was en route from San Francisco to Manila, P.I. Her first ten days out were devoted to a continuous fight against violent seas in the form of breakers which hammered night and day against her starboard bow and succeeded in tearing away most of her stack supports and smashing number one stack into uselessness.

Permission was obtained for the return trip to avoid the rough great circle route and to take the longer, balmy route due east from San Bernardino Straits to just south of the island of Hawaii. By that time the *San Jac* had seen her last rough seas, although she narrowly missed the fatal tidal wave which two days after her arrival in San Francisco devastated the city of Hilo on Hawaii.

For two years now the *San Jacinto* has been resting peacefully, inactivated, alongside a pier at the Alameda Naval Air Station, and the worst weather she experiences is the fog rolling in through the Golden Gate and condensing on her flight deck. She seems to have settled into a sort of blissful retirement.

VI

Typhoon Doctrine*

By Elmer W. Malanot

It is a fact that even the most experienced seaman in command of a ship sooner or later finds himself facing some problem where he will have to consult a textbook on seamanship; and in most cases, *Knight's* or *Crenshaw* will have the answer. This is not the case, however, if a man is looking for advice on what to do, and how to do it, when a typhoon or a hurricane has caught up with him.

Cyclonic storms are fully described, and also the method on how to avoid them, and how *sailing ships* can avoid them, but I have never yet seen anyone suggesting what to do, and how to do it, should one find himself caught in such a storm.

It is my assumption that the men who wrote these books on seamanship did not have sufficient experience passing through tropical storms and that their source of information was not complete enough to enable them to write on this subject.

If a man who has had such experience were to suggest stopping the engines when the wind in a cyclonic storm reaches a force of sixty knots and doing nothing until the center has passed and the force of the wind has reduced to about sixty knots, people would be skeptical. It would be argued that in stopping the engine, the ship would fall off into the trough and capsize; therefore to avoid falling off into the trough considerable power ought to be used to keep steerage way. It is not realized that this power hurls his ship against mountains of waves, like ramming one's head against a stone wall, and that in this way he would damage and perhaps even destroy her unwittingly.

Now, where is the trough in a cyclone that captains try to avoid? To find an

*From United States Naval Institute *Proceedings*—July 1955.

answer to this question, we should study the relation between wind and waves, and between waves and ship. Sea waves are formed by prolonged action of the wind. Once a sea wave is formed it will continue for some time, and travel great distances even when the wind that caused it has calmed down or changed its direction. Sea waves that travel at a speed of ten to twenty knots do not carry the water with them, as it is only the form that advances while the particles of water have a different motion from that of the waves.

This phenomenon can be seen in tidal estuaries, with waves rolling in from the sea against an ebb tide and floating objects being carried out to sea by the tide against the inward passage of the waves. This can also be seen in a ship dead in the water. The onrushing crest of a wave will not hit the ship; it will only lift it. But if the ship is moving, it will be the ship that hits the wave. This point of *who is hitting whom* is most important and is seldom understood by the average seaman.

In a typhoon, all observers concur in their reports, near the center the sea is confused. This confusion is caused by the changing direction of the force that forms the waves. In cyclonic storms, a wind blowing from north, for instance, will build up a heavy sea from that direction. Then, after the wind backs to northwest, and so on, there will be several distinct series of waves within the same area at the same time. This constant change of wind direction is what makes the terrible confused seas which just cannot be avoided no matter what the ship does.

HURRICANE IN THE CARIBBEAN

Many years ago when I was a comparatively young shipmaster, in command of a freighter of about 16,000 tons displacement on her maiden voyage in the Caribbean Sea, we had a hurricane warning. It was my first experience with a tropical storm, and with the help of *Bowditch* I put the ship on a course which would have brought it into the safe semi-circle out of the hurricane's path.

The motorship being deeply laden to the Plimsoll mark, worked heavily. Towering seas crashed on deck, and there was some damage to life boats and deck fixtures. During the voyage we had some difficulties with our diesel auxiliaries, and now the engineer reported that he had two out of commission, and it did not take long until the last auxiliary also failed. This of course stopped the main engine, and we were left at the mercy of that hurricane roaring down on us with winds of 120 knots. Visualizing what might happen to us when our ship fell off into the trough of those gigantic waves gave us quite a scare.

When we gradually recovered from that first shock and the ship was lying dead in the water, it seemed strange that the action of sea and wind decreased considerably and that there was no more smashing of waves on deck, although the center passed directly over us, with a short dead calm and blue sky. Then again came the tearing and screaming wind from the opposite direction. It seemed to us miraculous that there was no damage to the ship at all after the engine broke down. It took us some time to patch up the auxiliaries, and then we proceeded; but this lesson I have remembered all my life.

Later I read an account in the *Reader's Digest* about such a miracle happening to a destroyer during Admiral Halsey's battle with a typhoon in December, 1944. That destroyer had its boiler rooms swamped in the early stages of the storm, and although lying helpless and dead in the water, it survived the typhoon without further damage, while three other destroyers who had their 60,000 horsepower working to the last capsized with the loss of every man on board.* Those poor men died without knowing that it was suicide to use their powerful engines against the infinitely greater power of nature.

After V-J day I was assigned to the shuttle service between Manila, Okinawa, and Yokohama, then later extended to include Guam and Korea. From January, 1946, until May, 1954, except for five months' leave, I was in the typhoon area constantly and logged an average of two major typhoons a year. This offered excellent opportunity to study and observe typhoons in all their phases.

TYPHOON *LIBBY*

In October, 1948, we were caught in Naha, Okinawa, by *Libby*. We could not leave the port because there was a fifty-knot wind blowing three days before the typhoon struck the island, permitting no traffic to pass through the narrow channel of that harbor. There were, besides my ship (the USAT *Pvt. George J. Peters*), two Liberty-type ships manned by Japanese. These two ships tore from their moorings and piled up on Engineer Island in Naha harbor, heavily damaged. My ship had only superficial damage to the railings caused by one of the Liberties, for our moorings held. *Libby* was unusual because the center stopped over the island for about five hours, a most unusual occurrence. On October 3, 1948, the wind (northerly) increased gradually during the night to 120 knots, then in the morning of the 4th it suddenly dropped to a dead calm. The barometer was at about 28.40 and the sun was shining. At 1500 hours it started to blow from the SSW, then west and full force of about 140 knots from the WNW. At midnight the barometer started rising and the wind decreased to about forty knots at daylight, October 5. Those days in Naha, Okinawa, were dangerous, and I promised myself never to be caught again in a port by a typhoon.

TYPHOON *GLORIA*

The following year on July 22, 1949, the USAT *Pvt. George J. Peters* was again in Naha when *Gloria* came over the Island. This time we put out to sea and drifted with stopped engines while the center passed us at a distance of forty miles. The wind was up to 120 knots, the waves gigantic, of a height estimated to about 50 feet, but the ship floated like a duck, and there was not the slightest damage or even discomfort on board.

TYPHOON *RUTH*

The most violent and destructive storm I have experienced in those Far Eastern waters was typhoon *Ruth*. At that time I was in command of the USNS *Sgt. Joseph E. Muller*, a C1-MAV-1 class vessel of 4,500 tons displacement.

*The author is in error. There were a few survivors.

When we arrived in Okinawa, *Ruth* was 500 miles south, heading toward Formosa. We entered Naha harbor at 0700 hours on October 12, 1951, discharged our passengers, and were starting cargo operations when at 1000 hours the evacuation of Naha harbor was started. We proceeded to sea at about 1400 hours; our draft was 12'-2" forward and 17'3" aft. Our metacentric height (GM) about 4.84 feet.

Captain Henry T. Jarrell, USN, our passenger from Yokohama to Formosa, was offered quarters ashore by the Senior Naval Officer on Okinawa, but he returned to the ship to observe our typhoon-fighting tactics of which he had heard reports from officers ashore.

From Okinawa we proceeded to the island of Kume Shima, approximately fifty miles west from Naha, to take shelter behind the island until we had a clear indication of the proximity of the typhoon. We stayed near this island from 1840 hours on October 12 to 1747 hours on October 13. At that time we abandoned our shelter and let the easterly wind carry us out to sea with engines stopped. The barometer was falling rapidly, indicating the approach of the typhoon's center. The wind's force was about fifty knots, increasing continuously. There was a heavy swell from the south into which the ship was heading, being broadside to the easterly wind. The vessel was naturally rolling and pitching, but without taking any sea or spray on deck. Gradually the wind shifted counterclockwise, the barometer fell steadily, and the wind increased rapidly. By 0300 hours October 14, when we were at the closest point to the center, the wind had shifted to north; the force of it estimated at about 140 knots; the sea from all directions of a height estimated at 50 feet, and the barometer reading 28.02, the ship heading 090 degrees, drifting in a southerly direction with engines still stopped. At 0400 hours, the barometer began to rise, and the wind shifted gradually to NW and continued to back through W to SW. At 1030 hours the wind decreased to fifty knots, and we proceeded at full speed toward Naha, where we arrived at 1600 hours.

From various indications, it was established that the center of the typhoon had passed between Naha and our position, approximately 25 miles to the east of our vessel. From the damage caused by this storm on land and to shipping, *Ruth* was considered one of the fiercest typhoons Okinawa has had. Although the center passed us at a distance of only about 25 miles, we never experienced the slightest concern for the safety of our ship; we had no sea breaking on our decks, no jars or shocks to our hull, and no damage whatsoever. The only thing we did was to stop the engine and offer no resistance and no fight to the elements. Two fair-sized Japanese freighters which also evacuated Naha took shelter and anchored between the islands of Kerama Retto. During the night of October 13–14 they dragged their anchors and were smashed to pulp on the rocky shores of the island. Each was a total loss.

The following conditions were typical while drifting in typhoon *Ruth*:

a. Visibility zero to 300 yards.
b. Drifting at speeds of a maximum of five knots and in a semicircle of which the diameter was thirty miles.
c. Pitching heavily and rolling about 35° with a few rolls up to 43°. In general the

vessel adapted itself easily to the heavy confused sea. It did not ship any water except for a very few times in the heaviest rolls when a few inches of water above the gunwale were scooped off the crest of a wave. This was like an overflowing motion with no force or violence attached to it, would have gone to a depth not over a man's ankle, and would have amounted to less than a few hundred gallons. It certainly would not have damaged or disturbed any sort of deck cargo secured in the normal manner.

d. Radar and Loran were operative and gave us our position when required.

e. The floodlights were kept alight on deck, and thus the behavior of the ship continuously observed.

. . . the heavy swell in the vicinity of the center of a typhoon is always from a direction different from that of the wind. In our case, the wind was from WNW, still about 100 knots, while the ship pitched heavily to a swell from the NNE.

This is the point that should be impressed on seamen who believe that if they stop the engines, their vessel will fall off into the trough of the sea with disastrous results. The fact is that there exists a trough from all sides, and the only way to minimize the danger of this force is by not opposing it. If inexperienced commanders of small vessels with high power do not fully realize this point, they will, in their anxiety to avoid this trough, hurl their vessels against the gigantic power of nature and succeed only in their own destruction.

I am fully convinced now that a seaworthy ship of any size or draft with an adequate metacentric height, will be safer with stopped engines than by using them. Any book on seamanship teaches us how to calculate the metacentric height, and how dangerous a sluggish roll or, to the contrary, a quick jerky roll can be; and it teaches us also how easily both can be corrected: the sluggish roll by adding some weight in the bottom tanks, and the other by removing some weight from the bottom tanks. In a typhoon there is sufficient time to correct the stability of the vessel and also to obtain a safe margin of seaway. And so once a seaman, after getting sea room, has learned not to use any power in a cyclonic storm, he will have done all that can be done for the safety of his vessel and his crew, and will further find that he can then take any typhoon in his stride.

I think that this theory of not opposing such a force and of stopping the engine is one of the greatest importance to combat vessels, and especially destroyers, which for tactical reasons cannot concentrate on avoiding a typhoon, but have to stay at their post until the last minute, as during operations east of Luzon on December 18, 1944. I am convinced that if those commanding officers had been instructed, on the approach of that typhoon when the wind had risen to more than sixty knots, to stop their engines and just drift, there would have been no casualties and no damage.

I believe that it is high time to break with the old tradition of fighting a typhoon and introduce a new concept of riding it out, with stopped engines, drifting more or less broadside to the wind, which in a typhoon is always from a direction different from that of the biggest and most destructive waves. It will take courage by the Commanding Officer of any vessel to order the engines stopped, when close to the center of a typhoon, and even more courage to order a ship to test this "passive resistance," but I am sure that if this method is adopted, it will save money, lives, and valuable property, especially in time of war.

It is suggested that in this respect, the following simple instructions should be put in textbooks and typhoon doctrines:

When the center of a tropical storm approaches you, get thirty miles or more sea room around you, assure yourself of the ship's stability and watertight integrity, and when the wind force rises to sixty knots or more and the sea becomes confused, stop your engines, drift and wait for the storm's dangerous area to pass before you proceed.

VII

Discussions, Comments, Notes

Typhoon Doctrine*

In the July, 1955, *Proceedings* there appeared Elmer W. Malanot's "Typhoon Doctrine," an article which stimulated considerable comment from *Proceedings* readers. . . .

(Editor's Note: Mr. Malanot stated . . . that he had been inspired to write of his own experiences after having read an account of the typhoon which hit the U.S. Third Fleet off the Philippines in December 1944. Soon after the Malanot article appeared, the Naval Institute learned of a Pacific Fleet Confidential Letter written by the then Commander in Chief, Pacific Fleet, Admiral C. W. Nimitz, and dealing in detail with the lessons of that disastrous typhoon. With the cooperation of Fleet Admiral Nimitz and the Office of the Secretary of the Navy, the Naval Institute here publishes Admiral Nimitz' letter, now de-classified.)

18 February 1945

PACIFIC FLEET CONFIDENTIAL LETTER 14CL-45

From: Commander in Chief, U.S. Pacific Fleet.
To: PACIFIC FLEET and NAVAL SHORE ACTIVITIES, Pacific Ocean Areas
Subject: Damage in Typhoon, Lessons of.

1. On 18 December 1944, vessels of the Pacific Fleet, operating in support of the invasion of the Philippines in an area about 300 miles east of Luzon, were caught near the center of a typhoon of extreme violence. Three destroyers, the

---

*From United States Naval Institute *Proceedings*—January 1956.

HULL, MONAGHAN, and SPENCE capsized and went down with practically all hands; serious damage was sustained by the CL MIAMI, the CVLs MONTEREY, COWPENS, and SAN JACINTO, the CVEs CAPE ESPERANCE and ALTAMAHA, and the DDs AYLWIN, DEWEY, and HICKOX. Lesser damage was sustained by at least 19 other vessels, from CAs down to DEs. Fires occurred on three carriers when planes were smashed in their hangars; and some 146 planes on various ships were lost or damaged beyond economical repair by the fires, by being smashed up, or by being swept overboard. About 790 officers and men were lost or killed, and 80 were injured. Several surviving destroyers reported rolling 70° or more; and we can only surmise how close this was to capsizing completely for some of them. It was the greatest loss that we have taken in the Pacific without compensatory return since the First Battle of Savo.

2. In the light of hindsight it is easy to see how any of several measures might have prevented this catastrophe, but it was far less easy a problem at the time for the men who were out there under the heaviest of conflicting reponsibilities. The important thing is for it never to happen again; and hence, while it is impracticable herein to go into all the factors involved and the experiences undergone, some of the outstanding lessons will be discussed.

3. Possibly, too much reliance was placed on the analysis broadcast from Fleet Weather Central, Pearl Harbor. Weather data was lacking from an area some 240 to 300 miles in diameter (where the storm was actually centered); and the immediate signs of it in the operating area were not heeded early enough. Groups of the Third Fleet tried to avoid the storm center, but neither radically enough nor to best advantage, since their information as to its location and path was meager. Fleet damage and losses were accentuated by the efforts of vessels and subordinate commanders to maintain fleet courses, speeds, and formations during the storm. Commanding officers failed to realize sufficiently in advance of the fact that it was necessary for them to give up the attempt, and give all their attention to saving their ships. There was a lack of appreciation by subordinate commanders and commanding officers that really dangerous weather conditions existed, until it was too late to make the preparations for security that might have been helpful.

4. The following conditions were typical during the typhoon:

(a) Visibility zero to a thousand yards.
(b) Ships not merely rolling, but heeled far over continually by the force of the wind, thus leaving them very little margin for further rolling to leeward.
(c) Water being taken in quantity through ventilators, blower intakes, and every topside opening.
(d) Switchboards and electrical machinery of all kinds shorted and drowned out, with fires from short circuits. Main distribution board in engine room shorted by steam moisture when all topside openings were closed to keep out water.
(e) Free water up to two or three feet over engines or fireroom floor plates, and in many other compartments. It apparently all came in from above: there is no evidence of ships' seams parting.

(f) Loss of steering control, failure of power and lighting, and stoppage of main propulsion plant. Loss of radar and of all ability to communicate.

(g) Planes on carriers going adrift, crashing into each other, and starting fires.

(h) Wind velocities and seas that carried away masts, stacks, boats, davits, and deck structures generally, and made it impossible for men to secure gear that had gone adrift, or to jettison or strike below topside weights when the necessity had become apparent. Men could not even stay up where they would have a chance of getting clear of the ship.

(i) Maneuvering up to the time of sinking, in the attempt to maintain station, by all ships that were lost. DEWEY, saved by apparently a narrow margin, had given up the attempt.

(j) The storm "taking charge" and making impossible various evasive and security measures which might have been effective at an earlier stage.

(k) Testimony that the ships lost took a long roll to leeward, varying from 50 to 80°, hung there a little while, and then went completely over, floating a short time before going down.

5. The following tabulation does not purport to be the whole story, either for the ships mentioned or for the Fleet as a whole. It does, however, show that some ships, although of the same class as those lost, and undergoing the same punishment from the weather, survived nevertheless. It also indicates some differences in their condition and in the measures taken. Nobody can say, however, how far the outcome was due to these conditions and measures (or lack of them) and how far to blind chance.

6.

Class	All of Farragut Class				Both Fletcher Class	
	Hull	Monaghan	Dewey	Aylwin	Spence	Hickox
Outcome	Sunk	Sunk	Survived	Survived	Sunk	Survived
Fuel on hand (app.)	70%	76%	?	80%	15%	14%
Water Ballast	No	No	Yes	?	Very little	Fully ballast'd
Fuel to high side	No	No	Yes	Yes	No	?
Cond "A" taken	Yes	?	Yes	?	No	?
Top weight jettisoned or below	No	?	Yes	?	?	?
Free water in ship	Yes	?	Some	Yes	Yes	Some
Rolled and recovered	70°	?	75°	70°	Hung at 50° then capsized	70°

7. Various weaknesses were brought to light in our forecasting and dissemination of weather information, in structural details which permitted flooding with consequent loss of power, short circuiting, etc., and in the stability of some of our destroyers. Measures to correct these faults are being taken as far as possible. Yet the Commander in Chief, Pacific Fleet wishes to emphasize that to insure safety at sea, the best that science can devise and that naval organization can provide must be regarded only as an aid, and never as a substitute for the good seamanship, self-reliance, and sense of ultimate responsibility which are the first requisites in a seaman and naval officer.

8. A hundred years ago, a ship's survival depended almost solely on the competence of her master and on his constant alertness to every hint of change in the weather. To be taken aback or caught with full sail on by even a passing squall might mean the loss of spars or canvas; and to come close to the center of a genuine hurricane or typhoon was synonymous with disaster. While to be taken by surprise was thus serious, the facilities for avoiding it were meager. Each master was dependent wholly on himself for detecting the first symptoms of bad weather, for predicting its seriousness and movement, and for taking the appropriate measures, to evade it if possible and to battle through it if it passed near to him. There was no radio by which weather data could be collected from over all the oceans and the resulting forecasts by expert aerologists broadcasted to him and to all afloat. There was no one to tell him that the time had now come to strike his light sails and spars, and snug her down under close reefs or storm trysails. His own barometer, the force and direction of the wind, and the appearance of sea and sky were all that he had for information. Ceaseless vigilance in watching and interpreting signs, plus a philosophy of taking no risk in which there was little to gain and much to be lost, was what enabled him to survive.

9. Seamen of the present day should be better at forecasting weather at sea, independently of the radio, than were their predecessors. The general laws of storms and the weather expectancy for all months of the year in all parts of the world are now more thoroughly understood, more completely catalogued, and more readily available in various publications. An intensive study of typhoons and Western Pacific weather was made over a period of many years by Father Depperman at the Manila observatory, and his conclusions have been embodied in the material available to all aerologists. What *Knight* and *Bowditch* have to say on the subject is exactly as true during this war as it was in time of peace or before the days of radio. Familiarity with these authorities is something no captain or navigator can do without. The monthly pilot charts, issued to all ships, give excellent information as to the probable incidence and movements of typhoons. Stress on the foregoing is no belittlement of our aerological centers and weather broadcasts. But just as a navigator is held culpable if he neglects "Log, Lead, and Lookout" through blind faith in his radio fixes, so is the seaman culpable who regards personal weather estimates as obsolete and assumes that if no radio storm warning has been received, then all is well, and no local weather signs need cause him concern.

10. It is possible that too much reliance is being placed on outside sources for warnings of dangerous weather, and on the ability of our splendid ships to

come through anything that wind and wave can do. If this be so, there is need for a revival of the age-old habits of self-reliance and caution in regard to the hazard from storms, and for officers in all echelons of command to take their personal responsibilities in this respect more seriously.

11. The most difficult part of the whole heavy-weather problem is of course the conflict between the military necessity for carrying out an operation as scheduled, and the possibility of damage or loss to our ships in doing so. For this no possible rule can be laid down. The decision must be a matter of "calculated risk" either way. It should be kept in mind, however, that a ship which founders or is badly damaged is a dead loss not only to the current operation but to future ones, that the weather which hinders us may be hindering the enemy equally, and that ships which, to prevent probable damage and possible loss, are allowed to drop behind, or to maneuver independently, may by that very measure be able to rejoin later and be of use in the operation.

12. The safety of a ship against perils from storm, as well as from those of navigation and maneuvering, is always the primary responsibility of her commanding officer; but this responsibility is also shared by his immediate superiors in operational command since by the very fact of such command the individual commanding officer is not free to do at any time what his own judgment might indicate. Obviously no rational captain will permit his ship to be lost fruitlessly through blind obedience to plan or order, since by no chance could that be the intention of his superior. But the degree of a ship's danger is progressive and at the same time indefinite. It is one thing for a commanding officer, acting independently in time of peace, to pick a course and speed which may save him a beating from weather, and quite another for him, in time of war, to disregard his mission and his orders and leave his station and duty.

13. It is here that the responsibility rests on unit, group, and force commanders, and that their judgment and authority must be exercised. They are of course the ones best qualified to weigh the situation and the relative urgency of safety measures versus carrying on with the job in hand. They frequently guard circuits or possess weather codes not available to all ships; and it goes without saying that any storm warnings or important weather information which they are not sure everybody has received should be retransmitted as far as practicable. More than this, they must be conscious of the relative inexperience in seamanship, and particularly hurricane seamanship, of many of their commanding officers, despite their superb fighting qualities. One division commander reports that his captains averaged eight years or less out of the Naval Academy, and this is probably typical.

14. It is most definitely part of the senior officer's responsibility to think in terms of the smallest ship and most inexperienced commanding officer under him. He cannot take them for granted, give them tasks and stations, and assume either that they will be able to keep up and come through any weather that his own big ship can; or that they will be wise enough to gauge the exact moment when their task must be abandoned in order for them to keep afloat. The order for ships to be handled and navigated wholly for their own preserva-

tion should be originated early enough by the seniors, and not be necessarily withheld until the juniors request it. The very gallantry and determination of our young commanding officers need to be taken into account here as a danger factor, since their urge to keep on, to keep up, to keep station, and to carry out their mission in the face of any difficulty, may deter them from doing what is actually wisest and most profitable in the long run.

15. Yet if the O.T.C. is to be held responsible for his smaller vessels, he must be kept aware of their conditions, and the onus of this rests on the commanding officers themselves. Each of them must not only do whatever he is free and able to do for his ship's safety, but must also keep his superiors in the chain of command fully informed as to his situation. If there is anything in his ship's particular condition or in the way she is taking the weather that worries him, he should not hesitate to pass the information to his seniors. To let this be regarded as a sign of faintheartedness is to invite disaster, and seniors should indoctrinate their commanding officers accordingly. Going still further, it has been shown that at sea the severity of the weather may develop to a point where, regardless of combat commitments of the high command, the situation will require independent action by a junior without reference to his senior. This becomes mandatory if grave doubts arise in the mind of the junior as to the safety of his vessel, the lives of its crew, and the loss of valuable government property and equipment.

16. The commanders of all echelons in the Pacific Fleet will impress upon their subordinates the necessity for giving full consideration to the adverse weather likely to be encountered in the Western Pacific, particularly the presence of tropical disturbances and the formation and movement of typhoons. In this connection, each commanding officer should refresh himself on *Knight* and *Bowditch*, not only as to the "Laws of Storms," but also as to ship-handling in heavy weather. In order to know what outside weather reports are broadcast and what he should be getting, each commanding officer should be familiar with *Radio Weather Aids to Navigation* (H.O. 206), and its confidential supplement, H.O. 206-C-S(A). This publication, as well as the *Navy Weather Forecast Code No. 1* (CSP-946) should be on all DD's and DE's, *etc*. Even more important, a commanding officer should check up on his own ship's system of handling dispatches to make sure that every incoming dispatch about prospective weather is viewed and understood by himself or some other officer with experience enough to grasp its significance. It should by no chance get buried in files and overlooked. This applies even more strongly to local observations. Preoccupation with the job in hand, or a desire not to disturb the skipper, should never result in disregard of a rapidly falling barometer.

17. Steps must be taken to insure that commanding officers of all vessels, particularly destroyers and smaller craft, are fully aware of the stability characteristics of their ships; that adequate security measures regarding water-tight integrity are enforced; and that effect upon stability of free liquid surfaces is thoroughly understood. For preparing the ship against expected heavy weather, the basic written authorities are:

(a) *Damage Control Book* for ship concerned.

(b) Ballasting Instructions issued by the Type Maintenance Administration concerned.

(c) Notes on Stability of Ships in a Seaway (Pacific Fleet Maintenance Confidential Letter No. 7-44).

(d) *Booklet of Inclining Experiment Data* for either ship or class. Issued by BuShips.

(e) *Damage Control Instructions* (FTP 170-B).

(f) "Derangement of Electrical Equipment caused by Ventilation Conditions." *BuShips Bulletin of Information*, No. 12, p. 9.

(g) *Stability and Compartmentation of Ships* (C&R Bulletin No. 14).

18. In conclusion, both seniors and juniors must realize that in bad weather, as in most other situations, safety and fatal hazard are not separated by any sharp boundary line, but shade gradually from one into the other. There is no little red light which is going to flash on and inform commanding officers or higher commanders that from then on there is extreme danger from the weather, and that measures for ships' safety must now take precedence over further efforts to keep up with the formation or to execute the assigned task. This time will always be a matter of personal judgment. Naturally no commander is going to cut thin the margin between staying afloat and foundering, but he may nevertheless unwittingly pass the danger point even though no ship is yet in extremis. Ships that keep on going as long as the severity of wind and sea has not yet come close to capsizing them or breaking them in two, may nevertheless become helpless to avoid these catastrophes later if things get worse. By then they may be unable to steer any heading but in the trough of the sea, or may have their steering control, lighting, communications, and main propulsion disabled, or may be helpless to secure things on deck or to jettison topside weights. The time for taking all measures for a ship's safety is while still able to do so. Nothing is more dangerous than for a seaman to be grudging in taking precautions lest they turn out to have been unnecessary. Safety at sea for a thousand years has depended on exactly the opposite philosophy.

C.W. Nimitz

Commander C. R. Calhoun, USN—While I take no issue with the general theory that it frequently may be necessary in severe weather to give a ship its head (and in fact this is the gist of the now-famous Nimitz letter on the subject), I do wish to clarify Mr. Malanot's paragraph dealing with the Third Fleet's experience.

As Commanding Officer of the USS *Dewey* on 17–18 December 1944, I believe I can claim the distinction, along with my *Dewey* shipmates of having survived without capsizing, the greatest roll ever recorded by any U.S. naval vessel. I further believe that the *Dewey* probably came closer to disaster than any other ship which survived that storm, and feel that whoever wrote in *Reader's Digest* of a destroyer which "had its boiler rooms swamped in the early stages of the storm," was probably speaking of the *Dewey*. If this is the case then the use of the *Dewey* to illustrate Mr. Malanot's doctrine was an unfortunate choice. At no time during the entire storm were the *Dewey* boiler rooms "swamped" to the point where fires were extinguished, nor did she ever lose main propulsion power, nor did she lie "dead" in the water, for her port engine was kept one-third ahead throughout.

At about 0900 on the morning of 18 December 1944, I found it necessary to come left to avoid collision with the USS *Monterey*, whose Commanding Officer had just reported her dead in the water to fight hangar deck fires. The 40-degree course change thus made placed *Dewey* in the trough (there was no trouble in finding it—we were in it!) and also put the ship "in irons," with the wind generally on the port beam. Despite every possible engine and rudder combination, it was found impossible to move the ship's head more than ten degrees either way. I did discover that we rode just a bit more comfortably with the wind about one point abaft the beam and hence kept the port engine running at one-third ahead, with right 20 degrees rudder throughout the remainder of the storm. Although the seas became more confused as we approached the center, there still was a basic trough, and *Dewey* remained steadfastly wallowing in it.

To attribute *Dewey's* survival entirely to Fate, is to do an injustice to the gallant men whose efforts saved her. During countless giant rolls to starboard, the main forced draft blower intakes were submerged, and an estimated 500 to 1000 gallons of water poured into the firerooms. A brave little band of engineers, who never gave their personal safety a thought, remained in the firerooms, and by superb damage control techniques kept the flooding under control and maintained boiler steam pressure. I have the feeling that without the use of the port engine the ship would have been lost, for she came so close, so many times, to capsizing, that the loss of the slightest advantage would have been enough to tip the balance the wrong way. As I have already pointed out, the ship rode slightly better with steerageway and right rudder.

A few other facts might be of interest. The *Farragut*-class destroyers were known by their captains to possess a very small margin of stability. We were perhaps more stability-minded than any other skippers in the fleet, and we took unusual precautions to prepare our ships for heavy weather. The fact that two of them were lost was no surprise to those of us on the *Dewey*. Although the records are not now available to me, I believe it will be found that *Hull* (and possibly *Monaghan* also) did not have "60,000 horsepower working to the last," but rather capsized after her engine spaces had had to be abandoned! In my own personal opinion, the chief factor which contributed to the loss of the *Hull* and *Monaghan* was an inherently low margin of stability.

Contributing to (if not the direct cause of) the loss of the *Spence*, was her unballasted condition until in extremis when, if my memory serves me correctly, a last minute attempt was made to ballast her, and free-surface effect was thus added to the problem. *Spence*, a 2100 tonner, entered the typhoon with something like 10,000 gallons of black oil and no salt water ballast. Small wonder she was lost, and I doubt that the use of her engines had much to do with it!

As it stated in my second paragraph, I take no issue with the general "doctrine" proposed by Mr. Malanot. U.S. destroyermen have long recognized the advantage of letting the ship fight the storm as she seems to want to fight it. But let's correct the impression that *Hull*, *Monaghan*, and *Spence* were lost because their skippers pounded them against overpowering seas, or that *Dewey* survived simply because she had her boiler rooms swamped. It just didn't happen that way!

CAPTAIN JOHN V. NOEL, JR., U.S. NAVY—All blue water Navy men will enjoy Mr. Malanot's *Typhoon Doctrine*. He has described sound procedures for handling a ship in very heavy weather, although the practice of drifting with engines stopped is not considered as unorthodox as Mr. Malanot would have us believe.

A ship anticipating having to weather a typhoon or hurricane should first look for a lee, an island, or peninsula that will provide shelter. The alternative, of course, is to seek maximum sea room. This latter practice was axiomatic in the days of sail because of a seaman's dread of being caught on a lee shore as the wind shifts. It is still a consideration, particularly for a low-powered vessel, but should serve mainly to emphasize the need for understanding the structure of a tropical cyclone so that you can anticipate and understand the shift in the direction of the wind. Many small ships have survived severe tropical cyclones by seeking the shelter of land, moving to new positions as the wind shifts. This shift in wind, together with the first signs of the barometer checking its plunge and starting to rise, is usually a most heartening sign and shows that the storm is moving away from you.

If there is no lee to be found the storm must be weathered in the open sea. There are no hard and fast rules to guide a commanding officer faced with a rising wind and a falling barometer. Certainly, up to a point, maximum speed should be made away from the estimated path of the storm. It is normally more comfortable to head downwind, and this course should be chosen when practicable. Eventually it may be found advisable to head up into the sea at minimum speed. The lowest speed at which steerageway can be maintained should be used. In a twin-screw ship the engines may have to be employed separately to keep the ship headed into the large storm waves. There may come a time, in very high seas, when the ship persists in falling off and nothing can be done to avoid coming around into the trough of the sea. Under these circumstances many ship captains have stopped their engines and allowed their ship to drift. In most ships the drag of the propellers will cause them to lie with the wind and sea on the quarter. Some ships are reported to drift remarkably comfortably in this position, with little solid water coming aboard in spite of heavy rolling and pitching. This is natural since there is little resistance on the part of the ship to the action of the waves. As Mr. Malanot so aptly expresses it: "for a ship dead in the water the onrushing crest of a wave will not hit the ship, it will only lift it."

REAR ADMIRAL S.C. RING, USN—In substance, Mr. Malanot by virtue of the experience which he has gained, recommends lying to as the best maneuver to avoid damage on the approach of a tropical storm. He would resort to that action only under stated conditions and only after assuring himself of the stability of his vessel.

I do not gainsay the efficacy of the action proposed in handling *single* ships although personally I have never tried it. On the other hand, it seems pertinent to me to recognize that in many instances vessels confronting typhoons (or better yet, maneuvering to avoid them) are travelling in company and have a definite tactical mission to perform.

There can be little doubt but that the blind execution of an assigned mission is unwarranted in the face of forecasts which would produce weather damaging to the material integrity of the command. Adequate weight must be applied by the commander to probable gains to be acquired through the execution of his orders versus the danger of damage to his vessels incurred by immediate fulfillment of his assignment. Axiomatically, the commander should advise his immediate superior of his conclusions in the premises. A factor worthy of consideration is that weather is, by and large, impartial in its application and if weather conditions are such as to preclude successful execution of the mission assigned one force, it is highly probable that the anticipated maneuvering of the opposing force will be likewise affected.

Basically, the Task Force Commander should so maneuver his force that in the absence of compelling reasons to the contrary, he will avoid placing his force in weather-jeopardy. Such maneuvering may involve the acceptance of minor damage as the Force attempts to escape the path of the approaching typhoon. But, except as a last resort, the integrity of the command should not be lost. Obviously the commander should be guided by the manner in which all vessels of his Force are responding to the weather and he should so adjust the course and speed of the Force as to minimize the damage incurred, minimize the hazard to personnel, and maximize the chances of successful completion of his assigned mission.

Granted that each individual commanding officer bears the burden of responsibility for the ultimate safety of his vessel, and that under certain conditions he may elect to lie to in order to minimize the damage and danger to his ship and crew. But I believe that it is the reponsibility of the Senior Officer Present so to maneuver his charge that the extreme conditions are not met. I further believe that danger is increased rather than lessened if the commander orders his group stopped. In a formation, operating to avoid typhoon damage, components of the formation should maintain steerageway in order to minimize danger of collision, and should remain as well prepared as possible to continue the execution of the mission assigned when weather permits.

CAPTAIN H.B. LYON, USN—In 1952, as Chief Inspector for MSTSNORPAC-SUBAREA, I had the opportunity to take passage from Sasebo to Pusan and return with Captain Malanot in the *Sgt. Joseph E. Muller*. Captain Malanot regaled me with this typhoon doctrine of his and his many, many experiences which bear it out.

He is a delightful person, with old-style continental manners, with a lifetime of sea experiences, and a burning desire that the discoveries that he has made may be shared by all ship masters everywhere. To talk to him is to be convinced.

At the time that I met this fine gentleman, he was at a loss to know how to get his findings the type of recognition that he thought they deserved. I have endeavored, from time to time, to promote Captain Malanot's principles in discussion and in local articles. However, I have discovered two things:

(1) A second-hand story carries little weight.

(2) A person with some typhoon experience is usually so completely over-awed by the tremendous destructive power and majesty of a typhoon that it is difficult for him to think objectively about it.

Any Captain, in skirting a typhoon, will derive a great deal of security from the knowledge that "Typhoon Doctrine" imparts. It will give him assurance that he may survive even if his engines fail at the critical moment. However, Captain Malanot believes that his method is the only safe method of traversing a typhoon area, if that condition becomes a necessity.

Needless to say, I was very pleased to see his article in print. It is my sincere hope that more data by more people will become available to support his position. It must be available somewhere for the Gloucester Fishermen have been doing this for centuries.

Lt. Cdr. A.G. Graham, USNR (Ret.), Master, SS *African Enterprise*, Farrell Lines.—With regard to Mr. Malanot's "Typhoon Doctrine" I am qualifiedly in accord, having had one experience of breaking down in violent weather with the astonishing and comparatively favorable results which he describes.

The "doctrine" has one weakness and that is the heavy rolling that results. I know nothing about naval vessels, but a cargo ship loaded with bulk ore could shift her cargo and founder (as happened recently to the *Mormackite*) and a passenger vessel could seriously injure too many paying customers (most of whom seem to have a personal GM of 0.1 at sea) for the good of future business. I have found that a modern merchant vessel, with its raked stem and flaring bows, can be hove to differently than was possible with the straight-stemmed and flat-bowed ships of pre-war days. For what it may be worth, I will quote from an article I wrote for our house organ, *Farrell Lines News* (January, 1955) on the subject of heaving to in heavy weather.

"When heaving to, head to sea, the recommendation usually found in seamanship books is to keep the sea from two to four points on the bow. The purpose of this is to give the bow a chance to rise to the oncoming sea instead of poking her nose right into it. I disagree with this recommendation, however. I have found it best to head directly into the sea. With a gale force wind on the weather bow, you have to keep way on her to prevent her from falling off into the trough, and the stronger the wind the more way you require. By heading directly into the weather you can cut speed to a bare minimum, which means fewer—and much less forceful—seas coming aboard. Another advantage is that it reduces rolling materially. I have followed this practice for years and am convinced of its superiority.

"In Hurricane Carol we made good 1½ miles in 5 hours (by accurate Loran fixes) which is as close to stopped—ultimate ideal—as one could wish. I estimated the wind at 90 knots (it was clocked over Long Island a few hours later at 94 knots and attained 117 knots in gusts at Block Island according to the August, 1955, *Pilot Chart*) and the seas at 50 feet high. These seas were about 1000 feet, or roughly two ship's lengths, from crest to crest and were remarkably steep. This gave the ship no time to recover from the down slope of one sea before the next one was on her, and there were times when I thought she would stick her nose into it clear up to the bridge. Being all but stopped, however, gave her the few seconds needed to get her bow started upwards before it was engulfed, and we took only the tops of the breaking seas aboard. We suffered some damage forward, but it was of a minor nature.

"Prior to this I had been running before it at slow speed (though we still made 7 knots) simply because it was a 'fair' wind for us to New York. Finally, however, a sea pooped us heavily and carried away the hand steering wheel, the docking telegraph, and a few other useful items, and I figured it was time to turn around and face it like a man.

"Turning around under such conditions is always a heart-in-mouth proposition. This time I waited for 40 minutes (after alerting the Steward and Engine Departments to stand by for some heavy rolls) for a 'smooth' of sufficient extent to make the turn. Oddly enough, such smooths come along at intervals in the worst of blows. When it did come I gave her full ahead and hard left and crossed my fingers. She made the 180 degree turn in time to cut her to slow again before the first big one hit her. It snapped off our jackstaff and crushed a ventilator, but that was all, and my heart went back where it belonged. Running too long is an error and should be avoided if possible. However, lack of sea room or other considerations may make it necessary at times."

The above is applicable only when wind and sea are from the same direction, of course, but that is the normal situation. In or near the eye of a storm, however, with dangerous seas coming from different directions, it is impossible to avoid heavy rolling. Under such circumstances, I can appreciate the wisdom of stopping and drifting, as is recommended in "Typhoon Doctrine."

JOHN F. WILSON, MASTER, SS *Pioneer Lake*, U.S. LINES.—In the past ten years I have commanded five C-2 vessels, in the North Atlantic, South Pacific, and U.S. East Coast to the Far East. I am presently master in a C-2 in the Far East service, having spent the past eight years in the service. My early training was as an officer in passenger vessels such as the *Leviathan* and *Washington*; there I observed how the outstanding masters of those vessels handled them in major storms. Those masters had been trained by other outstanding men. From this experience I have concluded that no rules can cover all vessels. All depends on the vessel's size, her cargo, how it is stowed, and her handling qualities which only her master can know.

In a loaded C-2 I fear rolling more than pitching or pounding. Experience has taught me just about how much working my vessel can stand. As long as possible, I "weather a gale" by maintaining steerageway on 40 RPM, with a man at the phone and a throttle watch, to increase should she go off. We make every effort to dodge the typhoons, but sometimes get caught—even with our booms up. I can control my vessel's behavior as far as pitching is concerned, but rolling, the cargo may shift or other circumstance beyond my control start forces to work that may cause my vessel to founder. If my C-2 were light, then I would act differently, fearing pitching and possible cracking.

Like Captain Malanot, my greatest experience was in the Caribbean Sea. It was September, 1933. I was an officer in the T.E.S. *Virginia* (32,500 tons displacement). We were caught in the center of a hurricane; the barometer, corrected, fell to 27.40; the wind force was more than 125 MPH, proved by the fact that the anemometer on Swan Island, near us, broke down at this force. The ship went out of control; the rain, driven by the wind, cleaned the paint off steel stanchions, as though they had been sandblasted. Rain water ran over the thresholds and under the outside doors, spilling into the main lobbies and cascading down the main stair cases. Our heads rang as though we had taken quinine tablets. To breathe more easily, men in the fireroom had to remain near the floor plates. The hurricane bridge rails were folded back to the deck by the wind. Lifeboats were torn from their chocks and smashed against the boat deck house. I attempted to go down the outside ladder, and my 140 lbs. was virtually supported by the wind; I had to haul myself down. Fantastic and freakish damage was sustained. Since that time whenever I hear of surface winds of over 100 knots, I feel skeptical.

If a moderate size vessel is caught in a major storm there is not much choice but to stop, let her find herself, put out oil, if necessary, and hold on. In December, 1952, in the Pacific, I "guessed" correctly; a C-3 did not. We were near one another, running parallel to a storm center which weather reports from Guam stated held winds of 180 knots. The center was 400 miles south of us. *Pilot Chart* tracks showed most of these storms moved due west. Except one, that went right across our course. I slowed down, taking the chance that I might be held up for days. The C-3, larger and faster, continued on. The next day we exchanged weather reports. He was out of control, in high confused seas, winds of over 100 knots, and 150 miles from the center. He lost 165 tons of deck cargo over the side. As the Army tanks worked loose they moved his deck winches, this permitted water to enter number one hold and flood it. 250 miles east, I was having force 7 to 8 winds and heavy seas and swells, but no damage.

An authority has explained that swells are not raised by the hurricane winds revolving about the center of the typhoon, but rather by the pulsatory vertical motion of the lower part of the typhoon, causing "pumping" in the barographs and acting as a kind of piston on the water, thereby causing concentric waves to radiate outward from the center. And so, the swells in the vicinity of the center are always from a different direction than the wind.

If I were asked for advice by a young shipmaster I should say, "When possible—and I know it is not always possible—stay at least 250 miles from the center of a major storm, or at least clear of the confused seas, in order that you may escape."

But whatever decision you may make, if you get into trouble, you may be sure that someone, who was *not* there, will come up with something you *should* have done.

ROBERT E. HERBERT, JR.—The introduction and conclusion of Mr. Malanot to his "Typhoon Doctrine" in the July, 1955, *Proceedings* causes nearly as much of a confused sea as the storms he writes about.

My experience has shown the propeller to be a very good drogue, and under normal loading the ship's bow and forward areas present more windage than the after half. Therefore, the average vessel will lay to and ride comfortably with the wind and sea on the quarter. In steam-powered vessels, I have had the engines ticking over dead slow to keep them warmed up for emergency. I refer to the old "ups-and-downs" as I have not had any turbine ship experience. With diesels, of course, you just start them when you want them, though on one ship I was in, it was a gamble as to how much air she'd use before that old Atlas would fire.

It is a good article for the modern day, mechanically powered mariner and gives further weight to my constant argument that the graduates of our maritime schools, including the Naval Academy, would be better officers and ship handlers if they had some training in sail such as the Coast Guard has. In their case, they have made a good beginning, but I agree with Allan Villiers that the *Eagle* is not used nearly enough.

UP TO DATE TYPHOON DOCTRINE*

(Editor's Note: The writer of the following comment is the author of the article "Typhoon Doctrine" which appeared in the July, 1955 *Proceedings* and brought forth numerous comments which were published in the January, 1956 *Proceedings*.)

CAPTAIN ELMER W. MALANOT.—It appears that, unfortunately, there was no one who actually shut down completely, or at least to a dead slow, the power of his engines, near the center of a cyclonic storm, so that he could have judged the wisdom of such action.

We had this opportunity again on this vessel on October 18, 1955, on a voyage from Saigon to Yokohama, when sixty miles south of Myako Shima, we ran into Typhoon Opal. We had no previous warning when at 180600 I the barometer started to fall rapidly, and the wind from NNE increased to full gale force. The engine power was gradually reduced and, when the sea became confused at 181137 I, completely shut down to a dead slow. This vessel being powered with turbines, this was done merely to keep the engines warm. The vessel drifted in a southwesterly direction at the rate of three knots. At 1600 I, the wind was at its maximum of about 100 knots. Then the wind backed to NNW. The vessel was heading between 230 degrees and 265 degrees, and drifting in a southeasterly direction. The sea was mountainous and confused. The vessel pitched heavily and rolled to a maximum of 35 degrees.

Although this vessel was only ten miles from the center of this moderate typhoon, we had absolutely no damage whatsoever, while the ship had a full deck load of heavy Army trucks, lashed in the usual manner. And so again the only thing we did was to stop our engines.

*From United States Naval Institute *Proceedings*—March 1956.

At 182120 I, the force of wind and sea gradually moderated, and we proceeded to Yokohama.

This theory of evading damage by shutting down the power that primarily produces such damage, is so simple that, because of its simplicity, many people who have had experience in heavy weather, are so overawed by the gigantic force of nature, that they are reluctant to accept this simple fact.

I am including a letter I received from a Naval Architect, in which you might be interested, and you have my permission to reprint any of the above in your *Proceedings* if you so desire.

(Editor's Note: The following are excerpts from a letter Captain Malanot recently received.)

Recently I read your very enlightening article "Typhoon Doctrine." Your observations and recommendations are not only of value to seafaring men but also to Naval Architects.

Your observations and theory supporting your "Doctrine" are very convincing. Oftentimes observations do not seem to support a theoretical analysis; such divergences are passed over by the overworked proverb "practice and theory do not agree." In reality, when this is the case, there is something wrong with either one or the other.

I can well imagine that it is difficult to convince the crew that passive defense, as you put it, is the way to weather a typhoon. I am sure that you have considered the comments I wish to make.

If I may, I will briefly consider the stress aspect set up in machinery. Ship machinery is designed to withstand stresses due to torsion of the machine, shock stress due to load surges, inertia stresses due to rolling and pitching of the ship and others. Except for torsional stresses of the machine under consideration, the other stresses are difficult to evaluate since the sea forces inducing these stresses are difficult to evaluate and are impossible to control. These stresses are not always accumulative, but potentially there is the ever present chance that they can be. For heavy machinery, or for lightweight high-speed machinery in motion, inertia stresses due to rolling, especially for a "stiff ship," can attain tremendous values. In fact this stress can be of such proportions that structurally it can not be resisted. With stopped engines the torsional stresses due to rotation are zero, load surge stresses are zero, and pitching and rolling inertia stresses are lessened since minimum resistance is offered to the irresistible typhoon sea waves. Another type of machinery failure can also be avoided by your doctrine. Heavy rotating masses, like shafts, can have induced deflections by the forces mentioned to the extent that bearings will fail immediately. Also rolling sea suctions out of the water, loss of oil pressure and similar failures experienced in storms will result in major machinery derangements which in themselves can cause the loss of a ship. Rolling a boiler loose from its foundation is not uncommon. Plowing into a typhoon is just asking for such failures. Following such machinery derangements, uncontrollable engine room fires and similar disasters surely follow which spell doom for the ship. A dead plant or a minimum operative one while in a typhoon, should lessen the ever impending machinery failures mentioned.

I am sure that every Naval Architect would be relieved of much doubt if he knew that all ship Masters had your respect for the forces of the sea. Again, I want to assure you that your article made me realize that a designer does not have to do the impossible; namely, to build a ship to withstand almost irresistible forces.

Sincerely yours,
HOWARD A. PETERSON

DISSENT FROM THE MALANOT TYPHOON DOCTRINE*

COMMANDER W. J. RUHE, USN.—Malanot's theory that a ship can safely lie to in a trough of typhoon waves appears to be based on experience in broad-beamed types of ships, not with narrow-beamed, topside-heavy warships. Subsequent printed discussion on this theory interpreted Admiral Nimitz's letter as furthering the idea that ships might be given their head *in extremis*. However, on analysis, it appears that the Admiral's letter merely says that there are times when the skipper of a warship must leave formation by changing speed or course in order to save his ship. To this I agree. But where has Nimitz's letter recommended that a warship be allowed to lie to?

There is further evidence in Admiral Nimitz's letter which indicates that the worst thing for a warship is to go dead and lie to, thus losing its head and falling off into the trough. The *Monaghan* and the *Hull*, it can be presumed, lost all power and fell off into the trough. Since both were well fueled (75%) the finger cannot be placed on their being improperly ballasted. The *Dewey's* skipper, it is noted, attributed his survival to keeping way-on with full rudder. But the general tenor of all of the articles is that a warship skipper might benefit from Malanot's theory.

Let this be a dissenting vote to provide some form of sanity to the discussion. As a destroyer skipper I fear that just one other skipper will believe the theory and lose a ship.

Would a single naval constructor go along with Malanot's theory as it applied to ships like destroyers?

*From United States Naval Institute *Proceedings*—July 1956.

VIII

Extracts from *Typhoon**

By Joseph Conrad

Chapter Two—Observing the steady fall of the barometer, Captain MacWhirr thought, "There's some dirty weather knocking about." This is precisely what he thought. He had had an experience of moderately dirty weather—the term dirty as applied to the weather implying only moderate discomfort to the seaman. Had he been informed by an indisputable authority that the end of the world was to be finally accomplished by a catastrophic disturbance of the atmosphere, he would have assimilated the information under the simple idea of dirty weather, and no other, because he had no experience of cataclysms, and belief does not necessarily imply comprehension. The wisdom of his county had pronounced by means of an Act of Parliament that before he could be considered as fit to take charge of a ship he should be able to answer certain simple questions on the subject of circular storms such as hurricanes, cyclones, typhoons; and apparently he had answered them, since he was now in command of the *Nan-Shan* in the China seas during the season of typhoons. But if he had answered he remembered nothing of it. He was, however, conscious of being made uncomfortable by the clammy heat. He came out on the bridge, and found no relief to this oppression. The air seemed thick. He gasped like a fish, and began to believe himself greatly out of sorts.

The *Nan-Shan* was ploughing a vanishing furrow upon the circle of the sea that had the surface and the shimmer of an undulating piece of gray silk. The sun, pale and without rays, poured down leaden heat in a strangely indecisive light, and the Chinamen were lying prostrate about the decks.

. . . The lurid sunshine cast faint and sickly shadows. The swell ran higher

*Reprinted by permission of J.M. Dent & Sons, Ltd., London.

and swifter every moment, and the ship lurched heavily in the smooth, deep hollows of the sea.

"I wonder where that beastly swell comes from," said Jukes [Chief Mate] aloud, recovering himself after a stagger.

"North-east," grunted the literal MacWhirr, from his side of the bridge. "There's some dirty weather knocking about. Go and look at the glass."

. . . At its setting the sun had a diminished diameter and an expiring brown, rayless glow, as if millions of centuries elapsing since the morning had brought it near its end. A dense bank of cloud became visible to the northward; it had a sinister dark olive tint, and lay low and motionless upon the sea, resembling a solid obstacle in the path of the ship. She went floundering towards it like an exhausted creature driven to its death. The coppery twilight retired slowly, and the darkness brought out overhead a swarm of unsteady, big stars, that, as if blown upon, flickered exceedingly and seemed to hang very near the earth. At eight o'clock Jukes went into the chart-room to write up the ship's log.

. . . "Ship rolling heavily in a high cross swell," he began again, and commented to himself, "Heavily is no word for it." Then he wrote: "Sunset threatening, with a low bank of clouds to N. and E. Sky clear overhead."

Sprawling over the table with arrested pen, he glanced out of the door, and in that frame of his vision he saw all the stars flying upwards between the teak-wood jambs on a black sky. The whole lot took flight together and disappeared, leaving only a blackness flecked with white flashes, for the sea was as black as the sky and speckled with foam afar. The stars that had flown to the roll came back on the return swing of the ship, rushing downwards in their glittering multitude, not of fiery points, but enlarged to tiny discs brilliant with a clear wet sheen.

Jukes watched the flying big stars for a moment, and then wrote: "8 P.M. Swell increasing. Ship labouring and taking water on her decks. Battened down the coolies for the night. Barometer still falling." He paused, and thought to himself, "Perhaps nothing whatever'll come of it." And then he closed resolutely his entries: "Every appearance of a typhoon coming on." . . .

Chapter Three—. . . The strong wind swept at him [Captain MacWhirr] out of a vast obscurity; he felt under his feet the uneasiness of his ship, and he could not even discern the shadow of her shape. He wished it were not so; and very still he waited, feeling stricken by a blind man's helplessness.

To be silent was natural to him, dark or shine. Jukes, at his elbow, made himself heard yelling cheerily in the gusts, "We must have got the worst of it at once, sir." A faint burst of lightning quivered all round, as if flashed into a cavern—into a black and secret chamber of the sea, with a floor of foaming crests.

It unveiled for a sinister, fluttering moment a ragged mass of clouds hanging low, the lurch of the long outlines of the ship, the black figures of men caught on the bridge, heads forward, as if petrified in the act of butting. The darkness palpitated down upon all this, and then the real thing came at last.

It was something formidable and swift, like the sudden smashing of a vial of wrath. It seemed to explode all round the ship with an overpowering concussion and a rush of great waters, as if an immense dam had been blown up to windward. In an instant the men lost touch of each other. This is the disintegrating power of a great wind: it isolates one from one's kind.

. . . The rain poured on him [Jukes], flowed, drove in sheets. He breathed in gasps; and sometimes the water he swallowed was fresh and sometimes it was salt. For the most part he kept his eyes shut tight, as if suspecting his sight might be destroyed in the immense flurry of the elements. When he ventured to blink hastily, he derived some moral support from the green gleam of the starboard light shining feebly upon the flight of rain and sprays. He was actually looking at it when its ray fell upon the uprearing sea which put it out. He saw the head of the wave topple over, adding the mite of its crash to the tremendous uproar raging around him, and almost at the same instant the stanchion was wrenched away from his embracing arms. After a crushing thump on his back he found himself suddenly afloat and borne upwards. His first irresistible notion was that the whole China Sea had climbed on the bridge. Then, more sanely, he concluded himself gone overboard. All the time he was being tossed, flung, and rolled in great volumes of water, he kept on repeating mentally, with the utmost precipitation, the words: "My God! My God! My God!"

. . . The motion of the ship was extravagant. Her lurches had an appalling helplessness: she pitched as if taking a header into a void, and seemed to find a wall to hit every time. When she rolled she fell on her side headlong, and she would be righted back by such a demolishing blow that Jukes felt her reeling as a clubbed man reels before he collapses. The gale howled and scuffled about gigantically in the darkness, as though the entire world were one black gully. At certain moments the air streamed against the ship as if sucked through a tunnel with a concentrated solid force of impact that seemed to lift her clean out of the water and keep her up for an instant with only a quiver running through her from end to end. And then she would begin her tumbling again as if dropped back into a boiling cauldron. Jukes tried hard to compose his mind and judge things coolly.

The sea, flattened down in the heavier gusts, would uprise and overwhelm both ends of the *Nan-Shan* in snowy rushes of foam, expanding wide, beyond both rails, into the night. And on this dazzling sheet, spread under the blackness of the clouds and emitting a bluish glow, Captain MacWhirr could catch a desolate glimpse of a few tiny specks black as ebony, the tops of the hatches, the battened companions, the heads of the covered winches, the foot of a mast. This was all he could see of his ship. Her middle structure, covered by the bridge which bore him, his mate, the closed wheelhouse where a man was steering shut up with the fear of being swept overboard together with the whole thing in one great crash—her middle structure was like a halftide rock awash upon a coast. It was like an outlying rock with the water boiling up, streaming over, pouring off, beating round—like a rock in the surf to which shipwrecked people cling before they let go—only it rose, it sank, it rolled continuously, without respite and rest, like a rock that should have miraculously struck adrift from a coast and gone wallowing upon the sea.

The *Nan-Shan* was being looted by a storm with a senseless, destructive fury: trysails torn out of the extra gaskets, double-lashed awnings blown away, bridge swept clean, weather-cloths burst, rails twisted, light-screens smashed—and two of the boats had gone already. They had gone unheard and unseen, melting, as it were, in the shock and smother of the wave. It was only later, when upon the white flash of another high sea hurling itself amidships, Jukes had a vision of two pairs of davits leaping black and empty out of the solid blackness, with one overhauled fall flying and an iron-bound block capering in the air, that he became aware of what had happened within about three yards of his back.

. . . They [Captain MacWhirr and Jukes] held hard. An outburst of un-chained fury, a vicious rush of the wind absolutely steadied the ship; she rocked only, quick and light like a child's cradle, for a terrific moment of suspense, while the whole atmosphere, as it seemed, streamed furiously past her, roaring away from the tenebrous earth.

It suffocated them, and with eyes shut they tightened their grasp. What from the magnitude of the shock might have been a column of water running upright in the dark, butted against the ship, broke short, and fell on her bridge, crushingly, from on high, with a dead burying weight.

A flying fragment of that collapse . . . enveloped them in one swirl from their feet over their heads, filling violently their ears, mouths and nostrils with salt water. It knocked out their legs, wrenched in haste at their arms, seethed away swiftly under their chins; and opening their eyes, they saw the piled-up masses of foam dashing to and fro amongst what looked like the fragments of a ship. She had given way as if driven straight in. Their panting hearts yielded, too, before the tremendous blow; and all at once she sprang up again to her desperate plunging, as if trying to scramble out from under the ruins.

The seas in the dark seemed to rush from all sides to keep her back where she might perish. There was hate in the way she was handled, and a ferocity in the blows that fell. She was like a living creature thrown to the rage of a mob: hustled terribly, struck at, borne up, flung down, leaped upon. Captain Mac-Whirr and Jukes kept hold of each other, deafened by the noise, gagged by the wind; and the great physical tumult beating about their bodies, brought, like an unbridled display of passion, a profound trouble to their souls. One of those wild and appalling shrieks that are heard at times passing mysteriously overhead in the steady roar of a hurricane, swooped, as if borne on wings, upon the ship, and Jukes tried to outscream it.

"Will she live through this?"

The cry was wrenched out of his breast. It was as unintentional as the birth of a thought in the head, and he heard nothing of it himself. It all became extinct at once—thought, intention, effort—and of his cry the inaudible vibration added to the tempest waves of the air.

He expected nothing from it. Nothing at all. For indeed what answer could be made? But after a while he heard with amazement the frail and resisting voice in his ear, the dwarf sound, unconquered in the giant tumult.

"She may!" . . .

Chapter Five—. . . Nobody—not even Captain MacWhirr, who alone on deck had caught sight of a white line of foam coming on at such a height that he couldn't believe his eyes—nobody was to know the steepness of the sea and the awful depth of the hollow the hurricane had scooped out behind the running wall of water.

It raced to meet the ship, and, with a pause, as of girding the loins, the *Nan-Shan* lifted her bows and leaped. The flames in all the lamps sank, darkening the engine-room. One went out. With a tearing crash and a swirling, raving tumult, tons of water fell upon the deck, as though the ship had darted under the foot of a cataract.

Down there they looked at each other, stunned.

"Swept from end to end, by God!" bawled Jukes.

She dipped into the hollow straight down, as if going over the edge of the world. The engine-room toppled forward menacingly, like the inside of a tower nodding in an earthquake. An awful racket, of iron things falling, came from the stokehold. She hung on this appalling slant long enough for Beale [Third Engineer] to drop on his hands and knees and begin to crawl as if he meant to fly on all fours out of the engine-room, and for Mr. Rout [Chief Engineer] to turn his head slowly, rigid, cavernous, with the lower jaw dropping. Jukes had shut his eyes, and his face in a moment became hopelessly blank and gentle, like the face of a blind man.

At last she rose slowly, staggering, as if she had to lift a mountain with her bows.

Mr. Rout shut his mouth; Jukes blinked; and little Beale stood up hastily.

"Another one just like this, and that's the last of her," cried the chief.

... There was no wind, not a breath, except the faint currents created by the lurches of the ship. The smoke tossed out of the funnel was settling down upon her deck. He [Jukes] breathed it as he passed forward. He felt the deliberate throb of the engines, and heard small sounds that seemed to have survived the great uproar: the knocking of broken fittings, the rapid tumbling of some piece of wreckage on the bridge. He perceived dimly the squat shape of his captain holding on to a twisted bridge-rail, motionless and swaying as if rooted to the planks. The unexpected stillness of the air oppressed Jukes.

"We have done it, sir," he gasped.

... After the whisper of their shouts, their ordinary tones, so distinct, rang out very loud to their ears in the amazing stillness of the air. It seemed to them they were talking in a dark and echoing vault.

Through a jagged aperture in the dome of clouds the light of a few stars fell upon the black sea, rising and falling confusedly. Sometimes the head of a watery cone would topple on board and mingle with the rolling flurry of foam on the swamped deck; and the *Nan-Shan* wallowed heavily at the bottom of a circular cistern of clouds. This ring of dense vapours, gyrating madly round the calm of the centre, encompassed the ship like a motionless and unbroken wall of an aspect inconceivably sinister. Within, the sea, as if agitated by an internal commotion, leaped in peaked mounds that jostled each other, slapping heavily against her sides; and a low moaning sound, the infinite plaint of the storm's fury, came from beyond the limits of the menacing calm. Captain

MacWhirr remained silent, and Jukes' ready ear caught suddenly the faint, long-drawn roar of some immense wave rushing unseen under the thick blackness, which made the appalling boundary of his vision.

. . . The worst was to come, then—and if the books were right this worst would be very bad. The experience of the last six hours had enlarged his [Captain MacWhirr's] conception of what heavy weather could be like. "It'll be terrific," he pronounced, mentally.

. . . He [Captain MacWhirr] released it [box of matches] at last, and letting himself fall on the settee, listened for the first sounds of returning wind.

Not yet. He heard only the wash of water, the heavy splashes, the dull shocks of the confused seas boarding his ship from all sides. She would never have a chance to clear her decks.

But the quietude of the air was startlingly tense and unsafe, like a slender hair holding a sword suspended over his head. By this awful pause the storm penetrated the defences of the man and unsealed his lips. He spoke out in the solitude and the pitch darkness of the cabin, as if addressing another being awakened within his breast.

"I shouldn't like to lose her," he said half aloud.

. . . "It will come very sudden," said Captain MacWhirr, "and from over there, I fancy. God only knows though. These books are only good to muddle your head and make you jumpy. It will be bad, and there's an end. If we only can steam her round in time to meet it. . . ."

A minute passed. Some of the stars winked rapidly and vanished.

. . . A hollow echoing noise, like that of a shout rolling in a rocky chasm, approached the ship and went away again. The last star, blurred, enlarged, as if returning to the fiery mist of its beginning, struggled with the colossal depth of blackness hanging over the ship—and went out.

"Now for it!" muttered Captain MacWhirr. "Mr. Jukes."

"Here, sir."

The two men were growing indistinct to each other.

"We must trust her to go through it and come out on the other side. That's plain and straight. There's no room for Captain Wilson's storm-strategy here."

"No, sir."

"She will be smothered and swept again for hours," mumbled the Captain. "There's not much left by this time above deck for the sea to take away—unless you or me."

"Both, sir," whispered Jukes, breathlessly.

"You are always meeting trouble half way, Jukes," Captain MacWhirr remonstrated quaintly.

"Though it's a fact that the second mate is no good. D'ye hear, Mr. Jukes? You would be left alone if. . . ."

Captain MacWhirr interrupted himself, and Jukes, glancing on all sides, remained silent.

"Don't you be put out by anything," the Captain continued, mumbling rather fast. "Keep her facing it. They may say what they like, but the heaviest seas run with the wind. Facing it—always facing it—that's the way to get through. You are a young sailor. Face it. That's enough for any man. Keep a cool head."

IX

Recommended Books and Information Sources

Some books are to be tasted, others to be swallowed, and some to be chewed and digested.

—Francis Bacon, *Essays: Of Studies*

The following books and sources of information should be "chewed and digested" by those who sail the seas for recreation and pleasure, for commerce and trade, or for military purposes.

Admiralty Manual of Seamanship, vol. 3. London: Her Majesty's Stationery Office, 1964.

Annual Tropical Cyclone Report. Guam, Marianas Islands: U.S. Navy and U.S. Air Force Joint Typhoon Warning Center (Annually).

Anthes, R.A. *Tropical Cyclones*. Boston: American Meteorological Society, 1982.

Bigelow, Henry B., and W. T. Edmondson. *Wind Waves at Sea, Breakers and Surf*. Hydrographic Office Pub. No. 602, 1947.

Bowditch, N. *American Practical Navigator*. Washington, D.C.: U.S. Government Printing Office, 1958.

Brindze, Ruth, ed. *Experts Book of Boating*. Englewood Cliffs, N.J.: Prentice-Hall, 1959.

Bruce, Erroll. *Deep Sea Sailing*. New York: D. Van Nostrand, 1967.

Calhoun, C.R. *Typhoon: The Other Enemy*. Annapolis: Naval Institute Press, 1981.

Coles, K. Adlard. *Heavy Weather Sailing*. Tuckahoe, N.Y.: John De Graff, Inc., 1981.

Dabberdt, W.F. *Weather for Outdoorsmen*. New York: Charles Scribner's Sons, 1981.

Dent, N., ed. *The Yachtsman's Pocket Almanac*. New York: Simon and Schuster, 1981.

Douglas, M.S. *Hurricane*. New York: Rinehart and Co., 1958.

Dunn, G.E., and Miller, B.I. *Atlantic Hurricanes*. Baton Rouge: Louisiana State University Press, 1960.

Fisher, Bob. *The Fastnet Disaster and After*. London: Pelham Books, 1980.

Henderson, R. *Sail and Power*, 3rd ed. Annapolis: Naval Institute Press, 1979.

———. *Sea Sense*. Camden, Me.: International Marine Pub. Co., 1979.

Hiscosk, Eric. *Voyaging under Sail*. Oxford: Oxford University Press, 1959.

Hurricane Havens Handbook for the North Atlantic Ocean. Monterey: U.S. Naval Environmental Prediction Research Facility, 1982.

Huschke, R.E., ed. *Glossary of Meteorology*. Boston: American Meteorological Society, 1959.

International Meteorological Codes and Worldwide Synoptic Broadcasts. Bay St. Louis, MS: Commander, U.S. Naval Oceanography Command, 1981.

Kendrew, W.G. *The Climates of the Continents*, 5th ed. Fair Lawn, N.J.: Oxford University Press, 1961.

Kirkman, Karl L. *Sailing Yacht Capsize.* New England Section of Society of Naval Architects and Marine Engineers, 1982.

Kirkman, Nagle, and Salsich. *Sailing Yacht Capsizing.* Annapolis: 6th Chesapeake Sailing Yacht Symposium, 1983.

Kotsch, Rear Admiral W.J. *Weather For The Mariner*, 3rd ed. Annapolis: Naval Institute Press, 1983.

La Dage, John and Lee Van Gemert. *Stability and Trim for the Ship's Officer.* New York: D. Van Nostrand.

Lindemann, Kåre, et al. *Summary of a Course in Shiphandling in Rough Weather.* Det Norske Veritas, National Technical Information Service, U.S. Department of Commerce, 1981.

Mariner's Weather Log. Washington, D.C.: NOAA Environmental Data Service (monthly).

Mariner's Worldwide Climatic Guide to Tropical Storms at Sea. Washington, D.C.: U.S. Government Printing Office, 1974.

National Geographic Atlas of the World. Washington, D.C.: National Geographic Society, 1981.

Neumann, C.J., et al. *Tropical Cyclones of the North Atlantic Ocean, 1871–1977.* Washington, D.C.: U.S. Government Printing Office, 1978.

Noel, Captain J.V., Jr., ed. *Knight's Modern Seamanship*, 14th ed. New York: D. Van Nostrand, 1966.

Operations of the National Weather Service. Washington, D.C.: U.S. Government Printing Office (annually).

Pike, Dag. *Power Boats in Rough Seas.* Camden, Me.: International Marine Pub. Co., 1974.

Robb, Frank. *Handling Small Boats in Heavy Weather.* New York: New York Times Book Co., 1977.

Rousmaniere, John. *Fastnet Force 10.* New York: W. W. Norton & Co., 1980.

Royal Yachting Assoc. & Royal Ocean Racing Club. *1979 Fastnet Race Inquiry.* London: T. H. Brickell & Sons Ltd. and U.S. Yacht Racing Union, 1980.

Smithsonian Meteorological Tables. Washington, D.C.: The Smithsonian Institution, 1951.

Stephens, Kirkman, and Peterson. *Sailing Yacht Capsize.* Annapolis: 5th Chesapeake Sailing Yacht Symposium, 1981.

Sverdrup, H.U. *Oceanography for Meteorologists.* Englewood Cliffs, N.J.: Prentice-Hall, 1942.

Tannehill, I.R. *Hurricanes, Their Nature and History*, 8th ed. Princeton: Princeton University Press, 1952.

Technical Committee of the Cruising Club of America. *Desirable Characteristics of Offshore Cruising-Racing Yachts.* New York, 1977.

Tobin, W.E. III. *The Mariner's Pocket Companion.* Annapolis: Naval Institute Press (annually).

Typhoon Havens Handbook for the Western Pacific and Indian Oceans. Monterey: U.S. Naval Environmental Prediction Research Facility, 1982.

U.S. Navy. *Marine Climatic Atlas of the World*, volumes on the *Atlantic, Pacific, and Indian Oceans.* Washington, D.C.: U.S. Government Printing Office, published beginning 1955.

Voss, John C. *The Venturesome Voyages of Captain Voss.* London: Rupert Hart-Davis, 1955.

Worldwide Marine Weather Broadcasts. Silver Spring: NOAA National Weather Service, 1981.

X

Conversion Tables and Conversion Factors

Table X-1. Mariners' Measures

6 feet	= 1 fathom
120 fathoms	= 1 cable length
7.5 cable lengths	= 1 mile

1 statute mile	= 5,280 feet
1 statute mile	= 1,760 yards
1 statute mile	= 1,609.34 meters
1 statute mile	= 0.868 nautical mile
1 statute mile	= 1.609 kilometers

1 nautical mile	= 6,076.1 feet
1 nautical mile	= 2,025.36 yards
1 nautical mile	= 1,852 meters
1 nautical mile	= 1.152 statute miles
1 nautical mile	= 1.852 kilometers

1 kilometer	= 3,280.84 feet
1 kilometer	= 1,093.61 yards
1 kilometer	= 1,000 meters
1 kilometer	= 0.621 statute mile
1 kilometer	= 0.540 nautical mile

Table X-2. Meters to Feet

Meters	Feet	Meters	Feet	Meters	Feet
1	3.3	10	32.8	100	328.1
2	6.6	20	65.6	200	656.2
3	9.8	30	98.4	300	984.3
4	13.1	40	131.2	400	1312.3
5	16.4	50	164.0	500	1640.4
6	19.7	60	196.9	600	1968.5
7	23.0	70	229.7	700	2296.6
8	26.2	80	262.5	800	2624.7
9	29.5	90	295.3	900	2952.8
				1000	3280.8

Table X-3. Nautical Miles to Statute Miles and Kilometers

Nautical Miles	Statute Miles	Kilometers	Nautical Miles	Statute Miles	Kilometers
1	1.15	1.85	10	11.52	18.53
2	2.30	3.71	20	23.03	37.07
3	3.46	5.56	30	34.56	55.60
4	4.61	7.41	40	46.06	74.13
5	5.76	9.27	50	57.58	92.66
6	6.91	11.12	60	69.09	111.20
7	8.06	12.97	70	80.61	129.73
8	9.21	14.83	80	92.12	148.26
9	10.36	16.68	90	103.64	166.79

NOTE: For larger distances, merely shift the decimal point.

Table X-4. Knots to Miles Per Hour and Meters Per Second

Knots	Miles Per Hour	Meters Per Second	Knots	Miles Per Hour	Meters Per Second
1	1.2	0.5	70	80.6	36.0
2	2.3	1.0	80	92.1	41.2
3	3.5	1.5	90	103.6	46.3
4	4.6	2.1	100	115.2	51.5
5	5.8	2.6	110	126.7	56.6
6	6.9	3.1	120	138.2	61.8
7	8.1	3.6	130	149.7	66.9
8	9.2	4.1	140	161.2	72.1
9	10.4	4.6	150	172.7	77.2
10	11.5	5.1	160	184.2	82.4
20	23.0	10.3	170	195.8	87.5
30	34.5	15.4	180	207.3	92.7
40	46.1	20.6	190	218.8	97.8
50	57.6	25.7	200	230.3	103.0
60	69.1	30.9			

Table X-5. Speed and Distance Table

Knots	Nautical Miles Per Day	Nautical Miles Per Week	Knots	Nautical Miles Per Day	Nautical Miles Per Week
3	72	504	14.5	348	2,436
3.5	84	588	15	360	2,520
4	96	672	15.5	372	2,604
4.5	108	756	16	384	2,688
5	120	840	16.5	396	2,772
5.5	132	924	17	408	2,856
6	144	1,008	17.5	420	2,940
6.5	156	1,092	18	432	3,024
7	168	1,176	18.5	444	3,108
7.5	180	1,260	19	456	3,192
8	192	1,344	19.5	468	3,276
8.5	204	1,428	20	480	3,360
9	216	1,512	20.5	492	3,444
9.5	228	1,596	21	504	3,528
10	240	1,680	21.5	516	3,612
10.5	252	1,764	22	528	3,696
11	264	1,848	22.5	540	3,780
11.5	276	1,932	23	552	3,864
12	288	2,016	23.5	564	3,948
12.5	300	2,100	24	576	4,032
13	312	2,184	24.5	588	4,116
13.5	324	2,268	25	600	4,200
14	336	2,352			

Table X-6. Approximate Distances (in Hundreds of Nautical Miles) Between Major Ports*

ATLANTIC, MEDITERRANEAN, and CARRIBBEAN PORTS — distances to other Atlantic/Mediterranean/Caribbean ports:

	Suez Canal	Southampton	Rio de Janeiro	Recife	Piraeus	Panama Canal	Norfolk	New York	Naples	Montreal	Mayport	Magellan Strait	Key West	Halifax	Guantanamo	Gibraltar	Copenhagen	Cape of Good Hope	Buenos Aires	Bermuda
Azores	30	14	39	28	26	33	24	21	21	21	27	61	29	17	27	11	21	52	50	18
Bermuda	48	30	41	30	44	17	7	7	39	16	8	63	11	8	10	29	37	62	52	
Buenos Aires, Argentina	72	62	12	22	68	54	58	59	63	65	58	14	57	57	53	53	68	38		
Cape of Good Hope	54	60	33	33	66	64	68	68	62	71	68	43	67	65	63	51	67			
Copenhagen, Den.	38	7	57	47	34	52	40	39	29	37	44	79	47	32	46	19				
Gibraltar	19	12	42	31	15	44	33	32	10	32	37	64	39	27	37					
Guantanamo, Cuba	38	39	41	31	52	8	11	13	47	25	9	47	6	16						
Halifax, N. S.	58	27	46	36	42	23	8	6	37	10	13	68	16							
Key West, Fla.	58	36	46	35	54	11	9	16	49	24	5	50								
Magellan Strait	83	73	22	33	79	39	69	69	74	75	69									
Mayport, Fla.	56	38	47	36	52	16	5	9	47	22										
Montreal, Can.	51	29	54	43	47	32	17	15	42											
Naples, Italy	11	22	52	41	6	54	43	42												
New York, N. Y.	51	33	48	37	47	20	3													
Norfolk, Va.	52	34	47	37	48	18														
Panama Canal	63	46	44	33	49															
Piraeus, Greece	6	27	57	46																
Recife, Brazil	50	40	11																	
Rio de Janeiro, Brazil	61	50																		
Southampton, England	31																			

PACIFIC and INDIAN OCEAN PORTS — distances among Pacific/Indian ports:

	Wellington	Vladivostok	Valparaiso	Sydney	Suez	Singapore	Shanghai	Seattle	San Francisco	San Diego	Saigon	Pusan	Perth	Panama	Nome	Manila	Magellan Str.	Honolulu	Hong Kong	Guam	Cape of Good Hope	Cam Ranh Bay	Callao	Bombay	Aden
Bombay, India																									17
Callao, Peru																								107	90
Cam Ranh Bay, Vietnam																							106	32	44
Cape of Good Hope																						63	73	46	40
Guam																					77	21	84	50	62
Hong Kong																				18	70	7	109	39	51
Honolulu																			49	33	111	53	52	83	95
Magellan Strait																		64	99	81	46	97	27	92	86
Manila, Philippines																	105	48	6	15	68	7	103	37	49
Nome, Alaska																44	87	27	41	37	109	48	66	80	93
Panama Canal															58	94	39	47	92	80	64	100	13	84	67
Perth, Aust.															95	95	29	78	65	35	48	26	90	40	49
Pusan, Korea													43	81	30	14	103	40	11	16	80	18	89	49	61
Saigon, Vietnam												20	24	100	50	9	98	55	9	23	61	2	107	30	42
San Diego, Cal.											73	53	86	28	31	66	58	23	64	54	92	69	36	101	98
San Francisco, Cal.										4	69	49	85	32	26	62	62	21	60	51	96	65	40	97	93
Seattle, Wash.									6	10	66	46	84	40	23	60	70	24	58	49	104	63	48	95	100
Shanghai, China								51	54	58	17	5	40	86	35	12	105	43	8	17	76	15	94	46	58
Singapore, Malaya							22	71	73	77	6	25	21	105	56	13	96	59	15	26	56	8	107	24	36
Suez Canal, UAR						50	72	103	95	91	56	75	63	63	106	63	83	110	65	76	53	58	76	30	14
Sydney, Australia					84	42	46	68	64	65	44	46	22	77	63	40	54	44	45	30	67	47	69	61	69
Valparaiso, Chile				63	89	98	101	59	51	47	106	100	77	26	77	97	14	59	102	85	60	105	13	110	93
Vladivostok, USSR			96	51	80	30	10	42	46	51	25	5	48	78	27	19	108	37	16	20	85	23	86	54	66
Wellington, N.Z.		57	50	12	93	52	54	64	59	53	52	52	30	65	65	49	46	41	54	53	73	51	57	70	78
Yokohama, Japan	50	10	93	43	79	29	11	42	45	49	24	7	45	77	27	18	96	34	16	14	83	22	83	53	65

*To find the distance between an Atlantic and Pacific port, use both sides of the table, combining the distances to a selected junction. (Source: *The Mariner's Pocket Companion, 1983,* Naval Institute Press, 1983.)

Table X-7. Visible Distance to the Horizon (Based on Height of Observer's Eye)

Height (Feet)	Visible Distance			Dip of Horizon (Min./Sec.)
	Nautical Miles	Statute Miles	Kilometers	
5	2.57	2.96	4.77	2' 10"
10	3.63	4.18	6.73	3 04
15	4.45	5.12	8.24	3 45
20	5.13	5.92	9.53	4 20
25	5.74	6.61	10.64	4 51
30	6.29	7.24	11.65	5 18
40	7.26	8.36	13.46	6 07
50	8.12	9.35	15.05	6 51
70	9.61	11.06	17.81	8 06
100	11.48	13.22	21.28	9 41
150	14.06	16.19	26.07	11 52
200	16.23	18.69	30.09	13 42
300	19.88	22.90	36.87	16 44
400	22.96	26.44	42.57	19 32
500	25.67	29.56	47.59	21 39
1,000	36.30	41.80	67.30	30' 37"

Table X-8. Temperatures: Degrees Centigrade to Fahrenheit

Conversion Formulae: Centigrade = (5/9) (Fahrenheit − 32)   Fahrenheit = (9/5) Centigrade + 32

Degrees Centigrade	0	1	2	3	4	5	6	7	8	9
+40	104.0	105.8	107.6	109.4	111.2	113.0	114.8	116.6	118.4	120.2
+30	86.0	87.8	89.6	91.4	93.2	95.0	96.8	98.6	100.4	102.2
+20	68.0	69.8	71.6	73.4	75.2	77.0	78.8	80.6	82.4	84.2
+10	50.0	51.8	53.6	55.4	57.2	59.0	60.8	62.6	64.4	66.2
+ 0	32.0	33.8	35.6	37.4	39.2	41.0	42.8	44.6	46.4	48.2
− 0	32.0	30.2	28.4	26.6	24.8	23.0	21.2	19.4	17.6	15.8
−10	14.0	12.2	10.4	8.6	6.8	5.0	3.2	1.4	− 0.4	− 2.2
−20	− 4.0	− 5.8	− 7.6	− 9.4	−11.2	−13.0	−14.8	−16.6	−18.4	−20.2
−30	−22.0	−23.8	−25.6	−27.4	−29.2	−31.0	−32.8	−34.6	−36.4	−38.2
−40	−40.0	−41.8	−43.6	−45.4	−47.2	−49.0	−50.8	−52.6	−54.4	−56.2

NOTE: The vertical axis lists degree centigrade in ten-degree increments; the horizontal axis lists degrees centigrade in one-degree increments. For example, to convert −23 degrees centigrade to Fahrenheit, read down the vertical axis to −20 and across the horizontal axis to 3. The answer in this case is −9.4 degrees Fahrenheit.

Table X-9. Temperature Differences: Degrees Centigrade to Fahrenheit

Degrees Centigrade	Degrees Fahrenheit	Degrees Centigrade	Degrees Fahrenheit
1	1.8	6	10.8
2	3.6	7	12.6
3	5.4	8	14.4
4	7.2	9	16.2
5	9.0	10	18.0

NOTE: This table indicates the number of degrees Fahrenheit the temperature will rise for each increase in degrees centigrade. For instance, if the temperature increases 7 degrees centigrade, the comparable temperature in degrees Fahrenheit will increase 12.6 degrees. (A temperature increase from 10°C to 17°C equals an increase from 50°F to 62.6°F.)

Table X-10(a). Inches of Mercury (in Round Numbers) to Millibars

Inches of Mercury	Millibars	Inches of Mercury	Millibars	Inches of Mercury	Millibars
1	33.86	11	372.50	21	711.14
2	67.73	12	406.37	22	745.01
3	101.59	13	440.23	23	778.87
4	135.46	14	474.09	24	812.73
5	169.32	15	507.96	25	846.60
6	203.18	16	541.82	26	880.46
7	237.05	17	575.69	27	914.33
8	270.91	18	609.55	28	948.19
9	304.78	19	643.41	29	982.05
10	338.64	20	677.28	30	1015.92
				31	1049.78
				32	1083.65

Table X-10(b). Inches of Mercury (in Tenths and Hundredths) to Millibars

Inches of Mercury	0.00	.01	.02	.03	.04	.05	.06	.07	.08	.09
0.0	0.00	0.34	0.68	1.02	1.35	1.69	2.03	2.37	2.71	3.05
0.1	3.39	3.73	4.06	4.40	4.74	5.08	5.42	5.76	6.10	6.43
0.2	6.77	7.11	7.45	7.79	8.13	8.47	8.80	9.14	9.48	9.82
0.3	10.16	10.50	10.84	11.18	11.51	11.85	12.19	12.53	12.87	13.21
0.4	13.55	13.88	14.22	14.56	14.90	15.24	15.58	15.92	16.25	16.59
0.5	16.93	17.27	17.61	17.95	18.29	18.63	18.96	19.30	19.64	19.98
0.6	20.32	20.66	21.00	21.33	21.67	22.01	22.35	22.69	23.03	23.37
0.7	23.70	24.04	24.38	24.72	25.06	25.40	25.74	26.08	26.41	26.75
0.8	27.09	27.43	27.77	28.11	28.45	28.78	29.12	29.46	29.80	30.14
0.9	30.48	30.82	31.15	31.49	31.83	32.17	32.51	32.85	33.19	33.53

NOTE: Table X-10(a) converts inches of mercury in round numbers to millibars. Table X-10(b) converts inches of mercury in tenths and hundredths to millibars. Both tables can be used together to solve a conversion problem.

Example: Convert 29.73 inches of mercury to millibars.

Solution: First determine from table X-10(a) the number of millibars in 29 inches of mercury. Then determine from table X-10(b) the number of millibars in .73 inches of mercury. In table X-10(b), the vertical axis lists inches of mercury in tenths of an inch. The horizontal axis lists inches of mercury in hundredths of an inch. To convert .73 inches, read down the vertical axis to .7, and across the horizontal axis to .03.

Now, add the data from both tables for the answer.

From table X-10(a):   982.05 mbs
From table X-10(b):   24.72 mbs
                    ─────────────
   Answer: 1006.77 mbs

Table X-11. Miles Per Liter (MPL) to Miles Per Gallon (MPG)*

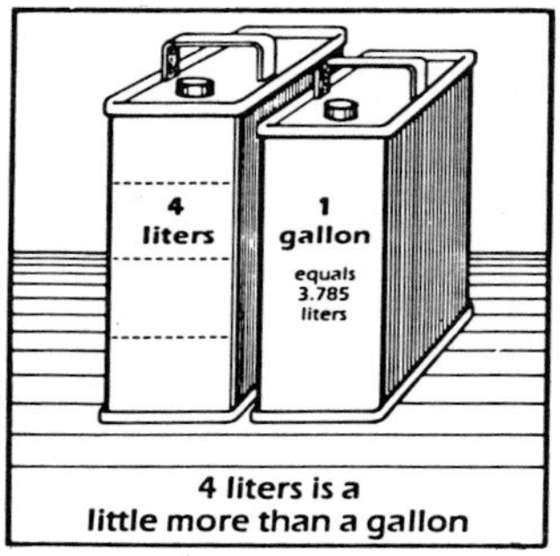

	MPL		MPG
	2.5	=	9.5
	3	=	11.4
	3.5	=	13.2
	4	=	15.1
	4.5	=	17.0
	5	=	18.9
	5.5	=	20.8
	6	=	22.7
	6.5	=	24.6
	7	=	26.5
	7.5	=	28.4
	8	=	30.3
	8.5	=	32.2
	9	=	34.1
	9.5	=	36.0
	10	=	37.9
	10.5	=	39.7
	11	=	41.6
	11.5	=	43.5
	12	=	45.4
	12.5	=	47.3
	13	=	49.2
	13.5	=	51.1
	14	=	53.0
	14.5	=	54.9
	15	=	56.8
	MPL × 3.785	=	MPG

4 liters | 1 gallon

equals 3.785 liters

4 liters is a little more than a gallon

*For a rough estimate, multiply MPL by 4 to get MPG.

Table X-12. Price Comparison Chart (Liters and Gallons)*

Price per liter		Price per gallon
$0.28	=	$1.06
.29	=	1.10
.30	=	1.14
.31	=	1.17
.32	=	1.21
.33	=	1.25
.34	=	1.29
.35	=	1.32
.36	=	1.36
.37	=	1.40
.38	=	1.44
.39	=	1.48
.40	=	1.51
.41	=	1.55
.42	=	1.59
.43	=	1.63
.44	=	1.67
.45	=	1.70
.46	=	1.74
.47	=	1.78
.48	=	1.82
.49	=	1.85
.50	=	1.89
.51	=	1.93
.52	=	1.97
.53	=	2.01
.54	=	2.04
.55	=	2.08
.56	=	2.12
.57	=	2.16
.58	=	2.20

*The gallon price equivalents are rounded to the nearest penny.

Table X-13. Converting Liters to (*Approximate* Equivalent) Gallons to Determine Tank Capacity in Liters*

Liters	Gallons	Liters	Gallons
1	0.26	50	13.2
4	1.1	55	14.5
10	2.6	57	15.0
15	4.0	60	15.9
19	5.0	65	17.2
20	5.3	70	18.5
25	6.6	75	19.8
30	7.9	80	21.1
35	9.2	85	22.5
38	10.0	90	23.8
40	10.6	95	25.1
45	11.9	100	26.4

*For larger capacities, shift the decimal point.
NOTE: 3.785 liters = 1 gallon
      1 liter = 0.2642 gallon

Table X-14. Handy Equivalents for Mariners

Mass (or Weight)

1 gram = 0.035 ounce
1 ounce = 28.35 grams
1 kilogram = 1,000 grams
1 kilogram = 2.20 pounds
1 pound = 0.454 kilogram
1 long ton = 1,016 kilograms
1 long ton = 2,240 pounds
1 short ton = 907.2 kilograms
1 short ton = 2,000 pounds
1 metric ton = 0.984 English ton
1 English ton = 1.016 tons
1 cubic foot of water = 62.4 pounds weight
1 cubic foot of water = 28.32 kilograms weight

Power

1 kilowatt = 1,000 watts
1 horsepower = 0.746 kilowatts
1 kilowatt = 1.34 horsepower
1 H.P. (British) = 1.014 H.P. (metric)
1 H.P. (metric) = 0.986 H.P. (British)
1 foot-pound = 0.138 kilogram-meters
1 H.P. (metric) = 75.0 kilogram-meters per second
1 H.P. (British) = 550 foot-pounds per second
1 foot-pound = 1.356 Joules
1 Joule = 0.783 foot-pounds

Volume

1 cubic centimeter = 0.061 cubic inch
1 cubic inch = 16.39 cubic centimeters
1 cubic inch = 0.0036 imperial gallons
1 cubic inch = 0.004 U.S. gallons
1 cubic decimeter = 0.035 cubic foot
1 cubic foot = 28.317 cubic decimeters
1 cubic foot = 6.229 imperial gallons
1 cubic foot = 7.481 U.S. gallons
1 cubic foot = 28.32 liters
1 cubic meter = 1.308 cubic yards
1 cubic meter = 35.31 cubic feet
1 cubic yard = 0.765 cubic meter
1 liter = 0.908 quart (dry)
1 liter = 1.057 quarts (liquid)
1 liter = 0.264 U.S. gallons
1 dry quart = 1.101 liters
1 liquid quart = 0.946 liter
1 U.S. gallon = 3.785 liters
1 U.S. gallon = 0.379 dekaliter
1 imperial gallon = 1.200 U.S. gallons
1 imperial gallon = 4.55 liters
1 U.S. gallon = 0.833 imperial gallon
1 U.S. gallon = 3.785 liters

Acknowledgments

Seldom is a book of nonfiction written that does not incorporate the comments and suggestions, both pro and con, and prior related work, of others. This is the nature of progress in nonfiction, and an attempt on the part of authors to have their work be, among other things, timely, accurate, informative, and inclusive.

The first edition of *Heavy Weather Guide* is out of print. It is also very much out of date. The dramatic increases in scientific knowledge and the extremely rapid developments in high technology in the last twenty years have dictated that this book be updated and expanded in scope. Consequently, a new edition is necessary to provide a current and easily understandable reference—of use to weekend sailors as well as deep-draft skippers—for dealing with heavy weather at sea and in coastal waters.

Prior to and during the course of this revision, many helpful comments and suggestions—both solicited and unsolicited—were received from users of the first edition, friends, and colleagues.

The authors are deeply grateful to the following individuals, listed alphabetically in the following paragraph, for their unfailing kindness, helpful comments and suggestions, generous cooperation, and permission to use material. To these friends, colleagues, and critics, we extend our sincerest thanks.

Walter C. Ahlin, formerly director, NADUC Photographic Laboratory of the GE/Management and Technical Services Co.;

John Alden, president, Alden Electronics and Impulse Recording Equipment Co.;

Armand D. Bouchard, manager, Marine Sales, Alden Electronics and Impulse Recording Equipment Co.;

Monica Byrne, Rights & Permissions Dept., Louisiana State University Press;

Robert A. Carlisle, Head, Still Photo Branch, Office of Information, Navy Department;

Edward Carlstead, commander, USN (Retired), assistant director, NOAA National Meteorological Center;

Charles R. Dale, commander, USN (Retired), Headquarters, U.S. Naval Oceanography Command;

William S. Dehn, lieutenant commander, USN (Retired), president, Sea Ice Consultants, Inc.;

Captain Robert O. Elsensohn, director of Maritime Institute of Technology and Graduate Studies;

Dr. R. Cecil Gentry, consultant and former director, National Hurricane Research Center;

Will G. Gould, lieutenant commander, USN (Retired), meteorologist, National Air Survey Center Corp.;

A. Alan Green, secretary, The Royal Ocean Racing Club, London;

Dr. Richard E. Hallgren, administrator for Weather Services, NOAA;

Dr. Glenn D. Hamilton, captain, USN (Retired), chief, Data Systems Division, NOAA Data Buoy Center;

Sarah L. Henderson, freelance editor, researcher, and typist;

Captain K.G. Hinman, Jr., USN, commanding officer, U.S. Naval Oceanography Command Center/Joint Typhoon Warning Center, Guam;

Donald R. Jones, commander, USN (Retired), formerly project manager, GE/Management and Technical Services Co.;

Donald J. Jordan, consulting engineer and yacht capsize researcher;

Karl L. Kirkman, naval architect and codirector of the Committee on Safety from Capsizing (sponsored by SNAME and USYRU);

Deborah E. Kotsch, consultant in cartography;

Kåre Lindmann, principal research engineer for Det Norske Veritas;

Captain John J. Maloney, USN (Retired), vice president, Finance and Administration, Oceanroutes, Inc.;

The Marine Superintendent, British Meteorological Office, Bracknell;

Chuck Mattes, president, National Air Survey Center Corp.;

Richard C. Newick, designer of multihulls and high-performance sailing vessels;

Arnold G. Oakes, Applications Directorate, NASA Goddard Space Flight Center;

John Rousmaniere, author of *Fastnet Force 10*;

Dr. Robert C. Sheets, hurricane specialist, National Hurricane Center;

Dr. Kenneth C. Spengler, brigadier general, USAFR (Retired), executive director, American Meteorological Society;

Roderick Stephens, Jr., yacht designer associated with Sparkman and Stephens;

R.J. Taylor, president of R.J. Taylor Co., safety equipment suppliers for ships and yachts;

Captain K.L. Van Sickle, USN, commanding officer, U.S. Naval Environmental Prediction Research Facility;

The *Washington Post*, Washington, D.C.;

Captain George E. White, master mariner, surveyor, and consultant;

A. Woodroffe, meteorologist, British Meteorological Office, Bracknell; Admiral Joseph M. Worthington, USN (Retired).

Index